1
RECONSTRUCTION IN GEORGIA

STUDIES IN HISTORY, ECONOMICS AND PUBLIC LAW

EDITED BY THE FACULTY OF POLITICAL SCIENCE
OF COLUMBIA UNIVERSITY

Volume LXIV]   [Number 1

Whole Number 154

RECONSTRUCTION IN GEORGIA

ECONOMIC, SOCIAL, POLITICAL

1865-1872

BY

C. MILDRED THOMPSON, Ph.D.,

Instructor in History in Vassar College

GLOUCESTER, MASS.
PETER SMITH
1964

PREFACE

THE material for this monograph would never have been collected had it not been for the kind assistance of many friends in Georgia. In Atlanta, Miss Sallie Eugenia Brown and Mrs. V. P. Sisson put at my disposal their interesting and valuable papers, and Mr. Clark Howell of the *Atlanta Constitution* helped materially in giving me access to newspaper files. Mrs. Maud Barker Cobb, Miss Dailey, and Miss Thornton of the Georgia State Library, have been untiring in their services. In Savannah, I am indebted to Mr. William Harden of the Georgia Historical Society Library, and especially to Mr. Wymberly Jones DeRenne of Wormsloe for his generous hospitality in allowing me to use his unique and extensive collection of material pertaining to the history of Georgia. I am under obligations to Professor Robert Preston Brooks of the University of Georgia for helpful suggestions, and to Professor Ulrich B. Phillips of the University of Michigan, who put at my disposal copies of valuable letters. To my colleague and friend, Professor Eloise Ellery of Vassar College, I am indebted for help in the joyless task of proof-reading. Without the constant encouragement and helpful criticism of my teacher, colleague and friend, Professor Lucy M. Salmon of Vassar College, this labor would not have come to completion.

Anything of bias or inaccuracy or limited vision in this essay is the fault of the author. Anything of fairness or wisdom or truth that it may contain must be ascribed to Professor William Archibald Dunning of Columbia University, in whom many students of Reconstruction History have found their guide and inspiration.

C. MILDRED THOMPSON.

POUGHKEEPSIE, N. Y., *March 15, 1915.*

TABLE OF CONTENTS

PART I.—ECONOMIC READJUSTMENT AND REORGANIZATION, 1865-1866

CHAPTER I

INTRODUCTION—GEORGIA IN THE WAR

CHAPTER III
LABOR AND LAND

CHAPTER IV
COMMERCIAL REVIVAL

CHAPTER V
SOCIAL READJUSTMENT

PART II.—MILITARY AND POLITICAL RECON-
STRUCTION, 1867-1872

CHAPTER VII

MILITARY RULE

CHAPTER VIII

ORGANIZATION OF THE RECONSTRUCTION GOVERNMENT

CHAPTER IX

STATE ECONOMY UNDER THE BULLOCK RÉGIME

CHAPTER X

REORGANIZED RECONSTRUCTION ; RESTORATION OF HOME RULE

PART III.—ECONOMIC PROGRESS AND SOCIAL CHANGES

CHAPTER XI

CHAPTER XII

CHAPTER XIII

PART I

ECONOMIC READJUSTMENT AND REORGANIZATION

1865–1866

CHAPTER I

Introduction—Georgia in the War

RECONSTRUCTION in Georgia can be understood only by seeing, in the first place, what were the effects of the war on the state—how population, white and black, was altered; to what extent a war economy injured the great agricultural and commercial interests and developed or transformed industrial enterprise; what were the resources of the state, its debit and its credit; and in what political temper the people of Georgia met the new business of statehood in 1865.

The effects of the war on population can be determined only approximately, as no census was taken until five years after the close of the war. The census of 1870, however, shows a gain in the ten-year period of over one hundred thousand in the total population, a little less than twelve per cent increase, much less than in the preceding and the following decades—thirty-one per cent in 1840-50, sixteen per cent in 1850-60, and thirty per cent in 1870-80.[1] Estimates of the loss in white population by war vary from thirty to forty thousand.[2] Apart from the consideration of actual numbers lost, the absence of thousands of adult white men in the armies seriously affected the producing capacity of the state during the war, and the ten or fifteen years after paid the price of the loss of young men from the

---

[1] *U. S. Census,* 1870, vol. i, pp. 4, 5.

[2] *Macon Telegraph,* December 29, 1865; *Joint Committee on Reconstruction,* 1866, pt. iii, p. 131.

workers, made up only in part by immigration from the North. Moreover, progressive citizenship suffered not only from the death of thousands of young men in battle, but also from the lack of education and peaceful training which was the cost of four years of military service to many youthful volunteers. Effects of the war on the blacks can be even less accurately computed. Some of the negroes wandered off with the Northern armies in 1864, comparatively few, however, out of the total number; some were transferred by their owners to plantations in the South and the West, but on the whole, their number was probably not much less in 1865 than in 1860.

Georgia, an agricultural, exporting state, found difficulties during the war not so much in raising a crop, for her territory was practically free from invasion until the last year of the conflict, as in marketing what she raised. Under normal circumstances the greatest agricultural asset of Georgia was cotton, produced in the broad belt of rich black land stretching across the central part of the state, diagonally from southwest toward northeast. To the north and west of this belt was the grain-producing area and to the southeast, piny barrens, with sea-island cotton and rice along the coast lands and islands. When a state of war closed the Northern market and when the extension of actual blockade of Southern ports became effective, need of agricultural adjustment was apparent. In the season of 1861, the Georgia planter was not deterred by any fear of war from putting his usual acreage in cotton. The common attitude, as reflected in the newspapers, was that the Yankees would not fight, and even if they did the South could whip them in short order. Then, too, that cotton was king was the chief article in the creed of every Southern planter. If a fight should come on, the need of Northern manufacturers and the necessity of England would soon aid Southern arms in restoring peace on the South's own terms. But by the end of the first year, the gravity of the situation called for a resolution in the state legislature, recommending planters to reduce the cotton crop for 1862, and plant more grain for home consumption and for the Confederate armies.[1] This advice was not followed to any appreciable extent, for by 1862 the agricultural problem of Georgia was rapidly growing serious. During the year the Federal army cut off connections with Kentucky and a large part of Tennessee, the source of much of the grain and meat consumed in Georgia, and at the same time two cotton crops on hand presaged low prices, even if the constant expectation of a removal of the blockade by English intervention should be fulfilled. In response to a request for his views, Governor Brown wrote a public letter in February, 1862, at the beginning of the planting season, urging the people of Georgia to reduce the cotton acreage so as to double the usual crop of Indian corn, produce a larger crop of potatoes and yams, increase the usual amount of beets, turnips, peas, and pay more attention to raising hogs and cattle.[2] In December, 1862, the legislature made its recommendation of the previous year mandatory in an act " To prevent and punish the planting and cultivating, in the State of Georgia, over a certain quantity of land in Cotton during the war with the Abolitionists." The amount was limited to three acres to each hand between fifteen and fifty-five years, and of hands older or younger two should be counted as one. Violation was declared a misdemeanor with a fine of $500 for every acre over and above the amount allowed, one-half of which was to go to the prosecutor or informer and the other half for

[1] *Acts of the General Assembly*, 1861, p. 137.

[2] Letter of Gov. Brown to Linton Stephens, February 25, 1862, in *Brown Scrap Books.*

the support of indigent soldiers in the county.[1] It is impossible to determine how far this law had effect. The comptroller general attempted to collect crop statistics, but returns were too incomplete and unsatisfactory to print.[2] Still other official measures were taken to protect the food supply of the state. On February 28, 1862, a proclamation of the governor ordered all distilleries closed and instructed the management of the state road (Western and Atlantic R. R.) not to transport whisky, and recommended other railroads to follow the instruction.[3] The proclamation was followed by an act of the legislature, intended to prevent unnecessary consumption of grain by prohibiting distillation, except for medicinal, chemical, hospital, and mechanical purposes.[4] Supplementary laws to enforce this act in 1863 show that the matter was not one to be settled by a single legislative measure. In the northern part of the state in regions where transportation was especially difficult, the only way by which the farmer could dispose of his grain to advantage was by distilling it, as he found more certain sale and easier transportation for whisky than for corn in bulk. Recognizing this hardship on the farmer in remote districts, the act of November 22, 1862, provided that distillation allowed under contract for the Confederate government must be carried on at places at least twenty miles from a railroad or navigable stream.[5]

Labor difficulties played no great part in the agricultural problem of Georgia until the end of the war. Practical unanimity of opinion testifies that the slaves continued

[1] *Acts of the General Assembly*, 1861, p. 137; 1862, pp. 5-6.
[2] *Report of the Comptroller General*, 1863, p. 28.
[3] *Southern Confederacy*, March 4, 1862.
[4] *Acts of the General Assembly*, 1862, p. 25.
[5] *Ibid.*, p. 26.

faithful during the years of war, causing no disturbance until 1864, and then only in the path of Sherman's invasion, where droves of them wandered away from the plantations to follow the soldiers. In the northern part of the state, where there were few blacks, a dearth of labor was caused by the drain of the armies on the white population, and women worked in the fields in the place of the men of the family who had gone to the war.[1] The cultivation of rice and sea-island cotton was practically abandoned after 1862. Many of the planters transported their slaves inland, and the fields and rice swamps were left to themselves or to the negroes that remained in actual freedom. On these abandoned coast lands General Sherman established colonies of free blacks in 1865.

The decade before the war saw the beginning of many new mills and factories of various kinds in Georgia. But when trade with the North was cut off, those already in existence were quite inadequate to the demands for war supplies, cannon, guns, ammunition of all kinds, cloth and clothing, and the multitude of manufactured articles that had long come into the South from Northern factories and shops. New cotton mills were not opened during the war, but those already equipped were run to their fullest capacity. Manufacturers were hindered by the scarcity of cards for carding cotton and other machinery for their plants. In 1862 the state came to the rescue by advancing $100,000 for the manufacture of woollen and cotton cards for factories and for procuring machinery and materials for the manufacture of cards.[2] That there was no conspicuous increase in the number of cotton mills during the war seems

[1] *Southern Confederacy*, April 22, 1862.

[2] *Acts of the General Assembly*, 1862; Executive Order, February 9, 1863.—*Brown Scrap Books*.

apparent from the census figures, showing 33 mills with
85,186 spindles in operation in 1860, and 34 mills with
85,602 spindles in 1870. Woollen mills, of which 30 were
listed in 1860, increased in the following decade to 46.[1]
The greatest industrial growth occasioned directly by
the war was in foundries, rolling mills and factories for
making army supplies of all kinds, situated mostly in the
inland towns, Macon, Atlanta, Athens, Augusta, and Columbus. These enterprises, more and more necessary to the
security of the state and the Confederacy, were gradually
impressed by one government or the other. In Macon more
than 350 workmen were constantly employed in making
cannon, shot, shell, saddle harness, and leather articles, while
the laboratory and the armory kept as many more busy
in the manufacture of smaller weapons and cartridges. In
1862 the arsenal at Savannah was moved to Macon. Macon
also had smaller establishments for the manufacture of buttons, enamelled cloth, wire, matches, soap, and other necessaries.[2] Columbus profited by unusual business activity.
The city was filled with transient residents who found employment in factories that worked night and day, employing two sets of hands. Many laborers were kept busy at
the Confederate Naval Works under military command.
Some new industries sprang up in Columbus, such as a cap
factory and a sword factory, and others were greatly stimulated. The Columbus Foundry and Machine Works had to
increase its working force to meet the great demand for
machinery and war supplies. Many women and girls,

[1] *U. S. Census*, 1860, Manufactures, p, 82; 1870, vol. iii, pp. 488-9,
508, 596-7, 630. The increase in woollen manufactures was in wool
carding more than in the manufacture of woollen goods.

[2] Butler, *Historical Record of Macon and Central Georgia*, pp. 257-8;
Von Halle, *Baumwollproduktion und Pflanzungswirtschaft in den
Nordamerikanischen Südstaaten*, vol. ii, pp. 58-9.

mostly wives and daughters of soldiers, found employment in the quartermaster's establishment in Columbus.[1] Atlanta was one of the military supply depots of the Confederacy, where arms, ammunition, alcohol, vinegar, spirits of nitre and other necessaries were manufactured for the government. The city was headquarters for the Confederate quartermaster and commissary, and as a chief hospital point, it gave employment to a large labor force and stimulated trade through large disbursements. Before 1861 its manufacturing interests were comparatively small, with four machine shops, two planing mills, three tanneries, two shoe factories, a soap factory and a clothing factory. During the war its industry was increased by the special demands of the time, but after the evacuation by Sherman's army nearly all the factories were in ruin. During the war the Atlanta Machine Works, managed by a Unionist, J. L. Dunning, refused to cast shells for the Confederacy, whereupon the works were seized by the government.[2] Athens had three second-rate cotton mills of limited capacity, all of which flourished under the excessive demand for cloth and yarn.[3]

The dearth of coal, iron and other minerals, occasioned by the war, seemed to offer opportunity for good investment in mining in North Georgia, and between 1861 and 1863 at least eight different companies were incorporated by the state legislature to carry on mining operations in the northern counties.[4] But capital was too scarce to make such ventures immediately profitable and no important results came from any of these operations.

---

[1] Martin, *Columbus, Georgia*, pp. 142-3, 166.

[2] Clarke, *Atlanta Illustrated*, p. 41, *et seq.*; Reed, *History of Atlanta*, pp. 456, 458.

[3] Hull, *Annals of Athens*, p. 390.

[4] *Acts of the General Assembly*, 1861, 1862, 1863.

Thus, the war greatly stimulated industrial enterprises in Georgia, but the most thriving industries were those of a temporary character, fostered by the special needs of war, only to subside as soon as peace returned. Many such factories, too, were destroyed in 1864-5. Industrial activity served partially to offset agricultural depression when the cotton market was stagnant and helped in the readjustment of labor by giving occupation to women and girls, whose support was removed when husbands and fathers were in the army. Still another result of the industrial activity of this period, important later in the dominant interests of the state, was the formation of a new class of rich men whose wealth did not rest in land and slaves.[1]

Before the war, the great bulk of Georgia's exports, bound eventually for European markets, was shipped from Savannah, Brunswick, or Charleston, to Northern ports, and thence across the ocean. A very small per cent of the shipping from Savannah was bound for England direct. This commercial dependence on the North loomed up full of dangers in the fall of 1860 when war was brewing, and plans were agitated for securing direct trade with Europe from Savannah, at first by private initiative, then by governmental sanction and aid. Governor Brown's annual message to the legislature in the fall of 1860 called attention to the fact that the Cotton Planters' Association of the state, in making efforts to establish direct trade with Europe, had sent a commissioner to Europe. The governor recommended in aid of the enterprise a law like one in Alabama, to exempt from all state, county, and corporation taxes all goods from any foreign country imported directly into Georgia through any of the ports of the Southern states.[2]

---

[1] *Cf. infra*, p. 118.

[2] *Journal of the House of Representatives*, 1860, p. 23.

No action seems to have been taken under this recommendation, but through the incorporation of the Belgian American Company, a further move was made for direct trade between the Southern states and Europe, the state guaranteeing for five years five per cent interest on the capital stock ($100,000), and supervising the company by a commissioner appointed by the governor.[1]

For a short time after secession vessels from the North continued to come to Savannah with goods on which custom duties were collected. In the spring of 1862, when the fall of Fort Pulaski below Savannah closed that port, and other ports on the Georgia coast were effectually blockaded, commercial difficulties became very serious.[2] The state sent Mr. T. Butler King on a mission to Europe to try to carry into effect the act of December, 1860, for the purpose of establishing direct intercourse with Europe. The Belgian American Company refused the terms offered, but the French government was more amenable, and changed in favor of Savannah, a subsidy previously granted a line to New York. In England a contract was made with Frederick Sabel, of Liverpool, for a direct line to Savannah on the payment of a subsidy of $100,000 as soon after peace as possible. This latter contract was not ratified, and indeed the possible benefits of Mr. King's mission came to nought, for by the autumn of 1862 the Federal blockade of the Georgia coast was so effective that none but the most daring blockade runners could break through.[3]

The coast blockade, by severing connection with the North, shut out manufactured articles in general usage, as well as machinery of all sorts, cloth and clothing, fine gro-

---

[1] *Acts of the General Assembly*, 1860, pp. 7-10.

[2] Wilson, *Historical and Picturesque Savannah*, p. 199.

[3] *Southern Confederacy*, December 4, 1862.

ceries, medicines, and other articles of household consumption, at the same time shutting in the cotton that went to pay for these imported articles. Georgia's other avenue of approach to the outside world was by railroads to the North and the West, by which came a large part of the grain and meat supply of the state. In the winter of 1861 food ran short, and in the next year, when Northern armies occupied Kentucky and part of Tennessee, conditions, already serious, were aggravated by a failure of the corn crop in part of North Georgia. Moreover, in these first two years of the war planters did practically nothing toward adjusting themselves to the situation by planting more grain and less cotton. In the short market speculation was rife. The legislature tried to control this abuse by enacting laws against monopoly and extortion, declaring it a misdemeanor with heavy fine as penalty to attempt to corner the market or artificially to raise prices in breadstuffs or other articles of general use and consumption.[1] Under such conditions mercantile business was at a standstill, many stores were closed or used as headquarters of various departments of the government.[2] Prices for all articles of ordinary consumption began to rise rapidly in December, 1860, when banks suspended specie payments, and continued upward as the double effect of a scarcity of commodities and an inflated currency.

A salt famine early threatened the people of the state when the blockade stopped the importation of this very necessary commodity. So serious was the difficulty as the packing season approached that the state legislature took measures to provide salt. To encourage the manufacture of salt

---

[1] *Acts of the General Assembly*, 1861, pp. 66-7; *Southern Confederacy*, February 5, 1862.

[2] Hull, *Annals of Athens*, p. 257; Wilson, *Historical and Picturesque Savannah*, p. 201; and newspapers.

in Georgia, the legislature in 1861 appropriated $50,000 to be advanced as a loan without interest.[1]   In 1862 the governor offered a reward for the discovery of salt wells in the state, and in December of that year a legislative appropriation put $500,000 in the hands of the governor to provide salt for the packing season.[2]   The state entered into a partnership with the Planters' Salt Manufacturing Co. and the Georgia Salt Manufacturing Co. to manufacture salt in Washington and Smythe counties in Virginia, and the governor was authorized to impress cars and engines to transport the salt in the state.[3]

Georgia, prior to 1861, was ahead of the other Southeastern states in the completeness and efficiency of its transportation system.[4]   The Western and Atlantic R. R., owned and operated by the state, brought food supplies from Tennessee, Kentucky and the West for distribution through the cotton belt, and the Georgia R. R. and the Central of Georgia R. R., together with branch feeding lines in the cotton region, carried cotton from the producing area to the sea-ports.   The extent of these railway lines in Georgia is seen by the following table:[5]

[1] *Acts of the General Assembly*, 1861, pp. 7-8.

[2] *Southern Confederacy*, April 6, 1862 (Proclamation of March 31st); *Acts of the General Assembly*, 1862, p. 6, *et seq.*

[3] *Ibid.*, pp. 105, 108.

[4] For a full and valuable account of the development of transportation facilities in Georgia before the war, see Phillips, *History of Transportation in the Eastern Cotton Belt to 1860.*

[5] *Ibid.* and Sherwood, *Gazetteer of Georgia*, 1860, p. 6 *et seq.*

RAILROADS IN GEORGIA IN 1860

Georgia R. R. Branches:	Augusta to Atlanta Camak to Warrenton Cumming to Washington Union Point to Athens	171 mi.
Western and Atlantic R. R. Branches:	Atlanta to Chattanooga Dalton to Cleveland, Tenn. Kingston to Rome	138 mi.
Central of Georgia R. R. Branches:	Macon to Savannah Millen to Waynesboro to Augusta Gordon to Milledgeville to Eatonton	191 mi.
Macon and Western R. R. Branch:	Atlanta to Macon Barnesville to Thomaston	103 mi.
Atlanta and West Point R. R.	Atlanta to West Point	87 mi.
Southwestern R. R. Branch:	Macon to Eufaula, Ala. and to Albany Smithville to Fort Gaines and Georgetown	163 mi.
Muscogee R. R.	Macon to Columbus	100 mi.
Savannah and Gulf R. R.	Savannah to Thomasville (completed in 1860 as far as Valdosta)	150 mi.

Other roads, chartered, surveyed, and partially constructed before 1861, were held up during the war by lack of capital and were not completed until later. Of the Macon and Brunswick R. R., about fifty miles were built. The Air Line R. R., to connect Atlanta with the Northeast, chartered in 1856, was surveyed into South Carolina before 1861. Construction was delayed until 1868, and five years later the road was completed to Charlotte, N. C. The Brunswick and Albany was chartered, a part of the grading done

and some miles of track laid. Later, aided by state endorsement of its bonds, the road was finished as far as Albany.[1]
    Between 1861 and 1865, practically no progress was
made in railway extension further than the granting of
charters to some new companies, the Ocmulgee River R.
R. from Macon to Griffin, the Atlanta and Roswell R. R.
to connect with the Western and Atlantic R. R., and the
Columbia and Augusta R. R.[2]
    The policy of Georgia toward railroads in the two decades
before the war was one of active aid and encouragement,
by subscribing to the stock of railroad companies and by
favorable tax agreements. Not until 1850 was any state
tax levied on railroad stock, and the companies chartered
before that year were secured against a tax greater than
one-half of one per cent on the net annual income. After
1858 all roads were taxed alike at this rate.[3] In general,
railroads prospered in the years just before the war. In
1859, the dividend declared by the Georgia R. R. was 8 per
cent; by the Macon and Western, 16 per cent; by the
Central of Georgia, 20 per cent;[4] and in 1860, under the
efficient management of Governor Brown's régime, the state
road paid into the treasury 10 per cent on the whole sum
paid out by the state and raised by bonds.[5]
    The invasion of Georgia by Sherman's army in 1864
wrought terrible havoc on railroads. In the northern and
central parts of the state the main lines of transportation
were broken up for almost two years. Sherman's march
of destruction followed the line of the Western and Atlan-

[1] Janes, *Handbook of Georgia*, pp. 173-6.
[2] *Acts of the General Assembly*, 1862, pp. 219-222; 1863-4, pp. 137-148.
[3] *Report of the Comptroller General*, 1860, pp. 20-21.
[4] Sherwood, *Gazetteer of Georgia*, 1860, pp. 149-154.
[5] Governor Brown, Annual Message, 1860, *Journal of the House*, 1860, pp. 7-9.

tic R. R. from Chattanooga to Atlanta, part of the Macon
and Western R. R. between Atlanta and Macon, and almost
the entire length of the Central R. R. to Savannah. The
left wing of the army did serious damage to the Georgia
R. R. between Madison and Augusta, and also to the Augusta and Savannah R. R. The line of march was marked
by " Sherman's hairpins ", *i. e.,* rails torn up, heated over
burning cross-ties, then bent around trees. Yard houses
and road-buildings were burned, bridges torn away, and
rolling stock carried off or destroyed.[1] The Atlanta and
West Point R. R. suffered like treatment at the hands of
General Wilson's raiders in 1865. The state road, the
Western and Atlantic, had been the bone of contention between the two armies, destroyed by each in turn. Later it
was put in temporary running order by the Federal authorities, and in September, 1865, was turned over to the state,
the United States government furnishing rolling stock, for
which the state gave bond.[2] Thus, by the end of the war,
the Western and Atlantic R. R., together with some por-
tions of the Southwestern R. R. and of the Atlantic and
Gulf R. R., constituted the usable parts of the transportation system, though these roads, too, suffered heavily from
loss of rolling stock.

No kind of business suffered more heavily by reason of
the failure of the war for secession than did banking. In
1860, twenty-five banks were doing business in Georgia
with an actual capital of $9,028,078. Of these, nine were
in Savannah, the commercial capital of the state, six in Augusta, two each in Macon and Dalton, and the others in
Columbus, Atlanta, Rome, Athens, La Grange, and Ring-

---

[1] Andrews, *War-Time Journal of a Georgia Girl,* pp. 47-8; Trowbridge, *Picture of the Desolated States,* pp. 501-502; *New York Times,*
October 13, 1865, and November 23, 1865.

[2] *Acts of the General Assembly,* 1866, pp. 14-15.

gold., The State of Georgia was not encouraging in its
policy toward banking corporations, taxing them 39½ cents
on $100 capital stock paid in, about six times the rate paid
by all other property, except railroads.[1] In the fall of
1860, when threatening war put the banks under a severe
strain, the legislature came to their relief by an act, passed
over the governor's veto, legalizing the suspension of specie
payments for one year, a privilege that was extended from
time to time to the end of the war.[2] In a very short time
after suspension, practically all coin disappeared from circulation, leaving a shortage in the currency in 1861. But
by the following year there was a flood of paper money of
all kinds, bank change bills in small denominations of 5, 10,
25 and 50 cents, bank bills in larger amounts, change bills
issued by the state road, state notes and bills, Confederate
notes, city and town currency, as well as bills and notes of
individuals and firms, called " shinplasters ", many of which
had better credit than public currency.[3] During the war
banks invested their funds largely in Confederate bonds
and state securities, so that, at the close of the war, when
the securities in their vaults were worthless, the banks were
almost entirely wrecked. In 1861, as a measure of relief to
cotton planters, a bank was organized in Thomasville,
known as the Cotton Planters' Bank of Georgia. Its purpose, as stated in the law of its incorporation, was to give
steadiness to the value of cotton, to make it the basis of a
circulating medium, and to enable the planters to control
their own cotton until the removal of the blockade. No one
could hold stock except planters, who might subscribe in

---

[1] *Report of the Comptroller General*, 1860, pp. 26, 27.

[2] *Acts of the General Assembly*, 1860, p. 22; 1861, pp. 18-19, 25-7;
1862, pp. 19-21.

[3] *Ibid.*, 1862, pp. 19-21; *Southern Confederacy*, December 2, 1862.

cotton of their own raising at the rate of $30 per bale (500 lbs.) of upland, and $45 per bale (300 lbs.) of sea-island cotton.[1] This was planned as an attempt to protect the planters from the grip of speculators.

Georgia, under normal conditions, derived her income for running expenses from a general property tax, from special taxes on bank stock, railroads, lotteries, foreign insurance companies and foreign bank agents, and from the earnings of the state road. The assets of the state in 1860 included taxable property assessed at more than $600,000,000, the valuable state-owned railroad, the Western and Atlantic, and stock in various banks and railroads amounting to about $800,000. Over and against these assets was a public debt of $2,670,750 in bonds maturing between 1861 and 1880.[2] During the first two years of the war, Georgia, like other states and like the Federal and the Confederate governments, showed unwillingness to meet war demands by increasing taxes, preferring the indirect method of bonds and paper currency. At the first session of the legislature after the war began, the state assumed the Confederate war tax, meeting the obligation by an issue of bonds; and the general appropriation bill of the same session authorized the governor to issue bonds or treasury notes to cover any shortage in the treasury for general appropriations.[3] The total debt in bonds incurred during the war was $3,308,500. In currency in the form of non-interest-bearing notes, treasury certificates of deposit and change bills, nearly fifteen millions were issued during the war, making a total indebtedness in bonds and notes for war purposes of about $18,000,000.

[1] *Acts of the General Assembly*, 1861, pp. 20-22.

[2] *Report of the Comptroller General*, 1860, pp. 3, 4, 6, 11.

[3] *Acts of the General Assembly*, 1861, pp. 13, 79.

STATE DEBT, 1861-1865 [1]

Bonds

7% bonds, issued under Act approved December 11,
1861, for payment of Confederate tax assumed by
the state—due 1872 .... $2,441,000.00
6% bonds, for state defence—due 1881 .... 25,000.00
7% bonds, for state defence—due 1881 .... 842,500.00
These two sets of bonds were issued February, 1861
and May, 1862, under Acts approved November 16,
1860 and December 16, 1861. Interest at 6% was too
low to make bonds salable, so rate was raised
to 7%.

Total in bonds $3,308,500.00

Currency

Non-interest-bearing treasury notes and treasury certificates of deposit, payable in 8% bonds and specie
six months after treaty of peace or when banks of
Savannah and Augusta resume specie payment 3,758,000.00
Treasury notes and treasury certificates of deposit, payable in specie or 6% bonds of the state six months
after treaty of peace between the United States
and the Confederate States 4,800,000.00
Treasury notes, payable in Confederate treasury notes
if presented within three months after maturity;
otherwise not redeemable except in payment of
public dues (outstanding in 1865) 5,171,500.00
Change bills, payable only in Confederate treasury notes
(outstanding in 1865) 997,775.85

Total in currency $14,727,275.85
Total war debt $18,035,775.85

Direct taxes, as a means of supporting the extra demands
of war, were not increased until the end of 1862, when
the legislature widened the scope of the general property
tax, declaring cotton, grain or other produce held for
barter or sale on April 1st of each year, not belonging to
the original producer, to be merchandise, and hence subject

---

[1] *Report of the Comptroller General*, 1865, pp. 11-18.

to taxation as other property. The amount of the general tax levied on property was fixed at $1,000,000 for 1862, and for 1863 at $1,500,000.[1] The first income tax was instituted by the legislature in special session in April, 1863. In its earliest form it provided for a graduated tax on the net income or profits of 20 per cent or more from the sale of goods, wares, merchandise, groceries, and from the distillation and sale of spirituous liquors. This was aimed primarily at speculation and excessive profits, but the aim seems not to have been well directed, for the comptroller general reported that the law produced misunderstanding, dodging, and fraudulent returns. In December of the same year, at the regular session of the legislature, the income tax was extended and changed in basis. Profits, instead of being taxed by the per cent of gain on capital, as in the April measure, were taxed at the specific amount of profit, and the rate was increased with the amount of profit. All profits over 8 per cent were taxed in the following scale:[2]

Less than $10,000,	taxed	at	5%
10,000-15,000	"	"	7½%.
15,000-20,000	"	"	10%
20,000-30,000	"	"	12½%
30,000-50,000	"	"	15%.
50,000-75,000	"	"	17½%
75,000-100,000	"	"	20%
over 100,000	"	"	25%

A slight change in the Tax Act of March 11, 1865, freed profits of less than 10 per cent from any income tax.[3] Most of the tax collected under this item, $125,241.64 in 1863 and $455,593.98 in 1864, came from the fifteen counties

[1] *Acts of the General Assembly*, 1861, p. 80; 1862-3, pp. 57, 59-60.

[2] *Ibid.*, 1862-3 p. 176, *et seq.*; 1863-4, pp. 80, 81; *Report of the Comptroller General*, 1863, pp. 28-31.

[3] *Acts of the General Assembly*, 1864-5, p. 66.

out of the total one hundred and thirty-two, where there
were factories or large mercantile establishments.[1] The
comptroller general, who disapproved of the income tax,
felt sure that there was much dodging and estimated the
returns as only one-fifth of the legitimate number. As
against 69,712 property tax payers, only 3,758 persons paid
any tax on income.[2] The assessment of the general tax for
1864 and 1865 was left to the governor and the comptroller
general, provided it did not exceed one per cent for all taxable property estimated in Confederate currency for 1864,
and one-half of one per cent for 1865.[3] In addition to
these state-imposed taxes, each county, through the justices
of the inferior court, issued bonds and levied extra taxes
to equip volunteers and to support indigent families of soldiers. In some counties the property of private soldiers
was exempt from the extra county tax, and in others property less than $2,000 was exempt when the holder was in
military service, and execution for default of taxes was delayed in case of those serving in the army.[4]

Popular opinion in Georgia supported the war with a
fair degree of unanimity, though there was strong opposition to secession in 1861, chiefly on the question of the expediency of immediate state action as against co-operation
with other Southern states.[5] After the beginning of hostilities the active Unionist element largely disappeared, fall-

[1] *Report of the Comptroller General*, 1863, p. 7; 1864, pp. 6, 30-31.

[2] *Ibid.*, 1864, p. 30.

[3] *Acts of the General Assembly*, 1864-5, p. 18 and 1863-4, p. 79. Act
of March 11, 1865, authorized additional tax of two-fifths of one per
cent on property. *Acts of the General Assembly*, 1864-5, p. 69.

[4] *Ibid.*, 1861, pp. 30, 76, 122, *et seq.*

[5] For the secession movement in Georgia, see Phillips, *Georgia and
State Rights*, chs. vii and viii.

ing in line with the mass of individuals who "went with their state". Though Unionists were still numerous in the upper counties, they were not a real political power and offered no appreciable obstacle to the general spirit of fighting to be free, which marked the early period of the war.[1] But during 1863 a spirit of querulous discontent with the Confederate administration developed strongly and widely. Georgia, through the action of her governor, presented the attitude of chronic objector, if not direct obstructionist, to the chief measures of the government at Richmond. At times the tension between the executives of the state and of the Confederacy was extremely high, particularly over the questions of conscription, suspension of the privilege of the writ of *habeas corpus,* and control of the state militia. Two hostile groups were formed in the state, with Robert Toombs, Alexander Stephens and his brother, Linton, on the side of Governor Brown, upholding the principle of state rights as against the extension of Confederate authority; while Howell Cobb, commander of the state troops, with H. V. Johnson and B. H. Hill, the two Confederate senators from Georgia, supported Jefferson Davis's policy.[2] The state legislature was generally more conservative in action than either of these two factions, watching jealously the centralizing tendencies of the Confederate government, and yet lagging behind the impatient hostility of the governor to Confederate policy. Military as well as political dissatisfaction was rife. Desertion from the army became threatening. The mountains in North Georgia were so infested with bands of deserters and stragglers that Governor Brown issued a proclamation

[1] Rhodes, *History of the United States since 1850,* vol. v, p. 449.

[2] Johnston and Browne, *Life of Alexander H. Stephens; New York Times,* December 3, 1863, speech of Robert Toombs delivered in Atlanta.

in January, 1863, ordering them to disperse and return to military service.[1]

The question then arises—Did this spirit of dissatisfaction and criticism mean a desire for peace and reunion? Discontent and a desire for reunion were not identical in the feelings of the people, though they tended to merge as time went on. The quarrelsome attitude of Georgia toward the Confederate power was, however, frequently misinterpreted by politicians and military commanders of the North, who regarded it as the presage of submission by independent state action. A clearer reading of this disaffected state of mind is given in a letter written early in 1863 by Alexander Stephens, who was always keenly sensitive to the pulse of popular sentiment in Georgia. In this letter he writes:

What do you suppose a Yankee paper would say over Governor Brown's proclamation about bands of traitors and tories in our State that require the military to put them down? Nothing of that sort has occurred in any part of the North yet; and we know, or ought to know, how little confidence is to be attached to it from what we see among ourselves. The great majority of the masses, both North and South, are true to the cause of their side,—no doubt about that. The great majority on both sides are tired of the war; want peace. I have no doubt about that. But as we do not want peace without independence, so they do not want peace without reunion. There is the difficulty. I think the war will break down in less than a twelvemonth; but I really do not see in that any prospect for peace, permanent peace. Peace founded upon a treaty recognizing our separate independence is not yet in sight of me.[2]

[1] *Official Records of the War of the Rebellion*, series iv, vol. ii, p. 360.

[2] Johnston and Browne, *op. cit.*, p. 435, a letter written by Stephens to R. M. Johnston, January 29, 1863. See Peace Resolutions intro-

In 1863 the leading apostles of discontent were the most ardent advocates of war to the goal of independence, but in the next year military disasters and threatened invasion of Georgia brought evident signs of weakening, and talk of reunion spread there as elsewhere. The idea was not promulgated as the tenet of any particular group or party, and the discussion was more by covert insinuation than by outright appeal or propaganda. The newspapers give little direct evidence of change of heart. However, growing reunion sentiment is inferable from the very loudness of the editorial calls for good cheer and the insistence of public speakers on the principle that nothing short of independence should be tolerated, even in thought.[1] Evidence is too scant to conclude that disaffection in Georgia went so far as to lend itself to the organization of secret peace societies, such as existed in North Carolina, Alabama, and elsewhere. Such societies may have existed along the Alabama border, but they seem to have played no decisive part in organizing a peace movement in Georgia.[2] The results of the gubernatorial election of 1863 throw some light on the extent of this peace feeling. The leading opponent to the re-election of Governor Brown was Joshua Hill, one of the strongest Union men in the state and one of the few leaders who had not gone with the state in sympathy after secession was voted. Mr. Hill's platform was a defence

duced by Linton Stephens in the Georgia Legislature, approved March 19, 1864. *Acts of the General Assembly*, 1864, p. 158; Waddell, *Biographical Sketch of Linton Stephens*, pp. 271-4.

[1] Speech of A. H. Stephens at Charlottesville, Va., July, 1863. Moore, *Rebellion Record*, vol. vii, pp. 216-7; letter of Robt. Toombs to A. Bees of Americus, Ga., in *New York Times*, September 12, 1863; extract from a Macon newspaper of August, 1863 in *Annual Cyclopedia*, 1863, p. 448.

[2] *Official Records of the War of the Rebellion*, series i, vol. xxiv, pt. iii, p. 588; series iv, vol. iii, p. 393.

of his Union policy in 1861 and a declaration of the futility
of the war, while Governor Brown stood out against anything short of independence as the aim of the war. The
outcome of the vote was the re-election of Governor Brown
by a large majority, but the fact that the outright Unionist
candidate carried more than one-fourth of the total vote
cast shows that the people of Georgia in 1863 were by no
means unanimous in wishing to push the war to the end of
independence, dubious of achievement as it then seemed.[1]
In 1864 a more definite peace sentiment developed. After
all expectation of foreign intervention had vanished, there
appeared to be two means by which peace might be attained,
directly by military success of the Confederate armies, and
vicariously by the triumph of the Northern Democrats in
the election of 1864. When the military victories of the
Southern armies became infrequent and when lines of Federal advance pushed farther and farther upon the soil of
the Southern states, hope of peace by the first means was
lost to all except the constitutionally sanguine. Then the
Southerners who still clung to the idea of independence put
their trust in the Northern Democratic party. The Democrats, however, did not promise to sanction the separation
of the sections, but declared officially for restoration on the
basis of the federal union of the states.[2] But whatever were
the words of the platform, both South and North felt that
the election of McClellan and Pendleton would mean that
the vast body of people in the North were weary of the
war to the point of abandoning the attempt to whip the re-
calcitrants into submission. This regard for political conditions in the North and the hope for the overthrow of the
Lincoln government played an important part in determin-

[1] *Annual Cyclopedia*, 1863, pp. 447-8.
[2] Platform of the Democratic Party in McPherson, *Political History
of the Great Rebellion*, p. 419.

ing the character of the peace feeling in Georgia in 1864.[1] By September, however, it became evident that no dependence could be placed on the success of the Northern Democrats. At the same time came a far more potent factor in developing the desire to end it all. The march of Sherman's army through Northwest Georgia, culminating in the fall of Atlanta, weakened the courage of the most stout hearted. The path of desolation which Sherman left behind him was a most terrifying threat to the rest of Georgia. It was no wonder that many began to cower and murmur peace in less exacting terms. The capture of Atlanta by the Federal army had a strongly depressing effect in the state and reunion talk was less disguised. Appeals were made to A. H. Stephens and H. V. Johnson for their views as to the propriety of attempting a peace movement, but both advised against it. While they were eager for peace, neither was disposed to head a movement toward independent state action.[2]

The critical point in the direction of the reconstruction sentiment came after General Sherman's occupation of Atlanta. Sherman thought that by playing upon the discordant feelings in Georgia toward the Confederate government, and by pointing a menacing finger toward the line of ruin from Chattanooga to Atlanta as a threat of what awaited the rest of the state, he might lure Georgia away from her confederate states. He wrote in a letter to Lincoln, September 17, 1864: "It would be a magnificent stroke of policy if we could, without surrendering principle or a foot of ground, arouse the latent enmity of Georgia

[1] Avery, *History of the State of Georgia*, p. 314; Reed, *History of Atlanta*, p. 174; letter of H. V. Johnson in *New York Times*, October 22, 1864.

[2] Avery, *op. cit.*, p. 286; Rhodes, *History of the United States*, 1850-1877, vol. v, p. 65.

against Davis." [1] Using Joshua Hill and William King, prominent Unionists, as intermediaries, Sherman invited Alexander Stephens and Governor Brown to an interview in Atlanta, suggesting that the state would be spared if the Georgia troops were recalled from the Confederate armies. [2] Stephens and Brown both refused to meet General Sherman, on the ground that neither he nor they had competent authority to settle such a matter. But before indicating his rejection of Sherman's proposition, Governor Brown called a special session of the legislature, and issued an order declaring a thirty-day furlough for the state militia under General Hood's command near Atlanta. This summons of an extra session of the legislature was not in itself a sign of weakening, for the extraordinary conditions arising from the pressure of an invading army might necessitate the meeting of the assembly. But the Governor's recall of the militia and the grant of a furlough are inexplicable unless they be taken as preliminary moves toward peace. His own explanation is entirely unconvincing, that the state troops, turned over to General Hood for the defence of Atlanta, were needed at their homes which they had left without preparation. So ran the Governor's order of September 10th. [3] Just eight days after the fall of Atlanta, when the enemy might at any moment march in any direction to spread the destruction that marked its path to Atlanta, the state troops were sent home to gather sorghum! It seems probable that could Governor Brown have proceeded on his own responsibility, he would have acted favorably toward the proposition made by General Sherman. He had a rare facility for divining on which side of the

---

[1] Sherman, *Memoirs*, vol. ii, p. 139.

[2] *Ibid.*, pp. 137-8; Johnston and Browne, *op. cit.*, pp. 471-2.

[3] *New York Times*, September 25, 1864.

bread the butter is spread, and to a mind such as his, less controlled than most by sentimental or ideal impulses, it must have been clear that the war was hopeless, a cheerless end not far off, and that a voluntary submission on the part of Georgia when the chance was given, instead of forced subjugation some weeks or months later, would save the state untold suffering in loss of life and property. But at the same time, the natural shrewdness of the Governor, sharpened by long political practice, made him see that the people of Georgia were not ready for such action as his own practical wisdom and regard for material consequences might dictate.

While weariness and discouragement with the war were increasing daily, there was strong objection to treating with an invading enemy, and stronger and more extensive still was the feeling that, whatever happened, the seceded states must stick together. This sentiment was voiced in Governor Brown's public note on the Sherman matter:

The fact must not be overlooked, however, that while Georgia possesses the sovereign power to act separately, her faith, which never has, and I trust, never will be violated, is pledged by strong implication to her Southern sisters, that she will not exercise this power without consent on their part, and concert of action with them.

Clear and direct as this statement is, the effect was rendered rather equivocal by the closing paragraph of the same letter:

If those on both sides who have the constitutional power of negotiation, from obstinacy or ambition, refuse to recognize the sovereignty of the states, and to leave the settlement of the question to the states when they cannot themselves agree and insist on continual effusion of blood to gratify their caprice, all the states, North and South, in their sovereign capacity, may then be justifiable in taking the matter in their own hands and settling it as sovereigns in their own way.[1]

In the middle of November the Federal army abandoned the ruined city of Atlanta and set out to " make Georgia howl ", as Sherman aptly stated the purpose of his march to the sea. The fate that awaited Georgia was not immediately appreciated. Many people thought, as did the military authorities at Washington, that Sherman was marching into a cul-de-sac and would be entrapped long before he reached the coast. But after Savannah had fallen late in December, affairs wore a different aspect. There was little question then about the fate of Georgia. Sufficient answer lay in the path, three hundred miles long and forty miles wide, of smoking ruins and trampled fields. The year 1865 dawned with little encouragement, except the certainty that the end was near. Some wished to hasten the end by calling a state convention, but others were unwilling to do anything to meet submission half way. The surrender in April brought the end which many greeted with the sense of relief that at least the worst had come.

Developing out of the despondency produced by the military disasters of 1863, helped on by the disaffection of the Georgia government toward the Confederate administration, and precipitated by the direful experience of Sherman's march, there existed in Georgia before the end of the war a strong trend toward reunion, a willingness to abandon the attempt to establish the independence of the seceded states. This readiness for submission implied no more than a return to the Union as it was, changed in nature only by the elimination of slavery. From lack of organization, and from the absence of declared leaders and a fixed

[1] *New York Times*, October 8, 1864, from the *Milledgeville Confederate Union*; Fielder, *Life and Times of Joseph E. Brown*, p. 311.

purpose to achieve a definite end, the peace feeling in
Georgia before the surrender was more in the nature of a
reunion sentiment than an actual movement towards reconstruction.

In April, 1865, when resistance to the Union ceased in
Georgia with the news of General Johnston's surrender to
General Sherman in North Carolina, the war left Georgia
poorer by the loss of 40,000 of its white population, and
burdened it with a serious labor problem, on the solution
of which the whole agricultural, and hence, chief economic
interest of the state depended. If her half million of blacks
continued to work in the fields as before, then her people
would be none the worse off and the estimated value of
slave holdings would not be reckoned as loss, but merely
transferred to enhance the value of land.[1] But if freedom
to the negro meant freedom from work, then land would
be worthless and Georgia itself would be ruined. In the
spring of 1865, lands in the rich southwest region were
untouched by the hand of the enemy, but across the middle
of the state, from the northwest corner to Savannah, lay a
land of waste thirty or forty miles broad. In this region
destruction involved not only stores of cotton and food
supplies and growing crops, but the annihilation of all implements and means with which to make a new crop.
Fences and barns were burned and live stock carried away.
For the soldier or refugee returning to the Sherman belt,
nothing was left but the mild climate and an occasional
well of water which the Yankees had been unable to de-
molish or appropriate.[2] Northeast Georgia, though not in-

[1] *Report of the Comptroller General,* 1860, p. 6; taxable value of land
in 1860, $161,764,955; of slaves, $302,694,855.

[2] For destruction wrought by Sherman's march, see Moore, *Rebellion
Record,* vol. ix, p. 7; *New York Times,* October 14, November 23, 1865;

vaded, was desolate and poverty-stricken, and just at the end of the war in April, 1865, Wilson's raiders burned cotton, warehouses and factories in the west and central part of the state, at West Point, Columbus, Griffin, and Macon. The destructive work of a hostile army disrupted the main lines of railway, destroying the chief means of transportation to the coast. Banks were thoroughly ruined and capital vanished. The state was eighteen million dollars in debt, with assets short in the weakened condition of its income-producing property, the Western and Atlantic R. R., and the taxable property of its citizens already burdened beyond the last point of endurance by war taxes and uncertain income.

In all this disaster, the people of Georgia felt relief that the end had come at last, but doubt and uncertainty for what the future might bring. In general, there was a willingness to return to the Union, even though the abandonment of slavery should be the price exacted for reunion. That reconstruction would enforce more than such a reunion was not foreseen.

Avery, *History of the State of Georgia,* p. 306; *Annual Cyclopedia,* 1864, p. 407; 1865, pp. 392-3; Wilson, *Historic and Picturesque Savannah,* p. 203; Andrews, *War-Time Journal of a Georgia Girl,* pp. 32-4; Reed, *History of Atlanta,* p. 194; newspaper clippings in *Brown Scrap Books.*

CHAPTER II

Transition from Slavery to Freedom

THE problems of peace were far more difficult and intricate than were those of war, and in 1865 when hostilities ceased, instead of the worst having passed, as the people of the South thought, the worst had only just begun in the region subject to reconstruction. Of all the problems before the South and the Nation, the foremost, not yet completely solved after fifty years, were the adaptation of the slave-driven negro to free labor, the adjustment of the land and planting system to new conditions, and the settlement of social relations between the two races living side by side when the old bond of master and slave was destroyed. These economic and social problems were complicated by political difficulties, the relation of the rebel state to the Union, the constitution of political citizenship in the state, and the struggle for party domination. In attempting to solve these problems, the process of reconstruction in Georgia, as in every other Southern state, was worked out through two revolutions. In 1865, the abolition of slavery overthrew the whole ante-bellum economy of Georgia; and since Georgia was primarily an agricultural state, a change in the labor system meant nothing less than a far-reaching economic revolution. In 1867, when the radicals in Congress undertook to make over the conquered provinces, the political enfranchisement of the former slaves induced a second revolution, fundamentally political and social in character.

[42

The half-million negroes in Georgia were not actually free until the end of the war, for the Emancipation Proclamation had no effect except in a limited region. In districts not penetrated by the Federal armies agricultural labor continued during the war as under normal conditions. But wherever the army appeared negroes left the plough in the field to follow the soldiers to freedom. The path traversed by Sherman's army was not through the region where blacks were most numerous, hence disorganization of labor was not general until the summer of 1865, when military posts were established. To the negro, freedom meant all that slavery had not been. Slavery signified work, generally in the field, labor under constant supervision, restriction in habitat, and subjection to patrol. Therefore, if freedom meant anything at all it must be idleness, roving from place to place, flocking into towns, and doing generally as pleasure dictated.[1] Vagrancy and loafing, natural reactions when the restraint of slavery was removed, were fostered among the negroes by the belief, as tenacious as their certainty of judgment day, that at Christmas time the white folks' lands would be divided and every negro would have his share, commonly estimated at forty acres and a mule.[2]

The negroes, especially as they came in contact with the soldiers of the garrisons and the agents of the Freedmen's Bureau, had some understanding that the war had been fought for the negro against the white man, and as outcome, what had been the property of the master would be turned over to his slaves. When the negroes were told by their masters or by Federal agents or by general rumor that

[1] Mr. Fleming's account of the negro testing his freedom in Alabama is substantially true for Georgia as well. Fleming, *Civil War and Reconstruction in Alabama*, p. 269, *et seq.*

[2] *New York Times*, October 14 and 24, 1865 (correspondent writing under the pseudonym, "Quondam"); *Milledgeville Federal Union*, July 18, 1865; Hull, *Annals of Athens*, p. 303.

they were free, the most general and immediate response
to the news was to pick up and leave the home place to go
somewhere else, preferably to a town.   The lure of the
city was strong to the blacks, appealing to their social
natures, to their inherent love for a crowd.

The first and only means by which the negroes could test
their freedom was migration, to go where they were not.
They put into practice the cynic's moral, " There's no place
like home—thank God ! "   With no sense of foresight, but
in simple trust that freedom must be good, there were
thousands of negroes, who, as Sidney Andrews remarked,
" had clearly let go the bird in hand without any prospect
of finding even one in the bush ".[1]   In the black belt of
Georgia, where slavery was as little burdensome to the
negro as anywhere in the South, multitudes of negroes were
on the march, leaving comfort and security in joyful quest
of the unknown.   Starve or steal they must before the
winter was over, for work they would not.   On the out-
skirts of almost every town there were throngs of these
wanderers huddled together in rude huts or with no shelter
at all.   In one such wretched hovel in Macon, Andrews
found eleven negroes.   With one of the men he had the
following conversation : [2]

" Well, Uncle," said I, after he had told me that he was
raised near Knoxville, some thirty miles away,—" well, Uncle,
what did you come up to the city for?   Why didn't you stay
on the old place?   Didn't you have a kind master?"

" I's had a berry good master, mass'r," he said, " but ye see
I's wanted to be free man."

" But you were just as free there as you are here."

" P'r'aps I is, but I's make a livin' up yer, I dun reckon; an'

[1] Andrews, *The South since the War*, p. 349.

[2] *Ibid.*, pp. 350-351.

I likes ter be free man whar I can go an' cum, an' nobody
says not'ing."

" But you would have been more comfortable on the old
place: you would have had plenty to eat and plenty of clothes
to wear."

" Ye see, mass'r, de good Lo'd he know what's de best t'ing
fur de brack, well as fur de w'ite; an' He say ter we dat we
should cum up yer, an' I don't reckon He let we starve."

The very essence of the negro's *Wanderlust* was expressed in the reply of an old darky, who was asked why
she left the old place: " What fur? *Joy my freedom!* " [1]
Hence, by the fall of 1865, when cotton-picking time came,
a large majority of the freedmen had left their former masters. Thousands of able-bodied negroes were living in in-
dolence, getting a living by picking and stealing from unpro-
tected corn-fields and hen-roosts; and hundreds more aged
and infirm and children were cared for by the Freedmen's
Bureau.[2] Thus, in the summer and fall of 1865, vagabondage was the general condition of the freedmen. Plantations
suffered from the loss of labor, from their depredations on
the crops, while towns were overwhelmed with throngs of
idle blacks that crowded everywhere.[3] Newspapers reported that most of the offenders brought before the provost courts in towns were negroes, accused of stealing,
quarreling, and disturbing the peace generally.[4] The *Augusta Constitutionalist* urged the need of turning to the
military authorities for protection against vagrants, and
suggested as a remedy that the commander of the post re-

[1] Andrews, *op. cit.*, p. 353.

[2] B. C. Truman said that about one-third of the slaves were with
their former masters. *New York Times*, November 23, 1865.

[3] Andrews, *War-Time Journal of a Georgia Girl*, p. 253, and newspapers.

[4] *Macon Telegraph*, December 1 and 30, 1865, and other papers.

quire all negroes coming into the city to register, allow
them reasonable time to secure work, and then send all
those still idle to plantations on the coast or hire them for
work on the railroads.[1] In Athens in one week one hundred and fifty negroes were arrested for theft. The problem of punishment was a trying one for provost marshals,
some of whom devised odd penalties, such as tying the of-
fender by his thumbs on tiptoe, or shaving off one-half of
his head, or putting him in a barrel with armholes and
labeled—" I am a thief ".[2] Somewhat later, judges of the
Freedmen's Court in Savannah punished freedmen by making them work in the chaingang on the streets, each one
bearing a placard stating his crime.[3]

Idleness and vagrancy brought to the freedmen much suffering and hardship from which slavery had protected them.
As valuable property, slaves were well fed and comfortably
housed, but as free persons, many of them abandoned all
comforts, satisfied because they were free. The rate of
mortality among the blacks in the latter part of 1865 was
frightfully high, and especially in towns, where pressure
for existence was heaviest, they suffered greatly from starvation and disease. In Macon, for instance, during December, about five hundred negroes died, whereas ordinarily the death rate was only about forty a month.[4] With
soldiers returning from the armies and negroes wandering without restraint, smallpox spread widely during the
latter part of 1865 and was responsible for many deaths
among the blacks.

[1] *Macon Telegraph*, May 24 and June 1, 1865.

[2] Hull, *Annals of Athens*, p. 303.

[3] *Macon Telegraph*, January 13, 1866.

[4] *New York Times*, December 31, 1865, from *Macon Telegraph* and
Augusta Constitutionalist; Joint Committee on Reconstruction, pt. iii,
p. 173 (Test.: Sidney Andrews).

One of the difficulties in the transition from slavery to freedom was the care of the dependent classes among the freedmen, the aged, helpless and young children. Some of these were supported by the Freedmen's Bureau, and many more, who remained in their old homes, were looked after by their former masters as they had always been. It was probably a rare case for a former slave-holder to turn out the old darkies or the sick, and, if he had any means of subsistence whatever, he willingly cared for those who had been dependent on him.[1] But it was a different matter when the charity given freely was demanded as an obligation by the Freedmen's Bureau. General Tillson directed that the Bureau was not to remove the helpless and the aged freedmen and young children from the homes of their masters: dependent adults should be supported by their sons or daughters, if they had any, or by former masters until the state should make provision for them; if children were not supported the agent should try to bind them out.[2] Newspapers, in commenting on this order, said that no case had been heard of where a master had refused to care for the helpless among his former slaves. " We wonder," said the *Columbus Enquirer,* " how many such examples there are at the North—how many poor Irish or German ' helps ' are provided for in their old age by former employers who for a score of years had the benefit of their faithful service when able to work." [3] The following observation of the *Milledgeville Union* on General Tillson's order was thoroughly sound in principle:

[1] B. C. Truman observed that in the whole state the Freedmen's Bureau had only about 1000 paupers, because generally the aged and young were cared for by their former masters. *New York Times,* December 5, 1865.

[2] Asst. Commissioner Tillson, Circular no. 5, in *Milledgeville Federal Union,* January 9, 1866.

[3] Quoted in *Milledgeville Federal Union,* January 9, 1866.

The plantation economy was an integral system, all parts of which were necessary to sustain it. When the government took away the effective working force, it knocked away the prop that upheld the whole system; it withdrew the effective workers, and with them the *means* by which the owner was enabled to provide for those who could not provide for themselves.[1]

And another comment on the order was:

The law which freed the negro, at the same time freed the master. At the same moment, and for both parties, all obligations springing out of the relation of master and slave, except those of kindness, ceased mutually to exist. If any officer can make the master support the old and infirm slave, he can also make the slave continue under and support the old and infirm master.[2]

Under these conditions the great troublesome question of the day, discussed in newspaper editorials and talked over wherever planters met together, was—What is to be done with the negro? On this point the *Southern Cultivator* observed:

Our servants are giving us not a little trouble, nowadays. Poor, misguided creatures! who imagine that " freedom " consists in no work, plenty to eat, and going where they please! . . . . The whole question of our future agricultural labor is one of the deepest import to every landholder and resident of the South; and deserves the calmest consideration of the wisest, best, and most experienced men of our country.[3]

It was agreed that some action must be taken to prevent a large part of the negro population from lapsing into per-

[1] *Milledgeville Federal Union,* January 9, 1866.
[2] *Southern Cultivator,* July, 1865.
[3] *June* 1, 1865.

manent vagabondage, and from the experience of the first few months of the negroes testing their freedom, the only possible method, apparently, was by some scheme of compulsory labor. Various suggestions for labor control were made. The editor of the *Savannah Herald* urged the appointment of officers in every militia district to supervise labor.[1] In most of the Southern states laws to control vagrancy in the Black Codes made some approach to compulsory labor. But in the meantime, the military authorities, as guardians of the black wards of the government, before the Freedmen's Bureau was thoroughly established in the state, were active in attempts to make the negroes work. Some parts of Georgia were fortunate in having officers at the posts who were energetic in trying to adjust labor difficulties and settle the negroes at work. In Milledgeville, for instance, blacks could not enjoy ease without labor, for the military officer there put vagrants to work on the streets without compensation.[2] Military orders in some places forbade negroes to go from one plantation to another without passes, and provided for daily inspection of negro cabins to stop the stealing and killing of stock. To prevent plundering on the plantations, trading with negroes from the country was prohibited. All blacks had to have written permits from their masters to sell things, and the commander of the post at Milledgeville ordered, " Freedmen that will use any disrespectful language to their former masters will surely be punished." Runaways who broke labor contracts and those who harbored runaways were arrested.[3] On June 26, 1865, General Molineux, in Augusta, issued strict regulations to control vagrancy. Passes were

[1] January 3, 1866.

[2] *Milledgeville Federal Union*, October 17, 1865.

[3] The above orders are mentioned in Avery, *History of the State of Georgia,* p. 343.

required from all persons out after nine o'clock.[1] Such restrictions on the freedmen, made by their national protectors, went further toward re-establishing the old slavery in some respects than even the severest of the Black Codes.

When General Tillson took charge as Assistant Commissioner of the Freedmen's Bureau in Georgia, he started energetically to improve the condition of the blacks by making them earn their living. In his order of October 3, 1865, he gave the following commands to his agents: to get work for unemployed negroes so as to prevent death and starvation in the approaching winter; to refuse rations to able-bodied negroes for whom work could be found; to disabuse the negroes of the false impression about the distribution of lands at Christmas; to help and not to interfere with the fulfilment of contracts already made, whether written or verbal; and to see that contracts for 1866 be written in a set form and duly registered by the superintendent of the district.[2] But nothing, not even the Bureau, could induce the freedmen to settle down to work, and planters were able to make very few contracts in the summer and fall when the negroes were filled with expectations of the distribution of land and other good things at Christmas time.

Rumors were current among the whites that a general insurrection was being planned by the negroes at Christmas and newspapers in various sections warned the people to make ready to protect themselves. There is no evidence that the Christmas uprising was anything more than mere rumor, a bogey to which the nervous and uncertain state of mind of the white people gave reality. But true or false

[1] *Official Records of the War of the Rebellion*, vol. xlvii, pt. iii, p. 665.
[2] *Milledgeville Federal Union*, January 9, 1866.

as rumors might prove, the white people took precautions against what the season might bring forth. In the country districts militia was organized to picket roads and patrol the country. During the last week of 1865 a number of negroes were killed and other outrages were reported.[1] But probably the disorder was not much greater than was usual at that season of the year. In towns Christmas passed more quietly than was expected. In Milledgeville, for instance, fewer negroes appeared than at Christmas time before and had less money to spend.[2] In Macon the rollicking, jovial negro of Christmas time was no longer seen. One good old negro, looking back to the palmy days of the past, said to a white friend: " Ah, Masser, niggers were niggers in dem days. Den dey enjoyed demselves and had somebody to take care of em. Now dey is just vagabonds —all gwine to de debil together." [3]

At any rate, the holiday season passed without undue disorder and after the beginning of the new year negroes began to look around for jobs and made contracts for 1866. Doubtless the determined order of General Tillson on December 22d greatly influenced them towards facing the necessity of work. One section of the order was as follows: [4]

Freed people have the right to select their own employers; but if they continue to neglect or refuse to make contracts, then, on and after January 15th, 1866, officers and agents of the Bureau will have the right, and it shall be their duty, to make contracts for them, in all cases where employers offer good

---

[1] *The Nation*, February 1, 1866 (contributed articles by J. R. Dennett on " The South as It Is ").

[2] *Milledgeville Federal Union*, January 2, 1866.

[3] *Macon Journal and Messenger*, December 31, 1865.

[4] *Milledgeville Federal Union*, January 9, 1866.

wages and kind treatment, unless the freed people belong to the class above excepted [those who have sufficient property to support themselves and their families without contracting to labor], or can show that they can obtain better terms. Contracts so made shall be as binding on both parties as though made with the full consent of the freed people.

In the early aftermath of emancipation most planters looked with despair upon the future of agriculture with free labor. Freedom and labor were considered incompatible in the negro. All the characteristics of the negro slave, as his owner knew him, were believed to be inherently racial, rather than adventitious, the product of slavery. "The negro won't work." "Cotton can never be raised with free labor." "Niggers won't work and everything is going to ruin." These opinions were heard on all sides in the summer and fall of 1865. Slavery was considered the natural and best condition for the negro. The point of view expressed in the following letter, written by Howell Cobb to General J. H. Wilson, echoed the opinion of the great mass of Southern people: [1]

By the abolition of slavery—which either has been—or soon will be accomplished, a state of things has been produced, well calculated to excite the most serious apprehensions with the people of the South. I regard the result as unfortunate both for the white and the black. The institution of slavery, in my judgment, provided the best system of labor that could be devised for the negro race. But that has passed away, and it will tax the ability of the best and wisest statesmen to provide a substitute for it. It is due both to the white population and the negroes that the present state of things should not remain. You will find that our people are fully prepared to conform to

[1] Letter dated from Macon, June 14, 1865. In Johnson MSS. in the Library of Congress. This letter has been published in Fleming, *Documentary History of Reconstruction*, vol. i, pp. 128-131.

the new state of things;—and as a general rule will be disposed to pursue towards the negroes, a course dictated by humanity and kindness. I take it for granted, that the future relations, between the negroes and their former owners, like all other questions of domestic policy, will be under the control and direction of the State governments.

In commenting on Cobb's letter, General Wilson made this statement as to the attitude of the people of Georgia toward slavery: [1]

The people express an external submission to its Abolition, but there is an evident desire on the part of some to get the matter within their own control, after the re-organization of the State. Others are anxious to substitute a gradual system of emancipation, or a modified condition of Slavery, similar to Peonage, and still others seem to doubt that the President's proclamation of freedom, and the laws of Congress have been final in disposing of the Slavery question. There must be no hesitation on any of these points either by military or civil authorities. The whole system of Slavery and slave labor must be effectually destroyed, and the Freedmen protected from the injustice of evil men, before the people of Georgia get the State Government under their own control. If a single particle of life is left in the institution, or the original guardians of it are allowed any influence in the reorganization of the State, they will resuscitate and perpetuate its iniquities if possible.

Some years later many of the slave-owning class came to think that emancipation was good for the master, whatever it might be for the slave; that it relieved the white man of a heavy responsibility. But in 1865 this opinion was shared by only a few slaveholders. Joseph LeConte,

[1] Letter of Bvt. Maj. Gen. J. H. Wilson to Brig. Gen. W. D. Whipple, from Macon, Ga., June 15, 1865. Johnson MSS.

who owned a large plantation in Liberty County, went even further and declared, to the astonishment of his friends, that emancipation entailed no real loss; that the exchange from the slave to a wage system, if labor remained reliable, would simply transfer the value of slaves to the value of land.[1] Few, likewise, were the slave owners who faced the new order of things with an open mind. Alexander H. Stephens was one of this class, who, as far as his own negroes were concerned, was glad to try the experiment, to see what could be done for them under the new conditions. As he wrote to President Johnson from Fort Warren, where he was imprisoned, in June, 1865:[2] " Slavery has been completely abolished. If any other system or measure can be devised for the better amelioration of the condition of the colored portion of our population, consistent with the best interests of both races, then I shall be content." In 1866, when Stephens was called before the Reconstruction Committee of Congress, he stated that relations between the whites and the blacks in Georgia were as good as the relations between employers and employees elsewhere, much better than in the previous fall when negroes were idle, refusing to make contracts in the expectation that the convention would distribute land among them at Christmas.[3]

In fact, the whole tone of comment on the labor situation changed completely in the early months of 1866. Despair gave place to hopefulness as the blacks made agreements to work and settled down on the plantations. As the *Augusta Chronicle* observed, General Tillson's order was having good effect, and consequently planters were feeling more encouraged than a few weeks previous. The real test

[1] LeConte, *Autobiography,* pp. 232-3.

[2] Avary (*ed.*), *Recollections of Alex. H. Stephens,* p. 201.

[3] *Joint Committee on Reconstruction,* 1866, pt. iii, p. 160.

would come in the summer and early fall. Patience and forbearance were necessary. The result would probably be mixed, however, with some failures and other successes under the new system of labor.[1] The *Milledgeville Federal Union* reported that in Baldwin County most of the negroes had gone to work though a score or more were still hanging around the sunny corners in town. The editor gave his opinion that the negroes should be taught that they must work, and that even being a " preacher " should not save a negro from a bad name if he didn't work.[2] In the Macon region negroes pretty generally contracted and went to work, but even then only about a third of a crop was expected. Delay was caused in some places where agents of the Freedmen's Bureau insisted that contracts be submitted to them.[3] In Talbot and Jefferson and other counties of Central Georgia, negro men settled to work early in January, but there, as elsewhere, difficulties were found in getting negro women to go back to their ante-bellum duties.[4] Reports from South Georgia, from Thomas, Early, Baker and other counties, said that the labor question was adjusting itself more rapidly than had been expected, though planters were not supplied with as many hands as they wanted and many large farms were idle for want of laborers.[5]

Still some of the larger towns continued to be troubled with crowds of loafing negroes. In Augusta at the end of January the streets were thronged with negro vagrants when everyone was clamoring for laborers. Negro hucksters harangued the loafers on street corners, telling them

---

[1] January 9, 1866.

[2] January 9, 1866.

[3] *Macon Journal and Messenger*, January 16, 1866.

[4] *Augusta Chronicle*, May 13, 1866; *Macon Telegraph*, February 3, 1866.

[5] *Ibid.*, January 10, 27 and February 14, 1866.

not to work for the whites unless they could get extravagant privileges.[1] But all of the negroes that remained in the towns after the holidays were not loafers. Some who settled down there were skilled mechanics of the plantation who found a good market for their craft in the city. This advertisement, for instance appeared in an Augusta paper, evidently written by a white friend of the persons whose names are signed:[2]

Work wanted—We have established a shop at Turnwold where we are prepared to do all manner of wood and iron work—wagon making and repairing included. We have not turned fools because we are free, but know we have to work for our living, and are determined to do it. We mean to be sober, industrious, honest, and respectful to white folks, and so we depend on them to give us work. (signed) William & Jim.

Town life afforded many opportunities to blacks who acquired skill of one sort or another as slaves. For instance, in the Hull family in Athens, the house servants found various means of living in the new conditions after emancipation. The seamstress and her daughter moved into a house belonging to Mr. Hull and took in sewing enough to support themselves. The carriage driver found work in a livery stable, and the old carpenter, who stuck to his master and was supported by him, made tubs and buckets for ready cash to buy dram and tobacco.[3] These are only a few instances of the many capable negroes who, having been household servants in towns or skilled mechanics on plantations, found profitable employment in towns and cities after emancipation. This new or greatly augmented class of black inhabitants changed the character of negro dwell-

Augusta Chronicle, January 31, 1866.

[2] *Ibid.*, April 17, 1866.

[3] Hull, *Annals of Athens*, p. 292.

ings in towns, which had formerly been small houses in the rear of white people's houses. Later, separate negro tenements were built in a distinct section of the city, the beginning of the " Shermantown " or " darktown " settlements of Southern cities.[1]

Plantations on the sea-islands and coast lands where rice and long staple cotton were raised were abandoned when the Federal fleet in 1862 blockaded the Georgia coast. All planters who had facilities transported their slaves to the safer inland region or else left the plantations to the negroes to get along as best they might. At the end of the war, when owners returned to the islands, difficulties arose over claims to lands that were occupied by the negroes as their own. General Sherman, after his march to the sea in 1864, assigned abandoned lands to negroes who had followed in his train.[2] But since he gave only a possessory title, rights were finally restored to the owners. After the war, conditions in the island and coast settlements were thoroughly chaotic, for vicious agents of the Freedmen's Bureau or men acting under its authorization did much to disturb the blacks and hinder instead of help them to make themselves self-supporting. Colored troops established at Darien and at other coast points also were contributing factors towards disturbance. But by the end of 1865 the colored troops had been recalled, giving place to white regiments. Some of the negroes, who had been transported up state during the war, came wandering back, many of them with no means of support, saying that their masters had dismissed them without any share of the crop or wages.[3]

[1] *Macon Journal and Messenger*, March 2, 1866.

[2] *Macon Telegraph*, February 10, 1866, quotes a letter from Gen. Sherman to President Johnson of February 2, 1866; Trowbridge, *Picture of the Desolated States*, pp. 508, 509.

[3] *Joint Committee on Reconstruction*, pt. iii, p. 42, report of C. H. Howard of the Freedmen's Bureau.

In the summer of 1866 General Steedman and General Fullerton, in investigating the working of the Freedmen's Bureau under commission from the War Department, made a careful tour of inspection of the Sea Islands of Georgia.[1] At the Ogeechee River Settlement, the largest colony established by General Sherman's order, they found that the negroes had been duped by the agent, who left them at the end of the year with no share in the rice crop they had raised. The agent, who provided the workers during the season with government rations, had hired twenty-five freedmen as guards and armed them with U. S. muskets, so as to prevent whites from entering the settlement. Even U. S. officers were refused admittance except by pass from the agent. On St. Simon's Island freedmen held eighteen valid land grants, encumbering four plantations. By the middle of 1866 most of the five or six hundred freedmen on the island were working for owners who had returned to occupy their plantations. They appeared well-fed and contented. On two plantations, though no formal contracts had been made, the negroes had confidence in fair treatment. Sapelo Island was exclusively cultivated by two Northerners, who were running a big plantation, promising some success. The negroes were working for two-thirds of the crop. In 1865 the freedmen of Sapelo Island had fallen into the hands of some unprincipled men who came with permits from the Freedmen's Bureau and bought their cotton at 10 cents per pound, paying mostly in whisky.[2] St. Catherine's Island was in the grip of the notorious Tunis

[1] The Steedman-Fullerton Report, on which this account is based, is printed in full in the *New York Herald*, beginning June 13, 1866; parts dealing with Georgia appear in the *Savannah News and Herald*, May 19, 21, and August 15, 1866, and *Augusta Chronicle*, June 16, 1866.

[2] *New York Herald*, June 2, 1866. Correspondent with Steedman and Fullerton.

G. Campbell,[1] a negro from Canada, appointed agent of the Bureau by General Saxton. Campbell had set up an autocratic government with an absurdly elaborate constitution, senate, house of representatives, courts of various kinds, and what not, with himself as chief autocrat. Seventeen valid land grants, 515 acres in all scattered over the island, were consolidated by General Tillson to cover one end of the island, leaving the remainder to the original owners. Two Northerners, who had rented part of the Walburg plantation and worked 147 hands, planted 530 acres in cotton and 115 acres in corn; whereas the 475 freedmen working for themselves, more than three times as many, planted only 200 acres of cotton and the same amount of corn: a commentary on the industry of the negro when left to himself. A special correspondent for the *New York Herald*, traveling with Steedman and Fullerton on their inspection tour, wrote the following as his opinion of the negro as land owner:[2]

This is but another illustration of the fact which I have previously mentioned, namely, that the experiment of making the uneducated plantation negro a planter on his own account is an utter and unmitigated failure, injurious to the negro himself and to the community in which he lives. The sooner the few valid land certificates issued under Gen. Sherman's order are bought up by the government, the better. It will remove a fruitful source of jealousy and ill-feeling among the blacks themselves, lessen the risk of unfriendly collision with the whites, and in the end be much better for all concerned.

The journal which Frances Butler Leigh kept of her residence on her father's plantations on St. Simon's Island and Butler's Island (near Darien) is a valuable account of con-

---

[1] Notorious in the later reconstruction period of Georgia.

[2] *New York Herald*, June 2, 1866.

ditions on the Sea Islands after the war.[1]   Early in 1866
letters from a neighbor and from a Bureau agent informed
Mr. Butler, who had resided in the North during the war,
that all his slaves had returned to the island and would
hire to no one else though they were badly in need of provisions.   When Mr. Butler returned, in addition to his own
negroes there were some whom he had sold eight years
before.   Seven had worked their way from the up-country.
Since it was too late to plant a full crop, only enough was
planted to make seed for another year and to clear expenses,
the negroes to have one-half of what was raised.   The negroes seemed happy to get back to the old place and to
their master.   Everything which had been left in their
charge was restored, and one old couple, " Uncle John and
Mum Peggy ", came with five dollars in silver half-dollars
tied up in a bag, which had been given to them in the second
year of the war by a Yankee captain for some chickens.
The negroes on St. Simon's Island, who had come under
the influence of Northern soldiers during the war, seemed
disappointed that the land was not really theirs as the
Yankees had told them.   They had planted some corn and
cotton, which Mr. Butler allowed them to keep, provided
they should plant twenty acres for him, for which he would
feed and clothe them.   After the first year's experience,
when Mr. Butler found that it was decidedly more difficult
to carry on a plantation with free than with slave labor,
he arranged with a Northerner who had leased a place on
St. Simon's to manage the Butler place for him on shares.
Mr. Butler's experience was not by any means unique.
After the war the prosperity of the rice and sea-island
cotton plantations vanished.

In the difficult period of transition from slavery to free-

[1] Leigh, *Ten Years on a Georgia Plantation since the War.*

dom, Georgia was particularly fortunate in having General David Tillson in charge of the Freedmen's Bureau from September, 1865, to January, 1867.[1] General Tillson was an enlightened man, fully in sympathy with the demands upon him to safeguard the interests of the negro, but intelligent enough to understand that the negro's welfare would not be advanced by stirring up the hostility of the former masters. It was his policy to secure the co-operation of the citizens of Georgia with the Bureau so far as possible. Hence, on October 25th he wrote to Provisional Governor Johnson, requesting him to instruct such justices of the peace and ordinaries of the counties, as might be designated by the Freedmen's Bureau, to act as agents. In selecting such civil officers as Bureau agents, Tillson promised to be guided by the competency and fitness of the officers to do simple justice without reference to condition or color.[2] Further co-operation was established between civil authority and the Bureau when the Assistant Commissioner asked the Provisional Governor to constitute the civil courts of the governor's appointment as freedmen's courts, whenever the judges were ready to accept such recognition. This was done with satisfactory results in most instances. In December, 1866, the legislature passed a law which made valid the contracts of apprenticeship made by citizens of Georgia with Freedmen's Bureau agents, the same as if made according to statutory provisions of the state.[3]

The main activities of the Freedmen's Bureau in 1865

[1] General Saxton was Assistant Commissioner for South Carolina, Georgia and Florida up to January, 1866, but was relieved in Georgia in December, 1865. Before that time Tillson was a subordinate under him.

[2] *Journal of the Proceedings of the Constitutional Convention of the People of Georgia*, 1865, p. 30.

[3] *Acts of the General Assembly*, 1866, p. 141.

and 1866 concerned the physical and economic needs of the negroes. It also directed educational opportunities for the freedmen in connection with Northern philanthropic societies. In the early months after emancipation, when the freedmen could not or would not earn their living, supplies from the Bureau kept many of them from starving. Between June, 1865, and September, 1866, 847,699 rations were furnished in Georgia; and in the next year from September, 1866, to September, 1867, about half that amount, less in Georgia than in the neighboring states. To care for the sick and helpless, the Freedmen's Bureau had five hospitals in Georgia in 1865, seven in 1866.[1]

Besides relieving distress among the freedmen, the most important work of the Freedmen's Bureau in 1865 and 1866 was its regulation of labor in getting the negro to work and in fixing the terms of contract. General Tillson used his utmost energy to disabuse the negroes of the idea that they did not have to work for their living. His second circular order of October 3, 1865, gave notice that rations would not be furnished to able-bodied negroes for whom work could be found; and his order of December 22d pronounced an ultimatum to idle negroes, giving them until January 15th to make contracts to labor.[2] This order, with the determination of Tillson to enforce it, was in no small part responsible for the betterment in the labor situation in 1866. Prior to issuing this order, General Tillson held a meeting with planters in Savannah, at which he offered to do his best to induce negroes to make contracts and to enforce them, if the planters for their part would offer good wages.[3] In Augusta, Milledgeville and elsewhere, other

[1] Peirce, *Freedmen's Bureau*, pp. 92, 98.

[2] *Milledgeville Federal Union*, November 17, 1865; January 9, 1866.

[3] *Joint Committee on Reconstruction*, 1866, pt. iii, p. 41, report of C. H. Howard of the Freedmen's Bureau.

officers of the Freedmen's Bureau addressed public meetings in an effort to bring seekers after labor and the laborers into harmony.[1] The planters appealed to the Bureau to help them in another difficulty which confronted them, which was to protect them against other employers who would entice the negroes away, after they had already contracted for the year, by offer of higher wages. Some unscrupulous men were ready to offer almost anything at the beginning of the season when hands were scarce, but were unable or unwilling to live up to their bargain when the day of reckoning came. As Ben Hill said: " How to make the negro observe his contract on the one hand, and how to make the bad white man fulfil his contract on the other, is just now the *pons asinorum* of our labor system ".[2] To cross this rather treacherous bridge, the employer and the laborer both needed some outside assistance, which only the Freedmen's Bureau was in a position to give in 1865, before the courts were ready to deal with the difficulty.

The trouble with the Freedmen's Bureau, like any other piece of machinery, was that its usefulness depended largely on the hands that operated it. Many of the subordinate agents were incompetent, unfit for what was a most difficult and delicate work. The system of payment of agents by fees, which continued in force until 1867, encouraged the worst class of agents to use their office for what they could get out of it. Their command over negroes was the source of great temptation to bribery.[3] Planters found that hands could be secured under favorable terms, sometimes, by greasing the palm of the Freedmen's Bureau agent. Some of the resident civil officers appointed as agents were ac-

[1] *Augusta Constitutionalist,* May 27, 1865; *Milledgeville Federal Union,* August 22, September 5, 1865.

[2] *Ku Klux Committee,* vol. vii, p. 758.

[3] Trowbridge, *Picture of the Desolated States,* p. 499.

cused by the head of the Bureau of abusing their powers in being unjust to the freedmen, and in inflicting cruel and unusual punishment upon them.[1] It was perhaps a rare experience for an agent of the Bureau to receive commendation from the white citizens in the district under his supervision. The fact that Captain Thos. W. White, in charge of the Bureau in Baldwin County, was a citizen of Milledgeville, and hence more in sympathy with the employer's point of view in settling difficulties that came before him than were non-resident agents, may account for the following resolution passed at a public meeting of the representative townsmen of Milledgeville:[2]

Resolved, That in view of the happy and quiet state of affairs in Baldwin County, in regard to the free negroes, resulting from the judicious exercise of his powers as Freedmen's Bureau Agent, by Capt. Thos. W. White, we, the people of the county, hereby tender to Capt. White our hearty thanks and commendation for the enlightened, moderate and useful administration of his office among us, and hereby acknowledge our public obligations to him, on his retirement.

The bad repute of the Freedmen's Bureau was due more directly to the political activities of its agents in 1867 and 1868, when they manipulated the helpless black voters for their own aggrandizement. But even in the first year and a half after the war, the Bureau, as a Federal organ coming between the white man and the blacks, was resented by most of the white people in the South. The judgment of General Steedman and General Fullerton after their investigation in the summer of 1866 was that the Bureau in Georgia, under the administration of General Saxton, was

[1] Report of Commissioner Howard in the *Report of the Secretary of War*, 1867, vol. i, p. 673.

[2] *Milledgeville Federal Union*, May 1, 1866.

badly mismanaged, granting unnecessary support and unnecessary tutelage and guardianship to the freedmen, and
teaching them to distrust the whites. But General Tillson's
management was commended in the warmest terms.[1] J. R.
Dennett, correspondent for the *Nation,* traveling in the
South, noted that the Bureau was generally denounced,
though some favorable opinions were expressed from a
man's personal experience.[2] A Northern resident in
Georgia testified before the Reconstruction Committee of
Congress that in Upper and Middle Georgia confidence was
expressed in the Freedmen's Bureau and in General Tillson.
It was good for both planters and negroes, necessary to
make the negro work, he thought.[3] Provisional Governor
Johnson said that something like the Freedmen's Bureau
was necessary. The law was all right, but its enforcement
was sometimes ineffective. Hostility toward its agents
was abating in 1866, especially among those who formerly
owned slaves.[4] B. C. Truman, sent south by the President
in the fall of 1865, remarked that the Freedmen's Bureau
and its agents were hated by a class of whites, mostly " poor
whites ", not the slave holders. In his opinion the Bureau
was well officered and managed, a necessity to both races.[5]
The *Macon Telegraph* on February 4, 1866, urging that the
Bureau be abolished as speedily as possible, said:

Georgia has taken the matter in hand, and, through the
agency of an enlightened committee of her citizens, devised a code for the government and protection of the black

[1] *New York Herald,* June 13, 1866.

[2] *Nation,* February 1, 1866.

[3] *Joint Committee on Reconstruction,* 1866, pt. iii, p. 110 (Test.:
Welles).

[4] *Ibid.,* p. 129.

[5] *New York Times,* November 23, 1865.

man that, if let alone, will do more in five years to secure his rights and revive prosperity in her borders than all the schemes that northern theorists could devise in a century.

The *Milledgeville Federal Union* of May 29, 1866, said that the Freedmen's Bureau was no longer needed in Georgia if it ever had been. A few military garrisons at two or three points in the state would be all that was necessary to protect the negroes. " If Congress would let us alone, we could work out our problem satisfactorily without even a soldier in the state. But people cannot object to orderly white soldiers—might prefer to have them for a time." The *Savannah News* was uncompromising in its judgment of the Bureau—" a social and moral evil, keeping alive antagonism between the races ".[1] Public opinion, as Sidney Andrews read it, was that the Freedmen's Bureau was a necessary evil that must be endured, though the people would rather have the negroes left to their own control.[2] To be left alone to work out the negro problem without interference from the North was the intense desire of the South. This was the keynote of the address of H. V. Johnson, President of the Constitutional Convention in 1865, who said:[3]

It is true our labor system has been entirely deranged, almost destroyed; and we are now to enter upon the experiment, whether or not the means of labor which are left to us, the class of people to which we are to look in the future as our laboring class, can be organized into efficient and trustworthy laborers. That may be done, or I hope it may be done if left to ourselves. If I could have the ear of the entire people of the United States, and if I might be permitted, humble though

[1] May 22, 1866.
[2] *Joint Committee on Reconstruction*, 1866, pt. iii, p. 173.
[3] *Journal of the Constitutional Convention*, 1865, p. 203.

I be, to utter an admonition, not by way of threat, but for
the purpose of animating them to the pursuit of a policy
which would be wise, and salutary, and fraternal, and best for
the country, I would implore them that, so far as providing
for this branch of our population is concerned, and their organization into a class of efficient and trustworthy laborers,
the Federal Government should just simply let us alone. We
understand the character of that class of people, their capac-
ities, their instincts, and the motives which control their conduct. If we cannot succeed in making them trustworthy and
efficient as laborers, I think it is not saying too much, when
we affirm that the Federal Government need not attempt it.
I trust they will not, and that we will have the poor privilege
of being let alone, in the future, in reference to this class
of our people.

Had all the inhabitants of Georgia been as fair-minded
and as humane toward the freedmen as H. V. Johnson,
Alex. H. Stephens, John B. Gordon, and the like, there
would have been no need of such an institution as the
Freedmen's Bureau.[1] But in conditions as they were, even
with the large bulk of evil influence justly charged against
some of its agents, the Freedmen's Bureau was, on the
whole, an important constructive force towards economic
adjustment in the immediate transition from slavery to
freedom.

[1] See address of Alex. H. Stephens before the Georgia Legislature on
February 22, 1866. *Journal of the House,* 1865-6, pp. 413-28; also
testimony of General Gordon, before the *Ku Klux Committee,* vol. vi,
p. 305, *et seq.*

CHAPTER III

Labor and Land

For the remainder of the season of 1865, after emancipation destroyed titles in slave property, Georgia planters attempted to continue their planting operations with as little change as possible from the old routine, by the substitution of some kind of payment to the freedmen for labor formerly exacted of them. This was the ideal of the planter in 1865, to cultivate on a large scale, to work the negroes in gangs as formerly under strict control, but to pay them some kind of wage, either a share of the crop or money. But the difficulty in achieving this ideal in most parts of agricultural Georgia was that the taste of freedom was sweet to the negro, and as a free agent he wished to get as far as possible from the old régime. The negro's ideal was to have a little farm or patch of ground of his own, to cultivate when and how he pleased, to establish his family as an independent social and economic group, without subjection to any master or overseer. The warring of these two ideals forced the remodeling of the agrarian system of Georgia that has taken place since 1865.[1] In the contest for supremacy the planter was at a disadvantage in many ways. He had little capital and but limited credit. He was rigid in his ideas and unadaptable to change. He had always cultivated his land in one way and lacked the

---

[1] On this subject two important monographs have been published, Banks, *Economics of Land Tenure in Georgia*, and Brooks, *Agrarian Revolution in Georgia*.

constructive power to create a new system instead of trying to resurrect the old. The new order came in spite of
him instead of because of him. The negro had the upper
hand. The white man wanted his work more than the
negro wanted to work. With the migration of freedmen
to towns and with the drain of the labor force to newer and
better paying fields in Mississippi and Louisiana, the demand for labor far exceeded the supply. On the other
hand, the freedman was handicapped by his ignorance and
by his defective bargaining powers. But this weakness of
the laborer was more than made up where the Freedmen's
Bureau was established. It was the business of its agents
to supervise the making of labor contracts so as to protect
the interests of the freedmen.

The first general order of Assistant Commissioner Tillson of the Freedmen's Bureau on October 3, 1865, directed
that labor contracts for 1866 should be in writing, and gave
the following as a model form for the use of agents: [1]

Know all men by these presents, that — of the county of —,
state of —, held and firmly bound to the United States of
America in the sum of — dollars, for the payment of which —
bind — heirs, executors, administrators firmly by these presents
in this contract: That — furnish the persons whose names
are subjoined, (freed laborers) quarters, fuel, substantial and
healthy rations, all medical attendance and supplies in case of
sickness, and the amount set opposite their respective names
per month during the continuation of the contract; the laborers
to be paid in full before the final disposal of the crop which
is to be raised by them on — plantation, in the county of —,
state of —.

[1] *Milledgeville Federal Union,* November 17, 1865.

No.	Names	Age	Rates of pay per month DOLLARS CENTS

This contract is to commence with this date and close with the
year.   Given in duplicate to — this — day of — 186—.
Registered —, 186—.

Witness: .... Supt. of Dist.

In places where the freedmen remained on the plantation
at the end of the war, chiefly in the southwestern part of
the state, the plantation was less disturbed than elsewhere.
Planters attempted to make arrangements with their former
slaves to continue cultivating the crop, promising a share
of the crop at the end of the year.   Payment by a share of
the crop was the general rule in Southwest Georgia in 1865.
Even in this section, where conditions were more favorable
than in other regions, many were the trials of planters who
tried to continue in the old way with free labor.   The following letters are an expression of the difficulties which
confronted Howell Cobb on his plantations in Middle and
Southwestern Georgia.[1]   There the old system was retained,

[1] Letters in MSS. in the possession of Mrs. A. S. Erwin of Athens,
Ga., to whom I am indebted, also to Professor U. B. Phillips of
the University of Michigan, for the use of the correspondence of
Howell Cobb.   These two letters have since been published in Brooks,
Agrarian Revolution of Georgia, pp. 20-2.   The letter from J. D.
Collins to John A. Cobb has appeared in the collection of Cobb's
correspondence, edited by U. B. Phillips, in *Annual Report of the
American Historical Association*, 1911, vol. ii, pp. 665-6.   Collins was
the overseer on one of Cobb's plantations, and John A. Cobb was the
son of Howell Cobb.

whereby the negroes worked under an overseer as formerly, the only difference being that they were paid one-third of the crop, out of which they had to maintain themselves.

[J. D. Collins to John A. Cobb.]

BALDWIN COUNTY, HURRICANE PLANTATION.

July 31, 1865.

Dear Sir,

Acordin to promis I write you to inform you how the negrows or freedmen air getting on. tha dont doo as well as tha did a few weeks back your propersition to hier them has no effect on them at tall tha say and contend that oneley three of them agreed to stay that was the three that spoke Sam, Alleck, and Johnson the rest claim tha made no agreement whatever an you had as well sing Sams to a ded horse as to tri to instruct a fool negrow Some of them go out to work verry well others stay at their houseses untell & hour by sun others go to their houseses and stay two & three days Say enny thing to them the reply is I am sick but tha air drying fruit all the time tha take all day evry Satturday without my lief I gave orders last Satturday morning for them to go to work when tha got the order eight went out I ordered tom to go to mill he said he would not doo so. tha air steeling the green corn verry rapped som of them go where tha pleas and when tha pleas and pay no attention to your orders nor mine: the commandant of post at milledgeville sent walker back under Gen Wilson order I explained the matter to him but he would send him back unless you had paid him for his work up to the time you ordered him off I told walker ef he came back he would not get a cent for his work not even his clothes nor those he came back in the face of all the orders had been given him. I drove him off the Secont time after you left before I received a written order to take him back I then went down and saw the officer in command an exsplained the hole matter to him but he said he could not allow him driven off without violating Gen. Wilsons order an he was compeld to carry them out as sutch the matter stands as above stated it would be best for you to visit the plantation soon or write a verry positive letter to be read to them requiering them to work or leave though I think I will get som of them by not feeding them which proses is now going on though tha is rather two mutch fruit and green corn to have a good effect. I send Alleck up with the wagon and mule pleas write back by Alleck I am sick at this time I have had fever for three days no other matters of importance at present.

P. S. We will need som barriels to put syrup in in about six weeks.

[Howell Cobb to his Wife.]

DOMINIE PLACE, SUMTER CO.
(December, 1865.)

My Dear Wife,

I avail myself of the first opportunity to send a letter to town. I find a worse state of things with the negroes than I expected, and am unable even now to say what we shall be able to do. From Nathan Barwick's place every negro has left. There is not one to feed the stock, and on the other places none has contracted as yet. I shall stay here until I see what can be done. By Tuesday we shall probably know what they will do. At all events I shall then look out for other negroes. I intend to send Nathan Barwick to Baldwin on Wednesday to see what hands can be got there, with the assistance of Wilkerson. I am offering them even better terms than I gave them last year, to wit, one-third of the cotton and corn crop, and they feed and clothe themselves, but nothing satisfies them. Grant them one thing, and they demand something more, and there is no telling where they would stop. The truth is, I am thoroughly disgusted with free negro labor, and am determined that the next year shall close my planting operations with them. There is no feeling of gratitude in their nature. Let any man offer them some little more freedom, and they catch at it with avidity, and would sacrifice their best friend without hesitation and without regret. That miserable creature Wilkes Flag sent old Ellick down to get the negroes from Nathan Barwick's place. Old Ellick staid out in the woods and sent for the negroes and they were bargaining with him in the night and telling Barwick in the day that they were going to stay with him. The moment they got their money, they started for the railroad. This is but one instance but it is the history of all of them. Among the number was Anderson, son of Sye and Sentry, whom I am supporting at the Hurricane.

In these first contracts there was great variety in the terms of hiring. In addition to the scheme just mentioned, other agreements provided that the hand would receive his maintenance during the season as well as a stated share of the crop at the end. In this way, if the laborer broke his contract before the end of the season, he lost everything except the food he had consumed and the clothes he wore. Still other contracts called for so much a month or a year. When wage was agreed to by the month, the planter tried to hold the laborer by paying only half each month and the remainder at the close of the season.

From the experience of 1865 it was seen that both methods of payment, by share and by money, had their difficulties. It was about six of one and half a dozen of the other. Those who had paid by shares wished they had paid money; and those who bargained for money thought that things would have been better had they hired their laborers for shares. The authoritative agricultural paper of Georgia at the close of the season of 1865 carefully canvassed both methods in an editorial on " Contracts with Laborers ".[1] Of the two methods, the editor thought that it would be best, if possible, to pay hands a stipulated price per week, and reserve half until the end of the year, which would be forfeited if the agreement was not kept. Deductions ought to be made for idleness or tardiness, as with factory labor in the North. Then additional hands could be hired at special times for extra work. To the money

[1] *Southern Cultivator*, December, 1865.

wage system, however, there were three objections. The planter didn't know what kind of labor he could get—most hands had no regular hours of work and moved lazily; then the planter could offer only small wages, which would react badly on the negro, not encouraging him to take pains. Moderate wages would make the Northern Radicals think that the negro was being oppressed. And most people had not the means to pay money wage. On the whole, concluded the writer, the best thing for all parties under the circumstances would be share payment. Shares would vary on different plantations, less on more fertile ones, where more of the work was done by animals and less by hand.

The scheme of payment of laborers by shares is described thus by Frances Butler Leigh, as practised on her father's plantation:

Our contract with them is for half the crop; that is, one-half to be divided among them according to each man's rate of work, we letting them have in the meantime necessary food, clothing and money for their present wants (as they have not a penny) which is to be deducted from whatever is due to them at the end of the year.[1]

Where the old plantation system was kept as closely as possible, the former slaves simply became hired hands under contract for a year. Their payment was either in a share of the crop or in a stated money wage. In 1865 payment in a share of the crop was more common than money payments.[2] The shortage in money at the end of the war

[1] Leigh, *Ten Years on a Georgia Plantation since the War*, p. 26.

[2] See Brooks, *Agrarian Revolution in Georgia*, p. 18. "In 1865, therefore, in a great number of cases all the externals of the former régime were continued: the negroes lived in 'quarters', went to the fields at tap of farm bell, worked in gangs under direction, and were rationed from the plantation smokehouse, the charge for food being deducted from the wage. A money wage was usually paid in 1865

made some sort of payment in kind practically necessary
for a time. All the ready cash that the planter realized
from the sale of his cotton on hand and all the credit that
he could command were consumed in purchase of stock and
provisions for the season, with none left in the great majority of cases for the payment of hands. Then, too, the
extreme mobility and uncertainty of labor, together with
the negro's ignorance of money values, made payment in
the crop more practicable to the planter.[1] The method of
hiring, by which a share of the crop was offered to be paid
at the end of the harvest season, out of which the cost of
provisions furnished to the hands during the season was
deducted, the plan used by Howell Cobb on his plantations,
kept the negro more nearly in his former position than any
other; especially when the organization of the plantation
continued to be squad work under the direction of the
planter or his overseer.

The labor problem thus offered perplexing difficulties.
To discuss the question, General Tillson met with planters
in Savannah on December 9, 1865. He offered to do his
part to induce the freedmen to make contracts and to enforce them if the planters offered good wages. Planters
thought $8, $10, or $12 a month with food would be a
good wage for a full hand, the majority agreeing on $10
with food. But General Tillson said he would not help to
make contracts for less than $12 to $15 with food for
males, and $8 to $10 for females. Some few planters
agreed to this stipulation.[2] In the circular which General

and 1866, the payment being weekly, monthly, or yearly, according to
contract." From the many current accounts of farming operations
which were published in the Georgia papers, I am led to differ with
Mr. Brooks on this last point. While both kinds of payment were
used side by side, I think share payment was more common.

[1] Banks, *Economics of Land Tenure in Georgia*, p. 78, *et seq.*

[2] *Joint Committee on Reconstruction*, pt. iii, p. 41 (report of Brevet
Brig. Gen. C. H. Howard to Gen. O. O. Howard, December 30, 1865.)

Tillson sent to agents of the Bureau on December 22d, he set down the following as standard wages: in Upper and Middle Georgia, where land was not rich, $12-13 per month with board and lodging for full male hand, and $8-10 for full female hand, the laborers to furnish their own clothing and medicine; along the coast and in Southwest Georgia, $15 for full male and $10 for full female. In all parts of the state, since some planters preferred to pay in part of the crop, one-third the gross to one-half the net proceeds might be considered a fair equivalent to the wages stipulated.[1] But the standard set by the Freedmen's Bureau was by no means held where planters could secure hands for less. J. R. Dennett, writing for the *Nation* in his series of articles, " The South as It Is ", reported from Macon and Columbus that the $12 rule was not enforced, that the majority of contracts calling for a money wage were for $120 a year and board.[2] This was good wages, for reports in the newspapers of 1866 gave $100 with rations as the current wage for a full hand, though payments varied from $75 to $140 for men and from $50 to $100 for women. In South Georgia a large majority of laborers worked for a part of the crop, one-third if they provided for themselves or one-fourth with everything furnished. Where money was paid, it was a common practice to pay one-half at the end of each month and the other half at the end of the year. This was done to hold the negro if possible until the end of the harvest season.[3]

The experiment of cultivating land with free contract labor was beset with two great difficulties, to keep the negro

[1] *Milledgeville Federal Union*, January 9, 1866.

[2] *Nation*, February 1, 1866.

[3] Reports from various counties in *Macon Telegraph*, January 27, February 3, 1866; *Macon Journal and Messenger,* January 3, 1866; *Savannah Herald*, March 28, 1866; etc. Also conversation with Mr. S. M. Mays of Augusta, Ga., a planter in Columbia County.

to his contract and to make him work steadily and regularly. It was hardly to be expected that the blacks, after their long habits as slave-driven workers, would understand the obligation of a contract. They were fickle, ready to quit work under the least provocation and to break one contract to make another under the inducement of higher wages. When the farmer set out to plant cotton in the spring with sixty hands, he had no security that sixteen or six would remain to work it during the summer and to pick in the fall. The blame did not rest entirely with the irresponsible blacks, but with employers who induced negroes by offer of higher wages to break their contracts. Agents came from further south, from Louisiana and Mississippi, where labor was in great demand, and beguiled the negroes away in the night by offering $20 or $25.[1] Planters appealed to the Freedmen's Bureau for help, and General Tillson, in his circular order of December 22, 1865, gave the following instruction:[2] " All persons are forbidden to tamper with or entice laborers to leave their employers before the expiration of their contracts, either by offering higher wages, or other inducements. Officers will punish, by fine or otherwise, any person who may be convicted of such acts." Agents probably afforded some sanction to the binding force of contracts on the negroes, but still the difficulty continued during 1866, apparent in the numerous complaints registered in the newspapers of that year.

[1] *Macon Journal and Messenger,* March 21, 1866; *Savannah News,* August 3, 1866; *New York Times,* November 23, 1866 (Truman); *Joint Committee on Reconstruction,* pt. iii, p. 167 (Test.: J P. Hambleton).

[2] *Milledgeville Federal Union,* January 9, 1866. In 1866 a law was passed by the state legislature which made it a misdemeanor to entice another's servants. *Acts of the General Assembly,* 1866, pp. 153-4. A case is cited by Mr. Brooks in which a verdict was rendered for $5000 against a man who enticed another man's laborers. *Agrarian Revolution in Georgia,* p. 30.

When the compulsory methods of slavery disappeared, there was absolutely no power to keep the negro steadily and regularly at work. Everywhere negroes worked more lazily than they did as slaves. Where formerly a negro, properly supplied with mules, was expected to cultivate fifteen acres, after emancipation only ten acres could be counted on.[1] The crop, after it was planted, was neglected. Sometimes the whole force would put aside work and go off fishing for the day. There were many like Zeke, a hand on a plantation near Savannah, who left the field about eleven o'clock—said it was too warm to work, and besides he had promised " the lady " to go to school. Sometimes hands worked only half a day and sometimes less, and Saturday was always their day off.[2] The only means of control which the planter could exercise over loafing and irregularity was by docking the delinquent's wages. But such penalty, deferred to the end of the month or the year when pay time came, had no deterrent effect on the lazy, pleasure-loving freedmen. Planters, who had gone deeply in debt for their year's supplies, despaired of clearing anything at the end of the year, for cotton required constant and regular care and a fair crop could not possibly be raised with such haphazard labor. One disadvantage of the share system, so widely used in 1866, was that the negroes considered it perfectly fair if they lost three days out of a week, since they were losers as well as the owners. They could not understand that a crop could not be raised on half-time labor. They thought if six days would raise a whole crop, three days would raise half a crop, which would satisfy them. Half a day's work might keep them

[1] *Augusta Constitutionalist*, July 1, 1866; *Nation*, February 1, 1866 (Dennett).

[2] *Augusta Constitutionalist*, July 1 and October 5, 1865; *Augusta Chronicle*, April 19, 1866.

from starving, which was all they cared for, but it would not raise a successful crop for the owner who had staked heavily on the year's planting.[1]

Hiring for wages, either in money or in crop, made no material change in the plantation system, for wage or share laborers were worked in squads under direction of their labor as in slavery. From the planter's point of view this was the most desirable method of utilizing free labor, but the least desirable in the negro's estimation. It was the ambition of all enterprising negroes to own small farms of their own, which they could cultivate as a family, free from any outside control. But with their poverty and the disinclination of the whites to see the freedmen become property holders, by the end of 1866 very few negroes had managed to secure holdings in their own right. There were some small holdings in the neighborhood of towns and on the abandoned coast lands, which they held under the supervision of the Freedmen's Bureau. Mr. Hull, of Athens, tells of two hands on his father's plantation who came to buy lands for themselves. One had coins amounting to fifty dollars which he had saved for years; the other bought on credit a few acres where he built a rude cabin and worked hard all the rest of his life with few comforts.[2] In the first year and a half of freedom negroes had not accumulated enough to buy land, and then there was not much marketable land at low prices until many planters were forced to give up a part of their lands after failure and heavy indebtedness at the end of 1866.

Between these two systems, in which the freedman was a hired laborer or else an independent property owner, an intermediate plan grew up wherein the negro freed himself

[1] Leigh, *op. cit.*, pp. 25-7.

[2] Hull, *Annals of Athens*, pp. 292-3.

in large measure from control by the planter and worked in a family group instead of the old associated labor group. This was accomplished in different kinds of tenancy, which varied as to amount and kind of capital furnished by the planter with the consequent degree of regulation over the tenant, and the amount and kind of payment made by the tenant.   While tenancy belongs more distinctly to the later period of the agrarian revolution in Georgia, it had its beginnings immediately after the war and existed to a considerable degree as early as 1866.   When it appeared it was almost always the sign of the inability of the planter to withstand the efforts of the negro to rise from the condition of subjection he was under as a wage or share laborer.   There were some exceptional instances where the landowner adopted tenancy voluntarily as an experiment looking towards the social as well as the economic betterment of the freedmen.[1]   When a negro became a tenant, he ceased to work in a group of laborers under the constant supervision of the owner or overseer, and received from the owner a special piece of land, generally stocked completely by the owner, for the use of which the tenant paid a share of the crop, varying generally from one-fifth to one-fourth. A newspaper reporter traveling in Georgia in the winter of 1865-66 found five cases of negro tenancy in which the rent varied from one-fifth to one-half.   In one instance the rent for forty acres was $250 and 48 bushels of meal.[2]   In 1866 there were not many instances of tenancy in which the tenant furnished part of the capital, paid a money rent, and received no control over his management from the landlord.

[1] Alex. H. Stephens was one of those who parceled out his lands among his former slaves as tenants, thinking it the best arrangement for the freedmen's interests. Avary (*ed.*), *Recollections of Alex. H. Stephens*, pp. 144, 201.

[2] *Nation*, February 1, 1866 (Dennett).

But tenancy, likewise, brought difficulties, as the following
incident shows:[1]

A tenant worked a piece of land, for which he was to pay one-
fourth of the corn produced. When he gathered his crop, he
hauled three loads to his own house, thereby exhausting the
supply in the field. When, soon after, he came to return his
landlord's wagon, which he had used in the hauling, the latter
asked suggestively:

"Well, William, where's my share of the corn?"

"You ain't got none, sah!" said William.

"Haven't got any! Why, wasn't I to have the fourth of all
you made?"

"Yes, sah; but hit never made no fourth; dere wasn't but
dess my three loads made."

But often it was the negro who suffered from his ignorance of arithmetic. A gentleman in Milledgeville tells of a
negro who failed to get anything after his year's labor, because by agreement he was to get one-half of the crop,
and his employer put him off without anything with the explanation that only half a crop was raised. Another story
is told of negroes on a plantation in Wilkes County who
quit work in high discontent when they discovered that the
hands on a neighboring plantation had contracted for one-
fifth of the crop, whereas they had been promised only one-
fourth.[2]

Tenancy grew from both above and below—from the
needs of the planter, his poverty, lack of capital, and the
uncertainty and instability of his labor force; and from the
demands of the negro to be free from supervision and his
inability to satisfy his demand for freedom through out-

[1] Barrow, "A Georgia Plantation," in *Scribner's Magazine, April,* 1881.
[2] Conversation with Capt. T. F. Newell of Milledgeville and Miss
E. F. Andrews of Washington, Ga.

right purchase of land.[1] With tenancy, when the negro no longer worked as a member of a group of laborers and when his work was not subject to constant supervision, two of the essential elements of the ante-bellum plantation system had disappeared, though the land still remained in the owner's possession. The importance of tenancy even in the first year and a half after the war is shown by the fact that landlords secured in 1866 the enactment of a law which gave them a lien on the crops of tenants.[2]

The family system of cultivation, which tenancy made possible, marked a distinct step forward in the social development of the negro. To establish the negro family as the industrial unit was the scheme which seemed to General Wilson, who was in command of part of Georgia at the end of the war, as the most promising for the freedmen's advance. The following letter, written by General Wilson from Macon in June, 1865, expresses his views on this subject:[3]

. . . It may not be improper in this connection to call attention to the present communal system of labor, practiced by slaveholders throughout the South. I believe it is susceptible of proof that nearly all of the crime and debasement of the Freedmen in their present condition is attributable to the fact that they are crowded together in villages offering every inducement and opportunity for promiscuous propagation, and allowing nothing like absolute protection to the family. Every individual of the community is made thereby subordinate to the brutalizing influence of the master's ignorance, cupidity and selfishness.

[1] For a discussion of tenancy see Banks, *Economics of Land Tenure in Georgia*, ch. v; and Brooks, *Agrarian Revolution in Georgia*, ch. ii and iii.

[2] *Acts of the General Assembly*, 1866, p. 141.

[3] This letter, addressed to Brig. Gen. Whipple, is in the Johnson MSS. in the Library of Congress.

I am convinced that the first step towards the civilization and elevation of the negro, by which he is to be made a useful and self-sustaining member of society, is to establish the family of every worthy man upon such a basis as will ensure it all the advantages of industry, good management, and virtuous aspirations.

Practically, every landed proprietor who has freedmen upon his estate should be compelled to give every respectable and trustworthy man a life-lease upon as much land as he and his family could cultivate; to build or allow the removal of houses and enclosures to the land, and require the lessee to live upon his own possessions, and paying a fair rate of rent either in money or in kind to the proprietor.

Along with the tendency among the negroes to work as a family was the ambition of the freedwomen to transfer their sphere from the field to the home. The withdrawal of women from field labor was a large factor in the scarcity of agricultural labor after the war. Freedmen generally refused to hire their wives, wishing to keep them at home to cook, tend the garden, do the washing, and the women liked to set themselves up as ladies with a home of their own. Where women did contract to labor, the wage was generally about $50 a year with provisions, though in some cases it was as high as $100 a year with board. Often women were paid by the month $3 or $4. One form of contract with women was to promise $4 a month cash when called for, at the end of one month or six, rations being furnished all the time and pay only when they worked. Household servants were in great demand and everywhere the complaints of housekeepers about no servants or unsatisfactory servants were as frequent as they are to-day.[1]

[1] *Macon Telegraph*, February 3, 1866; *Macon Journal and Messenger*, November 28, 1866; *Milledgeville Federal Union*, December 26, 1865; *Augusta Chronicle*, July 11, 1866.

In Atlanta and Augusta and other cities it was no uncommon thing for families to change cooks a dozen times in three months, and eight out of every ten were pronounced worthless. The trouble was not confined to cities and towns. A Jefferson County correspondent wrote that, while the freedmen were doing pretty well, the women were generally idle, lazy and crazy, delighting in new shoes and jockey hats.[1]

With all this irregularity of labor the amount of crop that could be raised was most uncertain. In Southwest Georgia the crop of 1865 was more nearly normal than in any other section of the state. Lands had not been plundered by either army, planters' houses, gin houses, and negro quarters were intact, and there in the first days of freedom the negroes were more inclined to stay on the home place and less given to roving about than elsewhere. By the end of the year a considerable crop was harvested; in fact, almost the whole cotton crop of Georgia in 1865 came from the Southwest.[2] In the eastern section of the cotton belt and in North Georgia prospects for any crop in 1865 were very bad indeed. Farming implements and stock had been taken or destroyed, plantations were overgrown with weeds, fences burned or fallen to pieces, cotton gins in ashes. Bad cotton seed, four or five years old, came up only about one in a thousand.[3] Much of what came to maturity was lost by neglect during the summer and through lack of labor to harvest in the fall. Along the coast much cotton in the fields was wasted for want of picking when negroes abandoned the plantations, and large quantities of sorghum

---

[1] *Augusta Chronicle,* May 13, 1866.

[2] For conditions in Southwest Georgia, see *New York Times,* October 28, 1865 (Quondam) ; *Savannah Herald,* February 8, 1866.

[3] *Joint Committee on Reconstruction,* pt. iii, p. 167 (Test.: Hambleton) ; and the Report of the Freedmen's Bureau for 1865.

cane were left standing in the field for the want of har-
vesters.[1]   In North Georgia land was cultivated as small
farms, the owners doing their own work with the aid of
their sons.   In this region slaves were few before the war,
so hardship in 1865 came from the desolation wrought by
the war, and not from the difficulties attendant upon emancipation.   In the northeast counties, though not devas-
tated by the armies, there was practically nothing growing
in 1865, the failure being due to severe drought and to the
depredations of lawless bands of bushwhackers.   Severe
distress among the whites resulted.[2]

Through the operation of the various causes mentioned
above there was a general failure of crops in 1865.   But the
coming of the new year brought brighter prospects for 1866.
The soaring price of cotton, 50 cents a pound in December,
and the willingness of the blacks to contract and settle
down to work after the Christmas holidays, gave new heart
to despairing planters.   Everywhere there was a mania
for cotton planting.   Everyone who owned a patch of
ground and could get anyone to work it put in cotton, and
lands were bought just for cotton.   In January and February there were optimistic expectations of a large crop, and
cotton lands advanced in price.[3]   Correspondents throughout the cotton region reported that vigorous preparations
were being made for a big cotton planting to the neglect
of provisions.   Many planters who were in debt at the end
of 1865, expecting to retrieve their losses, planted their
best lands in cotton, the rest in corn, preferring to buy corn

[1] *Macon Journal and Messenger,* November 28, 1865; *Milledgeville
Federal Union,* July 25, 1865.

[2] Avery, *History of the State of Georgia,* pp. 320-321.

[3] *Macon Telegraph,* January 10, 11, 1866; *Savannah Herald,* February 21, 1866; Hull, *Annals of Athens,* p. 308.

and meat in the fall.[1]   Many of the newspapers through their editorial columns warned against the policy of planting much cotton and little corn.   Planters, however, proceeded on the idea that cotton would bring almost as high prices in 1866 as in the previous year, without calculating that with everyone rushing into making cotton, a full crop would necessarily bring the market down with a tumble. Moreover, with cotton still the basis of credit, it was hard for the planter to alter his crop.

As the spring wore on, reports of the planting season and prospects of the crop became less and less cheering.   In Middle Georgia, a failure of the seed to come up brought discouragement; heavy rains in other regions were unfavorable.   Expectations of the crop varied from three-fourths to one-half or one-third of a normal ante-bellum crop.[2]   The hopefulness of early spring changed to doubt and despair in the fall.   The cotton crop was a failure, though, according to general testimony, the freedmen worked better in 1866 than was expected.   Very few planters managed to clear expenses at the end of the season.[3]   And in the grain fields of North Georgia a bad season of drought parched the growing crop early in August.[4]

Many Northerners, who were tempted by the conjunction of high cotton and cheap land at the end of the war, went to Georgia to begin planting operations in the fall of 1865, buying or leasing lands.   One of the number, whose experience was like that of many others, bought a plantation in

[1] *Macon Journal and Messenger*, January 3, 1866; *Macon Telegraph*, February 3, 1866; *Milledgeville Federal Union*, May 15, 1866.

[2] *Macon Journal and Messenger*, January 16, 1866; *Milledgeville Federal Union*, May 15, 1866; *New York Herald*, June 18, 1866 (special correspondent with Generals Steedman and Fullerton).

[3] *Atlanta New Era*, October 18, 1866.

[4] *Savannah News*, August 13, 1866.

Columbia County, in the eastern end of the cotton belt. According to the account of his operations in 1866, he found himself at the end of the season just one thousand dollars short. Though a thorough-going abolitionist, heartily in sympathy with free labor, he came to the conclusion that farming was not profitable in Georgia after slavery was abolished, since the cost of raising cotton was about doubled.[1]

One of the results of the difficulties and failure in planting in 1865 and 1866 was the extension of the credit system. The Southern farmer, even in prosperous years before the war, never accumulated much surplus, for he turned over his profits, when there were any, into more land and more slaves. The cotton planter generally received from his factor in Macon or Savannah or Charleston necessary supplies for running the plantation during the season, for which he paid when cotton was marketed in the fall.[2] But during the war and later the planter became all the more dependent on what he could borrow, having to pay in some places two per cent per month for the money advanced to buy mules, wagons, ploughs, seed, etc.[3] 1866 was a year of great expectations. Many and large debts were incurred in the hope of large returns, but the short crop of that year left the planter more deeply involved than ever. In 1866, to save the people from having the sheriff turned loose on them when probably not one man in ten could pay all his debts, the new state legislature enacted a stay law. The act of March 6th, passed over the governor's veto, sus-

[1] Stearns, *The Black Man of the South and the Rebels*, pp. 97, 150.

[2] For documents relating to the ante-bellum plantation economy, see Phillips, *Plantation and Frontier* (Documentary History of American Industrial Society, vols. i and ii) ; also *Records of a Rice Plantation in the Georgia Lowlands.*

[3] *Augusta Chronicle*, May 13, 1866.

pended levy and sale under execution on contracts or liabilities prior to June 1, 1865, provided the defendant pay
one-fourth of the debt annually, so that the whole be paid
in four years from January 1, 1866.[1] After the bad season of 1866 the legislature gave further relief to the debtor
by amending the stay law of March 6th to postpone the
first payment to January 1, 1868, when one-third should be
paid, and the remainder in thirds on January 1, 1869, and
January 1, 1870.[2] At the same session of the legislature a
lien law was passed, securing to landlords a lien on crops
of tenants for stock, farming utensils, and provisions furnished such tenants, for the purpose of making their crops,
and securing to factors and merchants a lien upon the growing crops of farmers, for provisions and commercial man-
ures furnished them for the purpose of making their
crops.[3]

One of the permanent results of the war and emancipation on land tenure in Georgia was the break-up of large
plantations into smaller units for cultivation.[4] The process
of disintegration went on to some extent in 1865 and 1866,
but the stay law helped to keep some plantations intact
and not until later did the break-up proceed with rapidity.
In the first year and a half of the reconstruction period in
Georgia, it was not so much execution for debts as it was
the difficulties of the labor problem that forced many owners to rent or sell. In the latter part of 1865 many advertisements appeared in the newspapers of lands for sale or
rent in all sections of the state. The *Macon Telegraph* of

---

[1] *Acts of the General Assembly*, 1865-6, pp. 241-2.

[2] *Ibid.*, 1866, pp. 157-9.

[3] *Ibid.*, p. 141. The term *farmer* used in this law was not interpreted
to include tenants. See Brooks, *Agrarian Revolution in Georgia*, p. 32.

[4] *Ibid.*, pp. 27, 32, *et seq.*; Banks, *Economics of Land Tenure in
Georgia*, p. 30.

December 30, 1865, gave notice of plantations for rent, 1,250 A. in Dougherty County, five miles from Albany, and in Stewart County, 2,300 A.; and for sale, cotton lands were offered in four different plantations, 1,000 A., 1,250 A., 2,500 A. and 2,200 A. The *Macon Journal and Messenger* of December 4, 1865, expressing regret that so many plantations were offered for rent or sale, urged that white labor from the North be secured in place of the negroes who would not work. In January, 1866, an owner offered for sale in Liberty County in the coast region, one plantation of 2,445 A. for rice and sea-island cotton and 3,118 A. in pine land, saying that he wished to sell because he could not spare time from his profession to inaugurate the free labor system.[1] Notices of three other plantations for sale or rent appeared in the same paper. In Cherokee Georgia, in the northwest, many farms were sold to persons from other sections of the state and from the North. 700 A. near Rome, of which 300 A. were in bottom lands, sold for $16,000; 160 A. of upland sold for $5,000; 480 A. in Polk County (upland) sold to a Boston man for $10,000; and in the same county 520 A. of upland to another man from Massachusetts brought $7,000. Near Madison two Northerners purchased a plantation of 2,700 A. for $12.50 and $20 per acre.[2]

These are only a few instances of the many plantations that changed hands. Where plantations did not actually break up into small farms during these first eighteen months after emancipation, many planters were able to cultivate only a small part of their acreage. The economy of tillage

---

[1] *Savannah Herald*, January 3, 1866.

[2] *Macon Journal and Messenger*, January 27, 1866, from the *Rome Courier* and *Augusta Chronicle*, June 5, 1866. The *Milledgeville Southern Recorder* of November 6, 1866, contained 68 separate advertisements of lands for sale. Brooks, *Agrarian Revolution in Georgia*, p. 38.

on a large scale was ceasing to exist, for with free labor, when the laborers were negroes, it was impossible for an overseer to superintend as many hands and as much land as under slavery. With the system of slavery broken down and no new system established, negroes needed more oversight and were less ready to take commands from their overseers, whom they regarded as hired men like themselves. The problem of securing competent overseers to deal with freedmen in the new conditions was quite as great at times as the difficulty of getting field labor. Many planters who had cultivated several different plantations found it necessary to confine their attention to one, leasing or selling the others.

Some thinking people felt that the South was trying to put new wine into old bottles in attempting to work old plantations with free labor. They thought that the whole system of living must be changed to meet new conditions. Instead of plantations, small farms well fertilized and cultivated intensively should be the method of agriculture. J. D. B. DeBow, editor of the commercial review of the South, wrote to Governor Perry of South Carolina, as follows, in a letter which the *New York Times* called significant of the " complete revolution effected in the South ": [1] " The South must throw her immense uncultivated domain into the market at a low price, reduce the quantity of land held by individual proprietors, and resort to intelligent and vigorous measures at the earliest moment, to induce an influx of population and capital from abroad." But in 1865 and 1866 the Southern planter did not realize the completeness of the revolution that had come upon him and tried vigorously though unsuccessfully to restore the essential features of the old order.

[1] *New York Times*, October 15, 16, 1865; also De Bow, *Review*, January, 1866.

Another difficulty came from the emigration of freedmen to Arkansas, Louisiana and Mississippi, where higher wages were offered, making planters fearful for the supply of labor in Georgia. At one time one hundred negroes were reported to have left Griffin in 1866 in care of Federal officers, bound for farms in Arkansas, and rumors were current that a body of a thousand blacks under similar escort left Atlanta for the Mississippi Valley about the same time. The movement of labor to a more profitable market was fostered by the Freedmen's Bureau. General Tillson said that he had sent enough negroes out of the state to alarm the people and so raise wages.[1]

White immigrant labor was looked upon by many people in the South as the only possible solution of the labor problem, attendant upon the emancipation of the blacks. One proposition was made to secure German laborers to settle the waste places of the state, to add to the prosperity of the community and still not displace the blacks; for, as the editor of the *Macon Telegraph* wrote: " The faithful negro must not be discarded—the South's duty is to its former slaves ".[2] Another Macon paper said that the South's greatest need was white immigrants, the more the better. The armies were turning loose thousands of young men, who should go south where fertile lands were offered for a song. But nine months after peace had been declared there seemed to be little foreign or Northern immigration, except traders and mechanics in towns or in the lumber business along the coast.[3] It was no wonder, however, that Georgia did not draw immigrants, since it had no free land to offer when there was plenty in the West.

[1] *Macon Telegraph*, December 29, 1865 and January 20, 1866; *Augusta Chronicle*, March 24, 1866.

[2] January 24, 1866; also February 16, 1866.

[3] *Macon Journal and Messenger*, November 28, 1865; June 30, 1866.

J. D. B. DeBow, editor of *DeBow's Review*, said that the need of the South in the difficult transition from slave to free labor was in immigrant labor, to secure which the South should follow the example of the West and appoint immigration commissioners.[1] In October, 1865, a corporation of prominent business men was formed with offices in Savannah to supply white labor in Georgia. This Georgia Land and Immigration Co., as it was called, published a prospectus which stated Georgia's need of white labor and the advantages which the state offered to white immigrants. To make the company self-sustaining and profitable, fees were to be paid by the immigrants, and commissions charged on the sale or rent of lands to those to whom laborers were furnished.[2] And in Augusta the Georgia Immigration Co. was organized in 1866 to furnish white labor for the South. Jacob R. Davis and Son advertised that they, as agents, were prepared to furnish promptly white laborers to planters who wanted hands; operators or mechanics to manufacturers; and cooks, seamstresses, nurses to housekeepers.[3] A notice of immigration prospects two months later stated that the Georgia Immigration Co. was expecting the arrival of over one hundred immigrants. Mr. Jonathan Miller, of Richmond County, was going north to procure more laborers, taking back with him one of the immigrants who had already braved so-called Southern atrocities.[4]

But white labor did not prove satisfactory and the attempt to make a business of importing white immigrants

[1] Letter to Governor Perry of South Carolina in the *New York Times*, October 15, 1865.

[2] *Augusta Constitutionalist*, October 7, 1865.

[3] *Augusta Chronicle,* January 31, 1866; *Macon Telegraph,* May 5, 1866.

[4] *Ibid.*, March 30, 1866.

was given up in June after the company lost about three
thousand dollars. Mr. Miller, mentioned above, related his
experience with white immigrant labor on his plantation on
Beech Island. At the beginning of 1866, after hiring negroes at $12.50 a month, he was forced to dismiss some
and try white labor. For the fifteen whites that he brought
from the North he paid passage, and as wages, agreed upon
$12.50 a month with rations for men, and $8 for women.
When the laborers insisted on an increase to $15 and $10
in spite of their contract, Mr. Miller acceded to their demands. As a member of the Immigration Co., he brought
down one hundred hands, nine of whom he kept as laborers
on his own plantation. In a short time they, too, demanded
more than their contract called for and became dissatisfied
with the rations furnished them. Miller dismissed all but
one, and came to the conclusion that whites did not work
any better than negroes, even at higher wages and better
rations. He gave up the business of getting laborers from
emigration companies in the North as a bad job.[1] After
the failure of white immigrant labor from the North, the
possibility of coolie labor for growing cotton and rice was
discussed, and was later put to trial along the coast.[2]

After all, it seemed that the negro was the only laborer
who could work the plantations in the South, and greater
willingness to work in 1866 made the planter hopeful of
successful results later.

Among the white people of the state, too, there was a
movement toward emigration to the North and to South
America. Many young men, who saw obstacles too great
in the way of establishing themselves in the turmoil of new
adjustments in 1865, went north where chances for business

[1] *Augusta Chronicle*, November 7, 1866 (supplement).
[2] *Savannah News*, November 8, 1866.

success seemed more favorable. In 1865 and 1866, and even more after the political revolution of 1867-8, many Southerners, who felt that new conditions in the South were intolerable, talked much and loud about emigration to Mexico and Brazil.[1] To encourage emigration to Brazil, the Brazil Emigration Society advertised in Southern papers, offering free passage to emigrants by the United States and Brazil Mail S. S. Co., and promising favors from the imperial government to emigrants from the United States. Unoccupied public lands would be sold at 23, 46, 70 and 90 cents per acre, with payments in five yearly installments, beginning one year after possession. The laws of Brazil granted exemption to immigrants from import duties on personal effects, implements, etc. No slaves or colored people would be received as immigrants.[2] But apparently the movement toward emigration southward was more talk than anything else, and few people actually left Georgia for Brazil.

[1] *Macon Journal and Messenger*, February 24, 1866.
[2] *Savannah News*, December 1, 1866.

CHAPTER IV

Commercial Revival

THE readiest resource toward beginning business under new conditions was in the sale of cotton on hand as soon as avenues of trade with the North were opened. In January, 1865, a limited opportunity for selling cotton was given to the Savannah region in control of the Federal army by the order of General Sherman, which allowed persons taking the amnesty oath to sell cotton to treasury agents at three-fourths of the market price in New York.[1] After the surrender, a general opening of trade, subject to treasury regulations, in the part of the South within military lines was proclaimed by President Johnson on April 29, 1865. A month later the first consignment of cotton appeared for sale to treasury agents in Savannah.[2] In January, 1865, shipping made some small beginning toward reopening connections with the outside world, and by May a partial connection with the back country was established by daily boats on the river between Augusta and Savannah. A weekly line to New York was put in operation and the custom house at Savannah resumed business.[3] On May 13th

[1] Gen. Sherman's Special Field Order, no. 13, Savannah, January 15, 1865, in *Official Records of the War of the Rebellion*, vol. xlvii, pt. ii, pp. 52-3.

[2] *Savannah Herald*, May 24, 1865; *Hunt's Merchant Magazine*, June, 1865.

[3] *New York Herald*, May 6, 1865 and *New York World*, May 6, 1865, in the Townsend Library of newspaper clippings, Columbia University.

[95

the *New York Herald* announced that merchant ships were again ready to trade in Southern ports. On the 29th General Grant ordered the commanding officers at Savannah, Augusta and other points to give every facility for marketing cotton and other produce, to make no seizure of private property or search for Confederate cotton, as the finances of the country demanded a speedy marketing of articles of export.[1]

It is impossible to estimate accurately the amount of cotton available in Georgia at the close of the war. Through the region of the Sherman and the Wilson raids there was practically none, but in South Georgia the accumulation of four years was still on hand, except what was consumed in home manufacture during the war. Since little cotton was made in 1865, at least one-half of the stock on hand was of the crop of 1860-61. An investigator of conditions in the South immediately after the war was informed that there was probably more cotton in Georgia at that time than in any other Southern state, and that the great bulk of Georgia's supply was in the Southwest. The amount on hand in forty counties of that section was estimated at about 200,000 bales. The crop raised in those counties in 1865 was thought to be only about 10,000 bales.[2] Another estimate put Georgia's stock at 300,000 bales.[3] The report of Neill Bros., an English cotton firm, reckoned that Georgia and Florida together had 330,000 bales, about half an ordinary crop.[4]

The hard terms of sale in the first two months after the war delayed cotton marketing and no one sold who was

---

[1] *Official Records of the War of the Rebellion*, vol. xlvii, pt. iii, p. 593.

[2] Andrews, *South since the War*, p. 318.

[3] *Macon Telegraph*, May 15, 1865.

[4] *New York Times*, October 17, November 23 (B. C. Truman), and December 12, 1865.

not forced by necessity. In New York practically no cotton was offered for sale until June, and then sales on government account, mostly Savannah cotton, brought 37½ cents in gold for good middling cotton. There were no private sales.[1] In June, notice was given by a treasury official at a meeting of cotton holders and warehouse merchants that the Federal tax of 25 per cent on cotton in the insurrectionary states was withdrawn and the intervention of government agents was abolished. In the next month the market was active and quotations began to appear regularly in Savannah, Augusta and Macon papers.[2] In Savannah, middling cotton brought 38-39 in July, continuing upward until it reached 50 in December and January. At the end of 1865, when labor difficulties gave little promise of successful planting in the next year, speculation was active and cotton was held by those not forced to sell, in the expectation that it would bring 75 cents by January.[3] But the Christmas season passed without the expected uprising among the negroes, and when they began to make contracts and settle down to work early in January and February, better prospects for a large crop in 1866 brought a fall in prices. Then, too, the discontinuance of the system of treasury agents stimulated the sale of cotton.[4] From September 1, 1865, to April 11, 1866, the Savannah market received 201,357 bales of upland and 8,154 bales of sea-island cotton, most of which was exported to the North or to Europe.[5]

[1] *Savannah Herald*, June 6 and 13, 1865.

[2] *Augusta Constitutionalist*, June 17, 1865; *Hunt's Merchant Magazine*, July, 1865.

[3] *Augusta Constitutionalist*, October 22, 1865.

[4] *Macon Journal and Messenger*, February 17, 20 and March 6, 1866.

[5] *Savannah Herald*, February 10, 23, March 20, April 11, 1866.

In cities and towns, immediately after the war, business began to revive with the incoming stocks of goods from the North as soon as the restrictions on trade were removed. Southern people had been forced to do without so many of the ordinary comforts of life during the four years of war that there was an avidity to buy when anything was offered for sale. Though the people were so poor that they had no money to pay their debts, still a stock of fine goods in the stores rapidly disappeared. Ten stores were doing business where there was formerly but one.[1] This zest for trade did much to raise from the stagnation of war times the most important cities, Savannah, Augusta, Columbus, and most speedily of all, Atlanta.

Though Atlanta was practically demolished by Sherman's army in 1864, with fully three-fourths of the buildings in ruins, resurrection came immediately in the first months after the war. The population of the city, which had been about 13,000 at the beginning of the war, had increased to 20,000 in 1866. In the fall and winter of 1865 business was booming. Retail stores, many of which were kept by Northerners, Jews and army sutlers, carried on active business. Rebuilding proceeded rapidly, generally with cheap, flimsy structures. Building material was dear, mechanical labor received high wages, and rents for stores and dwellings were exorbitant. The trade of the city was one-third greater than it had ever been in its most prosperous days before the war. At least 4,000 mechanics were at work, almost 200 stores were opened and its four railroads were taxed to their utmost capacity. Much property was in the market and speculation in real estate was lively. Many purchases of land were made by non-residents. In addition to retail stores there were new wholesale stores for the sale of groceries, hardware, crockery and dry-

[1] *Milledgeville Federal Union,* November 21, 1865.

goods. Pressing monetary needs brought banking facilities. Mr. John H. James re-opened his banking business in 1865, and later in the same year two national banks began business. In these months of rapidly reviving business and scarce money, the cost of living was high. Retail prices, quoted in greenbacks, were as follows: flour, $20 per bbl.; bacon, 40 cts. per lb.; beef, 15 cts. per lb.; corn meal, $1.25 per bu.; ordinary suit of clothes, $100; a pair of boots, $16.

Of the four railroads radiating from Atlanta, the Western and Atlantic, connecting with the northwest, was in running order; the Atlanta and West Point to the southwest was being rapidly repaired after the damage it suffered from Wilson's raid; the Macon and Western to the south, which had been partially damaged, was in running shape. The Georgia R. R., connecting Atlanta and Augusta with the east, was the only one of the four avenues of communication from Atlanta that was not in passable order in the fall of 1865, and that was rapidly repairing its breaks. Since Atlanta was not the center of the great agricultural region of Georgia, it was not so closely dependent on the prosperity of the planter as were Macon and Savannah. Its chief business was that of distributing center for grain and meat from the Northwest and for manufactured goods from the Northeast. It also came to be the financial center of the state, developing strong banking interests, and served as central headquarters for insurance companies and large wholesale establishments.[1] At this time Atlanta, calling herself the Gate City of Georgia, was pressing forward as a rival to Macon as the railroad center of the state. The following is a picture of Atlanta in the fall of 1865 as it

[1] For Atlanta after the war, see Reed, *History of Atlanta*, ch. xii; Clarke, *Atlanta Illustrated*, pp. 50-55; *Atlanta New Era*, October 9 and 26, 1866; *New York Times*, November 2, 1865 ("Quondam") and December 3, 1865 (Truman); *Nation*, January 25, 1866 (Dennett); Reid, *After the War*, p. 355, *et seq.*

appeared to Sidney Andrews, correspondent for Boston and Chicago papers:[1]

From all this ruin and devastation a new city is springing up with marvelous rapidity. The narrow and irregular and numerous streets are alive from morning till night with drays and carts and hand-barrows and wagons,—with hauling teams and shouting men,—with loads of lumber and loads of brick and loads of sand,—with piles of furniture and hundreds of packed boxes,—with mortar-makers and hod-carriers,—with carpenters and masons,—with rubbish removers and house-builders,—with a never-ending throng of pushing and crowding and scrambling and eager and excited and enterprising men, all bent on building and trading and swift fortune-making. Chicago in her busiest days could scarcely show such a sight as clamors for observation here. Every horse and mule and wagon is in active use. The four railroads centering here groan with the freight and passenger traffic, and yet are unable to meet the demand of the nervous and palpitating city. Men rush about the streets with but little regard for comfort or pleasure, and yet find the days all too short and too few for the work in hand. The sound of the saw and plane and hammer rings out from daylight till dark, and yet master-builders are worried with offered contracts which they cannot take. Rents are so high that they would seem fabulous on Lake Street, and yet there is the most urgent cry for store-room and office-room. . . . Atlanta seems to be the centre from which this new life radiates; it is the great Exchange, where you will find everybody if you only wait and watch. I saw it with wonder, and think of it with ever-increasing wonder. The very genius of the West, holding in the one hand all its energies and in the other all its extravagances, is there; not sitting in the supreme ease of settled pause, but standing in the nervous tension of expectant movement. What is thus affirmed of Atlanta is to a less extent true of twenty other places in that quarter of the State.

[1] Andrews, *op. cit.*, pp. 340, 375.

Columbus, too, suffered severely just at the close of the war. Situated at the fall line of the Chattahoochee River, with good water power, it was the busiest manufacturing town in Georgia at the outbreak of the war, having four cotton mills, a paper mill and others. During the war, factories for making war supplies sprang up and continued the prosperity of Columbus. As an important railroad center in the cotton belt it was a busy cotton market. After the destructive force of Wilson's raid, there was great energy in rebuilding, but recovery in the first eighteen months was not so rapid as in Atlanta. In December, 1865, B. C. Truman reported that business was active, the hotels were filled with cotton buyers and sellers, many newcomers and Jewish traders were conspicuous. At the beginning of 1866 the Eagle Cotton Factory, the largest of the cotton mills, was ready to resume business.[1]

Cotton shipping renewed business activity in Savannah in 1865. Early in that year a large number of Northern traders appeared in Savannah from New York, Boston and elsewhere. Whitelaw Reid, one of the many newspaper correspondents who traveled through the South to report conditions for Northern readers, observed that a dozen sutlers' establishments were in full blast, supplying customers with fashions which native merchants had lacked for four years. The city had large and gay-looking drug stores, rather meager jewelry stores with the stock of 1860 still on hand, plenty of coarse dry-goods and " wet groceries ". Business of all kinds was lively, hotels were crowded though shabby with old furniture, broken crockery and practically no silver. In December, 1865, Sidney Andrews wrote:[2]

[1] *New York Times*, December 3, 1865 (Truman) and December 31, 1865; *New York Herald*, June 18, 1866 (correspondent with Steedman and Fullerton) ; Martin, *Columbus, Ga.*

[2] *South Since the War*, p. 366.

Business in the city has been very brisk all the fall, and many a merchant has had all he could do who moaned last spring for the " good old days ".   One of them said to me yesterday, " There's been more done in the last six months than I believed last winter would be done in two years."   I have found no place in the South where early faith in the recuperative energies of the people has met with such large reward as here. Many men seem inclined to believe that the promise will not be kept, and are prophesying a dull season next year.   Others are more hopeful, and say that when the railroads connecting with Augusta, Macon, and Thomasville are repaired, the trade of the city will be fifty per cent greater than ever.   This latter view seems to me to be the correct one.

But in 1866 prospects were worse instead of better. In many lines of business there was stagnation in place of the great activity of the year before. Business houses, without great capital, that had bought when prices were high, suffered severely from the depression. Political uncertainty kept the market unsteady. With the Central of Georgia R. R. badly crippled, Savannah's railroad connection with the rest of the state was in bad shape during the greater part of 1866 and the cost of transportation was excessively high.[1]

In the latter part of the war Augusta was a depot for supplies brought in by blockade-runners.   Great quantities of cotton and tobacco went out and clothing and other goods were imported. The close of the war found a large stock of cotton stored in Augusta, probably about 50,000 bales, the sale of which stimulated business. Since Augusta was not in the path of Sherman's army it was spared the work of repair that Atlanta had to undergo. By

[1] In 1866 it cost $8 to carry a bale of cotton down the river from Augusta to Savannah, and tariff on returning freight was 8 cts. per lb. *Savannah Herald,* March 28, 1866; Wilson, *Historic and Picturesque Savannah,* p. 203; *New York Herald,* July 6, 1865; Trowbridge, *Picture of the Desolated States,* p. 509; Reid, *op. cit.,* pp. 136-7.

the beginning of 1866 Northern capital had begun to find its
way into Augusta investments. In December, 1865, the
National Bank of Augusta was organized under the National Bank Act with a capital of $500,000, in which North-
ern financiers were interested. W. B. Dinsmore, of New
York, head of the Southern Express Company, was its first
president. In the same year three savings banks were
opened in Augusta. The spring season of 1866 was active,
many traders coming in for a short stay, willing to pay any
price to secure shops for their wares. In the fall rents
were easier though there were no surplus houses in the city.[1]

Macon, Athens, and Milledgeville all experienced a revival in business in 1865 and 1866. Here, as elsewhere,
many Northerners engaged in trade. Rents were high and
business buildings and dwelling-houses were in great demand.[2] The growth in business activity between May,
1865, and the end of 1866, is clearly indicated in the number and variety of advertisements in the daily and weekly
papers. In the summer of 1865 newspapers were printed on
small sheets of two or four pages with very little advertising matter. In 1866 the daily papers in Georgia increased about one-third in size, and their pages were
crowded with advertisements of goods to sell and of opportunities to invest in new business ventures. Then as
now newspapers derived a large part of their income from
advertising patent medicines and quack doctors who guaranteed to cure anything and everything. In all cities and

[1] Jones and Dutcher, *Memorial History of Augusta*, pp. 359, 363;
Augusta Chronicle, July 4 and September 13, 1866; *New York Herald*,
June 2, 1865; *The Nation*, January 25, 1866 (Dennett); Andrews,
op. cit., p. 353.

[2] Butler, *Historical Record of Macon and Central Georgia; Macon
Telegraph*, May 6, 1865; *Macon Journal and Messenger*, February 13,
1866; Hull, *Annals of Athens; Milledgeville Federal Union*, May 1,
1866; *New York Times*, November 12 and December 3, 1865 (Truman).

towns there was a great increase in the number of grocery and dry-goods stores and retail stores of general merchandise. Business of this character gave employment as clerks to young men who drifted to towns after the armies disbanded. Editorial comment in a Milledgeville paper called attention to the fact that nine out of ten young men in the towns went into clerking in mercantile business when there was great need for men with mechanical skill.[1] There were three or four times as many grocery stores as before the war, and nearly the same was true of dry-goods stores. " Everybody seems to have a passion for keeping store," wrote Sidney Andrews, " and hundreds of young men are going into trade who should go into agriculture. If the coming season brings a ' smash ' in many towns, the prophecies of numerous business men will be fulfilled."[2]

Slight progress was made in manufactures in 1865 and 1866. Some of the cotton mills that had been destroyed in the latter part of the war were re-opened, but in new business the most that was accomplished was the incorporation of numerous companies for manufacturing and mining purposes, which had to wait for the incoming of the requisite capital to allow them to grow into active existence. The Georgia legislature in the two sessions of 1866 gave charters to more than seventy companies, most of which never put their charters into use. Mining excitement continued in North Georgia, principally in Hall, Lumpkin, Dawson and White counties, and in 1866 twenty-two companies received charters to carry on mining operations for gold, iron, coal, and petroleum.[3] A Milledgeville paper remarked that if one-third of the incorporated companies born in the 1866

[1] *Milledgeville Federal Union*, April 3 and 17, 1866.

[2] *South since the War*, pp. 365-6.

[3] *Acts of the General Assembly*, 1865 and 1866, *passim*.

legislature grew into active existence the state would reap great benefit.[1]

In 1860, Georgia had a greater railroad mileage than any other Southern state. The increase during the decade before the war was more than double, from 643 to 1,420 miles. There was no railway extension during the war, and in 1865 the increase in mileage was slight, making a total of 1,502 miles.[2] The war thoroughly paralyzed the transportation system of the South, both by destruction of road-bed and station equipment and by loss of rolling stock.[3] The chief progress of 1865 and 1866 was in repairing the damages of the last year of the war.

The Western and Atlantic R. R., under the efficient management of Major Campbell Wallace, did satisfactory business, using part of its earnings to replace temporary with permanent repairs. This property of the state was heavily involved, with a lien upon it of about $2,000,000 in bonds issued for its construction, $830,000 of which fell due in 1865, and also the bond of about $460,000 given to the United States for repairs made upon the road while it was in the possession of the Federal government. It further served as security for a loan of $100,000 made by the convention of 1865.[4]

The destruction of the Central R. R. in the last year of

[1] *Milledgeville Federal Union*, March 20, 1866.

[2] Poor, *Railroad Manual*, 1868-9, pp. 20-21.

[3] A prominent railroad man, who was called by business from Monroe, La. to Savannah in July, 1865, traveled by the quickest route, from New Orleans to Chicago, Niagara Falls, New York, thence by steamboat to Savannah, arriving at his destination just one month after he began his journey, with one week in New York. Wadley, *Life of W. M. Wadley*, p. 50.

[4] *Report of the Comptroller General*, 1865, p. 10; *Journal of the Convention*, 1865, p. 177; *Atlanta New Era*, October 12, November 1, 1866.

the war reached Sherman's standard in being " thorough ". A report of the condition of the road in May, 1865, was made as follows by the Chairman of the Board of Directors:

Mr. Schwabe has recently been over the road, and reports about one hundred and twenty miles between Gordon and this place torn up, all the warehouses except two, and all the water tanks destroyed. The bridge across the Oconee is burned down and three-fourths of the trestle work. Of the iron, about 80 miles uninjured, the balance bent and twisted, a good deal of which, doubtless, can be used. In addition to this the Augusta and Waynesboro Road will have to be rebuilt from Millen to Waynesboro.[1]

At the end of 1865 the books of the Central revealed a deficit of $77,863.49 in the year's account. The process of repair was delayed by the difficulty of procuring and retaining labor, so forty miles of track out of the total one hundred and thirty-nine that had been broken up were still unrepaired in December, 1865, when the president of the road made his report.[2] On February 1, 1866, the last rail was laid and connection re-opened with Augusta by a branch line, and in the course of the year the road was in final running order. In January, 1866, Mr. Wm. Wadley, an important figure in the railroad development of Georgia, was elected President of the Central.[3]

The Macon and Western R. R. between Atlanta and Macon was comparatively little damaged by the invading armies. Although its track was torn up for twenty-two miles, it suffered no great loss in rolling stock and was

[1] Letter from John W. Anderson to Wm. Wadley, in Wadley, *op. cit.*, p. 49.

[2] The annual report of the President of the Central of Georgia R. R. is published in the *Macon Telegraph*, January 10, 1866.

[3] *Savannah Herald*, February 2, 1866.

prosperous enough to declare a dividend of 8 per cent on January 2, 1866, for the preceding twelve months.[1]

The Georgia R. R., in 1865-6, not being as heavily damaged as the Central, had a surplus at the end of the year, though not enough to warrant paying a dividend. Its net profits were $374,919 as compared with $528,144 in 1859-1860. In the year after the war it transported 107,276 bales of cotton, about half its cotton traffic in 1859-60—219,774 bales.[2] The encouraging results of the year from May 15, 1865, to March, 1866, were due to special causes; to the immense amount of traveling just after the war with the return of refugees, and to the marketing of hoarded cotton. These conditions stimulated traffic on all the railroads in the South, but the Georgia R. R. enjoyed more than its share of the business at this time, owing to the extensive destruction of competing carriers.[3]

The business of the Southwestern R. R. suffered a considerable falling off in 1865-6 as compared with 1859-60. In the year before the war it carried 206,307 bales of cotton and only 87,250 in 1865-6. The Fort Gaines branch of the Southwestern was not in use during 1865-6, for iron removed from it during the war was not replaced until later. In February of 1866 conditions were sufficiently favorable for the directors to declare a semi-annual dividend of 4 per cent. In March of that year the legislature approved the terms of consolidation of the Muscogee R. R. with the Southwestern, by which the liabilities were assumed and the stock taken over by the Southwestern at 87½.[4]

[1] *Macon Telegraph*, January 7, 1866.

[2] Poor, *Railroad Manual*, 1868-9, p. 112.

[3] Jones and Dutcher, *Memorial History of Augusta*, p. 497.

[4] *Hunt's Merchant Magazine*, January, 1867; Poor, *Railroad Manual*, 1869-70, p. 53.

The Atlanta and West Point R. R. likewise was able to pay a 4 per cent dividend in 1866, half its normal dividend before the war, though its net earnings in 1865-6 amounted to only $54,628 as compared with $207,118 in 1860-61.[1]

The Macon and Brunswick R. R., a project started a few years before the war as a rival to the Central in diverting some of the carrying trade from Central Georgia to the port of Brunswick, made little headway before 1861.[2] In 1866 a vigorous campaign was waged by those interested in the railroad to secure aid from the state for its completion, and in December, 1866, despite the powerful opposition of the Central R. R., the legislature passed a bill authorizing the governor to place the endorsement of the state on Macon and Brunswick R. R. bonds to the amount of $10,000 per mile for as many miles as were completed, and to a like amount per mile for every additional ten miles as completed. As security the state held a prior lien on all property of the company.   By December, 1866, fifty miles from Macon were completed, equipped and running, and seventy additional miles were graded and ready for the superstructure.[3]

Work on the railroad connecting Macon and Augusta through Milledgeville, a branch of the Georgia R. R., progressed during 1866, as did likewise grading for the Georgia Air Line from Atlanta to the northeast. Several new charters were granted in 1866 to companies to build roads to act as feeders for lines already in existence—the Cherokee R. R. (chartered as the Cartersville and Van Wert R. R.) to go from Cartersville to Pryor, Ala.; the Gainesville and Dahlonega R. R., to connect with the Air Line R. R.; the Southern R. R. Co., from Bainbridge to Cuthbert; and the

[1] Poor, *Railroad Manual, 1871-2*, p. 219.

[2] Phillips, *History of Transportation in the Eastern Cotton Belt*, p. 359.

[3] *Acts of the General Assembly*, 1866, pp. 127-8; *Atlanta New Era*, November 16, 18, 1866; *Augusta Chronicle*, November 28, 1866.

Albany and Atlantic R. R., to a point where the Macon
and Brunswick crosses the Atlantic and Gulf.[1] The Atlantic
and Gulf R. R. had suffered damage to its rails for about
twenty-five miles south of Savannah. Bridges and trestle
work up to the Altamaha were down and had to be repaired in 1865.[2]

The railroads maintained their prosperity, such as it was,
at the expense of the traveling and shipping public. Passenger and freight rates were exorbitantly high. For instance, the fare between Milledgeville and Macon, 37 miles,
was three dollars, or eight cents per mile. In May, 1865,
the Central, the Southwestern and the Macon and Western
announced a reduction in fare to five cents a mile in specie
or national currency and double that in bills of the best
state banks. Freight charges payable in specie or national
currency remained at the same rate as in June, 1863, when
they were payable in redundant Confederate currency.[3]
The oppression of heavy freight rates, just at the time when
people were dependent on corn from the West and clothes
from the North, stirred up a movement to secure some sort
of regulation by the legislature.[4] But nothing was accomplished toward this end and the railroads continued to
charge what the traffic would bear. In December, 1866,
shares of Georgia railroads were rated in the stock market
as follows:[5]

Central R. R.	@ 97-99
Southwestern	91-93
Augusta and Savannah	84-86
Georgia	72
Muscogee	60-62
Atlantic and Gulf	47-49

[1] *Acts of the General Assembly,* 1866, p. 119, *et seq.*

[2] *New York Herald,* June 27, 1865.

[3] *Augusta Constitutionalist,* May 28, 1865.

[4] *Savannah Herald,* February 2, 1866.

[5] *Savannah News,* December 22, 1866.

Banks suffered more heavily than any other business in
Georgia by the failure of the war.   The greatest part of
their capital had gone into Confederate and state war securities, and when the fall of the Confederacy and state
repudiation made these worthless, with few exceptions the
banks in the state collapsed.   Those that survived the crisis
of 1865, the Georgia R. R. and Banking Co., and the Central R. R. and Banking Co., had only part of their capital
in banking operations.[1]   In 1865, banking business had to
start practically from the beginning.   In the first term of
the legislature more than twenty banking corporations were
chartered, besides numerous building and loan associations.
The number of savings banks showed a hopefulness that
the people of Georgia would soon have something to save.
By the end of 1866 nine national banks had organized in
Georgia under the National Banking Act, with a paid-in
capital of $1,700,000 and a note circulation of $1,124,000.[2]

Much Northern capital came to revive Georgia industry.
In November, 1865, Truman observed that Northerners
lent money freely to public institutions.   Corporations had
comparatively little difficulty in getting supplies, partly on
time.[3]   And in the acts incorporating new banking, manu-

[1] *Macon Telegraph*, January 30, 1866; *Augusta Chronicle*, February
14, 1866.   In January, 1866 the notes of the leading banks in Georgia
were rated as follows:

Central R. R. and Banking Co.	95	Bank of Fulton	20
Georgia R. R. and Banking Co.	93	Bank of Columbus	15
Marine Bank	70	Bank of Commerce	10
Bank of Middle Georgia	70	Planters Bank	10
Bank of Savannah	40	Farmers & Mechanics Bank	10
Bank of Athens	25	Merchants and Planters Bank	10
Southwestern R. R. bank	25	Bank of the Empire State	10
Bank of Augusta	25	State Bank	10
Bank of the State of Georgia	22	Timber Cutters Bank	5

[2] *Hunt's Merchant Magazine*, December, 1866.

[3] *New York Times*, November 23, 1865.

facturing and other companies appear the names of many residents of Northern states. There was some pressure on the legislature to amend the existing liability and usury laws so as to encourage the investment of outside capital.[1] In December, 1866, the legislature repealed the war measure forbidding aliens to hold property in Georgia.[2]

With the depreciation of bank-notes and the worthlessness of Confederate currency the shortage in a circulating medium was a great obstacle in the way of reviving business. Just after the surrender, returning soldiers had no money whatever. A card of buttons or a paper of pins could more readily buy a meal on the way than a pocket full of Confederate notes.[3] In the towns where Federal soldiers were stationed, greenbacks got readily into circulation when army pay-day came round. In the summer of 1865 newspapers notified their subscribers that, in the lack of a proper circulating medium, wheat-flour, meal, bacon, lard, butter and other articles of produce would be received at market prices in payment for subscriptions.[4] The movement of the cotton crop northward was the means of bringing much-needed currency to the South.

The total public debt of Georgia, reported by the comptroller in 1865, amounted to something over $20,000,000, but of this a little more than $18,000,000, considered as war debt, was repudiated by the constitutional convention of 1865 under pressure from Washington, leaving to the state a recognized indebtedness of about $2,000,000.[5] As

[1] *Macon Journal and Messenger*, November 28, 1865; *Augusta Chronicle*, January 10, 30, 1866 and February 28, 1866.

[2] *Acts of the General Assembly*, 1866, p. 1.

[3] Andrews, *War-Time Journal of a Georgia Girl*, p. 201.

[4] *Savannah Herald*, May 22, 1865; *Augusta Constitutionalist*, July 16, 1865.

[5] *Supra*, p. 29.

means of income in 1865 the state had practically nothing. All the earnings of its railroad were consumed in repairs, its railroad and bank stock brought in no dividends, and so little of the taxable property was able to produce an income in the first few months of re-adjustment that heavy taxes would mean bankruptcy. When the legislature met in November, 1866, the state treasury was in arrears for the expenses of the provisional government, for the convention of 1865, for the reorganized government, for repairs on the Western and Atlantic R. R., and for food supplies provided to relieve destitute people in the state.[1] The first legislature of 1865-6 authorized the governor to meet the ordinary obligations of the state by issuing mortgage bonds on the Western and Atlantic R. R., and by negotiating temporary loans in the meantime. Loans for three or four months were executed in New York at 7 per cent by both Provisional Governor Johnson and Governor Jenkins, and were paid in full at maturity. The issue of bonds was delayed for a time to allow Georgia's credit to appreciate, so that the state might not be forced to sell its bonds lower than 90. The $500,000 five-year bonds, authorized by the convention, were not popular and only $30,000 of these were issued. The legislature in March, 1866, authorized mortgage bonds on the state road as follows:[2]

Bonds ordered by the convention and authorized by the
    legislature $500,000
To meet appropriations of the legislature and repairs on W. &
    A. R. R. 1,500,000
For the payment of the Federal tax of 1861 600,000
To fund past due bonds and coupons 830,000
To purchase corn for the destitute 200,000

[1] Salaries of the provisional governors were paid by the United States government out of the army contingency fund.

[2] *Acts of the General Assembly,* 1865-6, pp. 18-20.

When the Federal government through the Secretary of the Treasury refused to sanction the assumption of the Federal tax by the state, the issue of $600,000 was diverted to create a fund for exchanging or redeeming old bonds due in 1868, 1869, 1870.[1] With these bonds issued, together with bonds owing as part of the state's subscription to the Atlantic and Gulf R. R., amounting to $134,500, and $2,676,500 issued before the war, not yet due, Georgia's bonded indebtedness at the end of 1866 amounted to $5,971,000. Of this $675,500 was due in the following four years.[2] Georgia bonds stood well in the market, rather better than the securities of other Southern states. In December, 1866, new Georgia 7's were rated at 89-91; old Georgia 7's at 88-89; and old Georgia 6's at 75-77.[3]

The cash balance in the treasury of $5,201,086.18, most of which was in Confederate currency, was worthless, with the exception of $44,750 in U. S. currency. Other assets of the state were of doubtful value. Its holding of $183,300 in stock in the Bank of the State of Georgia and $19,000 in the Bank of Augusta were valueless. $18,600 in the Georgia R. R. and Banking Co. was still good, and likewise $700,000 in the Atlantic and Gulf R. R., though the latter was not worth its face value since the stock was below par.[4]

The first legislature of the reorganized state government dealt lightly in taxes. A general ad valorem property tax to produce $350,000 was levied for 1866 in addition to the specific taxes—a poll tax of one dollar and various occupa-

---

[1] *Acts of the General Assembly*, 1866, p. 16.

[2] The message of Governor Jenkins to the legislature gives a summary of the condition of the state finances. *Journal of the House of Representatives*, 1866, pp. 10-15.

[3] *Savannah News*, December 22, 1866.

[4] *Report of the Comptroller General*, 1865, p. 14.

tion taxes as customary before the war. Unpaid taxes for
1864 and 1865 were remitted.[1] The next session of the
legislature in 1866 increased the general tax levy to produce $500,000 in 1867, with the usual poll and other specific
taxes. To meet the difficulty of the non-payment of poll
tax by the freedmen, the tax act of 1866 bore a provision
that the employer should pay for an employee who had not
paid and who had no property to levy on, the employer to
deduct the amount from the wages of the employee.[2]

Of the direct tax of $20,000,000 levied by the United
States in 1861 and apportioned among the states, $584,-
367.33 was due from Georgia. In June, 1865, tax commissioners were appointed by the Secretary of the Treasury
and work toward collection was begun in various Southern
states. The legislature of 1865-6 assumed for the state
the obligation which the United States put upon the citizens
of the state, but such action was disallowed by the Secretary of the Treasury. Then the legislature passed an act,
authorizing the governor to arrest collection of so much of
the state tax as was levied on lands in the state, if the
United States government proceeded to collect tax from
land owners. After about $82,000 had been collected in
Georgia the Secretary of the Treasury ordered, August 3,
1865, that the collection of the direct tax be suspended, and
this was not resumed.[3]

A matter of great importance, the payment of debts contracted by private individuals and corporations during the
war, came before both sessions of the assembly in 1866
and became one of the chief issues in the convention in

[1] *Acts of the General Assembly*, 1865-6, pp. 253-5.

[2] *Ibid.*, 1866, p. 164.

[3] *Ibid.*, 1865-6, p. 256; *New York World*, May 4, 1865 (Townsend
Library) ; Secretary of the Treasury, *Report of the Finances*, 1866, p.
62.

1867-8. In the first session after the war the legislature
passed a Relief Act, suspending levy and sale under execution for debts incurred prior to June 1, 1865, provided one-
fourth of the debt be paid annually. At the next session
in December, 1866, a second act was passed over the governor's veto by large majorities in both houses, which prohibited levy and sale, with the proviso that one-third might
be levied on after January 1, 1868, one-third in January,
1869, and the remainder in January, 1870.[1]

The year and a half immediately after the war was a
period of attempted recovery in commerce and industry, with
little in the way of real progress. The ideal was to go back
to the condition of 1860. The transportation problem was
to repair the damage of war; banking had to start from
the beginning; manufactures developed but little. Trading,
wholesale and retail, mercantile business in cities and towns,
was the one industry in which the activity of 1865-6 surpassed that of 1860. The state, like private corporations,
had to meet the difficulty of bearing extraordinarily large
expenditures with limited resources of revenue. Upon public and private enterprise alike the results of war had at
once enormously increased demands and cut off sources of
supply.

[1] *Acts of the General Assembly,* 1865-6, p. 241 ; 1866, p. 157.

CHAPTER V

Social Re-adjustment

1865 and 1866 were lean years for Georgia people. Though some few came out of the war rather richer than they went into it, poverty was the general condition among the great majority. Destitution in the parts of the state that had been ravaged by the armies was extreme. A traveler from Chattanooga to Atlanta in October, 1865, declared that there was not as much food growing in the whole region as on an ordinary farm.[1] In the summer of 1865 a Federal officer conducted an investigation of conditions in thirteen counties in North Georgia, adjacent to Atlanta. In these counties 5,768 families were reported to be absolutely destitute, and only 64 families had any surplus in food supplies. The people were doing little to ward off starvation; shiftless, lazy, and unwilling to work, whites and blacks alike.[2] The freedmen preferred to hang around sunny corners rather than plough in the field. Young white men, too, appeared unwilling to buckle down to work when there was the greatest need of it.[3] In some of the northern counties above Athens people took to " bushwhacking ", plundering and stealing, as the easiest means of getting a living. To provide food in the impoverished parts of the state the

[1] *New York Times*, October 14, 1865.

[2] *Official Records of the War of the Rebellion*, vol. xlix, pt. ii, pp. 1061-2.

[3] *Macon Journal and Messenger*, November 25, 1865.

legislature in 1866 advanced $200,000; and the North, too, where public meetings were held to raise funds for the destitute people of the South, lent a hand to relieve distress.[1]

Not only were the poor poorer, but many who had been rich were hard pressed to get the means of ordinary living. Howell Cobb, for example, before the war was considered one of the richest men in Georgia. He owned several large, fertile plantations, and over a thousand slaves; and in addition to his planting interests he had a lucrative law practice. The following letters, addressed by him to his wife, are indicative of the hard financial condition in which many formerly prosperous men found themselves after the war:

MACON, 24 NOVEMBER, 1865.

My Dear Wife,

I am sticking close to my office and books, with the ardor of a new beginner. The " nibbles " continue and I have no fears that you will be driven to the necessity of opening a day school. We refused a fee of three hundred dollars from Mr. G. B. Lamar, who wanted to employ us in a big case. He wanted our services, and we wanted his money, but the trouble was he wanted a thousand dollars worth of work for three hundred, and that we are not able to stand. If he raises his sights to the proper point, we may yet serve him *and ourselves.*[2]

MACON, 7 DECEMBER, 1865.

My dear Wife,

Nothing of interest has occurred since I last wrote to you. Everything moves on in a quiet way. We have some indications of business in our office; and if constant attendance and close attention to business will bring in more, we shall get it. Two fees,—one of five hundred dollars and another of two

[1] *New York Times,* October 17, November 14, 22, 1865.

[2] MS. Howell Cobb Correspondence.

hundred, with some smaller ones, have been ensured, and I
doubt not, others will follow in due season.[1]

But not everyone was poorer by reason of the war.
Some few prospered exceedingly by the industrial activity
of war time. Rolling-mills, foundries and factories for war
supplies coined money for their owners, who were shrewd
enough to invest their earnings in some other form than
Confederate or state bonds or bank stock. Speculators made
big profits in food supplies when markets were short and
uncertain.[2] By May, 1866, more than twelve hundred citizens of Georgia had received special pardons for their connection with the rebellion on the ground that they were
excluded from the general amnesty by being worth more
than $20,000. In this list are the names of a number of
men prominent in public life, C. J. Jenkins, Joshua Hill,
and Linton Stephens, for instance.[3]

One of the significant changes that have come in social
classes in Georgia since the war is the position of social and
political leadership achieved by men engaged in trade and
commerce. Before the war prestige was generally from
landed wealth or professional distinction. This shifting in
the basis of dignity and importance in the community was
beginning to show itself in 1865 and 1866, though its evi-
dences are more striking in the later period of reconstruction and after. City life, too, gained in distinction, and a
change was evident in the relative influence of important
cities and towns on social and political conditions. Re-adjustment in the old social order, brought about by the break-
ing up of the land system and the growth of new economic

[1] This letter is published by U. B. Phillips, *Annual Report of the
American Historical Association*, 1911, vol. ii, p. 672.

[2] Avery, *History of the State of Georgia*, p. 315.

[3] House Exec. Doc., 39 C., 1 S., no. 99.

interests, was furthered by the political measures of President Johnson's reconstruction policy. His exceptions from amnesty threw former leaders out of the running for a time, and gave more chance to the middle class than it had ever before had. While the period immediately after the war marks decided progress in the rise of a middle class in social and political power, still this shifting of social values did not begin with the end of the war, and the downfall of the so-called " slave oligarchy ". Its source lies further back. Georgia had never been thoroughly aristocratic in its controlling elements, and certainly before the war great changes had taken place in making way for the yeoman.[1] The election to the governorship in 1857 of "Joe" Brown, the up-state country judge and farmer, whose appeal was to the " plain man ", is significant of the deeplying social changes at work. With the shifting of the social, came also the shifting of sectional lines of leadership. More and more did the up-state country grow in dominating power at the expense of the older, more conservative, lowland region.

Before the war Georgia had no public school system, and not until 1866 did a scheme for general education at public expense become law. The state's contributions to education before 1865 were through its support of the University of Georgia at Athens and through its fund for the education of poor children. Schools were privately supported and managed. The educational fund of the state was distributed among counties pro rata, and parents who could not pay tuition for their children sent them to private schools at the expense of the county. In 1852 the legislature set apart

[1] Avary (*ed.*) *Recollections of Alex. H. Stephens,* pp. 421-3. Witness the strength of the Democratic party in Georgia as against the aristocratic Whig party, even before the slavery controversy scattered the Southern Whigs after 1850. See Phillips, *Georgia and State Rights.*

as a Poor School Fund the dividends from bank stock owned by the state in the Bank of the State of Georgia, the Bank of Augusta, and the Georgia R. R. and Banking Co. In 1858 the fund was increased by an annual appropriation of $100,000 from the earnings of the Western and Atlantic R. R., to be divided among the counties according to the number of white children between the ages of eight and eighteen. At the same time the legislature added to the fund the annual interest on new bonds which the governor might issue in lieu of bonds which were redeemed.[1]

In 1865 there were no bank dividends and the earnings of the state road were diverted to other purposes, so the whole fund for education was only $23,355, interest on the public debt redeemed since 1859.[2] Since many teachers in various counties received no pay in 1865, the legislature of 1865-6 authorized justices of the inferior court of each county to issue certificates of indebtedness at 6 per cent interest from January 1, 1866, due a year later. The rate of payment for teachers instructing beneficiaries of the Poor School Fund was not to be less than seven cents per day for each scholar.[3]

The establishment of a system of common schools was urged by Governor Brown several years before the war. In his message to the legislature in 1858 he suggested that a school fund should be established for common schools by the issue of new bonds as the standing debt was paid off, until the fund should amount to $4,000,000. The legislature did not act upon the plan proposed by the governor, though it did increase the Poor School Fund by $100,000.[4]

---

[1] *Report of the Comptroller General*, 1865, p. 23.

[2] *Ibid.*, pp. 23-4.

[3] *Acts of the General Assembly*, 1865-6, p. 77. By Act of December, the maximum charge was fixed at sixteen cents a day for each pupil.

[4] Fielder, *Life and Times and Speeches of Joseph E. Brown*, pp. 147-51.

In the first session of the legislature after the war, bills for
the establishment of common schools were introduced, but
the time of the assembly at this session was devoted to
pressing temporary measures of rehabilitation, and no constructive plan of permanent progress was considered until
the second session in November and December, 1866.   In
the first session, however, the House appointed a committee
of sixteen to digest plans for a common school system and
to report to the next session of the General Assembly; and
the Senate, likewise, appointed a committee on Public Education and Free Schools.[1]   In the second session, on November 15, 1866, the special committee of the Senate presented a report in the shape of a bill, which was made a
special order for November 26th, and passed on that day.
In the House on December 12th the Senate bill was
amended by the clause to postpone operation until January
1, 1868, and passed by a close vote, 62 to 58.   The vote in
the Senate, also, was close.   A motion to reconsider was
lost by 18 to 12.[2]   On December 12th, the governor signed
the bill, entitled, " An Act to provide for Education, and
to establish a general system of Georgia schools." [3]   It provided for a thorough-going system of common schools, with
a state superintendent appointed by the governor, a commissioner for each county, appointed by the grand jury of the
.superior court of the county, and three trustees in each district of the county, elected by the qualified voters in the
district.   Free instruction in the Georgia schools was offered to " any free white inhabitant being a citizen of the
United States and of this state, and residing within the

[1] *Journal of the House of Representatives,* 1865-6, p. 293.   *Journal
of the Senate,* 1865-6, pp. 23, 103.

[2] *Journal of the House of Representatives,* 1866, pp. 111, 378; *Journal
of the Senate,* 1866, pp. 120, 178, 179, 186, 418.

[3] *Acts of the General Assembly,* 1866, pp. 58-65.

limits of any county or school district organized under this Act, between the ages of 6 and 21 years, and any disabled and indigent soldier of this state under 30 years of age." Such public schools were to be supported by a county tax, levied by the inferior court at a per cent (not over 100 per cent) on the state tax, added to the share each county would receive from the state educational fund. The last section of the Education Bill contained the important proviso, "this act shall have nor force nor effect until after the first of January, 1868."

Postponement for a year was decided upon because the people of the state had not sufficiently recovered from the poverty brought upon them by the war to enable them to bear extra taxes for education. Before January 1, 1868, when the plan for a common school system in Georgia was to go into effect, a new revolution was brought upon Georgia by the reconstruction measures of 1867, and no general system of education organized by the state was established until 1873, and then by the plan of the reconstruction legislature of 1870. In view of this carefully planned scheme for a common school system, made law in December, 1866, but prevented from execution by circumstances over which the people of Georgia had no control, it is impossible to accept for Georgia the general conclusion so often stated that the public school system in the South was entirely the work of the reconstruction of 1868.

The University of Georgia at Athens was closed in October, 1863, when threatened invasion of the state took away members of the faculty and students to form part of the state troops and the home guard. After 1863 its dormitory buildings were occupied by families of refugees from New Orleans, Mobile, and Savannah, and no session was held until January, 1866. Then the campus was overgrown with weeds, the chapel and dormitories had been de-

faced by Federal soldiers, who had used the buildings as
quarters for a garrison. When the university re-opened,
seventy-eight students appeared, most of whom had gone
through the war and many of whom were grown men. Enrollment for the next year was increased by ninety-three
maimed soldiers, who received their education at state expense.[1] In December, 1866, the legislature provided that
$300 should be paid to the University and to several other
colleges for each indigent maimed soldier which the institution received. The recipient of the benefit was to pledge
himself to teach as many years in Georgia as he may have
been in college.[2] The smaller denominational colleges had
greater difficulty in recovering and did not get on their feet
again until 1867 and later.

In December, 1866, the legislature passed an act to provide for a college of agricultural and mechanic arts, ap-
propriating $2,000 for the purpose in order to take advan-
tage of the Federal grants of public lands for agricultural
schools, made under the acts of July 2, 1862, and April 14,
1864.[3]

The organization of public school systems in the cities
of Georgia made no headway in 1865 and 1866, except in
Savannah, where a " Board of Public Education for the
City of Savannah ", to superintend the education of white
children from sixteen to eighteen years, was established in
March, 1866. In December of the same year the act was
amended to extend authority over Chatham County as well.

---

[1] Hull, *Historical Sketch of the University of Georgia*, p. 73, *et seq.*;
Hull, *Annals of Athens*, p. 302, *et seq.*

[2] *Acts of the General Assembly*, 1866, pp. 143-4.

[3] *Ibid.*, pp. 64-5. In 1872 the state entered into a contract with the
trustees of the University of Georgia by which the State College
of Agriculture was to be established as part of the University.

During the first year two schools were opened with ten teachers and an enrollment of 520 pupils.[1] Soon after the surrender, in May, 1865, General Grover in command in Savannah attempted to help in providing school facilities for the white children of the city, since negroes were otherwise cared for. Of 2,000 white children of school age, only 600 were in school. General Grover's order to establish three free schools for white children in Savannah was disapproved by his superior officer, General Gillmore, who commanded that all schools provided should offer equal facilities to blacks and whites.[2]

The education of negroes was left to the Freedmen's Bureau and to Northern philanthropy. Some Southerners thought that since emancipation was a fact, the wisest policy for the South was to educate the negro so as to make him able to live up to that state of freedom into which it had pleased the North to call him. But this was the opinion of a small minority. The usual arguments against education as unfitting to the condition of hewers of wood and drawers of water were applied to their former slaves by most people of Georgia. Education of negroes, they thought, would be labor lost, resulting in injury instead of benefit to the working classes. C. H. Howard, of the Freedmen's Bureau, reporting in December, 1865, wrote:

Existing theories concerning the education of laborers and the prejudices against the blacks are such as absolutely to prevent the establishment of schools for the freedmen even though the

[1] *Acts of the General Assembly*, 1865-6, pp. 78-90; Wilson, *Historic and Picturesque Savannah*, p. 211; *Report of the Board of Education of Savannah*, 1869-70, p. 7.

[2] Correspondence between Gen. Grover and Gen. Gillmore, *Official Records of the War of the Rebellion*, series i, vol. xlvii, pt. iii, pp. 284, 418, 466-7, 492-3, 525, 568-9.

expense be paid by benevolent associations of the North, and
the many successful schools now in operation would be broken
up in most places on the withdrawal of the government
agencies. The same general observation will apply to all missionary work by Northern agents; and from special inquiry
and investigation of this subject, I am convinced that very
little in the way of moral and religious instruction for the
freed people is to be expected at present from the members
and ministers of the Southern churches. On the other hand,
it is for the interest of the whites for these agencies to remain,
and the better class of the thinking men expressed themselves
unhesitatingly in favor of it.[1]

For 1865 the Freedmen's Bureau reported 66 schools, 66
teachers and 3,500 pupils in Georgia. The New England
Freedmen's Aid Society and the American Missionary Association supported 62 schools for freedmen, which had 89
teachers and 6,600 pupils. In 1865-6 the American Missionary Association and the New England Branch of the
Union Commission and the Freedmen's Aid Society of the
Methodist Episcopal Church together spent $20,000 for
negro education in Georgia. The aid societies usually furnished teachers while the Bureau provided buildings.[2] In
some places there were self-supporting schools with colored
teachers, but these did not report to the Freedmen's Bureau.
In Savannah, out of 1,600 colored children, 1,200 were in
school and 350 of these were in the schools of the Savannah Educational Association, an organization supported by
the colored people and employing negro teachers.[3] Freedmen's schools in Macon, too, were flourishing, with 1,000
pupils and 11 teachers. The schools were provided with

[1] *Joint Committee on Reconstruction*, 1866, pt. iii, p. 47.

[2] Report of E. A. Ware, Superintendent of Education for Georgia,
Freedmen's Bureau, in the *Journal of the Georgia Senate*, 1868, pp. 78-9.

[3] Trowbridge, *Picture of the Desolated States*, pp. 490, 509.

teachers, women from the North, by the American Missionary Association. There were four morning schools, one in
each African church, one afternoon school for more advanced pupils, and a night school for those of all ages.
The freedmen paid for their own books and for fuel and
light.[1] In Augusta, schools were under the direction of
the Education Department of the Freedmen's Bureau. At a
meeting of the inferior court of the county, the judge
stated that the court was considering means to establish free
schools for colored people, and asked if the negroes would
accept their aid. In reply, some negroes objected that they
were too poor to pay taxes and the Northern people gave
them education free; other negro speakers favored the
proposition. In Atlanta a hospital and several good schools
were in operation, sustained chiefly by benevolent associations in the North. In South Georgia, too, the Bureau was
active in providing school facilities for the negroes. In
Quitman, Valdosta and Thomasville vacant buildings were
rented, the negroes furnishing labor to make necessary repairs. In Thomasville the Bureau representative proposed
to the white people that an academy building be used for
the negroes until another could be made ready. But the
white citizens objected, knowing that prejudice was such
that the white people would never consent to send their
children again to a school once used for negroes. Thomasville had a school for colored children taught by a colored
resident before the Freedmen's Bureau took hold, as had
Albany, also, where the teacher was a young woman from
New York. In Southwest Georgia the agent of the
Bureau heard of two planters who wished to establish
schools for colored children on their plantations. In these
plantation schools, by no means as rare as the Freedmen's

[1] *Ibid.*, pp. 465-6; *Macon Telegraph*, February 7, 1866.

Bureau agent thought, the expense was borne most frequently by the planters, the parents of the pupils paying a nominal sum monthly in money or provisions to the teacher. In Andersonville, too, a school was established for negroes in a Confederate building, where a sergeant of an Ohio regiment taught adults in the evening.[1]

In the early years after the war negro children were very much better off as to educational opportunities than were poor white children. To the blacks was extended the helping hand of Northern sympathy and the aid of a national bureau; but the poverty of his own father and the impotence of the state let the white child abide in ignorance.

Two important problems of social adjustment, the attitude of Southern people toward Northern immigrants and the treatment of the blacks by the white population, were subjects of investigation before the congressional committee on reconstruction in 1866. As to the former question, several witnesses called before the committee expressed the opinion that Northern residents in Georgia were dependent on the presence of Federal troops for the safety of their persons and property.[2] Still they had but few instances of maltreatment of Northerners to relate. Whether it was due to the presence of troops or not, the fact remains that many Northerners did take up residence in Georgia immediately after the war, and managed to preserve their lives and to secure some property. In some districts, cases were known where newcomers from the North were scared off by threats. In the newspapers were occasional harsh words about new Yankee residents, but to every one item of this tone were twenty clamoring for Northerners to come and

[1] *Joint Committee on Reconstruction*, 1866, pt. iii, pp. 43-6 (Report of C. H. Howard); *Augusta Chronicle*, April 26, July 1, 1865.

[2] *Joint Committee on Reconstruction*, 1866, pt. iii, pp. 7-8, 39, 47, (Test.: Gen. Hatch, Gen. C. H. Howard).

bring their business interests to the state. In Georgia to-day many persons who came from the North soon after the war to engage in business say that they were never maltreated or threatened in any way. Except in some few districts the personal safety of Northerners was not endangered. But socially their position was far from agreeable. Complaints were frequent that Northerners were not received in the homes of their neighbors. Women, who ruled the social world, were stricter than men in their aloofness from the Yankees and did not hesitate to show their displeasure by drawing their skirts aside to keep from brushing against the offensive Northerners on the streets, or by lowering a parasol to protect themselves from the distasteful gaze of a Yankee.

Ostracism of Northerners was greater in Savannah and the lowland region of Georgia, where social life was more conservative and more aristocratic than in the upper part of the state. An Atlanta paper said that it would welcome Northerners who were friendly to the South, though it wanted no hypocrites or radicals to come, and criticised Savannah people as acting in the wrong in ostracising newcomers simply because they were Northerners.[1] Much of the prejudice against receiving Northerners socially was doubtless due to the fact of their being Northerners, but in addition to that was the fact that many of the newcomers were persons who had no social position in their homes in the North, and in their persons bore no evidence of special presentability to make them eligible to social groups in Georgia. The dislike of Northerners was manifested often on occasions that gave an effect of fantastic incongruity. Thus, in Washington, Georgia, two Yankees entered a church and sat in a pew with a prominent young man of

[1] *Atlanta New Era*, October 20, 1866.

the town, who straightway rose and changed his seat. In the same town in June, 1865, during a revival meeting at a Methodist church, a former Confederate soldier, kneeling to profess his faith, was perceptibly chagrined to find a Northerner kneeling beside him. A sympathetic friend of the Southerner remarked that he was sorry to see a good Confederate going to heaven in such bad company.[1] The young women who came from the North to teach in schools for negroes, " Yankee school-marms ", were special objects of ostracism. It was often hard for them to secure board in white families, so they had to live with negroes whether they wished to or not.[2]

More serious than the relation of Southerners to Northerners was the question of race adjustment. Though there were many difficulties, the race problem in the greater part of Georgia, as the result of emancipation, was not acute in 1865-6. The immediate problem of emancipation was that of labor. But in 1867 and 1868, when the reconstruction program of Congress attempted to subvert the whole social order of the Southern states by making the former masters impotent and putting the instrument of power into the hands of the former slaves, and keeping it there by military force, then, indeed, came a social problem that the South and the nation have not yet in half a century been able to solve. The Southern white man did not consider that constitutional emancipation changed a particle the natural inferiority of the blacks to the white people. Freedom simply meant that the negro was no longer the property of an individual to be bought and sold, cared for and used by him. Natural inferiority of race and long habit made the negro dependent on the white. No legal measure could

[1] Andrews, *War-Time Journal of a Georgia Girl*, pp. 264, 288.

[2] *Henry County Weekly*, Memorial Number, April 24, 1908.

suddenly infuse into a weak, childish, irresponsible people, independence and competence. An act of Congress might affect the law of property, but it could not immediately alter social and psychological traits in any people. Slavery was the proper condition of the blacks, and even though the mechanism was destroyed, the principles on which it rested, inferiority of negroes to whites, incompetence to work without direction and compulsion, irresponsibility in protecting and caring for themselves, still remained. This was the point of view of the representative Southerner. Though some slaveholders welcomed emancipation as a relief from their burdens, this attitude was exceptional, and most Southerners accepted emancipation only of necessity. But however unwelcome emancipation was, Southerners who had owned slaves felt no ill will toward the irresponsible blacks who had freedom thrust upon them. Among the whites, however, who had owned no slaves, the " poor whites ", hostility toward the negro was felt and expressed. The emergence of the negro as a free laborer created a rival to the poor white man from which slavery had in a great measure protected him. Though there was, as a rule, no change in the friendly relations of the slave owner and the freedmen toward each other in 1865, altered circumstances intensified the mutual hostility of the poor whites and the negroes. This class of the white population feared the negro and hated him, whereas the negro felt and showed profound contempt for " poor white trash ".

To this animosity, intensified a hundred-fold when the political enfranchisement of the negro in 1867 aggravated the difficulty that already existed, were due many of the disturbances between whites and blacks in sections where blacks were few or evenly balanced in number with the whites. Fair-minded travelers from the North, like B. C. Truman, J. R. Dennett, correspondent for the *Nation,* and the cor-

respondent for the *New York Herald* with Generals Steedman and Fullerton, all agreed that in general the relations
of the white people and the negroes toward each other were
friendly; that it was a small minority, mostly of the non-
slave-holding class, that hated the freedmen and caused disturbances.[1]   Truman observed that negroes were treated
better by Southerners than by Northerners who went south.
Northerners who took up farms or plantations found themselves helpless in dealing with negroes and were less patient
with them than were those who were accustomed to negro
ways.   In her diary kept during 1865, Miss Fannie Andrews, of Washington, Ga., expressed indignation at the
way the Yankees treated the negroes whom they impressed
into service from her father's plantation.   They put at
hard work one old darky, Uncle Watson, who had been
humored and had never done anything but the very lightest
work when he felt like it.[2]

There were undoubtedly large numbers of fights and
rows between whites and blacks in the first year and a half
after emancipation, many of which were due to the hostility of the lower class of whites toward the negroes.[3]   But
the condition of Georgia, as it appears to one reading the
newspapers of different sections of the state day by day
was far from that of anarchy, absolute lawlessness, and
incipient civil war, as it was represented by the radical
members of Congress.   In the South, the tendency had always been strong to settle difficulties by the law of the fist
or the shot-gun, and naturally there was something more
of this kind of lawlessness in the months when courts were
disorganized and adjustment to peace conditions was being

[1] *New York Times,* November 23, 1865 (Truman); *Nation,* February
1, 1866 (Dennett); *New York Herald,* June 18, 1866.

[2] Andrews, *War-Time Journal of a Georgia Girl,* p. 252.

[3] *Joint Committee on Reconstruction,* 1866, pt. iii, pp. 42, 46, 129.

made. Garrisons of soldiers, instead of keeping order, frequently disturbed the peace and caused conflicts with negroes, and in the first few months after the surrender, negro troops were centers of disturbance wherever they were stationed. The following letter, written by a resident of Atlanta in July, 1866, tells of one case, typical of many such outbursts of rowdyism:

The great Fourth of July has come and gone, and what a time we had of it. The occasion was observed only by the negro population. They had a grand procession and with banners flying paraded the streets and went to a grove near the cemetery where speeches were made, songs sung, and a big dinner came off. I went out and spent an hour with them, expecting to hear Dunning, Markham, and perhaps " Free Dave " make speeches, but was disappointed. . . . When the procession returned to the city, a lot of drunken Yankee soldiers—with Fourth of July on the brain—attacked them, and there was a general row. I never witnessed more disgraceful scenes in my life. No one was killed, but more than twenty shots were fired, and many were injured. The affair took place on Decatur St., near where the circus tent was placed. It was enough to disgust any man with his country. There is a very bitter feeling between the negroes and the Yankees, and though I am no advocate of disorder, I can find it in my heart to stand complacently aside and see them kill one another just when they please. The negro population is being made sensible of who are their friends and where they may look for sympathy when trouble comes.[1]

Every kind of departure from order that took place and many that did not take place were dressed up for appearance in the pages of radical newspapers in the North, like

[1] Letter written by Mr. V. P. Sisson, Atlanta, July 8, 1866 (MS. in possession of Mrs. V. P. Sisson, Kirkwood, Ga., to whom I am indebted for the use of this and other letters).

the *New York Tribune* and the *Philadelphia Press,* as "Outrages on the Freedmen ". B. C. Truman, in December,
1865, remarked on the danger of Northern newspaper correspondents becoming " hireling incendiaries " to misrepresent the South, and an editorial in the *New York Times,*
representative of conservative policy toward the South,
made comment on the pernicious practice of Northern
newspapers in gathering up accounts of maltreatment of negroes. The same thing might be done for the North with
quite as unfair results.[1] Georgia newspapers were indignant and helpless at the misrepresentation of conditions
given in Northern papers. The *Atlanta New Era* said that
radicals in the North used stories of abuse of freedmen as
political ammunition against the Conservative party. The
whites were kind in their dealings with negroes, and ready
to adapt themselves to the new relation. Abuse of the negro
occurred as everywhere, but scattered cases were not indicative of the Southern mind. There was a strong suspicion that reports of outrages were made by subsidized
letter writers and by sub-agents of the Freedmen's Bureau,
whose only chance of employment was to keep up pretence
of need of the Bureau.[2] The *Milledgeville Federal Union*
said that while Congress was wrangling over the negro,
the freedmen were attending to their business, and all intelligent and respectable negroes would remain uncontami-
nated, in spite of Yankee school-marms, correspondents for
the radical press, agents of the Freedmen's Bureau and all
other evil spirits.[3] As to the misrepresentation of conditions in the South by the Northern press, the following

[1] *New York Times,* November 20, 1865 (Editorial) ; December 10,
1865 (Truman).

[2] November 15, 1866.

[3] April 24, 1866.

statement is significant, made before the Reconstruction Committee of Congress by Brigadier-General Tarbell, who purchased a plantation in Mississippi and intended to reside and open an office in Atlanta : [1]

It is also my impression that many people in the North very greatly overrate the present character and capacity of the plantation negro, as well as his capacity for future improvement. I think time will show that the most ardent in the North will be greatly disappointed in the improvement of these negroes, even under the most favorable circumstances. I wish to add, judging from my travels in these three states [Mississippi, Alabama and Georgia], that these reports of outrages upon the colored people, of ill-treatment of the northern settlers, are quite exceptional cases, and exaggerated, if not altogether false, and that all these statements in the newspapers of outrages upon the blacks and upon the settlers from the North, I think, do the educated people of the South very great injustice. There are, no doubt, disloyal and disorderly persons in the South, but it is an entire mistake to apply those terms to a whole people. I would as soon travel alone, unarmed, through the South as through the North. The South I left is not at all the South I hear and read about in the North. From the sentiment I hear in the North, I would scarcely recognize the people I saw, and, except their politics, liked so well. I have entire faith that the better classes are friendly to the negroes, and that through this feeling, and the laws of capital and labor, the relations of these classes, will settle down together on terms equitable and just to both. I have also faith that when the North and South come to know each other better their relations will be all that could be desired.

Temper in Georgia was continuously milder toward negroes and more friendly toward protecting them than in the states further south. For one thing, Georgia's black prob-

---

[1] *Joint Committee on Reconstruction*, 1866, pt. iii, p. 157.

lem was not so difficult as was the race question in Alabama
or Mississippi or Louisiana, because Georgia had fewer
negroes in proportion to the white inhabitants. In 1860,
negroes were not quite equal in number to the total white
population of Georgia, and in only thirty-seven out of one
hundred and thirty-two counties did the blacks outnumber
the whites.[1] The responsible press of Georgia and her
acknowledged leaders in the restoration period were all of a
mind to act wisely and justly toward the former slaves.
There was some loud bluster and harsh action toward negroes, outbreaks of race feeling, but such talk and action
did not come from the class that represented authority in
1865 and 1866. As the editor of the *Macon Telegraph* said,
it was the duty of good citizens to protect negroes from the
influence of a large class of whites who never owned slaves,
and who showed contempt and injustice toward the negroes.[2] It would be hard to find anywhere discussions of
the relations of the whites to negroes just after the war
more sound in common sense, more just or more humane
in spirit than in the final address of H. V. Johnson to the
constitutional convention of 1865, the inaugural address of
Governor Jenkins, or the speech delivered by Alexander
Stephens before the Georgia legislature on February 22,
1866.[3]

[1] Phillips, *Georgia and State Rights*, population map facing p. 206.

[2] December 28, 1865.

[3] *Journal of the Constitutional Convention*, 1865, pp. 201-207; *Journal
of the House of Representatives*, 1865-6, pp. 58-66; and 413 *et seq.*

CHAPTER VI

Political Reorganization

On April 30, 1865, news was received in Georgia through a dispatch from General Johnston to Governor Brown that hostilities against the United States had ceased. At this time Federal authority was already established in the region round about Savannah, which was held after General Sherman's occupation in December, 1864, and in Macon, which was taken by General Wilson on his cavalry raid in April just before the surrender. From Savannah and Macon as centers, military occupation was extended over the whole state during April, May and June. Augusta was occupied on May 3d, Athens on May 4th, Atlanta on the 16th and Milledgeville on the 21st. Central garrisons were established at these points, from which military lines radiated. Later in May, troops were ordered to occupy Brunswick and Darien on the coast, the towns along the Ocmulgee and Altamaha rivers, and along the railroad from Doctortown to Thomasville.[1]

Some disorder in various parts of the state marked the transition to military authority, when civil law was interrupted. In Augusta and other towns there were bread riots, ruffians broke into bakeries and grocery stores, and depots of Confederate supplies were raided in various places. Stragglers returning from the disbanded armies caused dis-

---

[1] For the military occupation of Georgia, see *Annual Cyclopedia*, 1865, p. 392; newspaper clippings in the Townsend Library; and *Official Records of the War of the Rebellion*, vol. xlvii, pt. iii, pp. 322, 387, 466, 473, 537, 561, 596, 597, 626, 641, 667; vol. xlix, pt. ii, pp. 718-9, 967, 970, 1023, 1059.

[136

turbance through the country and around railroad junction points. In the mountainous districts of North Georgia lawless bands kept the people in a turmoil by their pillaging. Idle negroes committed burglaries and wandered about at all hours of the night. In Chatham County depredations by lawless bands of men did great damage to property and threatened the loss of the year's crops. In November, disturbed conditions in Wilkes County were such that General Steedman ordered forces there to check the outrages of bands of jayhawkers and regulators.[1]

Frequent broils occurred between soldiers and citizens, between negroes and white soldiers and between white people and colored troops. Garrisons where colored troops were established were centers for disturbance. Hot-headed young Southern men would not brook the lording insolence of the blacks in brass buttons. And negro soldiers everywhere had a bad influence on the freedmen of the neighborhood, encouraging them in idleness and arousing in them a feeling of distrust or hostility to their white employers. Discontent among the Federal soldiers themselves did not make matters more comfortable. White volunteers were restive, thought they ought to be immediately mustered out, and regular soldiers did not get along with colored troops. General Grant, after his tour of inspection in the South, reported to President Johnson, December 18, 1865, that the presence of black troops, lately slaves, demoralized labor by their advice and by furnishing resorts for freedmen for miles around, whereas white troops generally excited no opposition. Negro troops had to be kept in large enough numbers for their own defense.[2] Though

[1] *O. R.*, vol. xlvii, pt. iii, pp. 595, 596, 665-6; *New York Times*, December 11, 1865; *New York Herald*, May 20 and 21, 1865.

[2] *New York Times*, December 3, 1865. Truman concluded that negro troops should be dismissed, since their service was "unnecessary, unpalatable, impolitic."—*Ku Klux Committee Report*, vol. i, pp. 294-5.

the relations of white citizens and white soldiers were far from cordial, still, in most places they got along together passably well. Conditions were represented thus by a distinguished Georgian in a letter to General Sherman on May 10th:[1]

. . . We are all very blue at the prospects before us—We who had labored to save the country from the terrible strife through which we have just passed; and who, after war commenced, labored and prayed for its termination, hoped, that, with the hush of arms would smile peace and quietude. That, though crushed and ruined in all our material prosperity, we should have cheerful hearts to begin to clear the wreck and get things in shape for our children. But we have not realized our hopes. True, there is no war upon us, but then it is not peace. Armed men still cover our whole land, and though they do not claim the right to take whatever they wish, they manage in one way or another to procure all they desire. Almost daily houses are entered and pilfered, and we meet at every turn the air of derision and defiance. Our people made almost superhuman exertions, after your army passed through, to gather up plough stock and get supplies to enable us to make a support for what of helplessness was left. Many of the farms were left crowded with helpless women and children, with a few old men. I counted the other day twenty-nine children in one yard, with only two decrepit negro men to labor with the proprietor for their support. Now the commander's cavalry squads, stationed at various points in the country, permit the negroes to take the plough stock from the farmer and swarm into their camps, and lounge about, abandoning all labor—Surely, whatever may be the final destiny of this people, they ought to be required to make a support— And the negro girls for miles and miles are gathered to the camps and debauched. In some instances this has occurred

[1] Johnson MSS. This letter was written by N. G. Foster of Madison, Morgan Co., Ga., May 10, 1865.

when ladies have taken the same pains to protect their virtue
that they exercised towards their own daughters. It surely
is not the wish of those persons who aim at an equality of
colors to begin the experiment with a whole race of whores.
. . . The cry of vengeance which has been raised, to keep
down future rebellion is all gammon. I have not conversed
with a soldier who had returned, that does not express a per-
fect willingness to abide the issue. They say they made the
fight and were overpowered, and they submit. Nothing will
again disturb the people but a sense of injustice. No people
who descended from Revolutionary fathers can be kept tamely
in a state of subjugation. And if it becomes necessary to
establish a military despotism South, any man with half an
idea must see that the North must eventually fall under the
same rule.

The relation of the military to the civil authority was not
clearly defined, and was all the more confused, owing to the
fact that Georgia responded to two commanding generals—
the east to General Gillmore, Department of the South, and
the west to General Thomas, Department of the Mississippi,
who held conflicting opinions as to their functions. General Gillmore acted on the principle that the government of
the state should be dominantly military, without recourse to
civil administration except where necessity compelled. General Thomas, on the other hand, instructed his officers that
" the military authority should sustain, not assume the functions of civil authority ", except where necessary to preserve peace. The milder of these two theories of military
control was the one applied more extensively in Georgia;
for on June 27, 1865, there was a reorganization, and the
Department of Georgia, under General Steedman, was
made part of General Thomas's command.[1] General

[1] *Official Records of the War of the Rebellion*, vol. xlvii, pt. iii, pp.
594, 596, 633, 667-8, 680.

Thomas took measures to restore civil organization in the counties, empowering all duly authorized judges, commissioners, and others to proceed to perform their duties according to the laws of 1861, except that the negro must be regarded as free. Where vacancies occurred, loyal people [those taking the amnesty oath] might elect new officers, subject to the approval of the military commander.[1]

In the actual administration of military rule the amount and kind of interference with civil affairs varied according to the temper of the officers in charge of the districts. In addition to the general business of the protection of life and property and the preservation of peace, military orders regulated and established courts, disbanded the state government, regulated newspapers to practices of loyalty, supervised mails, administered railroad affairs, made provisions and restrictions for trade and commerce, supervised schools, extended aid and relief in desolate communities, and performed various functions of ordinary civil administration. General Wilson, in his orders to one of his subor-

Military organization of Georgia by General Orders, no. 118, June 27, 1865 and General Orders, no. 130, July 28, 1865:

Military Division of Tennessee, Maj. Gen. G. H. Thomas commanding, comprising Departments of Tennessee, Kentucky, Georgia, Alabama.

Department of Georgia,—Maj. Gen. Steedman, commanding.

Military Districts—

(1) northwestern—Gen. Stevenson—
vicinity of Atlanta and Marietta—all counties on both sides of the W. & A. R. R.—Headquarters in Atlanta.

(2) southwestern—Gen. Wilson—
Griffin, Macon, Milledgeville, Albany, Columbus, Andersonville—Headquarters in Macon.

(3) southeastern—Gen. Brannan—
Headquarters in Savannah.

(4) northeastern—Gen. King—
Headquarters in Augusta.

[1] *O. R.,* vol. xlix, pt. ii, pp. 343, 582, 621.

dinate officers, May 4, 1865, designated the following as the duties of an officer in command: to arrest prominent agitators and rebels who try to evade terms of capitulation; to compel editors to publish papers in the interests of peace and national unity under the constitution and the laws, to exact parole to this effect or to prohibit publication of the paper; to encourage civil officers to urge others to accept the situation; to discountenance public meetings and keep down excitement; to protect property.[1]

In the matter of the administration of justice, in the west and the north, under General Thomas's command, county courts were from the outset encouraged to resume ordinary business; in the east, General Gillmore provided for provost courts for the trial of petty offences, and for the enforcement of civil claims and contracts that needed immediate decision. He proposed a concession to local autonomy by inviting local magistrates who had taken the amnesty oath to sit with the military officers, and by allowing civil magistrates to exercise their functions in places not conveniently reached by the troops.[2] After the President's policy toward the rebel states was announced, and after the provisional governor of Georgia assumed office in June, progress was made in reorganizing courts and local bodies of administration on the basis of loyalty, and military authority was more and more restricted to measures of maintaining peace and enforcing justice where the civil authorities failed. But even after the complete state government was reorganized, justice by military force was not rare. In August, 1866, the *Augusta Chronicle* noted the first military arrest under General Grant's order for the military to act where civil authorities failed.[3] The case

---

[1] *O. R.*, vol. xlix, pt. ii, p. 604.

[2] *Ibid.*, vol. xlvii, pt. iii, pp. 594, 633.

[3] August 22, 1866.

was one of an assault by one white man on another, in which civil authorities made no arrest. In this case the military turned the prisoner over to the civil courts for trial. In October, 1866, Judge Perry closed the county court of Burke because of interference from the garrison at Waynesboro.[1] In December, 1866, the first case under the Civil Rights Bill was reported. At the instance of J. C. Swayze, some citizens of Griffin were arrested, imprisoned in Ft. Pulaski, and released on bail to appear before the U. S. Court of the Northern District.[2]

Numerous instances occurred of military discipline exercised upon newspaper editors for articles that were considered disloyal. In Augusta, every editorial had to be submitted to the post commander for approval before publication, and for one fiery article the *Augusta Constitutionalist* was seized and a sentry put in the composing room.[3] Subscribers to the *Athens Watchman* were surprised one day to find in the columns of the paper words of high praise for the Federal soldiers and harsh criticism for the South, until they learned that the Federals had taken possession of the *Watchman* office and issued the sheet to express their own sentiments.[4] In July, 1865, the editor of the *Macon Journal and Messenger* was imprisoned and the paper suppressed. The " high crime against the United States ", of which the editor was guilty, was his statement in the paper of July 20th that in order to take the amnesty oath he had had to fortify himself with an extra amount of " Dutch courage ", and " immediately after the above performance we ' smiled ' and we were fortified in rear and front ".[5]

[1] *Milledgeville Federal Union*, October 2, 1866.

[2] *Savannah News*, December 15, 1866.

[3] Jones and Dutcher, *Memorial History of Augusta, Georgia*, p. 186.

[4] Hull, *Annals of Athens*, p. 301.

[5] *Milledgeville Federal Union*, August 1, 1865; Avery, *History of the State of Georgia*, p. 345.

Control of the mail, also, was in charge of the military after the disruption of the Confederate postal service. All mail had to go through the office of the provost marshal, and the privilege of the post was confined to those who had subscribed to the amnesty oath, which was required of all members of the family over eighteen. Young ladies found it very humiliating to take the oath, but some of them protected themselves from Yankee contamination by fumigating their letters before opening.[1]   Off the railroad and outside of military posts there was no mail service and people had no means of knowing what was going on. During the suspension of mail facilities, the Southern Express Company arranged to send letters to any part of the United States for twenty-five cents. In the latter part of 1865 advertisements for mail contracts appeared in Georgia papers, and in November of that year, a special agent of the Post Office Department was in Georgia arranging for the reopening of the U. S. mails. During the spring of 1866 mail facilities were generally restored in the state, though it was difficult to find postmasters able to take the oath, and in some places women were appointed.[2]

In the early months of military rule, orders of officers dealt with such matters as railroad regulation and supervision of trade and regulation of prices. The Western and Atlantic R. R. was in the hands of military officers and was repaired under their direction. Before returning property claimed by the Central of Georgia R. R., General Gillmore ordered that the board of directors be purged of disloyal men or those excluded from the amnesty proclama-

[1] *New York Times,* May 5, 1865; *Savannah Herald,* April 26, 1865; Hull, *op. cit.,* p. 305.

[2] *Macon Journal and Messenger,* November 10, 1865; *Savannah Herald,* February 12, 1866; *Milledgeville Federal Union,* October 17, November 7, 1865.

tion.[1] In matters of trade the military gave support to another branch of the Federal government—its treasury agents. Before the Freedmen's Bureau was well established in Georgia in June, 1865, affairs of the freedmen were administered by officers of the garrisons. In the matter of furnishing relief in parts of the state that had been ravaged by war, Federal officers were very helpful and co-operated with former Confederate officials. Mules, stock, and woollen goods belonging to the Confederate stores were distributed among the poor of North Georgia, and large amounts of food supplies were sent there to prevent the people from starving. Under the direction of General Winslow a careful investigation was made of the condition of the people in the burned region along Sherman's track.[2]

On May 29, 1865, President Johnson announced his policy for restoring the seceded states to their place in the Union in his proclamation for North Carolina, and on June 17th, the same measures were proclaimed for Georgia. At this time no authorized state organization existed in Georgia. The state legislature, summoned by Governor Brown, who acted on the assumption that the state was restored to its autonomy on the surrender of state arms, was prevented from assembling on May 22d by military order.[3] On May 11th Governor Brown was arrested and sent to Washington in custody, where he remained about a week.

[1] *Official Records of the War of the Rebellion,* vol. xlvii, pt. iii p. 644; vol. xlix, pt. ii, pp. 999, 1002.

[2] *Ibid.,* vol. xlix, pt. ii, pp. 734, 748, 890, 903, 945.

[3] *Ibid.,* vol. xlvii, pt. iii, p. 505 ; vol. xlix, pt. ii, p. 630. Gen. Gillmore wrote to Secretary Stanton, May 10th, that he had "no faith in the loyalty of Gov. Brown nor in that of the leading politicians of Georgia," vol. xlvii, pt. iii, p. 464.

After his return he issued to the people of Georgia a formal resignation of the governorship.[1] On June 17th, James Johnson was appointed Provisional Governor of Georgia by the President. The appointee represented the class consistently used by President Johnson as the medium of his restoration policy, those who had opposed secession in 1861 and who had taken no prominent part under state or Confederate administration during the war. Mr. James Johnson was a respected lawyer of Columbus, who stood well in

---

[1] *Ibid.*, vol. xlix, pt. ii, p. 1064. Gen. Thomas wrote to Gen. Wilson, July 4, 1865, that he thought that the President permitted Brown to resign as governor. The ex-governor continued to exercise great influence in Georgia, and some in Washington, as well. He kept in close touch with President Johnson by letter and telegram. The following telegrams are samples of many communications from Brown to the President in the Johnson MSS.

> "August 7, 1865.
> Macon, Ga.
>
> "I think it important that I have an interview with you about offices here. If my health will permit I should like to start to Washington in about ten days. Please send me passport to this place by telegraph. No telegraph office at Milledgeville."
>
> (Signed)   Jos. E. Brown.

> "Atlanta, Ga. July 21, 1865.
>
> "No opportunity is offered the people of many of the counties of the state to take the amnesty oath, the back woods counties whose people are most loyal and would send delegates on your line of policy, are neglected.
>
> "Please order a person with competent authority into each county in the State to administer it. If this is done soon there will be no difficulty in the Convention.
>
> "Hope you have received my letters by express—No mail to Milledgeville. Answer to Atlanta. On my way to Cherokee for few days. Where is Senator Patterson?
>
> (Signed)   Joseph E. Brown.

It is possible that ex-Gov. Brown may have been one of the influences that changed Johnson from severe to moderate measures toward the rebels. Brown as one of the "plain people", not of the slave oligarchy, had qualities to appeal to President Johnson, in addition to his astuteness in dealing tactfully with the stubborn president.

his profession. He had served one term in Congress, elected on the Union platform in 1851; had generally been on the unpopular side of agitated questions; had opposed secession in 1861, and lived quietly during the war.[1] Mr. Joshua Hill, the conspicuous leader of Unionist sympathies in the state, was looked upon as the probable choice of the President, and when it was noted that he had gone to Washington, his appointment was taken for assured. Meetings were organized which endorsed the candidacy of Joshua Hill and many personal recommendations were sent to President Johnson in his behalf. Mr. Hill himself was not slow in suggesting his suitable qualities to the President, as the following letter, written by Hill to President Johnson on May 10, 1865, shows:[2]

I take the liberty of addressing you on a subject of pressing importance to the people of Georgia—and to the Southern people generally. It is one that demands a speedy solution. I am prompted by no other motive than a desire to see tranquillity restored to a distracted land, and society relieved of the terrible evils of war. I am no sectionalist, and have never been a separatist in thought, act, or deed. I have never given a vote or taken an oath recognizing any other nationality than that of the United States. I say this much in vindication of my principles.

After discussing the labor question and the sentiment of Georgia people toward the Union, Mr. Hill finds it necessary to add in postscript:

This letter is written at Augusta, but from habit dated at my residence. I am at this point endeavoring to make myself

[1] Avary (ed.), Recollections of Alex. H. Stephens, p. 230, et seq.; Avery, History of the State of Georgia, p. 341; Fielder, Life and Times and Speeches of Joseph E. Brown, p. 410.

[2] Johnson MSS.

useful—to both country and people. You may rest assured
that the [*word not clear*] of this State, have abandoned all
idea of further following the fortunes of Mr. Davis, or the
phantom of Southern independence. I trust you may remember me, as one of the Representatives of Georgia at the time
of her secession—who condemned that movement—standing
alone—amongst her public men—in the national councils.

However, other delegations than that headed by Hill
made the pilgrimage to Washington and strong opposition
to him developed, possibly because of his radical unionism.
As one correspondent said, there was danger that Hill might
" play Brownlow ". Finally, a compromise was arranged.
On June 16th, O. A. Lochrane, as chairman of the united
delegations from Georgia to President Johnson, recommended James Johnson as Provisional Governor, and on
the following day the appointment was made.[1]

On July 13th, Provisonal Governor Johnson issued his
first official proclamation, calling for the election of delegates to a convention of the people on the first Wednesday
in October and for the meeting of such convention in Milledgeville on the fourth Wednesday of the same month.
Only those citizens who had taken the amnesty oath were
qualified to vote for members of the convention. Two days
later in a public address in Macon, Provisional Governor
Johnson said that he was appointed for the single purpose
of enabling the people of Georgia to form a government.
In his proclamation, he stated that until the new government was constituted, all redress of wrong was remitted to
military authority.[2] The line of demarcation between civil

---

[1] In addition to this letter from Lochrane to the President, the
Johnson MSS. contain many letters of May and June, 1865, and copies
of resolutions passed at meetings in Georgia concerning the appointment of a provisional governor.

[2] Avery, *History of the State of Georgia*, p. 341.

and military remained indeterminate. In some parts of the state local civil officers who subscribed to the amnesty oath continued to perform their duties, and where vacancies occurred, new appointments were made, sometimes by the officer in command, sometimes by the Provisional Governor.[1] But no one could ever be sure at what moment military power would step in to supersede civil regulation.

Elections for the constitutional convention were held as directed on the first Wednesday in October. The President's purpose of throwing control into the hands of those who opposed secession in 1861 was in the main successful. Of the members elected twenty-two had been delegates to the secession convention of 1861, and all but one of them had voted against secession on the test resolution. Fourteen, who had been defeated candidates for the 1861 convention on an anti-secession platform, were elected in 1865.[2] Very few chosen in 1865 were known as strong secessionists, and few, also, had been thorough-going Unionists during the war.[3] The great majority had disapproved of immediate secession, had voted the Bell-Everett or the Douglas-Johnson ticket in 1860, and had then gone with the

[1] President Johnson communicated to Gov. Johnson, August 22, 1865, a report that Union men were ignored in appointment to state offices and preference given to rebels—a practice likely to embarrass the reconstruction policy of the government. In reply Gov. Johnson wrote that he uniformly gave preference in appointment to Union men. Some of the state officers who continued in office were obnoxious and would be removed on application. Sen. Exec. Doc., 39 C., 1 S., no. 26, p. 234.

[2] *Journals of the Proceedings of the Constitutional Conventions* of 1861 and 1865; *Milledgeville Federal Union*, April 30, 1861, gives popular vote for candidates for the convention of 1861.

[3] Truman noted only 65 members that might be called "loyal". *New York Times*, December 10, 1865. "It would be a mockery to say that this was a convention of loyal men." Andrews, *South since the War*, p. 281.

state when war actually came, and a great many had served
in the army.   The convention to restore Georgia to the
Union was decidedly less brilliant in personnel than was
the convention that withdrew Georgia from the Union.   In
the great crisis of 1861 in every district the ablest and most
experienced leaders were chosen to make the momentous decision on secession.   Mr. U. B. Phillips in his *Georgia and
State Rights* characterizes the 1861 convention as " without doubt the most distinguished body of men which had
ever been assembled in Georgia.   Every Georgian of political prominence was a member, with the exception of Jos.
E. Brown, Howell Cobb, and C. J. Jenkins, while these gentlemen were invited to seats on the floor of the convention."[1]
With few exceptions, the ablest and most distinguished men
in Georgia had actively taken sides during the war, serving either in military or civil office in high rank, and so
were debarred from active participation in the work of restoration.[2]   Conspicuous by their absence from the 1865
convention were Robert Toombs, Howell Cobb, Alexander
and Linton Stephens, E. A. Nisbet, Ben. H. Hill, Jos. E.
Brown, and F. S. Bartow.   Of the delegates assembled at
Milledgeville to reconstitute Georgia, nearly three hundred
in number, the great majority were insignificant men who
were not prominent either before or after 1865.   The convention was described as a conservative body, unprogressive, mostly old men, with a conspicuous lack of prominent
men and rising politicians.[3]

[1] P. 202.

[2] Some were elected to the convention who had not been pardoned by
the President. Pardons were rushed so that they might take their
seats. Sen. Exec. Doc., 39 C., 1 S., no. 26, pp. 80, 81, 235.

[3] *New York Times*, November 17 and December 10, 1865. Truman
described the convention as " a select body of old fogies and malignant
demagogues ". A correspondent of the *Augusta Constitutionalist*,

In this body of respectable, substantial, mediocre citizens, leadership rested with two ante-bellum leaders, Chas. J. Jenkins and Herschel V. Johnson, who stood head and shoulders above all others. Both had had distinguished careers in Georgia, both opposed secession but went with the state when separation was declared.[1] Together they managed the convention, Johnson as presiding officer and Jenkins as chairman of the committee on business. Under their capable direction, the convention set to work to transact the business outlined in the message of the Provisional Governor.[2] With characteristic steadfastness to the doctrine of state rights, the convention repealed, but did not nullify, the ordinance of secession.[3] The form in which the convention declared the abolition of slavery, with the important proviso, is significant of the temper of the body. Article I, section 20 of the new constitution was as follows:[4]

The Government of the United States having, as a war measure, proclaimed all slaves held or owned in this State, emancipated from slavery, and having carried that proclamation into full practical effect, there shall henceforth be, within the State of Georgia, neither slavery nor involuntary servitude,

October 29, 1865, gives his impression: " It may be said that a very large majority of it are men who are the exactest types of the solid county representative—grave looking personages, clad to some extent in substantial homespun—though no few shine resplendent in northern ready-made clothes—decorous in demeanor, attentive to business, and anxious to get through and go home ".

[1] Phillips, *Georgia and State Rights*, pp. 146, 167, 168, 179; Fielder, *Life and Times and Speeches of Joseph E. Brown*, pp. 411, 416; Avery, *History of the State of Georgia, passim.*

[2] *Journal of the Constitutional Convention*, 1865, p. 8, *et seq.*

[3] *Ibid.*, pp. 17-18. This action indicates clearly that the majority of the convention, though anti-secessionists, had opposed secession on the ground of expediency and had not questioned the right to secede.

[4] *Ibid.*, p. 38.

save as a punishment for crime, after legal conviction thereof; Provided, this acquiescence in the action of the Government of the United States, is not intended to operate as a relinquishment, waiver or estoppel of such claim for compensation or loss sustained by reason of the emancipation of his slaves, as any citizen of Georgia may hereafter make upon the justice and magnanimity of that government.

A second article declared it to be the duty of the general assembly to protect and govern free persons of color, showing a disposition on the part of the convention to secure legal rights to the negro. A resolution was adopted ordering the appointment of a commission to draw up a code to show the changed relations between citizens and freedmen.[1]

The most difficult task before the convention was the settlement of the state war debt. The subject of repudiation was widely discussed before the election and was the biggest bone of contention during the whole session. The sentiment of the convention was strongly opposed to repudiation. The question was more than mere approval or disapproval of the purpose for which the debt had been incurred. There was the natural desire of those who held public securities to sustain the credit of the state; and important, too, was the fear that repudiation might scare capital away from the state, especially strong in counties with large towns where there was hope of building up strong industrial interests. In the state at large three different methods of disposing of the debt were discussed—redemption dollar for dollar in greenbacks, redemption at the gold value of the debt when incurred, and repudiation of the entire debt contracted during the war.[2] In spite of the appeal

[1] *Journal of the Constitutional Convention,* 1865, pp. 44, 125, 174.

[2] *Augusta Constitutionalist,* October 20 and November 3, 1865; *New York Times,* November 2, 1865 ("Quondam").

of Provisional Governor Johnson to President Johnson for aid and the President's peremptory reply that the debt should be set aside, the fight continued until the close of the session.[1] On November 6th, Judge Jenkins, as chairman of the committee of sixteen, reported that the committee was unable to agree on the question of the debt, and asked discharge.[2] Finally enough members were convinced that repudiation was an absolute condition upon restoration to pass the ordinance of repudiation, 135 to 117.[3]

These three measures—repeal of the secession ordinance, abolition of slavery, and repudiation of the war debt—constituted the most important work of the convention. Several measures of local significance also received attention from the convention—the investigation of the state finances, instituted by the political enemies of ex-Governor Brown, the enactment of a temporary stay law until the legislature should take action, the drawing up of a petition to present to President Johnson on behalf of Jefferson Davis, Alexander Stephens and others, resolutions to request relief for citizens excluded from amnesty, and the organization of a temporary militia in each county.[4] Also a recommendation was agreed upon to accede to the proposition of General Tillson, Assistant Commissioner of the Freedmen's Bureau, to employ certain state officers as agents of the Bureau,[5] and a recommendation to the legislature to pass measures of relief for widows and orphans of deceased soldiers and for infirm soldiers.[6]

[1] McPherson, *Reconstruction*, pp. 20-21.

[2] *Journal of the Constitutional Convention*, 1865, p. 163.

[3] The wording adopted was that of A. H. Chappell, amended: " to render null and void all debts of this State created for the purpose of carrying on the late war against the United States." *Ibid.*, pp. 135-6, 185, 234.

[4] *Ibid.*, pp. 56, 93, 106, 118, 143-4, 184, 192, 195.

[5] *Ibid.*, p. 58.   [6] *Ibid.*, p. 136.

On November 8th the convention adjourned, subject to call by the president of the body within six months, should the question of Federal relations demand further settlement.[1]

In the state election of November 15th, Judge Jenkins was the only candidate for the governorship. Others had been mentioned—notably Alexander Stephens and ex-Governor Brown, both of whom emphatically refused to be candidates for the office.[2] The unanimous choice of Judge Jenkins expressed a desire on the part of the people to unite on a safe, thoroughly conservative person, who stood for recognition of new conditions imposed as the result of war without disowning the career of Georgia in the previous four years. In the state election none were disfranchised by reason of the war, as had been the case in the election for delegates to the convention. Hence, the new legislature was less dominated by the element that controlled the convention, Union sympathizers or anti-secessionists. In counties where one candidate was an ex-Confederate and the other had kept out of the conflict, choice generally fell upon the former. This was partly an expression of loyalty to the past, but in greater part it meant that the best, most representative citizens in the state had actively taken part in the war, and those that managed to keep out were inferior men.

The temper of the legislature, which convened in Milledgeville on December 4, 1865, is evident in its choice of United States senators. Many candidates were in the field, actively or passively. Most prominent of all was Alexander

[1] *Journal of the Constitutional Convention,* 1865, p. 194.

[2] *Macon Journal and Messenger,* November 9, 1865; Avery, *History of the State of Georgia,* p. 351.

Stephens, who again on November 22d wrote a public letter to state that he would not allow the use of his name for any public office.[1] Joshua Hill, the leading Unionist in the state, was an avowed candidate, and other possibilities were H. V. Johnson, who had been president of the 1865 convention, General L. J. Gartrell, Thomas Hardeman, speaker of the lower house of the new assembly, and Provisional Governor Johnson, who was pushed forward as a candidate by President Johnson in his telegram of December 11th— "Why can't you be elected as Senator?"[2] Joshua Hill was the opponent of Stephens for the long term. On the first ballot Stephens secured 152 votes and Hill only 38. Mr. Hill seemed doomed to failure—he had not secured the provisional governorship nor had he succeeded to leadership in the convention. His steadfastness in Union sympathy was of little benefit to him, even when the Union cause was supposedly triumphant. Election for the short term was not made until the sixth ballot, when H. V. Johnson was finally chosen.[3] The choice of Alexander Stephens, Vice-President of the Confederacy, and Herschel V. Johnson, a senator of the Confederacy, was viewed in different lights by the North and the South. The Washington correspondent of the *New York Times* voiced conservative criticism in the North thus:

The election of A. H. Stephens and H. V. Johnson as Senators from Georgia is received here with regret by the best friends of the South connected with the government. That

[1] *Macon Telegraph*, January 23, 1866. President Johnson sent a despatch to the effect that it would not be politic for Stephens to be a candidate for senator. *Official Records of the War of the Rebellion*, series ii, vol. viii, pp. 8, 18.

[2] *Journal of the House of Representatives*, 1865-6, pp. 44-5.

[3] *Ibid.*, pp. 190-201.

two men should have been selected chiefly because of their prominence in the rebellion, and who cannot take the oath, simply embarrasses the work of restoration, and the Southern people in the end become the chief sufferers. The election of Prov. Gov. Johnson and Joshua Hill would have been a very encouraging sign of the moral effect of which the South is very much in need.[1]

The mistaken premise in the Northern argument was that Stephens and Johnson were chosen " chiefly because of their prominence in the rebellion ". But this was not true. They were fitting representatives of Georgia in 1866, primarily because they were conservative, cool-tempered leaders, who had opposed secession, and who looked back upon the war without animosity, willing to meet with dignity the demands of presidential reconstruction, and favorable toward securing to the negro full guarantee of civil rights by state law. Stephens especially was commended in Georgia as the man above all others who would be most useful in the trying process of reunion, conciliatory as he was in everything that he said or did.[2]

Of the seven congressmen elected in November, none was able to take the test oath, but only one, Solomon Cohen, of Savannah, a prominent member of the 1865 convention, had been an outright secessionist. The others were moderate men who had inclined toward the Union or had been co-operationists in 1861, afterwards following the state. W. T. Wofford of the seventh district was strongly Unionist, but had given distinguished service in the Confederate Army. E. G. Cabaniss of the fourth district, John Christy, editor of a newspaper in Athens, elected from the sixth dis-

[1] Quoted in the *Macon Telegraph*, February 6, 1866.

[2] *Macon Journal and Messenger*, December 7, 1865; *Augusta Constitutionalist*, November 25, 1865; *Augusta Chronicle*, February 8, 1866; *Macon Telegraph*, February 7, 1866.

trict, Jas. D. Matthews of the fifth and Phil. Cook of the second had been members of the convention of 1865. Hugh Buchanan of the third district was not well known except as a lawyer of good ability, reported as favoring secession in 1861 but moderate in temper.[1]

On December 14, 1865, according to instructions from President Johnson and Secretary Seward, Governor-elect Jenkins was inaugurated, though the Provisional Governor was not removed until five days later.[2]

The first action expected of the new legislature as part of President Johnson's program of reconstruction was the ratification of the Thirteenth Amendment. This was accomplished on December 5th and 6th in the two houses. In course of the discussion on the amendment, question was raised as to the implication of the second clause, granting power to Congress to enforce the article by appropriate legislation, and an attempt was made to qualify the ratification with an amendment to declare that all rights of citizenship rested with the states, not with Congress.[3] But better judgment dictated that ratification should be unqualified, and so it was voted almost unanimously.

[1] *New York Times*, November 23 and December 10, 1865 (Truman); *Joint Committee on Reconstruction*, 1866, pt. iii, p. 130 (Test.: Prov. Gov. Johnson).

[2] Sen. Exec. Doc., 39 C., 1 S., no. 26; Avery, *op. cit.*, pp. 352-4.

[3] *Journal of the House of Representatives*, 1865-6, pp. 16-17; *Journal of the Senate*, 1865-6, pp. 9, 16, 17, 18.
Howell Cobb wrote, December 7, 1865: " I have heard nothing from Milledgeville of any interest, except the passage by both houses of the constitutional amendment for the abolition of slavery. I think they will get the ' peculiar institution ' thoroughly disposed of after a while. It has now been abolished by Congress, the President, war, state conventions, legislatures, etc. If all that don't kill it, I should like to know what would?" *Annual Report of the American Historical Association*, 1911, vol. ii, p. 673.

The most significant work of the first session of the new
assembly was the enactment of legislation concerning freedmen. The commission appointed under the resolution of
the convention reported to Governor Jenkins on December
19, 1865, a series of eleven laws for the regulation of freedmen's rights.[1] After the hostile criticism which the Black
Codes of other Southern states aroused in the North, there
was a growing disposition in Georgia to refrain from enacting a separate code for freedmen.[2] The advice given by
ex-Governor Brown in a public letter issued February 14th,
was followed in the main by the legislature. Ex-Governor
Brown wrote that the labor system of Georgia had suffered
a complete revolution by reason of the war, effecting an
entire change in the relation of the white people to the
black population. Hence the people of the state must realize that the former slaves were equal in legal rights, though
they were not equals; and unless madness ruled the hour
they would never be placed upon a basis of political equality
with white people. As far as laws of rights and remedies
in courts were concerned, the two races should be on equal
terms. The negro should not be allowed to serve on juries,
nor should he have the right to vote; but he ought to have
the right to sue and be sued, to testify in court, leaving the
credibility of testimony to be adjudged by the jury, and to
be subject to the same penal enactments, and to have security in property and to enjoy the fruits of his labor. If
these rights were secured to the negro, then the state would

[1] Members of the commission appointed were Linton Stephens,
Ebenezer Starnes, Logan E. Bleckley, Wm. Hope Hull, Lewis N.
Whittle. Saml. Barnett took the place of the Linton Stephens, who
resigned. Report of the commission in *Macon Telegraph*, January
9, 1866, also pamphlet.

[2] *Savannah Herald*, February 13, 1866; *Macon Journal and Messenger*,
February 23, 1866.

probably be relieved of the Freedmen's Bureau and courts would be allowed to take cognizance of cases concerning the blacks. He thought it unwise for the legislature to adopt a distinctive Freedmen's Code.[1]

In the laws adopted by the legislature, negroes were secured in practically all civil rights as follows:

Persons of color [2] shall have the right to make, and enforce contracts, to sue, be sued; to be parties, and give evidence; to inherit; to purchase, lease, sell, hold and convey, real, and personal property, and to have full and equal benefit of all laws and proceedings, for the security of person and estate, and shall not be subjected to any other or different punishment, pain or penalty for the commission of any act or offense, than such as are prescribed for white persons, committing like acts or offences.

The privilege of the ballot and liability to jury service were not assigned to them, but these were likewise denied to one-half of the adult white population. The chief limitation on their legal status by reason of color was in the acceptance of their testimony in courts only in cases where persons of color were involved.[3] Other laws legalized marriage relations, established legal parental responsibility, and prohibited marriage between whites and blacks.[4] Vagrancy

[1] *Atlanta Intelligencer,* February 18, 1866 (*Brown Scrap Books*).

[2] "Persons of color" were defined as "all negroes, mulattoes, mestizoes, and their descendants, having one-eighth negro, or African blood, in their veins." *Acts of the General Assembly,* 1865-6, p. 239.

[3] *Ibid.,* pp. 234-5, 239-41. In the December term, 1866, the Supreme Court of Georgia upheld the competency of negroes to give testimony in cases where whites were involved. *Infra,* ch. xiii.

[4] A Jim Crow law to compel railroads to furnish separate cars for negroes passed the House but was reported adversely by the Senate committee. *Journal of the House of Representatives,* 1865-6, pp. 43, 185; *Journal of the Senate,* 1865-6, pp. 207, 235.

làws made no discrimination as to color. Thus, the reorganized legislature of Georgia put the freedmen on the basis of practical civil equality with white citizens, securing to them by state authority substantially the same rights that Congress guaranteed to them through Federal machinery in the Civil Rights Bill.[1]

Conservative papers in the North gave wide publicity to the inaugural address of Governor Jenkins, recognizing it as significant of the temper of the newly reorganized government of Georgia. An editorial in the *New York Times* in comment said:[2]

Each succeeding day brings additional proof that if the moderate men of the South, such as Governor Jenkins of Georgia, are allowed some discretion in determining the future status of the freedmen, it will fare at least as well with the emancipated population as if we provide a sumptuary code for their guidance and protection in Washington or Boston.

And again:

The great problem of keeping the two races together in the lately insurgent states on terms which shall be mutually advantageous, must be solved at the South—in the local Southern Legislatures, in the local courts of justice, in the Executive council chambers of just such governors as Governor Jenkins. And nothing that the philanthropy of the North can contribute

[1] Freedmen were excluded from the privileges of the Common School Law. Alex. Stephens wrote to his brother Linton from Washington, April 8, 1866:

" I don't attach any great importance to this measure [the Civil Rights Bill]. It will not affect Georgia, I think, or any other state that has done as she has. I have not read the bill carefully; but this is my understanding of it. The great error of the bill is the principle assumed in its passage, the jurisdiction claimed by Congress, etc." Waddell, *Biographical Sketch of Linton Stephens,* p. 295.

[2] December 18, 1865.

will be a compensation to the freedman for his forfeiture of the good-will and kindly co-operation of those who have heretofore directed his labor.

While Georgians were disposed to grant protection in ordinary civil rights to freedmen, sentiment was strongly opposed to granting them the suffrage, and even the proposition of restricted suffrage was vigorously rejected. Alexander Stephens was in a decided minority in advocating the extension of the franchise " to such members of the black race as could come up to some proper standard of mental and moral culture with the possession of a specified amount of property." [1]

In 1865 and 1866 the people of Georgia lent themselves in good faith to the demands made upon them by the President's scheme of restoration. Measures were accepted as necessary to restoration, quietly and submissively, and naturally without enthusiasm. Directors of public policy counseled acceptance of what was offered. Ex-Governor Brown, after his release from imprisonment in Washington, actively worked to persuade people to take the amnesty oath and to co-operate with the President in his policy toward the Southern states.[2] Alexander Stephens, while he was in prison in Fort Warren near Boston, wrote to President Johnson in his application for amnesty: " . . . If I were permitted to exert them, all my influence and power would be directed to a restoration of quiet, order, and government in Georgia upon

[1] Avary (ed.), Recollections of Alex. H. Stephens, p. 536. For further discussion of negro suffrage, see ibid., p. 267, et seq.; also testimony of Stephens before the Reconstruction Committee, reprinted in Johnston and Browne, Life of Alexander H. Stephens, pp. 610-23.

[2] Avery, History of the State of Georgia, p. 339.

the basis of accepting and abiding by the issues of war as proclaimed by the Executive ".[1] And this pledge he entirely fulfilled after his release and return to Georgia in October, 1865. His conciliatory spirit and his readiness to accept and adjust himself to new conditions were the qualifications which made him the pre-eminently suitable candidate for the United States Senate in 1866. H. V. Johnson and Chas. J. Jenkins likewise were apostles of full acceptance of the new order. Most of the ardent secession advocates of 1861 were quiescent in 1865. Governor Brown was the only one of the vigorous secessionists who came forward as a vigorous supporter of President Johnson's policy. But Brown was always vigorous and active in leadership in whatever policy was foremost, whether it was secession or presidential restoration or radical reconstruction. Of the other notable secession leaders, Robert Toombs was a fugitive, no one knew where, and Howell Cobb and others were paying more attention to the necessary business of earning their daily bread than to politics. Political views of the press were in conformity with the policy of the government. Editors were perforce submissive, for they were subject to discipline for any unguarded words that might slip off their pens.

The attitude of the people toward the government was a subject of inquiry before the Reconstruction Committee of Congress, and varied testimony was given according to the temper and prejudice of the witnesses. Provisional Governor Johnson testified that the feelings of the people toward the government improved in the first six months after the surrender. At first men were uncertain and reserved, but later were freer in talk and more ready to take part in re-

---

[1] Avary (*ed.*), *Recollections of Alex. H. Stephens,* p. 203.

organization, with better feeling toward the government.[1] H. S. Welles, a Northerner who went to Georgia to look after railroad interests, said that people in Georgia generally accepted the situation; the ex-Confederates were for peace, the common soldiers had had enough of war, business men were moderate, better satisfied than they had been; but the lower class of people were most bitter.[2] Other Northern witnesses testified that there was no "loyalty" in Georgia, though people were not so vindictive as in Alabama or Mississippi. People regarded themselves as subjugated, failing to acknowledge the wrong of secession though some lamented the war.[3] B. C. Truman, who was sent by President Johnson to investigate conditions in the Southern states, one of the most fair-minded and keenest sighted of all Northern travelers in the South who put their impressions in print, was of the opinion that people generally in Georgia supported the work of restoration. Among officers and soldiers of the Confederacy, among editors and other responsible people there was much real loyalty. In Western and Central Georgia he saw an improvement in the feeling and condition of the people of all grades. People in Georgia were rid of the excessive soreness of Alabama.[4]

Henry Watterson, likewise an investigator of conditions in Georgia and other parts of the South in the summer of 1865, was of the opinion that the trend of events in Georgia was satisfactory. The same judgment was pronounced by General Grant after his brief tour made at the suggestion

[1] *Joint Committee on Reconstruction*, 1866, pt. iii, p. 131 (Test.: Prov. Gov. Johnson).

[2] *Ibid.*, p. 109.

[3] *Ibid.*, pp. 1-2, 7-8.

[4] *New York Times*, November 23, 1865.

of the President. And General Steedman wrote to President Johnson from Georgia on August 15, 1865:

In my opinion, everything is moving satisfactorily toward the complete restoration of this State upon a basis that will be perfectly satisfactory to you and the country, as well as a triumphant vindication of the wisdom of your policy. . . . With the exception of a few isolated cases of outrages upon them—and these cases would have been as likely to occur in Ohio or New York as in Georgia—the Freedmen have been kindly treated, and have conducted themselves well.[1]

Carl Schurz, a thorough doctrinaire with fixed principles as to national loyalty and racial equality, gave a gloomy account of the progress of reconstruction in Georgia, which had wide influence in the North. The attitude of Georgia people whom Schurz met lacked much of meeting his standards of loyalty and social democracy. Because a Southerner, who had given his whole-souled allegiance for four years to the Confederacy, did not immediately shout— Hurrah for the Stars and Stripes!—and because the master of slaves, the instant emancipation became a fact, did not look upon the freedman as a friend and a brother as did the German idealist, Schurz saw omens of recurring rebellion and re-enslavement.[2]

Frances Butler Leigh, on her return to Georgia in March, 1866, wrote that people in Savannah seemed crushed and sad, though there was no bitterness against the North. Women lived in the past, men in the daily present, trying in a listless way to repair their ruined fortunes. Politics

[1] Letters from Watterson and General Steedman are in Johnson MSS. The report of General Grant appears in Sen. Exec. Doc., 39 C., 1 S., no. 2.

[2] Letters from Schurz in Johnson MSS. His report appears in Sen. Exec. Doc., 39 C., 1 S., no. 2; also *Speeches, Correspondence and Political Papers of Carl Schurz*, vol. i, pp. 279-374.

was not mentioned—they did not seem to care what was going on in Washington.[1] Indeed, this observation on popular indifference to politics is borne out for the rest of the state as well as Savannah, if the subject-matter in newspapers may be taken as the reflection of popular interests. News from Washington or from the state capital was less conspicuous than items giving news of the crops and discussions of the problem of labor and other items of everyday life. Some papers published regular news letters from correspondents in counties throughout the state, whose news consisted mostly of local reports of weather, progress of the crop—whether it promised well or whether it was swamped by rain, parched by drought, or devoured by the worm; the behavior of the freedmen, how many were working and how many hands were needed; the amount and kind of wages paid in the neighborhood. Contributors seemed interested in the dispute as to whether it was better to put all the land in cotton and buy corn or to give more attention to food crops and less to cotton; but ignored the endless chain puzzle—When is a state not a state?—that was perplexing the wiseheads in Washington. On this subject sound advice was given to the people of Georgia by Governor Jenkins in his message to the legislature, November 1, 1866, as follows:[2]

Our interest lies in eschewing political excitement, studiously avoiding all conflict with authorities unchosen by us, but placed over us, and employing our active energies in rebuilding our own waste places and developing our neglected resources. Whilst others rage and wrangle over ephemeral issues, let us be busy with the real, abiding concerns of life. Thus shall we emerge from this period of ostracism, wiser, more thriving, and more respected than ever.

[1] Leigh, *Ten Years on a Georgia Plantation since the War*, pp. 12-13.
[2] *Journal of the House*, 1866, p. 31.

More interest in the political situation was aroused in the fall of 1866 when the Fourteenth Amendment was submitted to the November session of the legislature.[1] By the end of 1866 it was evident that the cause of speedy restoration of the Southern states had failed with the defeat of the President's supporters and the success of the Radicals in the fall elections. When Congress failed to admit Senators and Representatives from Georgia and other Southern states, and when it put the Fourteenth Amendment for ratification before the legislatures of the states that it said were not states, then it decisively took the management of reconstruction out of the President's hands and President Johnson's attempt to restore the states by executive action failed.

The basis on which Congress acted in enforcing new reconstruction upon the Southern states in 1867 was that they were still in a condition of war—*bello non flagrante sed nondum cessante.* As far as Georgia is concerned, at the end of 1866, there was no condition of war, either flagrant or otherwise. There is no evidence that any attempt was on foot to stir up a new civil war. People generally accepted the results of former war. At the end of 1865, they were ready to make the best of things, and a year later they were hopeful of making things better. During the period of presidential restoration Georgia's political organization was rehabilitated: a governor, duly elected and inaugurated, administered the business of the state; the legislature in two sessions attended to law-making as under normal conditions; courts, organized under the regulation of the new

[1] The Fourteenth Amendment was rejected by both houses of the legislature, November 9, 1866, by the Senate unanimously and by the House, 147-2. *Senate Journal,* 1866, pp. 39, 42, 44, 65-72; *House Journal,* 1866, pp. 68-9.

constitution, were in operation to administer justice. From
this point of view, Georgia seemed to be managing its affairs of statehood as a normal state. But there were still
limitations on state authority. Federal troops were garri-
soned in the state, and military authority superseded civil
action in various cases. One-half of the population, the
freedmen, to whom the legislature had assigned all the
most important civil rights, were still under guardianship
of the national government through the Freedmen's Bureau.
So within its own bounds in local self-government, Georgia
was not yet completely a state at the close of 1866. Nor
was it a state in the Union, for its representatives were not
admitted to either house of Congress.

Socially, no great problems appeared in the early period
of reconstruction. Emancipation had in itself brought no
immediate upheaval in the relations of whites and blacks.
Except in some classes, the old feeling of friendliness between the two remained. In the first days of freedom the
negroes were given to "putting on airs", but in general
their position of inferiority was recognized and accepted
by them. Among the white population, changing fortunes
of war and the development of new interests began to give
evidence of shifting in dominant social classes, and town
life showed signs of increasing importance.

Economic re-adjustment was the greatest problem of the
early aftermath of the war, and herein was the greatest
achievement of the first attempt at restoration. Recovery
from the poverty left by the drain of war was under way
in the revival of commercial interests in towns and cities,
and partially in the great agricultural districts of the state.
The most revolutionary of all changes brought by the experience of 1861-5 was the abolition of slavery as a system
of utilizing negro labor. The labor question was not simply
how to adapt free labor to the plantation, but how to use

free laborers that were negroes. Management of negro labor was difficult in itself, and had been achieved by means of the compulsion and close supervision of slavery. But when negroes became free agents, then a difficulty mountain high arose before the Southern planter. Conditions in 1865 seemed hopeless, but the situation in 1866 was more cheering. Though there was still much to be done before the freedman could be counted a responsible, dependable laborer, still reports from all over the state gave news that the negroes worked better than had been expected of them.

While final adjustment was still remote, economic and social tendencies in 1865 and 1866 were decidedly on the upward curve of progress. After this period of hopeful convalescence came the critical relapse to unsettlement and upheaval, occasioned by the reconstruction measures of 1867.

PART II

MILITARY AND POLITICAL
RECONSTRUCTION

1867–1872

CHAPTER VII

MILITARY RULE

ON April 1, 1867, when General Pope assumed command of Georgia as part of the Third Military District, constituted by the Reconstruction Act of March 2, 1867, military rule was restored much as it was in May, 1865, when the Confederate power collapsed. And yet it was not the same, for in 1865 military force was intended to protect life and property in the transition from war to peace, and to assist in the reconstruction of civil authority. In 1867, the civil organization, which had been in successful operation since December, 1865, was declared provisional only, and upon it was superimposed the command of a major-general of the army and his subordinates. All the constructive work of rehabilitation, the painful labor of almost two years, was set aside and the process of reconstruction undertaken practically from the beginning, exactly as if the war had come to an end in 1867 instead of 1865.

Reconstruction, as ordained by the radicals in Congress in the Act of March 2, 1867, and its supplements of March 23d and July 19th, meant the remaking of the state through a new electorate, prescribed by Congress to include negroes and to exclude the most capable and respected citizens of the state; a new constitution, which should secure suffrage to the freedmen; and the ratification of the Fourteenth Amendment, rejected by the legislature in the previous October.

During the early part of 1867, while this new plan was

in process of formulation in Washington, people in Georgia were making up their minds as to what they would do about it.   The situation gave rise to three different parties: one group, headed by ex-Governor Brown, favored acquiescence in the proposed measure and advised that the state should meet Congress half way; another party vigorously denounced acquiescence as suicidal to the state; a third group remained neutral for the time being, not ready to take action, thinking that it was better to wait and see, yet continue to stand by President Johnson.[1]   Ben Hill summed up the situation: " The complying accept, the resolute reject, none approve, while all despise ".

In February, before the bill was finally passed, ex-Governor Brown returned to Georgia from Washington, where he had talked with men of all shades of opinion and had gotten a clear perception of the lie of the ground. A few days after his return he published a letter, addressed to some friends, in response to their request for his views on the situation.   Brown, in writing, said that he was not in a position to seek popularity, and so might express his opinions freely, though they were not acceptable to the people of Georgia.   The Radical party was clearly sustained by public sentiment in the North and had the necessary two-thirds in Congress to pass any measure over the President's veto.   The North had been enraged at the rejection of the Fourteenth Amendment by the Southern states, and now demanded universal suffrage, with no division of opinion on the subject.   Further, the Radical wing demanded that the state governments be declared null and void, that military government be established, and that all be excluded from office-holding, voting and jury service, who had voluntarily taken part in the rebellion, leaving the government

[1] *Atlanta New Era*, March 3, 1867; Reed, *History of Atlanta*, p. 217.

in the hands of the freedmen and a few loyal white men.
Their ultimate design included confiscation of the property
of the South to pay the war debt of the United States. The
extreme Radicals had not yet secured a majority, and the
moderates desired speedy adjustment under the power of
Congress by the Fourteenth Amendment and universal suffrage. Rejection by the Southern states would doubtless
be followed by greater rigor. It was no longer a question
as to whether the negro should vote — that was decided;
the question as to the rights of the white people who took
part in the war remained to be settled. Then what was to
be done? Brown's advice was: "Agree with thine adver-
sary quickly ". The state must abide by the United States
in good faith. In the great need of capital, people in
Georgia could get along only when political conditions were
adjusted. They must regard as friends all Northerners and
foreigners bringing capital into Georgia. Specifically,
Brown advised that the governor call the legislature, recommend a convention to change the constitution so as to include universal suffrage in conformity with the measures of
Congress, and to provide for an early election of a new
legislature to adopt the Fourteenth Amendment. If the
convention should ask for it, Congress would probably relieve the disabilities of judges, county officers, and others
necessary to the efficient administration of government.[1]

In this policy of meeting reconstruction half way, ex-
Governor Brown represented a decided minority of the
political leaders. The *Milledgeville Union,* a strong supporter of Brown during his governorship, made this comment on his letter:

We consider Governor Brown one of our wisest statesmen

[1] Letter of Governor Brown, dated February 23, 1867, in the *Atlanta
New Era*, February 26, 1867 and in *Brown Scrap Books*.

and purest patriots, and all advice coming from him claims our profound respect and earnest consideration. But we confess we cannot see, with the lights before us, how our situation will be improved by following his advice. . . . What would representation be worth to us if none could go except such as Ashburn and Co.? Better send no one to Congress than such as would misrepresent us. And we would rather risk ten military governors than one Brownlow.[1]

The great majority of the white people undoubtedly were in sympathy with this opinion of the *Milledgeville Union* and with the position taken by Ben. H. Hill, the leader of a vigorous anti-reconstruction campaign, carried on by public speeches and by a series of contributed articles to newspapers, entitled, " Notes on the Situation ".[2]   In the summer of 1867, Robert Toombs returned from Europe, where he had been since his flight after the downfall of the Confederacy, and announced himself as ready to organize in Georgia a Democratic Anti-Reconstruction Party.   He wrote: " I regret nothing in the past but the dead and the failure, and I am ready to-day to use the best means I can command to establish the principles for which I fought ".[3] Governor Jenkins and most of the public men in Georgia were not ready to bow their necks to the yoke voluntarily. They determined to resist by any lawful means in their power, and if they had no power of resistance whatever, then submission must come by force and not by consent on their part.   There was some talk of fighting, but that came only from a few hot-heads, not from the more reputable

[1] March 5, 1867.   Brownlow was the ultra-Radical governor of Tennessee.

[2] " Notes on the Situation," published in the *Augusta Chronicle and Sentinel,* beginning June 19, 1867.   See also Benj. H. Hill, *Senator Benjamin H. Hill, Life, Speeches and Writings,* Appendix.

[3] *Brown Scrap Books,* a clipping from the *Cincinnati Enquirer* copied in a Savannah paper, July 16, 1867.

citizens. In April, Governor Jenkins went to Washington, where he entered a petition before the Supreme Court for an injunction against the enforcement of the Reconstruction Act, the State of Georgia being plaintiff and Edwin M. Stanton, Ulysses S. Grant and John Pope, defendants. But no relief in the political situation came from the court, which dismissed the Jenkins petition on May 13th for want of jurisdiction.[1] From Washington, Governor Jenkins issued an Address to the People of Georgia on April 10th, advising them to take no action under the Act, "palpably unconstitutional and grievously oppressive", whatever might be the decision of the court.[2]

The military reconstruction of Georgia was directed by General Pope from April 1, 1867, to January 6, 1868. On his removal, General Meade was appointed to the Third Military District, acting until July 30, 1868, when civil authority was restored. For the first ten days of General Pope's command, Montgomery, Ala., was the headquarters of the Third District, with headquarters for Georgia in Milledgeville. On April 11th, Atlanta was made headquarters for the district. Georgia was organized into eight military districts, with posts established at Savannah, Augusta, Atlanta, Dahlonega, Rome, Athens, Columbus and Macon.[3]

The appointment of General Pope was received favorably, for he was understood to be conservative in politics and not inclined to compel too much military hardship. When he appeared in Atlanta to assume command, there

[1] 6 *Wallace*, 50.

[2] Opinions of prominent men, Martin, *Atlanta and its Builders*, p. 29; Reed, *History of Atlanta*, pp. 217, 228; *Atlanta Intelligencer*, July 16, 1867.

[3] Report of General Pope, October 1, 1867, in *Report of Secretary of War*, 1867-8, vol. i, pp. 320-374.

were enough who favored reconstruction for one reason or another to greet the general with a warm welcome. At a banquet given in his honor shortly after his arrival by those who wished to find favor with the military commander, a toast was proposed to " Reconstruction—Let it proceed under the Sherman Bill without appealing to the Supreme Court of the United States, the arbiter of our civil rights, and not of political issues ".[1] The response was made by none other than Joseph E. Brown, who, just two years before, was under arrest as a leading rebel. From April until August, General Pope and the civil officers got along in a fair degree of harmony. Two conservative newspapers agreed that, while not favoring military despotism, they thought Georgia was fortunate in falling to General Pope, who was inclined to be moderate and not too tyrannical.[2]

General Pope's policy was to allow civil officers to continue in the administration of their duties unless they attempted to obstruct the execution of the Reconstruction Acts, provided they exercised authority to the interests of all alike, with no discrimination as to race. Where vacancies occurred the governor was allowed to make appointments which fell within his jurisdiction, limiting his selection to those qualified to hold office under the Reconstruction Acts. Vacancies in elective offices were filled by the military commander. General Pope had to face many difficulties in his relation with civil officers, especially as popular irritation increased during the summer months as the work of registration got under way. He feared the disturbance that would result from wholesale removal of officials, and yet he found that they were all hostile to the Reconstruction Acts. In filling offices he found it hard to

[1] *Atlanta New Era*, April 14, 1867.

[2] *Macon Telegraph*, in *Savannah News*, July 8, 1867.

get competent men to take appointment from him, for the newspapers hurled abuse on all who would accept. Between competency and loyalty he preferred loyalty. As he wrote to General Grant, July 24, 1867: " It is surely better to have an incompetent but loyal man in office, than to have a rebel of whatever ability. In fact, the greater the ability, the greater the danger of maladministration ". On the whole, comparatively few civil officers were removed by General Pope, and those mainly for obstructing the process of reconstruction. In conflicts that arose concerning the jurisdiction of the governor and other civil officers, General Pope gave them to understand clearly that all civil authority was merely provisional, and that state laws held only until overruled by military order.[1]

Two orders of General Pope issued during August, the Newspaper Order and the Jury Order, helped augment the rising tide of hostility to him. On August 12th, in order to encourage favorable public opinion by nourishing a friendly press and disciplining hostile papers, General Pope commanded that all official patronage, publication of orders, proclamations, and advertisements be restricted to papers which had not opposed reconstruction under the acts of Congress nor attempted to obstruct civil officials appointed by military authority.[2] A howl of resentment and abuse went up from the reputable newspapers. As one editor said—it would be ridiculous to confine all public announcements to the four obscure and inferior radical journals. This act on the part of General Pope destroyed his reputation for conservatism.[3] A week later came the Jury Order,

[1] Reports and orders of General Pope in the *Report of the Secretary of War*, 1867-8, vol. i, pp. 24, 325-8, 333, 351; *Savannah News*, August 21, 1867.

[2] *Report of the Secretary of War*, 1867-8, vol. i, pp. 325-6.

[3] *Savannah News*, August 19, 1867.

giving negroes the right to jury service denied to them under the laws of 1866. General Pope commanded that jurors for trial cases, civil and criminal, or for administration of the law, be taken from lists of voters, without discrimination, registered under the Reconstruction Acts. Jurors were required to swear that they were duly registered.[1] As a result of this order came the most notable case of removal from office by General Pope. Judge Augustus Reese, of the Superior Court, Ocmulgee Circuit, one of the most prominent jurists in Georgia, wrote to General Pope that he could not consistently carry out the Jury Order, since it was contrary to the constitution and laws of Georgia which he had sworn to uphold. Accordingly, Judge Reese was removed from office.[2] From this time hostility to General Pope increased steadily. Early in January his removal from command over the Third Military District occasioned much rejoicing in Georgia.

The reason for the removal of General Pope probably was that his administration was too rigorous to suit the Johnson men in Washington as well as in Georgia, who pressed the President to remove him. The Washington correspondent of the *New York Herald,* in an article headed " Who killed Cock Robin? " suggested that the presence in Washington of H. S. Fitch, U. S. Attorney for Georgia, a Johnson man, might have some connection with the removal of Pope.[3]

The *Savannah News* voiced the sentiment of conservatives generally when it said that there was cause for rejoicing that a high-minded soldier had been substituted for a

---

[1] General Orders no. 53, Aug. 19, 1867, *Report of the Secretary of War*, 1867-8, vol. i, pp. 331-2.

[2] *Ibid.*, pp. 332-3.

[3] Copied in *Savannah News*, January 6, 1868.

military satrap.[1] General Meade was pleasing in appearance and attractive socially, and seemed, as one reporter
described him, " more like a Virginia gentleman than a
soldier ".[2] But General Meade's popularity was speedily
nipped in the bud when he removed Governor Jenkins and
other state officers. The controversy, left over from General Pope's régime, arose over the question of the disburse-
ment of funds from the state treasury to pay the expenses
of the constitutional convention. By the Reconstruction
Acts the convention was empowered to levy taxes to meet
its expenses, but before taxes could be collected the convention needed funds to pay its running expenses, especially
the per-diem of its members. The convention made a requisition upon the state treasury for $40,000, which requisition
was endorsed by General Pope. The treasurer declined to
honor the requisition without warrant from the governor,
and such warrant was refused by Governor Jenkins on the
ground that it was contrary to the constitution and laws
which he was bound by oath to enforce. The question was
still hanging fire when General Meade assumed command.
A week later the general removed both Governor Jenkins
and the treasurer, John Jones, appointing in their places,
Brevet Brig.-Gen. Thos. H. Ruger as governor and Brevet
Capt. Chas. F. Rockwell as treasurer.[3] Governor Jenkins
and Treasurer Jones then removed from the state and beyond General Meade's jurisdiction all funds, books and
records of their offices, hoping to force the case into court
and so obtain a hearing on the constitutionality of the Reconstruction Acts. A few days later, on the charge of obstructing the fulfilment of the Reconstruction Acts, Comp-

[1] *Savannah News*, January 9, 1868.

[2] *Atlanta New Era*, January 10, 1868.

[3] Report of General Meade in *Report of the Secretary of War*, 1868-9,
vol. i, pp. 74-130.

troller-General John T. Burns and Secretary of State N. C. Barnett were removed by General Meade and Captain Chas. Wheaton was appointed to fill both offices.[1] Governor Jenkins went to Washington, carrying the great seal of the state and about $400,000, which he placed in New York to secure the public debt. He filed a bill of complaint in the Supreme Court against U. S. Grant of Illinois, Geo. G. Meade of Pennsylvania, Thos. H. Ruger of Wisconsin, and C. F. Rockwell of Vermont for illegal seizure of the state's property and for imprisonment of the state treasurer, and asked injunction against said parties from furthe·spoliation of the state.[2]

The conservative press of Georgia commended Governor Jenkins and condemned General Meade vigorously. The hope for a milder administration vanished and no chance was left that Meade would not follow in Pope's arbitrary steps. In the appointment of military officers to the places of the removed officials, instead of Georgia radicals, the *Augusta Constitutionalist* took solace thus: " If Meade has outraged the Democratic element of the state, he has not given the expected comfort to the rapacious harpies who hungered and thirsted for the removal of Governor Jenkins and Treasurer Jones as a preliminary to stepping into the places thus vacated." [3]

So much pressure was brought to bear upon General Meade by ardent reconstructionists and thirsters after office for widespread removal of office holders, that he established a system by which all accusations against officers should be made in writing, and the accused have opportunity to make

[1] Report of General Meade, *op. cit.,* p. 88.

[2] 6 *Wallace*, 241.

[3] *Atlanta New Era*, January 14, 16, 1868, gives quotations from various Georgia papers on the removal of Jenkins.

defense.[1]   In all it was estimated that about twenty state
officers were removed and about seventy appointed.[2]   There
were numerous cases of the interference by military authority with ordinary civil government.   In Columbus the muni-
cipal government was run by military officers; in Augusta
the mayor and council appointed by General Pope were investigated under charges of maladministration by officers
under Meade's direction; also a military commissioner was
sent to examine the mayor of Savannah on the charge of
unfair treatment of negroes in the mayor's court; the tax
collector of Savannah was arrested on military authority
for refusing to carry out the general order to collect taxes
in conflict with the order of Governor Jenkins.   In Jasper
County the sheriff and the coroner were put under arrest by
the military, and in Georgetown, in Southwest Georgia, a
jailor was arrested for having chained a negro prisoner.
Further, General Meade caused the removal from the superior court of the case of a man charged with shooting a
colored woman, on the ground that prejudice against the accused would prevent a fair trial.[3]

In regard to the use of the military commission as a
tribunal of justice, General Meade, in answer to a charge
against him for tyrannical use of military power, reported
that in his whole district, Georgia, Florida and Alabama,
only thirty-two persons were so tried and only one sentence
was carried out.[4]   In cases where military superseded civil
authority under General Meade's command, there is no evidence of any attempt to oppress one class, the native whites
opposed to reconstruction, for the benefit of another, the

[1] *Report of the Secretary of War*, 1868-9, vol. i, p. 76.

[2] Woolley, *Reconstruction of Georgia*, p. 46.

[3] *Savannah News*, January 17, February 5, 18, June 11, 1868; *Augusta Chronicle*, February 7, 22, 1868; *Atlanta Constitution*, June 18, 1868.

[4] *Report of the Secretary of War*, 1868-9, vol. i, p. 80.

radicals. Interference was generally in behalf of order, justice and the full execution of the Reconstruction Acts. Some orders were issued looking especially to the protection of the freedmen. All civil courts and officers whose duty was to provide aid were ordered to grant it without discrimination as to race. In jails and prisons colored persons were to receive the same quantity and quality of food as whites, and sheriffs received the same fees for victualing all classes of prisoners. Near election time, an order forbade employers to interfere with the voting of employees, by threat to discharge or otherwise. And on the other hand, he issued an order to protect the employer from too frequent enticement of his hands to meetings by political agitators.

In matters concerning the freedom of the press and individual liberty General Meade was somewhat milder than General Pope. He modified the newspaper order of August 12, 1867, excluding from patronage only those papers which hindered civil officers appointed by military authority. As election time approached a warning was issued that persons detected in threatening violence, working with secret societies, or publishing incendiary material, would be punished by military officers. At this time General Meade notified General Grant of the need of an extra regiment. Secret organizations were causing disturbance in Georgia as in Alabama and Tennessee, with the object of driving out obnoxious men and intimidating voters. People were getting alarmed and negroes excited as election time approached. As a matter of public welfare, General Meade by military order declared certain provisions of the new state constitution immediately in force as soon as they were agreed upon in the convention. This was done in the case of the relief law. As soon as the convention passed the relief bill on December 12, 1867, creditors began immediate pressure upon their debtors before the law could be legally ratified. Upon petition from various sources General Meade, on January 16, 1868, declared the provisions of the relief act in force until action should be taken by popular ratification.[1]

Shortly before military control was withdrawn and the newly-elected state administration put into office, General Meade showed that he was out of sympathy with the radical group of Republicans, Governor-elect Bullock and his friends. When General Grant suggested to Meade that the newly-elected officers should displace the military governor, comptroller and others, Meade made the objection that Bullock would appoint officers on political grounds, whereas appointments should be made through the military commander on quite a different basis. Somewhat later, three weeks before military control was withdrawn, General Meade removed General Ruger to make room for Bullock as Provisional Governor.[2]

The differences between General Meade and Provisional-Governor Bullock became acute over the question of the eligibility of certain members of the legislature.[3] When investigating committees of both houses reported that none was ineligible, Meade refused to go behind the returns as Bullock wished, concluding it would be the wiser policy to accept the judgment of the legislature itself than to set himself against it.[4] In his report to the General of the Army, General Meade stated the case thus:

On reflecting upon this subject I could not see how I was to take the individual judgment of the provisional governor in

[1] *Report of the Secretary of War,* 1868-9, vol. i, pp. 75, 82-3, 100 ; McPherson, *Reconstruction,* pp. 320, 428; Woolley, *Reconstruction of Georgia,* p. 45.

[2] *Ibid.,* pp. 104-5.   [3] *Infra,* pp. 208-9.

[4] *Ibid.,* p. 112.

the face of a solemn act of a parliamentary body, especially as, from the testimony presented, I did not in several cases agree with the judgment of the provisional governor. The question was simply whether, in the construction of a law and in considering the facts of individual cases, I should make myself the judge, or take the opinion of the provisional governor, in the face of the official information that a parliamentary body had gravely and formally, through a committee, examined, reported, and acted on these cases. My judgment was decidedly that I had fulfilled my duty in compelling the houses to take the action they had, and that having thus acted I. had neither authority, nor was it politic or expedient, to overrule their action and set up my individual judgment in opposition.[1]

General Meade saw in the controversy, what was actually the case, that the dispute was personal, centering in the struggle to control the election of U. S. senators. The upper house especially, with a Republican majority, could have purged itself had it wished.

The real conflict was between the Bullock Republicans and the Anti-Bullock Republicans. The Anti-Bullock, or independent Republicans, supported by the Democrats, gained the balance of power and elected the moderate instead of the radical candidates for the U. S. Senate. And herein lay the chief cause of Georgia's subjection to a second reconstruction. Governor Bullock, in a public speech at Albion, N. Y., his old home, attributed the failure of Georgia to be properly reconstructed to General Meade's refusal to purge the legislature. Since Bullock's own friends had been relieved of disability by Congress, only his political opponents would have been eliminated. Again, General Meade acted conservatively in refusing to sustain Governor Bullock in

[1] *Report of the Secretary of War,* 1868-9, vol. i, p. 79.

the matter of the Camilla riot in South Georgia in September, 1868, after direct military control had been withdrawn and General Meade was acting as commander of the Department of the South. Governor Bullock appealed to the President for a military force to be stationed in Mitchell County where the disturbance occurred, representing the riot as a movement on behalf of the Democrats to prevent the Republicans from holding a peaceable meeting. The houses of the legislature investigated the matter, reporting troops to be unnecessary, as the civil authorities were quite equal to the occasion. General Meade sustained the legislature as against the governor and refused to interfere.[1]

In July, 1868, steps were taken to effect the substitution of civil for military control in Georgia. On July 3d, General Meade ordered Governor Bullock to effect the organization of the two houses of the legislature on July 4th; on the 21st, both houses ratified the Fourteenth Amendment; on the 22d, Bullock was inaugurated. General Meade reported to Washington that the state had complied with the demands of the Act of Congress of June 25, 1868, and on July 30th military authority was withdrawn. After Georgia and the neighboring states were organized under civil control, the Second and Third Military Districts ceased to exist, and the Department of the South was constituted of North Carolina, South Carolina, Georgia, Florida and Alabama. General Meade was in command with headquarters in Atlanta. Troops still remained, concentrated in Savannah, Atlanta, and Dahlonega.[2] On November 1st of that year, fifteen posts were held in Georgia, mostly along railroad lines.

Such having been the salient features of the military

[1] *Report of the Secretary of War*, 1868-9, vol. i, pp. 81, 124-5.
[2] *Ibid.*, pp. 114, 117.

administration of the ordinary governmental functions,
let us examine the process of political reorganization that
was in progress at the same time. In fulfilment of the
Act of March 23, 1867, General Pope appointed a board
of registration for each district, consisting of three members, two white and one colored, civilians where possible,
who were required to take the Iron Clad Oath of July 2,
1862. To encourage these officials to make a full registration, their pay was fixed by the fee system at an average
of twenty-six cents for each name enrolled. Colonel Ed.
Hulburt was appointed Chief Registrar for Georgia with
headquarters at Macon. Registration, which took place
in April, 1867, resulted in a white majority in the state of
less than two thousand: whites, 95,214; colored, 93,457.[1]
The counties in which registered negroes outnumbered
whites were those in the cotton-belt and the fringe of
coast-line counties, though several counties in the cotton-
belt had a white majority. As compared with the list of
polls (males between the years 21 and 60) of 1867 the
registration shows in most cases just what is to be expected, fewer whites and more negroes.[2] The smaller
number of whites was due to the fact that some were
disqualified and others voluntarily refused to register.
Negroes were naturally more eager to enroll as voters than
to be counted in the tax lists, especially when they were
assisted in the former function by Bureau agents and Republican managers. But in some counties the increase in
the number of negroes registered over those listed by the
comptroller was decidedly abnormal, as in Baldwin, Bibb,

[1] *Report of the Secretary of War*, 1867-8, vol. i, pp. 334-5.

[2] *Report of the Comptroller General*, 1869. Table A, registration and
elections in Georgia by counties, 1867 and 1868; Table B, number of
polls in 1867. After revision registration was—Whites, 102411; colored,
98507; polls, white, 120626; colored, 83168.

Brooks, Pulaski, Richmond, Spalding and Washington counties. In Richmond particularly, in which Augusta is situated, in 1867 there was a white majority in polls and in 1867 the registration list gave a majority of a thousand to the blacks.[1] Even allowing for the drift of negroes toward cities, on the face of these figures there seems to be some proof for the charge that the Augusta clique of radicals brought negroes from across the river in South Carolina to register; and in Baldwin county, that negroes were registered two or three times under different names. Of the five most important cities only Atlanta had a white majority in registration.[2]

Registration was probably fairly representative of the whites who were not disbarred. Leading conservative papers, such as the *Savannah News* and the *Augusta Chronicle*, counseled citizens to register, whatever policy might seem wiser later, to vote or to refrain from voting. In an editorial, " The Duty of Registration ", the *Savannah News* said: " Georgia expects every man to do his duty. Then register without delay, and show that you reverence your noble commonwealth still, though she has fallen in her fortunes, and the heavy hand of adversity is upon her." [3]

---

[1] Richmond County, registration, whites, 2491; colored, 3504; polls, whites, 1713, colored, 589; Bibb County, registration, whites, 1995; colored, 2596; polls, whites, 967; colored, 537. The marked decrease in the number of white polls from the number registered was due, perhaps, to the fact that whites, as well as blacks, were tax-dodgers, and also to the number of white men over sixty years of age in the cities, who could register but were not counted in the tax-list.

[2] *Milledgeville Federal Union*, July 16, 1867; *Augusta Constitutionalist* in *Brown Scrap Books*—registration

	white	colored
Savannah	2240	3091
Augusta	1574	1777
Macon	1353	1851
Columbus	635	653
Atlanta	1829	1653

[3] July 2, 1867.

Herschel V. Johnson, in an open letter of July 11th, advised citizens to register and vote against the proposed convention on the ground that military government, distasteful as it was, was preferable to such government as would be established under the Sherman measures.[1] The number of whites registered, 95,214, as compared with the average vote in Georgia before the war, 102,585, estimated by General Pope, shows, too, that the white people in general must have registered, if they were not disqualified. The number of those debarred from registering was variously estimated from 7,000 to 10,000.[2]

In the first election under the Reconstruction Acts, voters had to vote for or against holding a convention, and for delegates to serve in the convention, in case it should be held. In this election, held October 29 to November 2, 1867, the reconstructionists had everything their own way. In the greater part of the state conservative citizens, opposed to reconstruction, would have nothing to do with the election. This was in line with the policy advocated by most of the leading newspapers, such as the *Augusta Constitutionalist*, the *Macon Telegraph* and the *Milledgeville Federal Union*. The *Savannah News* advised its readers to go to the polls, vote for the best conservative, but refrain from voting on the question of holding a convention.[3] In most places no attempt was made by the conservatives to organize to defeat the reconstructionists at the election. The case seemed hopeless. But in Atlanta, where whites were in a majority and the conservatives had a better chance of holding their own, a Conservative-Union organization was formed for the dis-

[1] *Savannah News*, July 18, 1867.

[2] *Report of the Secretary of War*, 1867-8, vol. i, p. 334. Estimate given by Governor Brown, 7,000-10,000, in *Atlanta New Era*, January 11, 1868.

[3] *Savannah News*, October 17, 23, 1867, quoting other papers.

trict embracing Clayton, Cobb and Fulton counties. A public meeting was held in Atlanta on October 12th, followed by a district convention a week later. This convention nominated a ticket " anti-convention, anti-reconstruction, anti-radical ", for a " so-called state convention should such a body be decided by vote ".[1] In most of the black counties conservatives made no attempt to vote. In Baldwin County, for instance, only seven white people voted out of a total number of registered voters of 1,700; in Jefferson, but one white man voted; in McIntosh, only three against 524 blacks; and in Liberty, seven against 575 blacks. In Savannah, with 5,399 registered voters, 2,511 votes were cast, all but twelve of which were in favor of a convention, thus showing that the conservative whites refused to take part in the election.[2] The question of holding a convention was carried by a vote of 102,283 out of a total vote polled of 106,410.[3]

Of the one hundred and sixty-nine delegates to the convention thirty-seven were negroes, nine were white carpet-baggers, and about twelve were conservative whites. The great majority, then, were native whites, known as Scalawags, because they went over to the reconstructionists.[4] The counties most conspicuously controlled by negroes and carpet-baggers were Chatham and Richmond, in which Savannah and Augusta respectively are situated, and also Baldwin, Burke, Columbia, Dougherty, Houston, in all of which registered negroes largely outnumbered whites. Chatham with eight delegates had four negroes and three

[1] Reed, *History of Atlanta*, p. 232.

[2] *Milledgeville Federal Union*, November 5, 1867; *Savannah News*, November 4, 12, 1867.

[3] Official report of General Pope, *Journal of the Convention of 1867-8*, p. 6.

[4] This tabulation is made from the list in the appendix to the *Journal of the Convention of 1867-8*, compiled by Z. D. Harrison.

carpet-baggers. The Augusta delegation furnished the leaders of the radical wing of the convention and the strongest Republican leaders in the state, among whom were R. B. Bullock, elected governor in 1868; Benj. Conley, President of the Senate in 1868; and Foster Blodgett, a faithful aid of Bullock. Augusta also sent to the convention J. E. Bryant, an agent of the Freedmen's Bureau and a skillful manipulator of the negro vote. The fifth member of the Augusta contingent was S. W. Beard, a mulatto. Among the negroes prominent in striving for leadership in the convention were A. A. Bradley of Savannah, Tunis G. Campbell from McIntosh County on the coast, and H. M. Turner of Macon. Bradley, who boasted the name Aaron Alpeoria, was a notoriously disreputable organizer of the blacks in Savannah and made himself generally obnoxious in the convention. After being expelled from the convention for gross insults offered to that body and its members, he held his own among the black voters of Chatham County, so that he was elected to the legislature in 1868, from which he was expelled on the charge that he had been convicted of felony in New York state and had served a term in the state prison.[1] Tunis G. Campbell came to the sea-islands of McIntosh County soon after the war, where he organized a so-called republic on St. Catherine's Island with himself as the government. Generals Steedman and Fullerton, investigating the Freedmen's Bureau in 1866, and others gave Campbell a bad name for inciting negroes and disturbing the peace.[2] Turner was a better sort than Bradley or Campbell. He came south as chaplain of a negro

---

Journal of the Convention of 1867-8, pp. 294-6; *Senate Journal*, 1868, pp. 121-2, 138; *Savannah News*, December 14, 1867.

[2] *New York Herald*, June 2, 1866; Leigh, *Ten Years on a Georgia Plantation*, pp. 133-6; *Savannah News*, December 14, 1867; Campbell's own account in *Sufferings of the Rev. T. G. Campbell and his Family in Georgia*.

regiment, then engaged as missionary in the African Methodist Church; but like others, the opportunity of the time gave him a more active mission in politics than in religion. He was a member of the legislature in 1868 and the next year was appointed by President Grant postmaster of Macon.[1] He remained in Georgia, a leader of the colored people, and became a respected bishop of the African Methodist Church. To a reporter of the *Savannah News*[2] the negroes in the convention appeared well dressed and well behaved, with few exceptions. They usually sat together but looked to their white colleagues for their cues.

Among the carpet-baggers in the convention were J. E. Bryant and C. H. Prince from Maine, and A. L. Harris from Ohio. Bryant's introduction into Georgia and into politics was by way of the Freedmen's Bureau. In 1867 and 1868, as a member of the Augusta clique, he was an active supporter of Bullock and an efficient director of the negro vote in his district. His aspirations to the U. S. Senate were not furthered by Bullock, who favored Blodgett instead, and later Bryant became a virulent opponent of Bullock when the split came in the Republican ranks.[3] Prince served in the Union army, went to Georgia after the war, settled in Augusta and was elected to Congress in 1868 after his service in the convention.[4] A. L. Harris, delegate from Savannah, a capable and helpful member of Bullock's party, was awarded a position on the state road, and in 1870 ably assisted in the reorganization of the legislature.[5] On all questions in the convention, negro and car-

[1] *Macon Telegraph*, April 21, 1869; *Ku Klux Committee*, vol. vii, p. 1084.

[2] December 14, 1867.

[3] *Atlanta Constitution,* August 14, 1868.

[4] *Biographical Congressional Directory*, p. 937.

[5] Avery, *History of the State of Georgia*, p. 427; *Atlanta New Era*, March 5, 1868.

pet-bagger delegates, with few exceptions, voted steadily for Bullock's side.

Unlike the constitutional conventions of South Carolina, Alabama, Mississippi and other states subjected to reconstruction in 1867, the Georgia convention was not managed by carpet-baggers and negroes entirely. It is noteworthy that in Georgia the most influential leaders in the work of the convention were men who, while not natives of the state, had resided there long enough to have established permanent interests. Such men were R. B. Bullock, Amos T. Akerman, H. K. McCay, and Benj. F. Conley. Bullock, a native of New York, came to Georgia in 1859.[1] Akerman was born in New Hampshire, moved to Georgia in 1854, and practised law in Elbert County. An old-line Whig and Union man, he opposed secession, but served in the Confederate army during the last year of the war.[2] He probably was the ablest lawyer in the convention, was not a Bullock partisan, and led the fight against the relief measure, which he termed the robbing part of the constitution. In 1870 he was appointed Attorney-General of the United States by President Grant. H. K. McCay, another competent lawyer, a Pennsylvanian and a Princeton graduate, had lived in Georgia since 1839, and practiced law in Sumter County. In 1860 he supported Douglas, opposed secession, and was a defeated candidate for the convention of 1861 on the Union platform. B. F. Conley, who came to Georgia in 1830, was a merchant in Augusta. Unlike most of the leaders in the convention, he had held a political office in Georgia before the war, being mayor of Augusta in 1857-1859.[3] In 1868 he was elected President of the Senate, and hence was governor after Bullock's flight in 1871.

[1] Reed, *History of Atlanta*, pt. ii, p. 12.
[2] *Atlanta New Era*, March 7, 1868.   [3]*Ibid.*, March 8, 1868.

In the convention the chief line of cleavage was between the radical and the moderate Republicans, with the handful of conservatives acting as a small group by themselves. Some of the ablest men in the convention and the sincerest in sympathy with reconstruction were moderate Republicans. The moderation of the Georgia Constitutional Convention, in contrast to the conventions of other states, may be attributable in no small degree to the influence of ex-Governor Brown. Another important factor is to be seen in the large number of conservative Republicans, natives or long residents of the state, and the comparatively small number of negroes and carpet-baggers, always the tools, if not leaders, of ultra radicalism. After the convention had been in session for some weeks, before any important measures were agreed upon, Governor Brown was invited to speak before the convention. In his address on January 9, 1868, he urged the delegates to meet the demands of Congress by extending suffrage to negroes, but not to go over and beyond what was asked by conferring the right to serve on juries or to hold office. For the protection of the debtor class he recommended to the convention a liberal homestead exemption and provision against prosecution for debts incurred before June, 1865.[1]

The most important work of the convention concerned relief for debtors, the franchise, education, and organization of the judiciary. Of these the question of relief was the most vigorously contested and consumed more time in the convention than any other subject. In the election of delegates, relief was taken up by the radical Republicans to win over the whites who might not ordinarily be sympathetic with reconstruction. In October, just before the

[1] *Atlanta New Era*, January 11, 1868. For further discussion of the relief question, see letter by Brown to J. R. Parrott, president of the convention, in *Brown Scrap Books*.

election, Hulburt, who was chief registrar in 1867 under appointment from General Pope, issued the following circular:[1]

Let the motto of the Reconstruction Party be " Convention and Relief."

The country is heavily in debt. Multitudes of executions are ready to be levied.

The Stay Law is practically dead. Several Superior Court Judges, Honorable Hiram Warner among the number, have ruled the Stay Law unconstitutional.

Judge Warner is now Chief Justice of the Supreme Court.

General Pope has refused to grant relief in the premises.

Executions will now be levied and thousands sold out and rendered bankrupt, unless something be done speedily.

Good men will suffer seriously unless some aid is granted.

The Convention is now our only hope.

Let the platform of all reconstruction candidates for the Convention be " Reconstruction and Relief," and we will sweep the state by thousands.

Set the ball in motion.

One of the first acts of the convention was to pass an act for temporary relief, introduced by R. B. Bullock, to suspend levies until the convention should take action on relief.[2] On January 9th, the second day of the session after the Christmas holidays, the committee on relief, one of the standing committees of the convention, made its first report. After a heated contest, in which Bullock led the side in favor of relief and A. T. Akerman championed the opponents, a relief measure was finally agreed upon. The ordinance adopted became a section of the constitution.[3] It

[1] *Savannah News,* September 21, 1867.

[2] *Journal of the Convention of 1867-8,* pp. 23, 202-6, 250-4.

[3] Constitution of 1868, Article V, (Judiciary), sec. xvii. The greater part of this article was stricken out by the legislature of 1868, acting under the Act of Congress of June 25, 1868.

provided that jurisdiction should be denied to all courts in the state over contracts prior to June 1, 1865, with the following main exceptions and specifications: where the debt grew out of a trust for the benefit of minors and where the property or proceeds remained in the hands of the trustee; in debts against corporations; in debts for property sold, where less than one-third of the purchase money had been paid, and where the debtor still held the property or proceeds; in debts due to charitable institutions or institutions of learning, and to mechanics and laborers; in other cases the legislature might confer jurisdiction by two-thirds vote; courts might never have jurisdiction over debts arising from the purchase or hire of slaves; contracts made to encourage or aid rebellion were illegal; the General Assembly might assess a tax on debts dating prior to June 1, 1865, when collected by legal process.

An examination of the vote on relief shows plainly that it was passed largely as a political, rather than an economic, measure. With only two exceptions every negro voted in favor and all but two carpet-baggers likewise voted for relief. These two classes were presumably of all members in the convention the freest from debts contracted in Georgia prior to June, 1865. Those opposed to the relief measure declared it a cheat and a swindle, a trick to catch the vote of the ignorant debtor. Linton Stephens, in a speech before the Democratic clubs of Richmond County, said that the relief features of the constitution were a snare, that they would not hold for one moment before the U. S. Courts.[1]

In addition to the relief measure, the convention adopted as part of the constitution a homestead privilege of $2,000 in real and $1,000 in personal property, to be exempt, except

[1] *Augusta Chronicle*, April 5, 1868.

for payment of taxes and for money borrowed for improving, for purchase of, for labor or material used thereon.[1]

The report of the committee on franchise, made by the chairman, J. E. Bryant, was decidedly more radical than the section of the constitution finally adopted by the convention. In addition to the fulfilment of the Reconstruction Acts by extending suffrage to negroes, the committee's recommendation excluded from registration, voting and holding office, until January 1, 1869, those disqualified from office by the Fourteenth Amendment and those disqualified from registration under the Reconstruction Acts, until their rights should be restored by Congress. Another important section provided that all qualified electors, and none others, should be eligible to office.[2] By a vote of 116-15, the disqualification clause was dropped;[3] and by 126-12, the section concerning office-holding was stricken out.[4] Thus, by deliberate vote, with only twelve contrary, the clause distinctly conferring the right to hold office upon negroes was eliminated, negroes themselves voting in the affirmative. This vote is significant in connection with the action taken by the first legislature in expelling negro members on the ground of their ineligibility under the constitution. This, it seems, was nothing more nor less than a political trick. It was represented to the blacks that they were eligible anyway without distinct provision; and the omission was used as an appeal for ratification to the white voter, who would object to negro office-holding. At least it was so used as a two-edged sword in the campaign on the adoption of the

[1] *Journal of the Convention of 1867-8*, pp. 405-6; Constitution, Article VII.

[2] *Journal of the Convention*, pp. 148-150.

[3] *Ibid.*, pp. 299-300.

[4] *Ibid.*, pp. 311-2.

Constitution in April, 1868. There was a strong suspicion that ex-Governor Brown was behind this scheme to carry Cherokee Georgia, on the anti-negro-office-holding quality of the constitution.[1] Then, if the Augusta clique elected its men in the black belt, the legislature could bestow the right on negroes.[2] The franchise section of the constitution gave the suffrage to males, twenty-one years of age, who had resided six months in the state and thirty days in the county, and had paid taxes for the year next previous to the election.[3]

In the matter of education, the constitution contained a provision that the General Assembly at its first session after the adoption of the constitution should provide a general system of education, forever free to all the children of the state. As a school fund the constitution set apart the poll tax, the existing school fund, and some special taxes.[4]

In its main features the work of the constitutional convention was decidedly more moderate than the reconstruction work in other Southern states. No disqualifications were made in the right of suffrage and in no respect did the members of the Georgia convention out-radical the radicals of Congress. They fulfilled the demands of the Reconstruction Acts but did not go over and beyond the requirements made of them. This moderation was due to several circumstances: to the fact that negroes did not heavily overbalance the whites, as in South Carolina, Alabama, Mississippi and Louisiana; that many respectable

---

[1] The Cherokee section of Georgia was the northwest, where population was largely white, and where there was strong prejudice against negroes.

[2] *Savannah News*, February 20, 1868.

[3] Constitution, Article II.

[4] Constitution, Article VI. *Journal of the Convention*, pp. 151-4; 477-9.

white men, some of whom were of Northern birth but of long residence in Georgia, took active part in the business of the convention, assuming the leadership that in other states was held by adventurers from the North; and in large measure to the fact that the personal influence of ex-Governor Brown was potent with reconstruction leaders on the side of moderation.

CHAPTER VIII

ORGANIZATION OF THE RECONSTRUCTION GOVERNMENT

AFTER the work of the convention was completed and a new constitution framed, the next step in the process of reconstruction was the ratification of the constitution by popular vote and the election of state officers and representatives to Congress. The election of state officers and the vote on the constitution were ordered by General Meade for the same time, beginning April 20th and continuing four days. To secure a peaceful election and a large negro vote, General Meade issued various orders for the conduct of the election. He forbade the assembling of armed bodies of men to discuss political questions, and the carrying of arms at or near the polls on election day. Superintendents of registration and officers of the Freedmen's Bureau were ordered to instruct the freedmen in their rights, a function they were not slow to perform.[1]

As we have seen, the Conservatives allowed the election for delegates to the convention to go by default. But soon after it met, leading Conservatives determined upon an aggressive policy. They began to organize a vigorous campaign and to use their whole strength to get control in the state election. In November and December, 1867, Conservative clubs were organized all over the state.[2] On December 5, 1867, the Conservative

---

[1] McPherson, *Reconstruction*, pp. 320, 321, 428.

[2] *Milledgeville Federal Union*, December 31, 1867; *Savannah News*, January 1, 1868.

state convention met in Macon, the first state political convention after the war. It was not a fully representative body, however, for only about half of the counties sent delegates and very few of the northern counties were represented.

In March, 1868, the Democratic executive committee, of which E. G. Cabaniss of Macon was chairman, issued the following appeal to the voters of the state, nominating Judge Reese for governor:

Resolved, That the opinions and feelings of the National Democratic Party of Georgia, and the United States, upon the unconstitutionality and injustice of the Reconstruction Acts of Congress, are too decided and well known to require reiteration here. Their opposition to the actions of the several conventions called in pursuance of those acts, and to the effort to establish the supremacy of the negro race in the South, and to place the destinies of those states in the hands of adventurers and irresponsible persons, is equally decided and well known; yet warned by the fate of Alabama, and actuated by the instinct of self-preservation, we feel it to be our duty, to the extent of our power, to provide against every contingency; and therefore would urge upon our friends to participate in the election which is to be held on the 20th of April next to the end that the best and wisest men—men permanently identified with Georgia, and who will administer her government in the interests of the people and not for the purposes of plunder—may be chosen to organize the government, and to frame the laws under which we and our posterity may have to live.

Resolved, That in view of these principles and objects, we recommend to the people of every name and faith who have the honor and welfare of Georgia at heart, that able jurist, conservative statesman, and incorruptible patriot, Augustus Reese, of the County of Morgan, as their candidate for Governor at the approaching election.[1]

[1] *Atlanta Intelligencer*, March 14, 1868.

Judge Reese, however, had to withdraw his name, being ineligible under the Fourteenth Amendment, and Judge David Irwin was named in his stead by the Democratic Committee. When Judge Irwin, too, was pronounced ineligible by General Meade, the committee encountered great difficulty in finding a worthy leader who had not held some office before or during the war. Before nominating another candidate the committee consulted General Meade and received his sanction to the eligibility of General John B. Gordon.[1]

In the Republican ranks rivalry for the nomination for governor boded ill for the party for a time. Col. H. P. Farrow was a prominent candidate for the place and had a strong following in the state, but Rufus B. Bullock dominated the constitutional convention.[2] The Bullock men, with Foster Blodgett at the head, as chairman of the Union Republican Central Committee for Georgia, managed to convert the constitutional convention into a party nominating convention. On March 2d, the following notice was issued from the Union Republican Central Committee, signed by Blodgett as chairman and J. E. Bryant as secretary :

As delegates to the Constitutional Convention were elected by an almost unanimous vote of the Republicans of Georgia, the delegates of the Convention are requested to meet at noon on March 7th to form a nominating convention to nominate governor, candidates for Congress, and delegates to the National Republican Convention to meet in Chicago on May 2nd. All nominations for the state senate, legislature, and

---

[1] *Atlanta New Era*, March 15, 25, April 5, 1868; McPherson, *Reconstruction*, p. 320.

[2] *Savannah News*, March 11, 1868; Avery, *History of the State of Georgia*, p. 383.

county officers are to be made by the people in the districts
and counties.[1]

At the meeting, Bullock's nomination was carried, and
the threatened rupture between the two factions was
averted when Colonel Farrow announced a few days later
that he accepted the nomination of Bullock and would
stump the state for him.[2] For their platform in the campaign the Republicans put forward the new state constitution which they had framed, as a statement of their
political principles.[3]

In the greater part of the state the rule of radicals was
vigorously contested by Conservatives, whose policy was
to defeat the constitution and vote for the Conservative
ticket.[4] The complete success of their plan would render
the election of Gordon of no avail, would defeat the plan
of reconstruction mapped out by Congress, and would
continue military control. But military rule, frankly
tyrannical, was deemed preferable to civil government
run by negroes, Northern adventurers and unscrupulous
native politicians. The program of the Republicans was
to secure the ratification of the constitution and the
election of Bullock, though there was a group of moderates who advised voting for the constitution and for
Gordon, instead of Bullock.[5] The strength of these in-
dependents, together with some Democrats who thought
it best to accept the constitution, accounts for the fact
that the vote for Gordon was considerably larger than the

[1] *Atlanta New Era*, March 6, 1868.

[2] *Ibid.*, March 12, 1868. When Bullock became governor, Farrow was
appointed Attorney-General.

[3] *Ibid.*, March 11, 1868.

[4] *Augusta Chronicle*, March 6, 1868; *Savannah News*, April, 1868;
Avery, *op. cit.*, pp. 383-4.

[5] Avery, *op. cit.*, p. 384.

vote against the constitution.[1]   The fundamental issue in the campaign was the restoration of conservative white rule.   The relief feature of the constitution was pressed forward by the Republicans as a means of attracting the vote of the debtor class of whites.   During the campaign, newspapers were full of notes and campaign views, in contrast to the situation in the previous winter, when they paid scant attention to the proceedings of the convention or to politics in general.[2]   Numerous political handbills were circulated by both parties.   One, issued by the Democratic Conservatives, made the following arraignment of the constitution : [3]

It establishes social, political, and educational equality of whites and blacks.

It would result in depreciation of property and a fearful increase of taxation.

It did not originate with the people of Georgia, but in Washington—framed by adventurers from New England, by convicts from penitentiaries,[4] and by ignorant negroes from the cornfields.

At least 20,000 whites are excluded at this election.

The constitution is a falsehood to entrap people to accept it through the Relief promises, though it is known it will not stand court decisions, being contrary to the U. S. Constitution.

[1] In every district Gordon's vote outran the vote against the constitution and Bullock's vote was less than that for ratification. *Report of Comptroller General*, 1869, Table A.

[2] *The Savannah News*, for instance, in December, 1867, while the convention was in session, gave only brief notices of the proceedings when it was giving several columns to a Methodist Conference.

[3] This and the following handbills are in the possession of Mrs. V. P. Sisson of Kirkwood, Ga., to whom I am indebted for the use of them.

[4] Refers to A. A. Bradley, a negro delegate from Savannah, who served a term in a New York prison.

And another:

White men of Georgia! Read and Reflect! Rescue Georgia!

The issue involved in the election on the 20th of April is whether or not Georgia shall pass into the hands of negroes and Yankee political adventurers! Can Georgians rule Georgia? They can! Then go to the polls and vote the Democratic-Conservative ticket.

Both parties appealed to the passions of the poor whites, the Conservatives by arousing them against the domination of negroes, and the Republicans by stirring up jealousy against the former leading class. Of the latter kind of appeal the following [1] is a good example, addressed by the Republicans to the Poor White Men of Georgia:

Be a man! Let the slave-holding aristocracy no longer rule you. Vote for a constitution which educates your children free of charge; relieves the poor debtor from his rich creditor; allows a liberal homestead for your families; and more than all, places you on a level with those who used to boast that for every slave they were entitled to three-fifths of a vote in congressional representation. Ponder this well before you vote.

In the outcome of the election, the Republicans secured the state ticket, electing Bullock by a majority of 7171, and ratifying the constitution by a majority of 17,972.[2] The election of the members of the legislature was so close that it was doubtful which party would control. Bullock carried most of the counties where a majority of the registered voters were negroes, and also nine of the white counties in Northeast Georgia, three in the northwest and three on the southern border. It

[1] In *Brown Scrap Books.*

[2] *Report of the Comptroller-General,* 1869, Table A.

is noteworthy that fifteen counties in which negro registered voters outnumbered whites were carried by Gordon.[1]

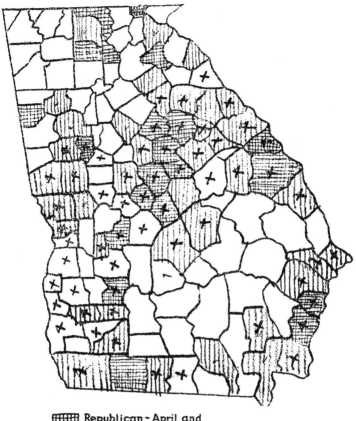

Republican - April and
November 1868

Republican - April
Democatic - November 1868

X   Majority of registered voters
colored in 1867

[1] These counties were Elbert, Spalding, Crawford, Upson, Houston,
Chattahoochee, Stewart, Quitman, Clay, Randolph, Baker, Early, Sumter,
Lowndes, Washington.

It is difficult to determine whether the result came with a moderate degree of fairness or not. In some of the black counties carried by the conservatives, Ku Klux bands doubtless did much toward achieving the result by intimidating negroes to keep them away from the polls. With all the machinery of election in their hands the Republicans had full opportunity to doctor the returns to suit themselves. Charges of unfairness were made on both sides. Savannah and Augusta papers stated that droves of negroes were brought over from South Carolina, and that negroes who appeared with a Democratic ticket were set upon by radicals and prevented from voting. In Augusta an affidavit was made by three citizens to the effect that Blodgett had four negroes from Lincoln County take the voter's oath and vote, although they had been in Richmond County less than ten days, the legal term of residence.[1] The same complaint that negroes were brought in from adjoining counties was made in Macon. A conductor on a train said that two-hundred negroes got on the train at Hawkinsville and other points in Pulaski and Twiggs counties and were taken to vote in Bibb County.[2] The Conservatives looked upon Hulburt, the Republican superintendent and manager of the election, as a skilful and unscrupulous manipulator of the returns. An example of his strategy is given by Avery in his *History of the State of Georgia*, citing the following communication from Hulburt:[3]

[1] *Augusta Chronicle*, April 21, 1868; *Savannah News*, April 23, 1868.

[2] *Macon Journal and Messenger*, April 21, 1868.

[3] Pp. 384-5. This document was published in the *Columbus Sun and Times*.

OFFICE OF SUPERINTENDENT REGISTRATION, }
ATLANTA, GA., *May 8, 1868.* }

JOHN M. DUER, ESQ., COLUMBUS:

Dear Sir: Yours of 6th at hand. We want affidavits proving force, fraud, intimidation, in violation of general orders. We must have them. Go to work and get them up at once.

The names of the parties making the affidavits will not be known to any person except yourself and the Board. They need have no fear on that score. You can swear them before Capt. Hill. Please go to work "sharp and quick." Get Chapman and other friends to assist you.

The election in your county will be contested. Defend yourselves by attacking the enemy.

Respectfully, etc.
(Signed)   E. HULBURT.

It was generally understood that the lower house had a Conservative and the upper house a Republican majority. But in April, 1868, parties were not definitely enough crystallized to make an accurate division possible. There was no doubt as to the straight-out radicalism of some and of the uncompromising conservatism of others. Between these two were the independent Republicans, who voted at times with one side and again with the other. The following classification is the result of an examination of the votes in the first session of the legislature on certain test questions, checked up by the classification in the Atlanta papers given at the time of the election:[1]

[1] The test questions considered were: ratification of the Fourteenth Amendment, election of U. S. Senators, relief for debtors, negro expulsion from the legislature. Avery gives the composition of the Senate as 26 Republicans and 18 Democrats. *History of the State of Georgia*, p. 395.

Senate—17 Radical Republicans.
10 Moderate Republicans.
17 Conservative Democrats.

House —75 Radical Republicans.
9 Moderate Republicans.
88 Conservative Democrats.

When the legislature convened, Bullock, acting as Provisional Governor under General Meade's appointment, notified the commanding general that no steps had been taken to test the eligibility of members under the Fourteenth Amendment.[1] General Meade issued certificates of election according to the returns sent him by the election managers, leaving inquiry into eligibility to each house.[2] Each house then appointed a committee of investigation. The majority of the Senate committee reported none ineligible; one minority member reported two ineligible;[3] and another minority member reported eleven.[4] The Senate, in which there was presumably a Republican majority, voted to accept the majority report, those members whose eligibility was under question not voting.[5] In the House three members of the investigating committee reported two to be ineligible, W. T. McCullough and J. M. Nunn; two of the investigating committee agreed that Long of Carroll County also was

[1] The Reconstruction Act of March 2d provided that "no person shall be eligible to any office under any such provisional government who would be disqualified from holding office under the provisions of the third article of said constitutional amendment."

[2] *Report of the Secretary of War*, 1868, vol. i, pp. 78-9.

[3] J. L. Collier and W. B. Jones.

[4] The two named above and J. C. Richardson, B. R. McCutcheon, Joshua Griffin, J. H. McWhorter, C. R. Moore, J. Harris, E. Thorn, J. G. W. Mills, E. D. Graham.

[5] *Senate Journal*, 1868, pp. 28, 32-5.

ineligible. The two minority members reported that they found none to be ineligible. The minority members based their report on the grounds that members of the legislature were not "officers" in the meaning of the law, and that all members of the House had been permitted to vote by the registrars, though the franchise was more exclusive than the right to hold office. By a vote of 95–53 the House accepted the minority report declaring none ineligible.[1] Accepting the judgment of the two houses as final, General Meade allowed the legislature to proceed to the transaction of regular business. In the organization of the two houses, the Radicals elected Benj. F. Conley as President of the Senate, by a vote of 23–13, though the moderate Republicans and Conservatives together elected their candidate for President *pro tem.* (24–19); and in the House, by a close vote and a mistake made by one of the candidates, a Republican Speaker was elected.[2]

On July 21st the legislature passed the joint resolution to ratify the Fourteenth Amendment, the Senate by 27–14 and the House by 89–71.[3] Those voting contrary were, of course, outright Conservatives, but in the Senate one Conservative voted for ratification, and two refrained from voting. In the House, six Conservatives voted for ratification and several did not vote.

The first action that showed definitely the line-up of members was the all-important election of U. S. Senators. The Bullock Republicans favored Jos. E. Brown for the long term, and Foster Blodgett for the short

[1] *House Journal,* 1868, pp. 31-45.

[2] *Senate Journal,* 1868, pp. 8, 48. Conley defeated Wooten for President; Wooten defeated Harris for President *pro tem. House Journal,* 1868, p. 12. R. L. McWhorter defeated W. T. Price, 76-74.

[3] *Senate Journal,* 1868, pp. 44-6; *House Journal,* 1868, pp. 49-51.

term.   Alex. H. Stephens was the choice of the Conservatives for the long term and for the short term they
supported H. V. M. Miller.   On the first ballot, Brown
had 24 votes from the Senate and 78 in the House, a total of 102, against Stephens' vote of 96, 15 in the Senate
and 81 in the House, Neither had a majority.   The
Conservatives and moderate Republicans then formed a
coalition, uniting on Joshua Hill, electing him for the
long term by 110 votes to Brown's 94.[1] On the first
ballot for the short term senatorship, Foster Blodgett
got 73 votes, H. V. M. Miller, 93, with scattering votes
for A. T. Akerman and Jas. L. Seward.   On the joint
ballot of the two houses most of this independent scattering vote went to Miller, who was elected by 120 to
Blodgett's 72.[2] So the anti-Bullockites, the Conservatives and the moderate Republicans, acting together,
showed in no unmistakable terms that they were in control of the situation.

The following letter from Robert Toombs to Alex. H.
Stephens, written August 9, 1868, gives Toombs' interesting comment on the senatorial situation:

As to the senatorship I preferred that Brown should be
beaten by Joshua Hill to almost any other man.   It is impossible for you [to] think worse of the scoundrel than I do, but
it could only be done by a Radical, and there was political
justice in making the earliest traitor[3] defeat the worst one and
break down his party.   I differed with you as to the policy of
beating Brown.   He had been [covert ?] Govr. of Georgia
nearly two years, administering the patronage of the military,

[1] *Senate Journal*, 1868, p. 91; *House Journal*, 1868, pp. 100-108.

[2] *Senate Journal*, 1868, p. 92; *House Journal*, 1868, pp. 106-108, July 29.

[3] Joshua Hill was candidate for governor on a Union platform
against Jos. E. Brown in 1863.

and had the whole patronage of Bullock at his feet,[1] and put all these with the whole patronage, if he had been senator [it] would have cost us not far short of 10,000 votes. His special knowledge, especially of all the rogues in the State, is prodigious, and I think it was about worth the State to beat him. Hill is a poor devil. His forlorn condition, powerless under the present circumstances, is conclusive evidence of his weakness, his inability to help himself or hurt us. I did my utmost to elect him, and ask of him no other favor than not to join us or speak to me.[2]

In the first legislature under the reconstruction constitution, three negroes were elected to the Senate and twenty-nine to the House. During the campaign, such supporters of the constitution as Jos. E. Brown maintained that negroes were not eligible to office by the new document.[3] The Conservatives in both houses from the very first looked for an opportunity to eliminate the black brothers from their midst. The first open attack was made in the Senate, when Milton A. Candler, the Conservative leader, included in the resolution concerning the eligibility of members under the Fourteenth Amendment the question of the right of the three negro senators to their seats by reason of their color.[4] This motion was incidental to the main question and nothing was done on the matter until July 25th, when Candler introduced the following resolution :[5]

[1] A resolution was introduced in the House, July 28th, (Williams, of Morgan, Moderate) for the appointment of a committee to wait on the governor to invite him to make explanation as to his using the patronage of his office in a partisan attempt to elect certain persons to the U. S. Senate.—*House Journal*, 1868, p. 97.

[2] From MS. for which I am indebted to Prof. U. B. Phillips. This letter has since been published in *American Historical Association Report*, 1911, vol. ii, p. 703.

[3] Speech of Brown of March 18, 1868, in the *Atlanta Constitution*, August 11, 1868.

[4] *Senate Journal*, 1868, p. 19, July 8.   [5] *Ibid.*, p. 84.

Whereas, ex-Governor Joseph E. Brown, one of the ablest lawyers of the Republican party of Georgia, as well as persons distinguished for their knowledge of constitutional law, held during the late election canvass that persons of color were not entitled to hold office under the existing Constitution ; and whereas such persons hold seats as Senators on this floor ; and whereas there are laws of vital importance to the people of Georgia to be enacted by the General Assembly, the validity of which should not be rendered uncertain because of the participation in their enactment by persons not entitled, under the Constitution, to so participate ; therefore be it

Resolved, That the Committee on Privileges and Elections be directed to inquire into the eligibility of the several persons of color holding seats as Senators, and report at the earliest day practicable.

At this time the resolution was laid on the table by a vote of 21–14, and the question of negro expulsion was not brought forward again until September 7th.   In the meantime one of the negroes in question, the notorious A. Alpeoria Bradley, was expelled on evidence that he had served a term in the New York State prison, convicted of the felony of seduction.[1]   His seat was taken by his Conservative opponent having the next highest vote in the April election, Rufus E. Lester.

On September 12th, after vigorous and lengthy argument on both sides, the Senate, voting 24–11, passed the resolution to expel Tunis G. Campbell of the 2d district and George Wallace of the 20th, as " ineligible to seats, on the ground that they are persons of color, and not eligible to office by the Constitution and laws of Georgia,

[1] *Ibid.*, pp. 13, 121-7, 129, 130, 134-5, 137.   The resolution to expel Bradley passed after a vigorous contest, August 13.   On the final vote Bradley was sustained by only five votes, Adkins, Higbee and Sherman in addition to his two negro colleagues.

nor by the Constitution and laws of the United States." [1]
In their places candidates having the next highest number of votes in the election were seated, thus adding two
more to the Conservative party in the Senate.[2]   In comparing the votes on the test resolution of July 25th and
the final vote on expulsion on September 12th, to find
how it was that the Conservatives finally got together
ten votes more and the Radicals ten less, we find that
five came from every Conservative being in place, whereas
five were absent on July 25th; Lester in the place of
Bradley added one more to the Conservatives at the
expense of the Radicals, and four changed sides—J.
Griffin (6th district), M. C. Smith (7th), W. C. Smith
(36th), and Richardson (32d).   On other questions the
first three had voted as moderate Republicans, but Richardson had voted with the Bullock men.   His divergence
from his party on the question of negro office-holding
was probably due to the fact that he represented the
northern mountainous counties, White, Lumpkin and
Dawson, where there was strong prejudice against
negroes.

In the House, where the Conservatives had more control than in the Senate, the expulsion of negro members
was carried with less difficulty.   On August 26th a resolution was introduced declaring ineligible the following
named persons, by reason of being persons of color: [3]
Allen of Jasper, Barnes of Hancock, Beard of Richmond,[4]

[1] *Senate Journal*, pp. 243-4, 273, 277-8.

[2] *Ibid.*, pp. 280, 324-6.

[3] *House Journal*, 1868, p. 222.

[4] The names of these four, Beard, Belcher, Davis and Fyall, were
later stricken out as they were so nearly white that their race was
indeterminate. They remained in the House after the others were
expelled. *Ibid.*, p. 229.

Belcher of Wilkes,[1] T. G. Campbell of McIntosh, Claiborne of Burke, Clower of Monroe, Colby of Greene, Costin of Talbot, Davis of Clarke,[1] Floyd of Morgan, Fyall of Macon,[1] Gardner of Warren, Golden of Liberty, Harrison of Hancock, Houston of Bryan, Joiner of Dougherty, Linder of Laurens, Lumpkin of Macon, Moore of Columbia, O'Neal of Baldwin, Porter of Chatham, Richardson of Clarke, Sims of Chatham, Smith of Muscogee, Stone of Jefferson, Turner of Bibb, Warren of Burke, Williams of Harris.

On September 3d the resolution to unseat the negro members passed the House, 83–23,[2] negroes not voting. It was clear enough that the Conservatives could carry the measure, so the opponents made no such resistance as in the Senate, where the outcome was doubtful.

When Governor Bullock, by request, reported to the House the list of candidates having the next highest vote, he took occasion to protest against the expulsion of negro members as unconstitutional and illegal. The House showed its temper toward the Governor by returning his message, with the tart resolution that "the Constitution declares that the members of each House are the judges of the qualifications of its members, and not the Governor. They are the keeper of their own consciences, and not his Excellency."[3]   But while the legislators of Georgia may have been the keepers of their consciences, as they averred, they were not the keepers of the State of Georgia. Congress was master, as it plainly demonstrated in its refusal to admit Georgia's representatives, and in its order for the second reconstruction of the state under the military management of General Terry in 1869. How-

---

[1] See note 4, p. 213.

[2] *House Journal*, 1868, pp. 242-3.

[3] *Ibid.*, pp. 296, 302-303. Vote, 71-32.

ever unsuited negroes were to the important function of making laws for the commonwealth, the two houses were most unwise in their act of expulsion, as events proved. The Conservatives of Georgia made their mistake in being strong enough to gain control too soon to suit the Radicals in Congress, who were still the real keepers of Georgia. The Conservatives made a like error of judgment when they elected A. H. Stephens and H. V. Johnson to the U. S. Senate in 1865; and again when they carried the state for Seymour and Blair in the presidential election of 1868. The trouble was that the Conservatives considered solely what was best for the white people of Georgia, instead of viewing reconstruction as a national political problem and consulting the pleasure of the Republican leaders in Congress and the effect of Georgia proceedings on public opinion in the North.

A test case was made by the Republicans in Georgia to have the courts decide the question of the eligibility of the negroes to hold office. In June, 1869, the case of White v. Clements was argued before the Supreme Court. Justices Brown and McCay decided in favor of the eligibility of negroes, with Justice Warner dissenting.[1] After the decision of the court was rendered, the question arose: What bearing did it have on the status of the legislature? Was the legislature bound to act accordingly and reinstate negro members, or could the *status quo* continue, on the basis that each house had the inalterable right to determine the qualifications of its members? The press was divided; the *Macon Telegraph, Athens Banner, Griffin Star, Atlanta Intelligencer,* and *Albany News* holding that the law must be obeyed, unpleasant though it be; and the *Augusta Constitutional-*

[1] 39 Georgia 232. See *infra,* p. 360.

ist, Columbus Sun and Times, Augusta Chronicle, Columbus Enquirer and *Savannah News* agreeing that the decision had no effect on the legislature.[1]   Alex. H. Stephens held the latter opinion.   Writing from Crawfordsville, June 29, 1869, to A. R. Wright of the *Augusta Chronicle*, he said that the decision of the supreme court seemed to him in accordance with law, for he himself thought the legislature in error in deciding colored members ineligible; yet the legislature was judge of the qualifications of its members and the court had no binding power on the legislature.[2]   However, the legislature had no opportunity to act or to refuse to act on the decision of the court, for it was not in session when the decision was rendered, and before the next session Congress passed the Reorganization Act.

A comparison of Georgia in the first two years of reconstruction, 1868–70, with her neighbors, Alabama, South Carolina and Florida, shows a marked moderation in her government, a lesser degree of reconstruction evils, less wanton corruption and extravagance in public office, less social disorder and upheaval.   In Georgia, negroes and carpet-baggers were not so conspicuous, and conservative white citizens were better represented. Facts do not warrant the description of the reconstruction government of Georgia as a negro-carpet-bagger combination.   There were some of both classes in the constitutional convention and in the legislature of 1868, already mentioned, and many in the Federal service, particularly as internal revenue officers, but they generally held minor positions.   The big plums of office went to

[1] *Macon Telegraph*, June 18 and June 20, 1869, cites opinions of other papers.

[2] Letter printed in *Macon Telegraph*, July 4, 1869.

native Republicans or to Northerners who came South before the war. Governor Bullock himself, strictly speaking, was not a carpet-bagger, though his opponents applied that opprobrious epithet to him. A carpet-bagger was, strictly speaking, a Republican adventurer who came South after the war and won political office by controlling the negro vote. But Rufus B. Bullock came to Georgia from New York State in 1859, and was connected with the Southern Express Company in Augusta. During the war he held a minor position in connection with the Confederate army, assistant quartermaster-general. Personally, Bullock was an affable, likeable man, by no means lacking in ability. His career in Georgia was a variation of ups and downs. When the Democrats gained the legislature in 1871, Bullock resigned from the governorship and fled from the State to escape certain impeachment. But unlike most reconstruction governors, he returned. In 1876 he came back to Georgia and underwent trial on the indictments made against him in 1872, and with insufficient evidence against him, was acquitted. He remained in Atlanta, engaged in business and enjoyed considerable esteem in the community until sometime in the nineties, when he left again under a cloud, having failed in business under rather questionable circumstances. In 1907 he died in his old home in New York State.[1]

The real head of Georgia at this time was not Governor Bullock, but his guide and advisor, intimate friend and financial agent, H. I. Kimball.

The state of Georgia seems to have had a dual executive, Rufus B. Bullock and Hannibal I. Kimball, from the 4th of

---

[1] *Atlanta Constitution*, April 28, 1907; Avery, *History of the State of Georgia, passim.*

July, 1868, until the last of October, 1871, and so inseparable were those, *par nobile fratrum*, that whenever you see the footprints of the one, you may look with confidence for the track of the other.

This was the conclusion of the joint committee of the legislature in 1872, "to investigate the official conduct of Rufus B. Bullock", based on the strongest of circumstantial evidence.[1] Kimball was one of the most interesting of the newcomers brought by the opportunities of reconstruction,—not a carpet-bagger, for he did not devote his energies to seeking political office. He was a friend and patron of office holders. Without the presence of such patrons as Kimball, membership in the legislature would have been decidedly less lucrative than it was with his encouragement. Among the Republicans at the state capitol Kimball was a great favorite, the epitome of munificent and open-handed wealth and unbounded success. The negro sang his glories in a popular song with the refrain:

> H. I. Kimball's on de floor
> 'Taint gwine ter rain no more.

Mr. Kimball's chief enterprises were the construction of railroads by state aid. He was president of the Brunswick and Albany R. R., of the Bainbridge, Cuthbert and Columbus R. R. and of the Cartersville and Van Wert R. R., all of which were involved in illegal use of state bonds. He purchased the Opera House, then in construction in Atlanta, remodeled it and sold it to the state for a capitol building. In a notorious case against the State of Georgia, the claims of the Mitchell heirs, he bought an interest in the claim, associated with ex-Governor Brown as a Mitchell "orphan", and managed to secure from

---

[1] Report of this committee, p. 2.

the legislature a favorable settlement. This claim for
property in Atlanta which was used by the state for ter-
minal purposes in connection with the Western and
Atlantic R. R., long lay dormant until the vitalizing touch
of Kimball and others awakened it to activity before the
legislature.[1] Kimball, likewise, was an important factor
in the company which secured the lease of the state road
in 1870. As was said of him in that connection, " he was
in pretty much everything about that time." [2] As a part-
ner in the so-called Tennessee Car Co. he secured funds
from the state road, though the cars paid for were not
delivered.[3] As semi-official financial agent for the State
of Georgia and for the governor, Kimball had free-handed
control over state bonds, rendering no account of his
transactions. In 1870 a great hotel, the Kimball House,
was built by him in Atlanta, and was commonly believed
to have been paid for with state bonds.[4] The spectacular
career of Kimball, who was so fittingly named Hannibal,
came to a close in 1871, just coincident with the decline
of the power of the Republican party, with the cutting
off of supplies from state bonds, and with the flight of
Governor Bullock from Georgia. Kimball, too, returned
to Georgia after the excitement of the investigating period
subsided. But in his later career, when he was no longer
the right hand of the chief executive, he cut no such
striking figure as he presented in the height of his glory
in 1870.[5]

[1] Committee to investigate the official conduct of R. B. Bullock, 1872,
testimony concerning the Mitchell claims, pp. 1-21; and report of
committee, pp. 12-17; *Senate Journal*, 1870, vol. iii, pp. 495-502, 518-9,
552; *House Journal*, pp. 1152-4.

[2] *W. and A. Lease Committee*, 1872, p. 7.

[3] *Bullock Investigating Committee*, p. 30.

[4] Avery, *History of the State of Georgia*, p. 457.

[5] *Ibid.*, pp. 447, 457; Turner, in *Why the Solid South*, p. 135.

In Governor Bullock's defence of his administration in answer to the charges made by the legislative committee of 1872,[1] he stoutly denied that there was ever a partnership existing between himself and Kimball. But if there was technically no partnership, whatever the relationship may be called, Bullock profited materially by the political influence he gave to Kimball. There was not a single enterprise of Kimball's which did not have the fullest support of Bullock and his friends in the legislature. Moreover, very damaging testimony as to the business relationship of Bullock and Kimball was given by the cashier of the Georgia National Bank, used for the business of the state and for the private accounts of Bullock and Kimball as well. The cashier stated that Kimball constantly made large deposits to Bullock's private account, kept Bullock supplied with funds, and the bank officials were given to understand in unmistakable terms that the bank account was open to both.[2] If Bullock used his whole political power to foster Kimball's interests so extensively without receiving financial benefit himself, he certainly was more fool, if less rogue, than is ordinarily credible. The committee of 1872 came to the conclusion that a partnership existed between the two, beyond the shadow of a doubt, basing its judgment on the cashier's statement

[1] Gov. Bullock, *Address to the People of Georgia*, October, 1872: A Review of the revolutionary proceedings of the late repudiating legislature—the slander and misrepresentations of the Committee exposed—A Republican administration contrasted with the corrupt and reckless action of the present usurping minority, under the lead of General Toombs.

[2] *W. and A. Lease Committee*, 1872, pp. 203-213. Cashier E. L. Jones said that Kimball paid to Bullock's account between $30,000 and $50,000 after the W. and A. lease was granted.

Kimball, by the way, purchased a large amount of stock in this bank in 1870.

of banking operations, on Kimball's activity as financial agent for the state in the matter of disposing of bonds, on the fact that fraudulent grants of state aid to railroads, all supported by Bullock, were in Kimball's interest, that Bullock was eager to have the Mitchell claim settled as soon as Kimball became one of the litigants, together with corroborative testimony as to their relations in the Western and Atlantic R. R., given by A. L. Harris.[1]

Foster Blodgett, Bullock's faithful Man Friday, was chairman of the Republican Executive Committee in 1868, doing more than anyone else to secure the nomination of Bullock as governor over the rival claims of H. P. Farrow. As a return for his services, he was the candidate of the Bullock forces for the short term in the U. S. Senate. Failing that, he was rewarded with a remunerative place in the state road, first as treasurer and later as superintendent. In the latter capacity, though only a figure-head acting under Bullock's immediate direction in important matters, such as making appointments and letting contracts, he came in for a large share of the charge of corruption and mismanagement against the reconstruction administration. Blodgett was a Georgian, resident in Augusta at the time that he made his first political appearance as member of the convention in 1867. Along with Bullock he was a member of the "Augusta ring" that carried things much their own way among Republicans at the first election. Others of the same group were J. E. Bryant and Ephraim Tweedy, members of the Augusta ring and henchmen of Bullock in 1868. A. L. Harris, familiarly known as "Fatty" from his weight of something over three hundred pounds,

---

[1] *Report of the committee to investigate the official conduct of R. B. Bullock, 1872, p. 3, et seq.*

a native of Vermont and later resident in Ohio, also belonged to the Bullock coterie. Trained for civil engineering, he drifted later into newspaper work and was editor and proprietor of several papers.[1] In 1867 he was a member of the convention from Savannah, and in 1868, when the plums were distributed, the supervisorship of the state road was his share. Though not a member of the legislature in 1870, he was the efficient instrument chosen by Governor Bullock to reorganize the senate. Though there was a large clearing-out of Democrats after General Terry's Purge, it was necessary for Bullock to make sure that his friends, rather than independent Republicans, secured control of both houses. In achieving this purpose Harris rendered faithful service. Ed. Hulburt, too, a Bullock friend in 1867, when he was superintendent of registration, found his reward in the state road as superintendent, a position which he held until differences with Governor Bullock led to his removal in Blodgett's favor. Hulburt was a carpet-bagger.

The state officials elected by the legislature in 1868 were not numbered among Governor Bullock's friends. The Comptroller-General, Madison Bell, the Treasurer, N. L. Angier, and the Secretary of State, D. G. Gotting, were independent Republicans.

Of the six representatives sent from Georgia to the lower house of Congress in 1868, two were carpet-baggers, J. W. Clift and C. H. Prince. Clift was a native of Massachusetts, whose trade as carpenter seemed to fit him to serve in the Union army as a surgeon. In November, 1866, he began to practice medicine in Savannah, and in 1867, he began to practice politics

[1] Avery, *History of the State of Georgia*, p. 427.

when General Pope appointed him registrar.[1] Prince from Maine was a man of limited education, a merchant before he entered the Federal army. After the war he settled in Augusta. Like many others of his kind he served his political apprenticeship in the constitutional convention.[2]

No enumeration of the influential leaders who determined the work of reconstruction can be complete without further mention of the most significant of them all, the power behind the throne, ex-Governor Brown. Of all public men in Georgia in this period he was the most astute and the most powerful. He was first in secession, first in reconstruction, and very nearly first in the restoration of Democratic home rule. Consequently he came up on top at every revolution of the wheel of destiny. In 1865 Governor Brown quickly acquiesced in the first scheme of restoration, made himself *persona grata* to President Johnson, and used his potent influence in Georgia for the successful achievement of Johnson's reconstruction policy. In the fall of 1866, when he saw that President Johnson had finally lost out with Congress, Brown counseled the adoption of the Fourteenth Amendment; and in the next stage, when the Reconstruction Acts were put forward, he became a reconstructionist of the new sort. When General Pope came to take charge of Georgia under military rule, Brown was among the first to give the general cordial greeting. Brown was friendly with Bullock and Blodgett and their contingent, and to him they looked for influence to carry the constitution by popular vote, especially in Cherokee Georgia, Brown's stronghold.

[1] *Biographical Congressional Directory*, p. 553.
[2] *Ibid.*, p. 937.

In return the Bullock party mustered all its strength in support of Brown for the U. S. Senate. In the next turn of events, when Republican rule was overthrown, among those in the vanguard for restoration, escorting the Democratic governor in triumph to the chair of office in 1872, was ex-Governor Brown. No one was more vilified by the Conservative press in Georgia in the years 1867 to 1871 than Jos. E. Brown. In June, 1868, the *Atlanta Constitution* published a series of articles in execration of Brown, entitled "A Prophet Foretelling his own Infamy"—Brown, in 1860, foretelling disaster when the government should pass into black Republican hands. The following is from the stinging pen of the *Constitution's* editor: "When a white man like Jos. E. Brown becomes the political foot-ball of dirty, insolent negroes, instead of giving him an additional kick, should not all good men rather lament his fallen state?"[1] At a Democratic rally in Atlanta, at which Robert Toombs, Howell Cobb and Ben Hill spoke, the following signs were displayed on transparencies:[2]

B's without Honey!

B – rown	B – ryant
B – lodgett	B – ullock
B – radley	B – ard[3]

Stings extracted in November.

The B's are hived! Perjured Blodgett, Traitor Brown, Convict Bradley, and the Thief Butler!

Joe Brown—a traitor to his section, and an outcast from society—Judas Escobes Brown.

[1] *Atlanta Constitution*, July 10, 1868.
[2] *Ibid.*, June 17 and July 10, 24, 1868.
[3] Samuel Bard was the editor of the *Atlanta New Era*, an organ of the Bullock party in 1868.

On the whole, as far as personnel is concerned, the reconstruction administration of Georgia was not entirely bad, was even quite good in some members.   This praise, faint as it is, is more than can be given to most of the governments in the Southern states in 1868.

CHAPTER IX

State Economy of the Bullock Régime

NUMEROUS charges of misconduct were brought against Governor Bullock; abuse of the pardoning power; the part he played in forcing the second reconstruction of Georgia, conniving at the so-called " slander-mill " to manufacture tales of outrages by the whites against negroes and Northern Republicans; assistance in defrauding the state through his transactions with H. I. Kimball in connection with the purchase of the state capitol in Atlanta, the Mitchell claims and state-endorsed railroad bonds; and his subsidy of the press and the bar by extravagant payments for unnecessary services. These and other charges were thoroughly probed by a committee of the legislature, appointed under a resolution of December 1, 1871, after Governor Bullock had fled from the state. Under the guiding hand of Robert Toombs, as attorney for the investigating committee, no stone was left unturned to reveal corruption in the administration of the Republican governor.[1] It was the financial policy of the Bullock administration, however, its general extravagance and illegal use of state bonds, and the corrupt and inefficient

---

[1] *Joint committee of the legislature to investigate the official conduct of Rufus B. Bullock,* report and testimony, printed 1872. Senate: J. C. Nicholls, Chairman, and C. J. Wellborn; House: E. F. Hoge, S. A. McNiel, W. H. Payne.

An earlier committee to investigate Bullock's financial transactions was appointed in 1870. A majority report supporting Bullock and a minority report against him were presented.

management of the state road, that most seriously affected the interests of Georgia.

In the matter of total expenditure Bullock's administration did not greatly exceed the Jenkins government of 1865-6. In the years immediately after the war, however, large disbursements were necessary to relieve distress and to meet other special needs not existing in 1868. It was more in certain classes of expenditure, in the cost of the civil establishment, in the contingent fund and in printing, that the Bullock management was either unduly extravagant or corrupt, probably both. Comparing 1870 with 1866, for instance, we find that the civil establishment cost the state $76,492.38 in 1870 and only $20,771.66 in 1866 : the contingent fund in 1870 was $36,284.44 and in 1866, $6,128.62 : for printing, $57,323.53 in 1870, and $1,021 in 1866. The special appropriations of the 1866 legislature, including large funds to relieve destitution and to care for needy Confederates, amounted to $304,955.05, a puny sum when compared with the generosity of the Republican legislature of 1870, on whose appropriations $1,073,595.18 was expended.[1] In the sole item of printing, exclusive of the amount paid to the official printer for matters of public printing, $140,397 was expended by Bullock during his term of office. Executive orders and proclamations were published in forty-two papers. Newspapers were paid for publishing for weeks the offer of reward for the arrest of a criminal, then for publishing the pardon of the same offender after his capture and the payment of the reward. The *Atlanta New Era*, which in 1869 became the property of Bullock and his friends, was the recipient of lavish patronage

[1] These figures are taken in part from Woolley, *Reconstruction of Georgia*, p. 101, checked up by the *Reports of the Comptroller General*.

from the state. Excessive attorneys' fees, not merely to Republican but to favored Democratic lawyers as well, were freely paid, it was claimed, in an attempt to subsidize the bar as well as the press.[1] One of the papers that evidently did not partake of Bullock patronage, published the following :[2]

Bullock's Soothing Syrup.

This is one of the greatest remedies recently invented. It is so effective that we give it a little " puff " gratis. It cures

Excessive indignation
Chronic disgust
Hatred for infamy
Persistence for right

and many other complaints to which the Southern people are subject. Many cases heretofore considered obstinate, have yielded to its influence, and are now thoroughly cured. It is composed principally of a powerful green substance, collected by the tax-gatherers of Georgia, compounded by Dr. Bullock, and given according to the extent of the affliction.

Price, Expressed favor for Bullock and the negro legislators.

When a cure is not effected after thorough trial, the remedy will be taken back and no charge made.

Special sources of leakage were pointed out by the state treasurer, N. L. Angier, in his controversy with Governor Bullock, as shown in the following items:[3]

[1] *Committee to investigate the official conduct of Rufus B. Bullock,* pp. 17-20, 24.

[2] *Milledgeville Federal Union,* October 5, 1869, copied from the *Americus Courier.*

[3] Angier's report in *Ku Klux Committee,* vol. vi, pp. 153-5.

	1855–60	1868–70
Amount expended for extra legal services	$17000	$36600
Rewards for fugitives	1400	51100
Advertisements of proclamations . .	5000	98300
Incidental expenses	2188[1]	23800

However, taxes were not heavily increased by the reconstruction government. The rate of taxation remained about the same as that fixed by the Jenkins government in 1866. To meet wasteful and extravagant appropriations the governor and the legislature had recourse to bond issues, throwing the burden of debt on future generations.

The issue of bonds by Governor Bullock was the center of a far-reaching controversy, which played an important part in reconstruction history. The treasurer, N. L. Angier, a Republican but not a Bullock partisan, in January, 1869, reported upon the state finances in such a way as to suggest that Governor Bullock was making corrupt use of public funds. Thereupon the two houses of the legislature appointed a joint committee to investigate the condition of the state finances. In 1870 the legislature was strongly Republican. Hence the majority report of the committee was favorable to Bullock. Two years later, after the Democrats gained control and Governor Bullock fled from the state, various committees of investigation were appointed, among which was the Bond Committee,[2] consisting of T. J. Simmons, Garnett McMillan and J. I. Hall. The published findings of the committee contain the testimony of witnesses examined, besides recommendations of the committee. The bonds under question were the state endorsed bonds of railroads,

---

[1] This includes incidental expenses for 1866-7, also.

[2] *Acts of General Assembly*, 1871, p. 14.

currency bonds of a temporary issue under act of 1870, and 7 per cent gold bonds of 1870.   Before the committee set to work it was impossible to know exactly what was the amount of the state debt, for bonds were issued irregularly, some without the signature of the state treasurer and without proper registration.   H. I. Kimball acted as semi-official agent for the state and for Governor Bullock, keeping no records, and Henry Clews was the financial representative of Georgia in New York.

The situation of the debt in 1872, according to the results of the committee's investigation, was as follows :[1]

Bonds issued before 1868[2]	$5,618,750
" " after July 4, 1868	
endorsed railroad bonds	5,733,000
other	6,831,250
	12,564,250
Total state and endorsed bonds	18,183,000

The real question of corruption and illegality arose in connection with the endorsed bonds of the railroads with which H. I. Kimball was associated, the Brunswick and Albany, the Bainbridge, Cuthbert and Columbus, and the Cartersville and Van Wert (later the Cherokee). In these three cases the committee recommended that the state repudiate its obligation, as the terms of the law granting state aid had not been fulfilled.   In the case of the Brunswick and Albany, the most conspicuous of all, the conclusions of the committee were as follows : (1) The claims for damages made by the company against the state were based on false assumptions : for the Con-

---

[1] *Bond Investigating Committee,* 1872, pp. 13-14; Report of Acting-Governor Conley on the state finances; *Report of the Treasurer,* 1871, p. 10.

[2] Of the bonds issued before 1868, $1,718,750 was issued before 1861, and $3,900,000 more before 1866.

federacy and not the state seized iron from the road; the iron taken was fully paid for; and contracts with Governor Brown for transporting troops in 1861 could not be enforced as they were in furtherance of rebellion. (2) The bonds were issued and endorsed, not in accordance with the terms of the law, on the completion of twenty-mile sections, but before sections were completed. (3) The cost of construction was not commensurate with the aid granted and no investment by private parties was made. (4) A strong suspicion existed that corrupt means were employed to effect the passage of the Brunswick and Albany grants in the legislature.[1]

Under the terms of the Act of March 18, 1868, aid was granted to the Bainbridge, Cuthbert and Columbus R. R. on the completion of twenty-mile sections. Before a single mile was completed, Governor Bullock, in the office of H. I. Kimball and Company in New York, endorsed 240 bonds, which were never sealed or signed by the Secretary of State. Hence these bonds were considered by the committee as not binding on the state.[2]

The bonds endorsed for the Cartersville and Van Wert, to the amount of $100,000, were given when only one and one-half miles of track were laid, and $275,000 more when three miles were laid, still incomplete, though the law called for endorsement on the completion of five-mile sections. No funds were ever paid in by private investors. The investigating committee declared that Governor Bullock personally knew the incomplete condition of the road when he endorsed the bonds, and that Henry Clews also, with whom Kimball placed the 275 bonds endorsed in August, 1870, knew that the endorse-

---

[1] *Bond Investigating Committee,* 1872, pp. 19-29, 49, 165; *Bullock Investigating Committee,* 1872, pp. 30-33.

[2] *Ibid.,* pp. 34-5.

ment was premature and illegal. These bonds were pronounced by the committee to be null and void.[1]

The Act of August 27, 1870, provided for an issue of currency bonds to the amount of $2,000,000, intended as temporary, to be taken up as soon as gold quarterly bonds were ready. In 1871 Acting-Governor Conley reported that $1,500,000 of these were still in the hands of the following New York firms, who were unwilling to exchange the currency for the gold bonds intended to take their place:[2]

$800,000 with Henry Clews and Co.
$530,000 "   Russell Sage
$120,000 "   J. Boorman Johnston and Co.
$50,000   "   Fulton Bank, Brooklyn

The investigating committee declared these bonds not binding, as they were canceled by the quarterly gold bonds. Further, there was no evidence that the state received any money on the bonds hypothecated by Kimball as agent for Bullock.[3]

The matter of the 7 per cent gold bonds was more complicated. The Act of September 15, 1870, provided for gold bonds without limit for the payment of bonds when due, for the payment of interest and coupons due, and for the appropriations made by the legislature. Before 1872, $3,000,000 of these were issued, of which $250,-000 was given to H. I. Kimball in payment for the Atlanta Opera House, purchased for the state capitol, and $100,000 to John H. James for purchase of the executive mansion in Atlanta. The rest were put on the market through H. I. Kimball and through Henry Clews

[1] *Bond Investigating Committee*, pp. 78 *et seq.*, 150-51.

[2] *Commercial and Financial Chronicle*, January 20, 1872.

[3] *Bond Investigating Committee*, 1872, pp. 152-4.

and Company, except $102,000, still unsold with Clews.
The total thus disposed of was $2,548,000.[1]   Clews and
Co., as financial agents for the state, sold 1650 bonds,
500 at 87½ and 1150 at 86½.   Out of the proceeds
delivered to the State's account ($1,432,250), Clews paid
$609,192.12 on drafts of Bullock and Blodgett, mostly on
account of the state road.   Since these bonds were authorized for the expressed purposes of paying bonds
when due, interest and coupons due, and for appropriations made by the legislature, the committee considered payment of any part of the proceeds to the
account of the State road as an illegal transaction.   The
remainder of the bonds were hypothecated by Kimball
for an amount unknown.   Of these quarterly gold bonds,
the committee recommended that those issued by Bullock
for property or sold in the market by his agents be recognized as good and binding; those hypothecated on
which money was borrowed by an agent of the state be
returned to the treasurer and the amount borrowed, with
interest and reasonable expenses for returning bonds, be
paid by issue of new currency bonds or by cash; those
still held by Clews without legal right as collateral security or otherwise constitute no liability against Georgia.
Further, the investigating committee decided that the
claims of Henry Clews and Co. for $47,145.50 and £1800
be ignored, as Clews was a party to the misappropria-
tion of state funds in paying drafts of Bullock and

---

[1] *Commercial and Financial Chronicle*, January 20, 1872. Report of
Acting-Governor Conley gives the following as the account of the 7%
gold bonds:

Held by Clews & Co. for sale to secure advances made by them on
    currencies and others $1,750,000
    by Russell Sage and others   500,000
    deposited with Fourth National Bank, N. Y.   300,000
    placed with A. S. Whiton, N. Y.   100,000

Blodgett on proceeds from quarterly bonds for other purposes than those for which they were intended.[1]

But the bond question was not settled by the report of the investigating committee. Even while the bonds were under investigation and after the report was presented, sales of bonds were made in New York. The *Commercial and Financial Chronicle* of July 22, 1872, noted that there was a fair amount of dealings in Georgia bonds in spite of the report of the committee. The opinion of the *Chronicle* was that the legislature would not carry out the recommendations of the committee, for it would impair the credit of the state to repudiate bonds on grounds purely technical. To direct public opinion against repudiation, Henry Clews and Co. published a card in the *Atlanta Constitution*, rehearsing their operations as financial agents for Governor Bullock. Admitting that proceeds of the bonds were misapplied and that the state failed to receive value for them, yet for the sake of the future credit of the state, they advised that the legislature should not resort to repudiation.[2] In Georgia there was a wide difference of opinion on the matter. There was a significant group, represented by ex-Governor Brown, that favored compromise, by recognizing the equity of the case by payment of the actual amount received on bonds with interest. Leaders urging no compromise, but repudiation, were Robert Toombs, Ben. H. Hill, and W. M. Wadley of the Central R. R. The repudiation party prevailed, and in August, 1872, the legislature passed bills declaring null

[1] *Bond Investigating Committee*, 1872, pp. 159-163.

[2] *Commercial and Financial Chronicle*, January 6, 1872. See pamphlet, Reply of Henry Clews & Co. to the Annual Report of the Treasurer, N. L. Angier, January 12, 1872; also, Clews, *Twenty-eight Years in Wall Street*.

and void the endorsed railroad bonds and others designated by the investigating committee.[1] To make the
action perpetually binding, the Constitutional Convention of 1877 inserted in the constitution a clause prohibiting the payment of the bonds thus pronounced illegal.[2]

State aid to railroads was a policy by no means distinctive of the reconstruction period. Before the war
encouragement was given by tax exemption or by sub-
scription on state account to railroad stock. In the first
period of reconstruction the policy used extensively in
1869 and 1870 was tried—state guarantee of bonds of
the railroad, for which the state secured a first mortgage
on the property of the road. In December, 1866, the
legislature agreed to the endorsement by the state of
bonds for the Macon and Brunswick R. R. at the rate of
$10,000 per mile for the fifty miles then completed, and
at the same rate in ten-mile sections as the road should
be finished.[3] In 1868, when the question of state aid
came before the legislature, the senate committee on internal improvements reported that all such bills ought to
be laid over until the next session. In the unsettled
political condition, with a treasury almost exhausted, the
policy of supporting the railroads would, the committee
believed, be injurious to the credit of the state. Already,
up to September 8th, bills had been introduced calling
for state aid to an amount in excess of three million dollars. One member of the committee presented a minority
report, urging that an exception be made of the Atlanta
and Richmond Air Line, which would open a valuable

[1] *Acts of the General Assembly*, 1872, pp. 5-8.

[2] *Constitution of 1877*, p. 44.

[3] *Acts of the General Assembly*, 1866, p. 127.

section of the state.[1] The Air Line had strong support in
the legislature and the act granting bond endorsement
to this road was passed by a substantial majority. A
few days later a bill to lend the credit of the state to the
South Georgia and Florida R. R. was passed. At the
same session endorsement was pledged to the Macon and
Augusta R. R.[2]

1869 and 1870 were the active years of state-aid grants.
By the close of 1871 endorsements were authorized by
the legislature to thirty-seven railroads. At the time
that grants were secured most of the railroad recipients
had existence only on paper or in the brains of their
promoters. While the state made itself liable under
certain contingencies for bond endorsement amounting to
over thirty millions, it was unlikely that much of it would
be called for within several years, if ever. The Macon
and Augusta R. R. resigned its claim, finding it could
make better loans independent of the state; and the
Atlanta and Richmond Air Line, having the same experience, returned $240,000 of bonds endorsed by the state.[3]

In pursuance of these grants the only railroads which
actually received endorsement of bonds before 1872 were
the following:[4]

Brunswick and Albany R. R.	$3,300,000
Cartersville and Van Wert.	275,000
Cherokee	300,000
Bainbridge, Cuthbert and Columbus	600,000
South Georgia and Florida	464,000
Alabama and Chattanooga	194,000
Macon and Brunswick.	600,000

[1] *Senate Journal*, 1868, pp. 248-9, 259.

[2] *Acts of the General Assembly*, 1868, pp. 143-7.

[3] Report of Governor Bullock, July 5, 1871, in *Commercial and Financial Chronicle*, July 22, 1871.

[4] *Bond Investigating Committee*, 1872, p. 14.

Very serious charges of corruption in the legislature were made in connection with the bill to grant aid to the Brunswick and Albany R. R., one of the pet enterprises of H. I. Kimball. In the Senate, on the motion of Milton A. Candler a leading Democrat, an attempt was made to recall the bill from the governor because charges were made that fraudulent means had been used to secure its passage. Hungerford, a Radical, retaliated with a resolution to investigate the means used by the Central of Georgia R. R. and allied roads to defeat the Brunswick and Albany bill. The result was that the whole matter was tabled by a vote of 20-19, Bullock's friends having the necessary majority.[1] It was commonly noised abroad that the Central led in an extensive and expensive lobby to prevent the grant of state aid to competing lines, while it was generally believed that Brunswick and Albany stock was freely distributed among members of the legislature.[2] The bond investigating committee was able to put its finger on little direct evidence of corruption. Two facts pointing that way, however, were brought out in the testimony given before the committee. R. B. Hall, a member of the legislature from Glynn County, held preferred stock of the B. & A. R. R., for which he paid nothing; and E. F. Blodgett testified that his father, Foster Blodgett, who took active part in securing aid to the Brunswick and Albany, owned $15,000 in B. & A. bonds, received, he thought, from H. I. Kimball.[3] The same charges were made concerning bills of aid to the other Kimball enterprises, the Cartersville and Van Wert and the Bainbridge, Cuthbert and Columbus, which passed the legislature about the same time.

---

[1] *Senate Journal*, 1869, pp. 630, 665.

[2] *Savannah News*, March 12, 1869.

[3] *Bond Investigating Committee*, 1872, pp. 28-9.

As a matter of policy it was perhaps wise for Georgia to lend its credit for the construction of needed railways, and so contribute to the economic development of the state. But as the principle was actually applied by the Bullock administration, credit was given on political rather than economic terms with little gain to the real progress of transportation facilities. Funds obtained by the hypothecation of Georgia bonds, unfortunately, did not all find their way into cross-ties and iron rails and engines for the new roads of Georgia. The affairs of the state-aid railroads, especially those with which H. I. Kimball was connected, were so badly managed that all, with the exception of the South Georgia and Florida R. R., soon defaulted in payment of the interest on their bonds and went into the hands of receivers.

Instead of being a financial asset the state road proved a heavy burden to Georgia during Bullock's administration. From 1868 until December, 1870, when it was leased to a private corporation, the history of the Western and Atlantic R. R. is replete with all the abuses to which publicly-owned utilities may be subject. It was managed primarily as an organ of patronage for the radicals in control of the state. Officials of the road were chosen, not because they knew anything about railroad business, but in the same way that U. S. consuls or postmasters were generally selected. Those high in office used the road to further their political interests and others used it for financial advantage as well. As a result of graft and incompetence, the road piled up for Georgia a debt of nearly three-quarters of a million dollars in 1868-70, instead of adding a substantial income to the state treasury, as it could easily have done under ordinarily honest management.[1]   Before the war, under Governor

[1] *Report of the joint committee of the legislature to investigate the official conduct of Rufus B. Bullock*, p. 29.

Brown's administration, the Western and Atlantic was
brought to a good paying level, turning into the state treasury $25,000 a month and more.[1]   In the first two years
after the war, mortgage bonds were issued by the state to
repair heavy damages, and over $800,000 was spent in
equipment and construction, placing the road in a fair
condition to transact business satisfactorily.

When Governor Bullock took charge of the state government in July, 1868, old employees of the road were dismissed to make way for his friends.   The superintendent,
Major Campbell Wallace, was replaced by Ed. Hulburt, the
Republican superintendent of registration in 1867, to whom
Bullock was indebted for substantial aid in his election as
governor; Foster Blodgett, Bullock's henchman and candidate for the U. S. Senate, was treasurer; and A. L. Harris,
another strong Bullock supporter, was supervisor.   When
the radicals split into two factions in 1869, Hulburt took
sides against the Bullock-Blodgett group, opposing the second reconstruction scheme, and was therefore removed
from office as superintendent.   On January 1, 1870, Foster
Blodgett took his place.   Hulburt, disgruntled and disaffected, turned to the other side and became a bitter witness
against Bullock before the investigating committee of 1872.[2]
Mr. Blodgett himself, testifying two years later before a
committee of the legislature, said he knew nothing about
railroad management—his business was to run the political
part of it.   The road had always had two or three times as
many employees as were needed, he said, and passes were
given freely to members of the legislature and to anyone
whom they or the governor wished.[3]   Several members of

[1] The W. and A. R. R. paid into the state treasury in 1859, $420,000; in
1860, $450,000. *Report of the Comptroller General*, 1865, p. 4.

[2] *Committee to investigate the W. and A. R. R.*, 1872, pp. 53, 152 *et seq.*

[3] *Joint committee of the legislature to investigate the fairness of the
W. and A. R. R. lease*, 1872, pp. 232, 235.

the legislature were given offices. McWhorter Hungerford, an ardent radical and Bullock supporter in the legislature, held a position as shipping clerk with a salary of $100 a month and expenses amounting to $100 a month more; and when Blodgett became superintendent, Hungerford was made business agent with a salary of $200 a month and expenses. When a witness before the friendly investigating committee of 1870, Hungerford said there were a good many carpet-baggers with places in the W. and A. R. R., though they were not fortunate enough to be passenger conductors. Those lucrative jobs in the days when many cash fares were paid on the train were mostly held, he said, by sons of members of the legislature.[1] In 1870, in the state senate, when a resolution was introduced that the superintendent of the state road should dismiss from employment all members of the legislature, Hungerford responded with a retaliatory proposal to dismiss all relatives of members.[2] Not only as an instrument of patronage did the road serve as a useful political adjunct. At election times it was a great convenience to the radicals as a means of carrying voters to strengthen points of weakness. Before the December election in 1870 a carload of negroes were brought from Chattanooga to vote in Atlanta. They held tickets instructing them to vote in Atlanta, which were recognized as passes by the conductor, according to instructions from headquarters.[3] At the same time one hundred negro laborers, employed on the Atlanta and Richmond Air Line, going back to Virginia for Christmas under contract with the company, received specially favorable transportation rates as a return compliment for their pause in Atlanta over election day. When A. L. Harris was candidate for alderman

[1] *Senate Journal*, 1870, vol. i, p. 890.

[2] *Ibid.*, pp. 131-2.

[3] *Committee to investigate the W. and A. R. R.*, 1872, p. 61.

in Atlanta, again a lot of negroes were brought in to vote. In 1870, according to the statement of a conductor on the road, about half of all the passengers traveled on free passes.[1]

With suspicions of mismanagement continuously in the air, several committees of the legislature, one after the other, investigated the management of the road. In February, 1869, a joint committee to examine the affairs of the road reported that wasteful management was due to an old evil— employing it for political purposes. At this time there was much talk of the state selling the property to remove a source of political corruption.[2] In 1870, when the Republicans had full control of both houses, a second investigating committee presented a whitewashing report.[3] The purpose of the investigation, as it worked out, was to show that the administration of Blodgett, covering the months of January to April, 1870, up to the time of the investigation, was no worse than the preceding administration. The committee did not ferret out any of the corruption then being talked about, but was content to report that it was gratified that no charges of corruption or mismanagement were sustained. The most serious findings of the report were that unduly large amounts were paid for lawyers' fees, not so large in 1870, however, as earlier; and that at one time there were too many hands employed in the car factory of the road, an abuse remedied as soon as it was called to the attention of Mr. Blodgett. The committee regretted that no money was being paid monthly into the state treasury, but felt satisfied that the earnings were being applied to

[1] *Committee to investigate the W. and A. R. R.,* pp. 61, 66-7.

[2] *Senate Journal,* 1869, pp. 468 *et seq.*

[3] *Senate Journal,* 1870, vol. i, pp. 920-930; testimony, pp. 819-920. Members of the 1870 committee were—Senate: W. Brock, J. M. Colman; House: A. H. Lee, R. M. Parks, E. Tweedy, J. A. Maxwell.

permanent improvement. The books show that the road
paid to a firm in Atlanta a bill of $1,650 for liquors, cigars,
etc., for the entertainment of the 1870 investigating committee.[1] Perhaps this offers some explanation for the rose-
ate hue in which affairs of the road appeared to the investigators. Furthermore, the chairman of the 1870 committee
was found later to be involved in fraudulent damage cases
against the W. and A. R. R., to which he lent his influence
in return for a share of the proceeds.[2]

The grossest corruption in the management of the road
took place in the latter part of 1870 under Blodgett as
superintendent. When it was apparent that the state was
going to lease its property, officials and employees tried to
get all they could out of the road into their pockets. Frauds
of all kinds, mostly in purchases and in claims and damage cases, were brought to light by the investigating committee, appointed by the Democratic legislature in December, 1871, after Bullock's flight.[3] Though this committee
was strongly partisan, the evidence it brought out of
wanton fraud was incontrovertible. The minority member
of the committee could not deny the evidence of fraud,
though he proved that Democrats, as well as Republicans,
enjoyed the spoils of corruption. Testimony before the
committee supported strong suspicion, if not absolute proof,
that money from the state road helped pay the expenses of
Governor Bullock and his friends in Washington in carrying out their campaign for prolonging Republican control
in Georgia. The worst graft was found in the department
of the purchasing agent, who was the son of the superin-

[1] *Joint Committee to investigate the W. and A. R. R.*, 1872, p. 187.

[2] *Ibid.*, p. 142 *et seq.*; also, *Milledgeville Federal Union*, July 12, 1871.

[3] The members of the joint committee to investigate the management
of the W. and A. R. R., 1872, were—Senate: Milton A. Candler, W. L.
Clark; House: Claiborne Sneed, R. W. Phillips, W. L. Goldsmith.

tendent. False accounts were made for goods never purchased, double prices were charged, the surplus divided between the firms making the sales and the agent for the road. One of the agents of the purchasing department, in collusion with an Atlanta merchant, acting under the name of a fictitious firm of New York, received several thousand dollars on fraudulent bills.[1] Business men of good standing in Atlanta and elsewhere were involved in these schemes of graft, not hesitating to secure patronage on the terms offered by employees of the road—fraudulent charges and a share of the rake-off, or expensive gifts to purchasing agents. Christmas presents were supplied liberally. A shotgun and a rifle, a silver tea-set, knives and forks were furnished to an agent, paid for by the road under charges for " assorted iron " and " block tin ".[2] There were frauds in pay rolls, frauds in damage and claim cases, in excessive lawyers' fees, and notorious graft in connection with the purchase of cross-ties and wood for fuel. As evidence of the harmonious business interests of H. I. Kimball and Governor Bullock, it appeared that the Cartersville and Van Wert R. R., one of the state-aid railroads in which Kimball was interested, was furnished with cross-ties and machinery, with several cars and one engine from the Western and Atlantic and with transportation of hands, without payment for such supplies and service.[3] Another of Kimball's enterprises, the so-called Tennessee Car Co., likewise defrauded the state road through contracts for cars, paid for to the amount of more than $30,000, but never delivered.[4]

[1] Testimony taken by the W. and A. Committee, 1872, p. 23.

[2] *Ibid.*, pp. 16, 19, 34, 42, 68.   [3] *Ibid.*, pp. 74-5.

[4] *Ibid.*, p. 111 *et seq.* Foster Blodgett and Varney Gaskill, indicted on charges of fraud in connection with the Western and Atlantic R. R., were pardoned by Gov. Conley.

W. and A. R. R., 1865–1870

	Gross earnings.	Expenses.	Expenditure for equipment and construction.	Excess of earnings over expenses.	Paid into state treasury.	Ratio of expenses to receipts.
Sept. 30, 1865–Sept. 30, 1866..........	$1,315,756.40	$854,379.23	$465,183.38	—	—	64.9 %
Sept. 30, 1866–Sept. 30, 1867..........	1,273,191.35	728,209.63	413,865.90	$544,981.72	—	57.1
Sept. 30, 1867–Sept. 30, 1868..........	943,607.24	677,493.45	20,251.73	266,113.79	$230,000	71.8
Sept. 30, 1868–Sept. 30, 1869..........	1,138,300.63	800,802.38	134,015.32	337,488.25	250,000	70.3
Sept. 30, 1869–Jan. 1, 1870 (3 mos.)....	378,245.04	318,751.06	53,848.86	59,493.98	—	84.2
Jan. 1, 1870–April 1, 1870 (3 mos.).....	437,902.05	389,188.33	79,030.36	48,713.72	45,000	88.8

Compiled from official reports of the W. and A. R. R., found in the journals of the Assembly and from reports of the legislative investigating committees of 1869 and 1870.

The mismanagement of this valuable property continued on an increasing scale during the reconstruction period, until in 1870 the state road seemed nothing more than a public grab-bag into which each one sufficiently favored politically might plunge a hand. Since the books of the road were so badly kept and no report was rendered, it is impossible to compute the amount of indebtedness which the political misuse of the Western and Atlantic by Bullock and Blodgett piled up for the state, between April and December, 1870.

In this condition of affairs strong public sentiment was aroused in favor of disposing of the state road either by sale or lease. A bill to lease it, introduced in the legislature by Dunlap Scott, one of the Democratic leaders, became law. Under the terms of the act, the governor was authorized to lease the property to a company, not to a connecting railroad, for a rental not less than $25,000 per month.   To guard against the danger of the road falling into the hands of outside speculators, the law required that a majority of the lessees should be bona-fide citizens and residents of Georgia of at least five years standing, and that lessees should give bond for at least $8,000,000, of which $5,000,-000 must be in Georgia, and should be worth in their own property, above all indebtedness, at least $500,000.[1]

The lease bill was primarily a Democratic measure, though it secured enough votes from the other side to carry it by a substantial majority, in the House, 90-31, and in the Senate, 25-7.[2] Well might the question be asked—How did it happen that the Republicans in the legislature, who partook so freely of the fruits of the state road, were willing to assent to such a self-denying ordinance as to yield

[1] Approved, October 24, 1870. *Acts of Assembly*, 1870, pp. 423-7.
[2] *House Journal*, 1870, pp. 1024-5; *Senate Journal*, 1870, vol. iii, p. 570.

the common source of profit to private lessees? On the face of it there must have been corruption somewhere to secure the passage of this law.[1] With such a legislature and state administration as that of 1870 the mere purpose of the public good was not enough to account for legislative action. In October, 1870, no bill could have passed without the assent of Governor Bullock and his friends, who controlled both houses of the legislature. Then why was Governor Bullock willing to let the state road go out of his hands to a private corporation? The possible answer may be two-fold. In the first place, it was evident, from the trend of politics in Georgia in the fall of 1870, that the Republicans could not hold on much longer, that the next election would remove Bullock's control in the legislature unless some prolongation legislation from Washington could be obtained, of which there was little hope at that moment; and secondly, a lease would not be a loss to the governor provided that it went to the " right " persons. About the time that the lease act was passed it became known that ex-Governor Brown was organizing a company to bid for the lease. Associated with him was H. I. Kimball. Perhaps in Kimball the " right " person was found.

The Democrats themselves were loath to leave the leasing of the road to the governor, but as Mr. Dunlap Scott explained, they could not hope to get enough votes from the Republicans to pass the bill if the governor were ignored.[2] At the time that the lease bill was before the Senate numerous attempts were made to amend the bill so as to provide against trickery in granting the lease. A resolution was in-

---

[1] A matter of some $50,000, said to have been expended by Kimball in connection with securing the lease, was never satisfactorily explained. See testimony of A. J. White, one of the lessees, *Joint Committee on Lease of the W. and A. R. R.*, 1872, p. 34 *et seq.*

[2] *Ibid.*, p. 119.

troduced to require the governor to place all bids and all information before the next session of the legislature; and another, to require the governor to accept the highest bid made by a company formed according to the terms of the law. But these amendments, as were all others, were tabled or defeated when put to vote.[1]

The most interesting and intricate part of the history of the state road lease arose in connection with the formation of the company of lessees and the controversy concerning the fairness in the award of the lease. On October 26, 1870, the governor advertised that bids would be received until December 25th, and on December 27th it became known that the company of which ex-Governor Brown was head had been awarded the lease at $25,000 per month rental. Before the lease act passed, the group in which Governor Brown was interested was the only one known to be possible bidders for the lease. When it was ascertained that John P. King, President of the Georgia R. R., was acting with Brown's company, the heads of the railroads radiating from Macon—the Central, the Macon and Western and the Southwestern—feared that the Western and Atlantic would be managed by such a company for the interests of the Georgia R. R. to the injury of other roads in the state. Whereupon, at a meeting of several representatives of the Macon roads it was determined that they should try to secure a half interest in Brown's company. With this purpose in view, a committee representing these roads sought an interview with Brown in Atlanta. When they saw it would be impossible for them to be admitted into the close corporation forming in Atlanta, they determined to form a company of their own to compete for the lease. From what they learned of the situation in Atlanta,

---

[1] *Senate Journal*, 1870, vol. iii, pp. 569, 571.

the Macon gentlemen concluded that business interests alone would not be sufficient to enable them to compete with the Atlanta company.[1]   Hence they, too, played politics. Their move at this point, one of remarkable shrewdness, finally brought them victory, and a half interest in the leasing corporation.   Influence in Atlanta being already engaged, the Macon company looked higher up, to the U. S. Senate and to the President's friends, in fact, and secured for their corporation Simon B. Cameron, John S. Delano, son of the Secretary of the Interior, and Thomas A. Scott, of the Pennsylvania R. R.   This combination did the work.   On the last day for the submission of bids, after hours of negotiation between the two parties, compromise and combination were achieved.   So the leasing corporation, as finally constituted, represented two somewhat hostile parties, the Brown party and the Macon, or Hill party.   The Macon party was made up of the railroad representatives already mentioned, the Washington group, and in addition B. H. Hill, W. C. Morrill,[2] a Republican politician and office-holder, and John T. Grant, a capitalist and railroad contractor.   In Brown's party the most prominent were Brown himself, H. I. Kimball and Kimball's father-in-law, Geo. Cook, and H. B. Plant, a friend of Bullock, with representatives of the Georgia R. R. and of the Nashville and Chattanooga R. R. and others.   Difficulty in the negotiations between the two

[1] Testimony of W. S. Holt before the W. and A. Lease Committee, 1872, p. 7 *et seq.* W. M. Wadley, President of the Central R. R., refused to have anything to do with the lease.

The account of the formation of the lease company is based on testimony given before this committee, especially from the evidence presented by W. B. Johnston, A. J. White, J. E. Brown, B. H. Hill, Wm. S. Holt.   Members of the committee to investigate the W. and A. lease—Senate: W. M. Reese, A. D. Nunnally; House: G. F. Pierce, Geo. M. Netherland, C. B. Hudson.

[2] Morrill, a Republican office-holder, was taken in because he secured the introduction of the Washington group.   Lease Committee, p. 137.

camps arose concerning the controlling interest in the board of directors. The final agreement called for twenty-three directors, each group to have eleven, with a twenty-third director in the person of W. B. Dinsmore, President of the Southern Express Company. Though it was never actually proved, it was currently believed that Director No. 23 was simply a cloak for Governor Bullock. Dinsmore himself was not present at the time of the negotiations and his name was not mentioned until the very end.

The twenty-three lessees, with the shares held at the time of the award of the lease and the personal wealth of each, were as follows: [1]

Jos. E. Brown, one and one-half shares, Atlanta, worth $100,000.

H. I. Kimball, one and one-half shares, Atlanta, worth $100,000.

Geo. Cook, one share, New Haven, Conn., worth $100,000.

H. B. Plant, one share, Augusta, worth $100,000, connected with the Southern Express Co.

John P. King, one share, Augusta, worth $250,000, President of the Ga. R. R. and of the A. and W. P. R. R.

Richd. Peters, one share, Atlanta, worth $100,000, Director of the Ga. R. R.

A. H. Stephens, one-half share, Crawfordsville, worth $10,000.

E. W. Cole, one share, Nashville, worth $40,000, representative of the Nashville and Chattanooga R. R.

Thos. Allen, one share, St. Louis, worth $500,000, representative of the St. Louis and Iron Mt. R. R.

Ezekiel Waitzfelder, one share, New York, worth $100,000.

Benj. May, one share, Columbus, worth $100,000.

W. B. Dinsmore, one share, New York, worth $500,000, President of the Southern Express Co.

[1] *Journal of the House of Representatives*, 1871, App. p. 24.

John S. Delano, one share, Mt. Vernon, O., worth $50,000.

Simon B. Cameron, one and one-half shares, Harrisburg, Pa., worth $500,000, U. S. Senator.

Wm. C. Morrill, one share, Macon, worth $8,000.

Thos. A. Scott, one share, Philadelphia, worth $500,000. Pennsylvania R. R.

Wm. T. Walters, one share, Baltimore, worth $500,000, Baltimore and Ohio R. R.

A. J. White, one-half share, Macon, worth $50,000, President of the Macon and Western R. R.

Wm. B. Johnston, one share, Macon, worth $100,000, Director of the Central R. R. and of the Mac. and Wes. R. R.

C. A. Nutting, one share, Macon, worth $100,000.

Wm. S. Holt, one share, Macon, worth $80,000, President of the Southwestern R. R.

B. H. Hill, one share, Athens, worth $100,000.

John T. Grant, one share, Walton County, worth $100,000.

It is a matter worthy of comment that the name of Alex. H. Stephens appears among the lessees. It seems that when it was known that ex-Governor Brown was forming a company to bid for the lease, Stephens wrote to Brown, saying that he would like to join such a company, willing to pledge himself to the amount of $10,000, his whole property above liability. Stephens thought the lease a good thing for the state, and regarded Governor Brown as an efficient manager of the railroad, as he had proved himself while governor. While Stephens and Brown differed politically, Mr. Stephens said that he never believed Brown to be a "rogue", but had confidence in his business honesty. The lease company was by no means loath to accept Stephens as one of their number in spite of his limited financial backing. No one stood higher in the minds of the people of Georgia for public-mindedness and scrupulous integrity than Alex. H. Stephens, who would lend moral support to any company of which he was a member. A few days after the lease was awarded to the Brown Company, Mr. Stephens, hearing more of the circumstances connected with the lease, wrote to Brown, withdrawing from the company of lessees.[1]

Meanwhile, a rival company, made up mostly of Atlanta merchants and bankers, made a bid for the lease, offering $35,000 per month rental, whereas the successful bidders offered but $25,000. This second group, the Seago-Blodgett Company, offered among its securities the Central R. R. and other railroad properties, which the officials of these roads declared were offered without their sanction. On the ground of unsatisfactory security, their bid was rejected by the governor in favor of the first company. Seago and his associates, in seeking political influence, added Mr. Blodgett to their number.[2] But Mr. Blodgett was of no weight at all when Kimball, Delano, Scott and Cameron were in the opposite balance. Just a few days before the lease was awarded, the state election had been held, resulting in defeat for Bullock's party. With some prolongation scheme still hoped for and the question of the admission of Georgia's senators unsettled, it would seem wise to Bullock to gain favor at court in every possible way. While Cameron, Scott and Delano were in Atlanta, much pressure was put upon them to use their influence in Washington to have the election in the fifth Georgia district set aside, so as to bring about some kind of reorganization.[3]

In 1872 all the circumstances attendant upon the leasing of the state road underwent careful review before an investigating committee of the legislature. The evidence before the committee revealed unmistakable crookedness in getting the lease bill through the legislature and in the

[1] Correspondence between Stephens and Brown in *Atlanta Constitution* and *Augusta Constitutionalist*, January, 1871.

[2] *W. and A. Lease Committee*, 1872, p. 216 *et seq.*

[3] *Ibid.*, p. 154.

formation of the Atlanta group of the lease company. Through all the conflicting and intricate mass of testimony it seems fairly conclusive that, whether or not Bullock held a share in the lease company, as was commonly believed, he and H. I. Kimball expected to control the company. Important light on the situation came from A. L. Harris, supervisor of the Western and Atlantic under Bullock.[1] He said that when he remonstrated with Bullock that it would be impolitic to allow the road to go out of his hands, the governor assured him that he and his friends would control it. Harris was first promised a share in the lease, and later, the position of superintendent. Up to January 10, 1871, when the lessees elected the officers of the company, both Bullock and Kimball assured Harris that he would be superintendent. Afterwards, according to Harris's account, Bullock said that the company had gone back on him—"had acted the hog". Their scheme, so Harris testified, was originally to "sweat" Governor Brown out of the presidency and to put Kimball in his place. But the plans of Bullock and Kimball, if such they were, went awry because of two unforeseen difficulties, the astuteness of Brown, accustomed to lead and to use others rather than to be used, and the strength of the Macon group supported by Washington influence. Events that followed substantiate Harris's statement of the case. When Kimball failed to secure control he sold his interest, part of which was attached for debt, as did also his father-in-law, Geo. Cook. Instead of Kimball "sweating out" Brown, that uncomfortable process seems to have been applied to Mr. Kimball himself.

The majority report of the joint committee to investigate the fairness of the Western and Atlantic lease, signed

---

[1] *Joint Committee to investigate the official conduct of Rufus B. Bullock*, 1872, pp. 68-70.

by four of the five members of the committee, declared that
Governor Bullock had acted unfairly in creating suspicion,
if not conviction, of his intention to grant the lease to certain bidders in any case; that the combination among bidders was unfair, thwarting competition; that the inference
was clear that the lease was unfairly procured; and that
H. I. Kimball had "manipulated" Governor Bullock in
procuring the lease. The committee concluded:

It is certainly established that Kimball had an absolute control
over Governor Bullock, in all matters of legislation and of
official patronage, from which money was to be made for himself, his relatives and friends. It is admitted that Kimball
secured for himself and his father-in-law, George Cook, two
and one-half shares in the lease company. It is certain that
no company which did not allow H. I. Kimball and his relatives an undue interest in it could have secured the lease. The
question arises, how did H. I. Kimball obtain such power
over Governor Bullock? This question is well answered by
E. L. Jones, cashier of the Georgia National Bank. This
witness says, "that Governor Bullock was constantly supplied
with money by H. I. Kimball; that they were mutually interested in all matters of business."

Hence, the decision of the majority was: "The present
lease of the Western and Atlantic R. R., obtained from
Rufus B. Bullock, Governor of the State of Georgia, on
the 27th day of December, 1870, was unfairly obtained." [1]
The minority member of the committee, A. D. Nunnally,
of the Senate, reported no unfairness in the award of the
lease, since the other competitors did not fully comply with
the terms of the lease act. On the main question at issue,
whether or not the legislature should sustain the lease as
granted by Governor Bullock, to a company offering but
$25,000 per month, when another bid for $35,000 was

[1] *Journal of the House*, 1871, App.

made, the Democratic legislature rejected the recommendation of the majority and voted to uphold the lease.[1]

There was widespread feeling in Georgia that the lease had been obtained unfairly. The *Atlanta Constitution* in January had bitter editorials concerning the transaction, pouring its venom especially upon Jos. E. Brown and Benj. H. Hill. The position of Mr. Hill was particularly open to attack. In 1867 and 1868 he was one of the most vigorous defenders of Georgia against reconstruction, and his "Notes on the Situation" in 1867, written primarily to oppose Governor Brown and the submissionists, was taken as the creed of those who would stand firm for resistance or masterly inactivity to the bitter end. In December, 1870, just when the lease company was in process of formation, a public letter from Mr. Hill came like a clap of thunder upon his friends in the state.[2] He, too, counseled submission and acceptance of reconstruction as the best policy. As the *Atlanta Constitution* said: "Joe Brown and Ben Hill, cheek by jowl, politically, is a merry piece of humor".[3] An apt quotation was cited by those who relied upon a sense of humor to relieve their chagrin: "Joseph is not, and now they take my son Benjamin".[4]

In general, however, the mismanagement of the road had aroused such disgust that most people in Georgia were glad to have it removed from the immediate sphere of politics, and to know that $25,000 would pour into the state treasury every month instead of many times that amount flowing out.

[1] *Journal of the Senate*, 1872, pp. 296-7; *Journal of the House*, 1872, p. 369.

[2] Letter of December 8, 1870 in *Augusta Constitutionalist*, December 14, 1870.

[3] January 11, 1871.

[4] A. R. Wright, testimony before the Ku Klux Committee of Congress, *Ku Klux Committee*, vol. vi, p. 144.

CHAPTER X

REORGANIZED RECONSTRUCTION AND THE RESTORATION OF HOME RULE

GEORGIA was one of the six states included in the Omnibus bill of Congress of June 25, 1868, to be admitted to representation when the Fourteenth Amendment should be ratified by the legislature. A further condition was made in the case of Georgia, requiring the annulment of the relief clause of her state constitution, the clause on which the Radicals had relied to carry the state for ratification.[1] On July 21st the legislature ratified the Fourteenth Amendment,[2] and annulled the relief clause of the constitution, limiting jurisdiction over debts incurred before June 1, 1865.[3] During the second session of the 40th Congress, Georgia's seven representatives were admitted to the House. Joshua Hill and H. V. M. Miller, the senators chosen in July, did not arrive in Washington until after the end of the session, and so the question of their admission did not arise until the beginning of the third session on December 7th, when Joshua Hill presented his credentials.

But between June and December, important things happened in Georgia. As we have seen, anti-Bullock men, controlling both houses of the legislature, refused Bullock's demand to declare members ineligible. The legislature rejected Bullock's favorites for the U. S. Senate, and ex-

[1] U. S. Statutes at Large, vol. xv, 40 C., 2 S., Public Laws, pp. 73-4. See *supra*, p. 195.

[2] *Senate Journal*, 1868, p. 46; *House Journal*, 1868, pp. 49-51.

[3] *Senate Journal*, 1868, p. 46; *House Journal*, 1868, p. 52.

pelled negro members from both houses. But most serious of all, Democratic electors were chosen in the presidential election in November. These circumstances, together with Ku Klux outrages, real and fictitious, were made much of by Governor Bullock in convincing his friends in Washington that the state which he had administered for six months as governor was not a state, but still a military district, " with no adequate protection for life and property ". In his communications to Congress and to the General Assembly he called himself Provisional Governor, the title used before the removal of General Meade's command in July, 1868.[1]

In the House of Representatives the case of Georgia was referred to the Committee on Reconstruction, which took testimony during January, 1869, concerning the condition of affairs in the state.[2] Governor Bullock, the most important witness demanding further action by Congress, declared that the Reconstruction Acts had not been fulfilled in Georgia; that the legislature was not duly constituted, since members had not taken the test oath required by the Reconstruction Acts, but only the oath of the state constitution. Thus, he claimed, about forty members of the House and fifteen or eighteen in the Senate held seats unconstitutionally. Further, negro members had been expelled illegally from both houses. The plan of action which he recommended was that the commanding general should reassemble the legislature as elected in April, 1868, require the test oath of all members, and thus reinstate colored members and eliminate those ineligible under the Reconstruction Acts.[3]

[1] Gov. Bullock's Address to Congress, Dec. 7, 1868. *House Journal,* Georgia Assembly, 1869, pp. 5-7.

[2] *Congressional Globe,* 40 C., 3 S., p. 10; *House Mis. Doc.,* 40 C., 3 S., no. 52, " Condition of Affairs in Georgia."

[3] *Ibid.,* pp. 2-5.

Other witnesses appeared before the committee to prove that conditions in Georgia demanded Congressional interference. Two of the expelled members of the legislature, Jas. M. Sims, a Baptist preacher of Savannah, and H. M. Turner, a missionary of the African M. E. Church in Macon, told of the hardships suffered by negroes in being denied the right to vote, in being discharged from work for their political affiliations, and of severe outrages perpetrated upon them.[1] A. T. Akerman, a prominent Republican member of the Convention of 1868 and later Attorney-General in Grant's cabinet, was not quite so satisfactory a witness for the reorganization party as Bullock might have wished. He testified that there was much lawlessness about the time of the presidential election, and in some places negroes were kept from voting by white men, who closed in around the polls and crowded them out; but after the election in November conditions materially improved, disorder subsided, people were becoming reconciled to negro suffrage, and many who considered the reconstruction government unsettled until the presidential election afterward regarded it as permanent. One of the best indications of increasing confidence in the established order, he thought, was the decided rise in real estate values.[2] Another witness, I. Seeley, brought quotations from the report of General Lewis of the Freedmen's Bureau in Georgia to prove lawlessness and harsh treatment of the blacks. Between January and November, 1868, 260 cases of outrages against freedmen were reported, averaging 17 a month under military rule and 46 a month after the restoration of civil authority [3]—rather a sorry commentary, after all, on the efficiency of the state administration, though Bullock did not see it in that light.

---

[1] *Congressional Globe,* 40 C., 3 S., pp. 7-9, 11.

[2] *Ibid.,* pp. 12-22.   [3] *Ibid.,* p. 41.

To combat the testimony given by Bullock's witnesses, Nelson Tift, of Albany, Ga., a Democratic congressman admitted at the previous session, introduced evidence obtained from one hundred or more civil officers, judges, mayors of cities, ordinaries, assessors of revenue and others. His questionnaire touched on the following points: impartiality in the enforcement of laws, organized or unorganized resistance to law, faithfulness of officers, attitude of whites toward blacks, toward Northerners and Republicans in general, desire of the people for peace and restoration, and justification for the re-establishment of military government. On all these points there was general agreement in the letters introduced by Mr. Tift as to favorable conditions in Georgia, not warranting further interference by Congress.

Ex-Governor Brown, though still a Republican, at this point in reconstruction departed from Bullock and the strong reconstruction party. In his letter in reply to Mr. Tift's questions, he stated that in some parts of the state lawlessness went unpunished, and at election time excitement ran high, negroes and white Republicans generally being the sufferers. But after the November election a marked change took place, excitement cooled and better order prevailed. The native white Republicans of Georgia, esitmated at about 25,000, were strongly opposed to any further reconstruction by Congress. Other letters expressed the opinion that Brown only hinted at, that the cry for more reconstruction was set up only from a fraction and a faction of the Republicans for personal interest. Judge Hiram Warner of the Georgia Supreme Court wrote that the main object of Bullock in urging General Meade to purge the legislature was to secure the election of his favorites to the U. S. Senate, and that the Democratic victory of 1868 showed ill feeling not to Grant but to the " Atlanta Ring ". The same testimony was given by one of the reve-

nue assessors, Mr. Bowles, who wrote: " I cannot see any
good reason why the government of Georgia should be destroyed, unless Congress does it to gratify a few disappointed politicians, and fulfil the prophecies of the most
bitter and persistent enemies of reconstruction ".[1]

During the third session of the Fortieth Congress no
action was taken by either house to straighten out the
Georgia tangle.   The Senate, in refusing to admit Joshua
Hill, pronounced against the restoration of Georgia.   When
it came to counting the electoral vote in February, 1869, the
two houses took a somewhat equivocal stand, by announcing
the result with and without Georgia's vote.   This showed
plainly that Congress was not ready to decide definitely
what was to be done with the troublesome state which had
managed to secure moderate instead of radical control in its
assembly, dared to expel negroes from its legislature, and
was so uncircumspect as to elect a Democratic electoral
ticket.   In the Senate, both Sumner and Edmunds introduced bills looking to the further reconstruction of Georgia;
and in the House, the matter was referred to the Committee on Reconstruction, of which B. F. Butler had become
chairman after the death of Thaddeus Stevens.[2]

In March, 1869, when the Forty-first Congress assembled,
the House was able to rid itself of the Georgia members by
the happy accident of a technical flaw in their credentials,
which failed to state to which Congress they were accredited.[3]   Not until the second session, however, did Congress
agree upon its treatment of Georgia.   New ammunition
came to the hands of the party desiring further reconstruction in the report of General Terry, who was assigned to

[1] *Congressional Globe,* 40 C., 3 S., pp. 141-55.

[2] *Ibid.,* 40 C., 3 S., pp. 10, 27, 144.

[3] *Ibid.,* 41 C., 1 S., pp. 16-18; 41 C., 2 S., pp. 853-4.

duty in Georgia, and new purpose impelled them in their need for votes for the Fifteenth Amendment.[1] Hence the Georgia Bill was passed, December 22, 1869, remanding the state to military jurisdiction under the Acts of 1867, and requiring the adoption of the Fifteenth Amendment as a further condition of admission.[2] For the third time military government was enforced—in 1865, from April to June; in 1867, when the civil reconstitution of 1865-6 was repudiated; and again in 1869 when the status of 1867 was resumed.

In the meantime, in Georgia during the year 1869 several things happened which played into the hands of those who were looking for excuses for Congressional interference. First of all, the legislature rejected the Fifteenth Amendment. On March 9th, " Provisional Governor " Bullock submitted the amendment, together with a message construing the amendment to include all political privileges, the right to hold office as well as to vote.[3] On March 11th, by a vote of 68-60, the lower house passed a resolution to ratify the amendment, with a proviso rejecting the construction placed upon it by the governor; and on March 16th, the motion to ratify unconditionally was passed, 64-53.[4] In the Senate, however, the amendment was finally rejected, 13-16.[5] The defeat of the amendment was by no means chargeable to the Conservatives, who were divided on the question. Some still held out against agreeing in any way whatsoever with the work of Congress, while

---

[1] Report of General Terry, October 31, 1869, in *Report of Secretary of War*, 1869-70, vol. i, pp. 83-95.

[2] U. S. Statutes at Large, 41 C., 2 S., vol. xvi, Public Laws, pp. 59-60.

[3] *House Journal*, 1869, pp. 575-80.

[4] *Ibid.*, pp. 601-2, 665-6.

[5] *Senate Journal*, 1869, p. 806.

others considered it good policy to accept the amendment, which simply fastened on the rest of the country what Georgia could not shake off. Evidence seems to uphold the charge made at the time that the defeat of the amendment was a political trick of the Bullock men. Be it remembered that in 1869 Bullock was trying in every possible way to secure the re-establishment of military government in order to overthrow the legislature which he could not control. If the amendment were adopted, Congress would be likely to maintain the status quo in Georgia. Hence it was to the interest of the " Provisional Governor " and his friends to reject the amendment. In the Senate the opposing influence of Bullock was patent. After the resolution for ratification was first agreed to by a vote of 21-16, on reconsideration a motion for indefinite postponement prevailed by the deciding vote of the chair, Benj. Conley, a strong Bullock ally. On this vote and on the final vote on March 18th, it was noticeable that the firmest friends and most diligent supporters of the governor failed to vote. Out of 44 members of the Senate, only 29 voted on the final resolution, 13 in favor.[1] It is noteworthy, likewise, that the House, where Conservatives were stronger, ratified the amendment, while the Senate rejected it. A Democratic newspaper contributed the following:[2]

[1] Vote on the Fifteenth Amendment—*House Journal*, 1869, pp. 601-2, 610, 618, 665-6; *Senate Journal*, pp. 688, 794, 806. Avery, *History of the State of Georgia*, p. 411, explains the vote as follows: House—first vote on amendment, 24 Republicans in favor, 4 opposed, 24 dodged. After the resolution to ratify was carried, on a vote to reconsider, one of the dodgers voted for reconsideration. Senate—on the vote for indefinite postponement, 13 Republicans in favor, 6 opposed. On final vote, 8 Republicans for amendment, 8 opposed, 8 dodged.

[2] *Macon Telegraph*, March 23, 1869.

Who killed the Fifteenth Amendment?

I, says Mr. President Conley
I, and I only
I, in the Senate
Killed it in a minute
With my little vote
I gave it a death stroke;
I killed the Fifteenth Amendment.

The question of negro eligibility to office still hung fire in 1869. Some of the Conservatives, who gleefully voted to expel the negro members from the legislature, became uneasy when they saw the effect of their action on public opinion in the North, and were willing to leave the matter to the state supreme court for decision. Such was the advice of Congressman Nelson Tift after a conversation with General Grant.[1] A resolution to that effect passed both houses of the legislature in February, only to be vetoed by the governor.[2]

Acting under the bill for the reorganization of Georgia, Bullock issued a call for the meeting of the legislature on January 10, 1870, to all members declared elected in 1868, including, of course, the negroes who had been expelled. On this occasion the question of eligibility of members was not entrusted to the two houses, but was taken in hand by Governor Bullock and General Terry, in command of the Department of Georgia under the Reorganization Act. Organization was directed by appointees of the governor, J. G. W. Mills in the Senate and A. L. Harris in the House. The test of eligibility applied was the oath of the Reconstruction Acts, not the Fourteenth Amendment. In order

[1] *Macon Telegraph*, January 19, 1869. Telegram from Tift to Gen. J. B. Gordon, E. G. Cabaniss, and J. I. Whitaker.

[2] *Senate Journal*, 1869, p. 263; *House Journal*, pp. 228 *et seq.*

to establish official interpretation of the terms of the oath, " civil office " and " aid and comfort to enemies ", Bullock called for an opinion from the attorney-general of the state, H. P. Farrow. Farrow's interpretation was the broadest possible, including notaries public, commissioners, state librarians, among " civil officers " in the meaning of the law.[1] This wide construction of the term, by which several members displeasing to Bullock could be excluded, was followed by the attorney-general and incidentally by the Republican Executive Committee as well, in working up evidence against suspected ineligibles.[2] On the other hand, Chief Justice Brown, at this period parting from his former radical allies, being called upon by a group of Conservatives from the legislature to construe the meaning of eligibility, gave an opinion directly contrary to that of Farrow.[3]

By General Terry's command, a military board, consisting of General T. H. Ruger, General T. J. Haines, and Major Henry Goodfellow, was ordered to investigate the eligibility of certain members—W. T. Winn, J. J. Collier, A. W. Holcombe, W. J. Anderson, B. B. Hinton, C. J. Wellborn, and others.[4] In its rulings the military board did not go as far as Bullock's friends wished, for it considered some offices, such as marshal of a town, notary public, and state librarian, not to be offices within the meaning of the law. Of those investigated under evidence presented by the attorney-general, four were declared by the military board to be ineligible, W. T. Winn in the Senate, R. A. Donaldson, E. M.

[1] *House Journal*, 1870, pp. 10-16.

[2] *Atlanta Constitution*, January 9, 1870; Avery, *op. cit.*, pp. 424-6.

[3] *Atlanta Constitution*, January 19, 1870.

[4] General Orders, no. 3, *House Exec. Doc.*, 41 C., 2 S., no. 288.

Taliaferro, and J. H. Nunn in the House.[1] In addition, sixteen other members, who filed petitions to be relieved from disability, were on the face of their own petitions declared by General Terry to be ineligible.[2] Two others failed to take the oath.[3]

In this instance the Republicans adopted the method which the Conservatives used to fill the seats of expelled negroes, seating the candidates having the next highest vote in the election of 1868. Thus, one Republican replaced a Conservative in the Senate, and twenty-one new Republicans took their places in the House. In addition, the negroes who were expelled in 1868 were restored to their seats. By this transformation, commonly known as Terry's Purge, strong Republican majorities were established in both houses, and now at last it would seem that the Bullock party could proceed without impediment.[4]

After the cases of eligibility were decided, permanent organization was effected in the two houses. Conley was again elected President of the Senate. In the House the contest over the speakership revealed the strength of the two parties. R. L. McWhorter, Speaker during the first session, was the choice of the Bullock men, while Conservatives united with moderate and anti-Bullock Republicans

---

[1] Report of the Military Investigating Board, January 22 and 23, 1870, *House Exec. Doc., op. cit.*, pp. 166-8.

[2] Burtz, Brinson, Bennett, George, Goff, Hudson, D. Johnson, Kellogg, Meadows, Penland, Surrency, J. R. Smith, H. Williams, Drake, J. T. Ellis, Rouse. *House Journal*, 1870, pp. 30-4.

[3] Crawford and McCulloch.

[4] Woolley, *Reconstruction of Georgia*, p. 94, gives a table to show the political composition of the legislature after the reorganization in 1870—House, 87 Rep.   Senate, 27 Rep.
           83 Consv.   17 Consv.
This does not take account of the Independent Republicans, who voted variably.

on J. E. Bryant. Bryant and J. H. Caldwell, who were staunch supporters of Bullock in the legislature in 1868, were now leaders of the disaffected Republicans and fought vigorously against Bullock both in Washington and Atlanta.[1] The Bullock forces won, electing McWhorter with 76 votes to Bryant's 52.[2]

The following letters, written by Robert Toombs to his close friend, Alex. H. Stephens, give an interesting sidelight on the political tangle in Atlanta as it appeared in this period of reorganization:[3]

WASHINGTON, GEO., Jan. 24, 1870.

. . . I went to Atlanta to see if I could be of any service in the present *coup d'état* of Bullock and his conspirators. It is a hard job. He is perfectly reckless, fully supported by the military, stakes all upon success, and offers all the offices, places, money, and the plunder of the people for help to aid him to obtain the dictatorship of the state. It has not been without its effect upon some of the so-called Democrats. Many outsiders bite at the bait, and some representatives, but our true men have banded together with a good deal of firmness, hold the weak and timid and overawe and intimidate some of the villains on their own side. They have also good prospects of strong defection among the enemy if they will "stick". Nearly all of the "ins" are against Bullock and his own, and [a] pretty good lot of those that could not get "in" when they wanted to. Bryant is the candidate of the Democrats

[1] See pamphlets presenting Bryant's case against Bullock—*Reply to Article in the Washington Chronicle; Bryant before the Judiciary Committee; Letter from Bryant to Sumner.* Bryant maintained that Bullock's purpose in reorganizing the legislature was to elect Blodgett to the U. S. Senate, to cover up his financial operations, and to carry certain railroad schemes.

[2] *Journal of the House*, 1870, pp. 33-4.

[3] *Annual Report of the American Historical Association*, 1911, vol. ii, pp. 707, 708.

for speaker of the House, and I and Joe Brown are trying to elect him! Rather a strange conjunction, is it not? But you know my rule is to use the devil if I can do better to save the country. Upon the whole the prospect was pretty good when I left there.

WASHINGTON, GEO., Feb. 8, 1870.

. . . P. S. I forgot to tell you about my political adventures in Atlanta. I got into consultations with Brown, Bryant, Caldwell, *et id omne genus.* Politics does make us acquainted with strange bedfellows. Brown seems really in earnest in his endeavor to defeat Bullock and his schemes. I don't [know] whether or not he sees where his present course will land him, but I suppose he does. There were many curious developments which I don't care to put on paper but will tell you all about when we meet. We thought we had the crowd pretty dead two or three times, but the spirit of evil at Washington was too strong for us and poor Grant could not " stick ".

In February the purged legislature promptly ratified the Fifteenth Amendment, and the Fourteenth as well, although the Fourteenth Amendment had already been proclaimed law with Georgia as one of the ratifying states.[1] Continuing on the basis that the legislature of 1868 was illegal, the reorganized body on February 16th proceeded to the election of U. S. Senators. Conservatives, with few exceptions, refused to vote. Now Bullock's friends had their own way and one, at least, of the main purposes for which reorganization was effected could be achieved. Ex-Governor Brown, who was the favorite of the Bullock party in 1868, now on the supreme bench, was out of the race, especially since his departure from the Radicals on the subject of further reconstruction. Foster Blodgett was

[1] *Acts of the General Assembly,* 1870, pp. 492-493.

elected for the term ending in 1877, H. P. Farrow for the 1873 term, and R. H. Whiteley for the short term, 1871.[1] Farrow and Whiteley were chosen for the terms of Joshua Hill and Dr. Miller, who had not been admitted to the Senate. By law the election for the 1877 term should not have been held until the session of the legislature in January, 1871, but the Radicals thought it wise to take all they could get while they had their innings.

The form of the provisional and military government was upheld by the legislature, which transacted no general business after ratifying the amendment and electing senators. It adjourned from February until April, awaiting the action of Congress. After a brief session of two weeks, it again adjourned, since Congress still had not dealt with Georgia, leaving government practically in the hands of General Terry and the provisional governor. The activity of General Terry in Georgia called forth resolutions of protest in Congress. The House of Representatives in January, 1870, requested from the General of the Army information as to the authority of army officers acting as an eligibility committee of the legislature, and the Judiciary Committee of the Senate declared that the Act of December 22d had been misconstrued.[2]

The second scheme of the reconstructionists, fathered by Governor Bullock and sponsored in Congress by B. F. Butler, was to prolong the power of the Radicals in Georgia by postponing the election of a new assembly, due by law in December, 1870. The wheels of the scandal mill continued to grind, not slowly, like the mills of the gods, but with all speed, and members of Congress were plied with accounts of dreadful happenings in Georgia. While the

[1] *House Journal*, 1870, pp. 95-7.

[2] *Congressional Globe*, 41 C., 2 S., pp. 575, 1029, 1128, 1624; *Senate Reports*, 41 C., 2 S., no. 58.

prolongation scheme was hanging fire in Congress, this item appeared on the editorial page of the *Atlanta Constitution:* [1]

Wanted—Ku Klux Outrages.

Wanted, a liberal supply of Ku Klux outrages in Georgia. They must be as ferocious and blood-thirsty as possible. No regard need be paid to the truth. Parties furnishing must be precise and circumstantial. They must be supplied during the next ten days, to influence the Georgia Bill in the House. Accounts of Democrats giving the devil to Republicans are preferred. A hash of negroes murdered by the Ku Klux will be acceptable. A deuce of bobbery is necessary. Raw head and bloody bones, in every style can be served up to profit.

The highest price paid. Apply to R. B. Bullock, or the Slander Mill, Atlanta, Ga., and to Forney's *Chronicle*, Benjamin F. Butler, or to the Reconstruction Committee, Washington, D. C.

Georgia Railroad Bonds traded for this commodity.

There was a feeling in Congress that Georgia had been tinkered with long enough. So in July, 1870, a bill finally restoring Georgia to representation was agreed upon. In this case the conservative Republicans in both houses, by voting for the Bingham amendment to the Georgia bill, carried the day against B. F. Butler. The Act of July 15, 1870, contained this section:

It is hereby declared that the State of Georgia is entitled to representation in the Congress of the United States. But nothing in the Act contained shall be construed to deprive the people of Georgia of the right to an election for members of the General Assembly of said state, as provided for in the constitution thereof.[2]

---

[1] April 23, 1870.

[2] *U. S. Statutes at Large*, 41 C., 2 S., vol. xvi, Public Laws, pp. 363-4.

The Radicals in the Georgia legislature took up the work of Butler and tried to prolong their own term by declaring no election until after representatives should be seated in Congress. Again prolongation failed, for the resolution lacked a majority in the lower house.[1]

At the third session of the Forty-first Congress, Georgia members, chosen in the state election in December, 1870, were admitted to the House of Representatives.[2]

In the Senate the question was, who were the properly accredited senators from Georgia—H. P. Farrow and R. H. Whiteley, elected by the reorganized legislature in 1870, or Joshua Hill and H. V. M. Miller, chosen by the first session of the reconstruction legislature before the negro members were expelled. The Judiciary Committee of the Senate recommended the admission of Hill, reporting that Miller was unable to swear to the Test Oath of 1862. By special resolution, Congress suspended the test oath for Miller, and in February, 1871, he and Hill took their seats, the first senators from Georgia to take their places after the withdrawal of Toombs and Iverson in 1861.[3]

Thus, it took Georgia six years, from May, 1865, to February, 1871, to re-establish normal relations with the Federal government. In May, 1865, President Johnson reorganized the state government by means of military power, and a new administration was established on the basis of the old electorate, excluding certain classes. The newly-organized legislature ratified the Thirteenth Amendment, abolished slavery, and insured the election of representatives to Congress and senators. Congress refused to admit Georgia's members and senators, and in March, 1867, remanded the

---

[1] *Senate Journal*, 1870, vol. ii, pp. 29, 50; *House Journal*, pp. 342-3.

[2] *Congressional Globe*, 41 C., 3 S., pp. 527, 530, 678, 703-7, 1086.

[3] *Ibid.*, 41 C., 3 S., pp. 663, 816-30, 848-51, 871, 1163-84, 1632; *Senate Reports*, 41 C., 3 S., no. 308.

state to the condition of military province. Again a state government was organized, this time on the basis of a new electorate, including negroes and excluding large classes of whites. Under this second government the Fourteenth Amendment, securing civil rights to negroes, was ratified. Representatives to the lower house of Congress were admitted, but senators were not seated. In this condition of suspended reconstruction, with one foot in and one foot out of Congress, Georgia remained until December, 1869. Then the state government was remodeled, again by military authority. Ratification of the Fifteenth Amendment, securing the right of suffrage to negroes, was exacted. And at last, by February, 1871, when representatives and senators were seated in both houses of Congress, the troublesome question, whether Georgia was a state or not a state, was finally settled and normal relations with the other states of the Union were resumed.

With the failure of prolongation schemes in Congress and in the state legislature, the Bullock administration had to face a popular election. It was a foregone conclusion that defeat was theirs. The term of the governor and half of the members of the Senate and of the House lasted until January, 1873, but the other half of the legislature, with the members of Congress, were subject to election in December, 1870. The result was as expected—a big Democratic majority in both houses and four out of seven members of Congress Democrats. The change in political complexion (racial, as well, in many cases) was marked in some counties. In Chatham, Richmond and Burke, three Democratic members took the place in the House of the three Radicals in each county elected in 1868. Columbia, Hancock, Jefferson, Muscogee, Newton, Oglethorpe, Pulaski, Talbot, Warren, Wilkes, each having two members in the lower house, substituted Democrats for Republicans. And the same replacing of Republicans by Democrats occurred in other counties having one representative each—in Banks, Bryan, Campbell, Henry, Laurens, Lincoln, Pierce. With very few exceptions counties which sent Conservative representatives in 1868 retained them. Five counties in which members were subject to election again returned a full Republican delegation—Bibb, Clarke, Morgan, Thomas, Decatur.[1] Of 86 members elected to the House, 71 were Democrats. In the Senate, 19 out of 22 elected were Democrats.

The legal date for the meeting of the new legislature was November 1, 1871. With full Democratic control in both houses, Governor Bullock foresaw clearly that impeachment awaited him. Accordingly, on October 23d, he filed with the secretary of the executive department his resignation, to take effect on October 30th, two days before the meeting of the legislature. The resignation was kept secret until the 30th, when B. F. Conley, President of the Senate, was sworn in as governor. It was then discovered that Governor Bullock had left the state some days before, not to return. This was a clever trick on Bullock's part, a last attempt to prolong Republican control in a state which clearly declared itself Democratic. By law, in case of the death or resignation of the governor, the office was filled by the President of the Senate, in this case, Bullock's Radical ally, B. F. Conley. As soon as the legislature came together, organizing with L. N. Trammell, Democrat, as President of the Senate, and James M. Smith, Democrat, as Speaker of the House, the question arose as to who should act as governor—Conley, President of the previous Senate and no longer member of the legislature, or Trammell, President of the Senate at the time. Conley held on, but was unable

[1] *Milledgeville Federal Union,* January 3, 1871, gives the party affiliations of newly elected members of the legislature.

to enforce his claim to office for the full unexpired term of Bullock. The legislature passed over Conley's veto a law requiring an election for governor to be held on the third Tuesday of December.[1] At a convention held by the Democrats prior to the election, James M. Smith, Speaker of the House, was nominated for governor. His closest rivals for the nomination were General W. T. Wofford, Unionist, prominent in the Johnson period of reconstruction and Conservative in the later time, and Herbert Fielder, a Democrat of long standing. Alfred H. Colquitt and Ambrose Wright of Augusta were also prominently mentioned for the nomination. James M. Smith, a lawyer of Columbus, had opposed secession but had gone with the state and served as an officer in the Confederate Army. He was a self-made man, representing no power of birth or wealth, one of the plain people.[2]

The Republicans were in a dilemma as to the best policy to pursue. Some of the leaders, mostly anti-Bullock men, held a caucus in Atlanta and decided to put a candidate in the field. Their choice, James Atkins, member of the legislature of 1868, declined the nomination. Thus the election fell to Smith without opposition.

With the inauguration of Governor Smith on January 12, 1872, the Democrats were in full control of both the legislative and executive departments of the government, and rule by the conservative whites was fully restored.

The first work of the Democratic government was to investigate the condition of affairs left by Bullock and to undo the work of the Republican government as far as possible. In accordance with a resolution passed December 1, 1871, several investigating committees were ap-

---

[1] *Acts of the General Assembly*, 1871, pp. 27-8.

[2] *Milledgeville Federal Union*, December 13, 1871; Avery, *History of the State of Georgia*, p. 466.

pointed, the chief one being instructed " to investigate the official conduct of Rufus B. Bullock." This committee, of which J. C. Nicholls of the Senate acted as chairman, examined many witnesses, whose testimony, published with the report of the committee, covers one hundred and sixty-one pages. The committee found Bullock guilty of corruption in connection with the purchase and equipment of the state capitol; it condemned the settlement of the claims of the Mitchell heirs against the state; it charged Bullock with wanton extravagance in publishing executive orders and proclamations in forty-two papers, paying $140,397 for printing in addition to the large sum that went to the state printer; it saw in the payment of excessive lawyers' fees an attempt by Bullock to subsidize the bar as well as the press; corruption was found in the use of the executive power of pardon, with some of the governor's political household engaging in pardon brokerage; the state penitentiary was plundered, with no intervention by Bullock when his attention was called to it; and convicts were leased at about one-fifth of the price offered by responsible bidders; in the matter of state aid to railroads, gross corruption was found in the payment to roads of subsidies contrary to the terms of the law, especially to those in which H. I. Kimball was interested; in connection with the " promotion of reconstruction " in 1870, Bullock was declared to be guilty of dishonest and illegal practices. In his whole administration the committee found that he was guilty of general extravagance in every department of his management.[1]

The presiding genius of the investigating committee was Robert Toombs, who gave his services free of charge as prosecuting attorney against Bullock. The report itself

[1] *Report of the Bullock Investigating Committee*, pp. 1-45.

shows the unmistakable imprint of Toomb's racy style. The committee was thoroughly partisan, but the Republicans themselves could make but small defense against the charges. In October, 1872, Bullock attempted to defend himself in an Address to the People of Georgia, " a review of the revolutionary proceedings of the late repudiating legislature—the slander and misrepresentation of the committee exposed—a Republican administration contrasted with the corrupt and reckless action of the present usurping minority, under the lead of General Toombs." A careful reading of Bullock's defense fails to bring conviction that he disproved a single charge of the investigating committee. The best that he could do to justify his administration was to insist that it was not so bad after all—six hundred miles of railroad had been constructed, property had increased in value by $50,000,000, and the rate of taxation had not increased.

Early in the process of investigating Bullock's career the committee found corruption in connection with the Opera House purchase, and a warrant was issued for Bullock's arrest for "larceny after a trust delegated".[1] The ex-governor remained beyond the reach of the arm of the law for several years, and not until 1876 was the arrest made. The case against him was then tried in Georgia, but at that late day proof to convict him of connection with criminal frauds against the state was insufficient, and acquittal resulted.[2]

By December, 1872, much had been accomplished toward the undoing of the political reconstruction of 1867-8. A Democratic governor and Democratic legislature controlled the government of the state. The Republican reconstruction

---

[1] *Report of the Bullock Investigating Committee*, p. 45.

[2] Avery, *op. cit.*, p. 462.

governor was a fugitive from justice, under indictment for fraud against the state. A large part of the debt which the reconstruction government had piled up against the state was repudiated. Negroes were no longer a significant element in the body politic. When their leaders were unhorsed, negro voters were timid and uncertain, quite willing to avoid difficulty by shunning the polls. Negro suffrage was not limited by statute, except by the law requiring the payment of a poll tax before registration. This requirement, withdrawn by the Republican legislature in 1870 in the negro's favor, was restored to work against him in 1871.[1] By intimidation and a thousand and one kinds of indirect influence, the negro was made to feel that his sphere was the field, not politics, and that polling places were not healthy resorts for black men.

By the close of 1872, with the negro no longer an important political factor and Republican control in the state broken, the two main achievements of congressional reconstruction were overthrown.

[1] *Acts of the General Assembly*, 1870, pp. 431-2; 1871, p. 74.

PART III

ECONOMIC PROGRESS AND SOCIAL CHANGES

CHAPTER XI

AGRICULTURE, 1867-1872

THE year 1867 saw no revolution in the agricultural system of Georgia at all commensurate with the upheaval in politics brought on by military reconstruction. On the whole, it is surprising that the political changes in these years were wrought without more serious damage to economic prosperity. The real cataclysm in agriculture came when the slave laborer first became free. The disturbance occasioned by the emergence of the freedman into a voter was but a slight tremor as compared with the upheaval of 1865-6. Tendencies which appeared in the first year and a half of free labor continued in 1867 and after with no particularly new development. But by the end of the reconstruction period changes going on slowly in the agricultural system became more apparent. Large plantations broke up into smaller farming units; the number of farms, especially of the smaller size, increased greatly, while the acreage under cultivation decreased; the supply of agricultural labor diminished steadily, and the scheme of employment increasingly tended toward payment in shares rather than in money wages, with less and less control by the planter over the laborers. With contraction in acreage under cultivation and decrease in the labor supply, farm land was much in the market and property values suffered a decided shrinkage. Still, cotton continued to hold its own as the dominant interest of land and labor.

Figures are not available for the comparison of the num-

ber and size of farms in Georgia at the beginning and at
the end of the reconstruction period, but by comparing the
figures of 1860 and 1870 we can approximate the result.
No change to amount to anything in this respect occurred
during the war, so it may be safe to assume that the situation at the beginning of the war continued practically the
same up to 1865. While the number of farms increased in
this decade, the total acreage in farms decreased by three
million acres.[1] Besides the total decrease in acreage, in 1870
the per cent of unimproved land to the total farm acreage
was greater—71.1 per cent in 1870, 69.7 per cent in 1860.
With free labor the farmer was unable to cultivate as much
land as he had tilled with slaves; hence the unit of cultivation was appreciably smaller. In 1860 the average size
of farms in Georgia was 430 A.; in 1870, 338 A.[2] But the

ACREAGE IN FARMS

	Number of acres in farms, total.	Improved.	Unimproved.	Per cent. of unimproved land to total land in farms.	Average size farms.
1860.................	26,650,490	8,062,758	18,587,732	69.7	430 A
1870.................	23,647,941	6,831,856	16,816,085	71.1	338 A
1880.................	26,043,282	8,204,720	17,838,562	68.5	188 A

average size of farms is by no means as fair an indication
of the contraction in planting as is the size of the dominant

[1] *U. S .Census*, 1870, vol. iii, pp. 340–41; *Compendium of the Census* of 1880,
pt. i, pp. 650–657.

[2] Mr. Brooks calls attention to the fact that some of the changes recorded by the
Census in 1880 must have taken place in 1870. Because of inaccuracy the Census statistics for 1870 can give only an approximate idea of the changes that
were taking place. Brooks, *Agrarian Revolution in Georgia*, p. 41.

farm unit.   In 1860, there were more farms in the group
100-500 A. than in any other class; ten years later the farm
of 20-50 A. was most common.   Further, it is noteworthy

NUMBER AND SIZE OF FARMS

	Total number.	3–10 A.	10–20.	20–50.	50–100.	100–500.	500–1000.	1000 and over.
1860............	62,003	906	2,803	13,644	14,129	18,821	2,692	902
1870............	69,956	3,257	6,942	21,971	18,371	17,490	1,506	419
1880	138,626	3,110	8,694	36,524	26,054	53,635	7,017	3,491

that the smallest farms multiplied most rapidly in number,
and the largest diminished to the greatest extent.   A farm,

PER CENT IN 1870 OF THE NUMBER OF FARMS IN 1860

```
3–10 A.......................................... 350 per cent.
10–20 A......................................... 240 per cent.
20–50 A......................................... 160 per cent.
50–100 A........................................ 130 per cent.
100–500 A.......................................  92 per cent.
500–1000 A......................................  55 per cent.
Over 1000 A ....................................  46 per cent.
```

in this sense, means a unit of cultivation, whether tilled by
the owner or by a tenant.

   The counties most affected by the break-up of the larger
into smaller units of cultivation were conspicuously the
coast counties, where labor was most disorganized in 1865
and demoralized in 1868.   In all the coast counties—Chatham, Bryan, Liberty, McIntosh, Glynn and Camden—the
number of farms more than doubled in this decade.   This
disintegration was due primarily to the failure of the rice

and sea-island cotton planting, and to the opportunity of negroes to take up small farms of their own. In four of these counties the dominant size of the farm was less than 10 A.; in Liberty County, 10-20 A.; and in Bryan, 20-50 A. In most of the counties of the pine barrens in the southeastern section the number of farms greatly increased, especially the small farm of less than 50 A. In many of the cotton-belt counties, likewise, the process of disintegration of large plantations was marked, in Burke, Columbia, Harris, Houston, Meriwether, Monroe, Muscogee, Washington, and Wilkes, as the following table indicates: [1]

	Number of farms of all sizes.		3-10 A.		10-20 A.		20-50 A.		50-100 A.		100-500 A.		500-1000 A.		Over 1000 A.	
	1860	1870	1860	1870	1860	1870	1860	1870	1860	1870	1860	1870	1860	1870	1860	1870
Burke.	675	847	2	3	8	83	80	245	99	467	315	39	100	10	71	—
Columbia.	388	617	—	7	4	26	53	158	76	153	208	228	35	25	12	20
Harris	683	960	10	18	10	22	80	211	144	324	360	370	62	15	17	—
Houston	487	782	1	—	5	—	33	149	83	201	229	345	96	74	40	13
Meriwether.	685	909	—	6	6	55	68	317	163	270	370	255	63	6	15	—
Monroe	662	800	1	1	2	22	53	230	105	274	380	266	94	7	27	—
Washington	697	1652	16	1	19	14	81	886	151	464	358	276	52	9	20	2
Wilkes	393	513	1	1	5	19	30	113	57	149	202	212	69	16	29	3

The explanation of the process of change in these counties as elsewhere is that tenancy had made a strong invasion as a scheme of cultivation, and with the contraction in planting, due to the high cost and uncertainty of labor, parcels of less productive land were taken up by negroes.

[1] *U. S. Census*, 1870, vol. iii, pp. 348–349; 1860, Agriculture, p. 196.

One of the first effects of emancipation was a fall in

PREVAILING SIZE OF FARMS, 1870

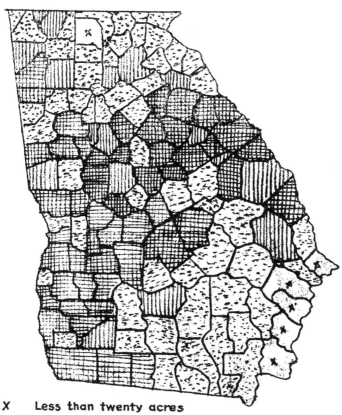

X   **Less than twenty acres**

      20-50 A.

      50-100 A.

      100-500 A.

land values in the entire state.   The average taxable value of land in Georgia, $4.85 per acre in 1860, fell to $2.87 per acre in 1872. The heaviest loss was borne by the cotton-belt. In most of the cotton-belt counties in 1860 the average per acre was $5-7; in 1872, $3-5. In five of the cotton-producing counties values decreased over 70 per cent during the war and reconstruction periods. In eleven counties the decrease was between 60 per cent and 70 per cent, and in nineteen more, over 50 per cent. Thirty-seven counties in all lost in land valuation more than half the value of 1860. For example, in 1860, in the great cotton counties, Dougherty, Lee and Houston, the average taxable value of land was over $9 per acre, the choicest area of the cotton-belt. In 1872, the average had fallen to only $3-5 per acre. The richest grain counties of the northwest held their own considerably better. Before the war land in Catoosa, Gordon, Floyd, Bartow and Polk averaged over $9, but in 1872 was worth only $5-7.[1]

It is an undoubted fact that there was a steady decrease in the amount of agricultural labor for hire in Georgia from 1865 to 1872. The year 1866 ended disastrously for both planter and laborer, hence many negroes availed themselves of the opportunity to get better pay in the neighboring states to the southwest. This drain by migration left many sections inadequately supplied with hands, and complaints came from all sides concerning the insufficiency of labor, in spite of the higher wages paid in 1867 than in the previous year.[2] The reports of the comptroller general confirm the day-by-day accounts of newspapers that labor

[1] *Reports of the Comptroller General*, 1860, pp. 38-9; 1872, pp. 25-9. In any comparison of values before and after the war it must be borne in mind that in the latter period gold was at a premium.

[2] *Augusta Chronicle*, March 9, 1867; *Milledgeville Federal Union*, February 12, 1867; *Southern Cultivator*, March and June, 1867; Report of the Freedmen's Bureau in the *Report of the Secretary of War*, 1867-8, vol. i, p. 675.

grew more and more scarce. Taking the years 1867 and 1872, for instance, there was a most decided diminution in the number of hands employed in most sections of the state. In almost all of the southwestern counties, where black population increased rapidly between 1860 and 1870, hired hands became fewer and fewer in the reconstruction period. In Dougherty County, one of the largest cotton-producing counties in Georgia, the number of hands decreased 47 per cent in these five years. Since migration did not affect the diminution of the labor force in Southwest Georgia, other circumstances must account for the abnormally large decrease in the number of hands employed after 1867. This was the newest cotton section of Georgia, with much wild land not opened to cultivation before the war. Here negroes found an easy opportunity to gratify their desire to take up holdings of their own. By 1874 the southwest and the southeast, the coast land and pine barrens adjoining, were the two centers of negro landholdings. In Decatur County, for instance, at the extreme southwest corner of Georgia, by 1873, 10,751 A. were owned by sixty negro proprietors.[1] Then railroad construction in this section drained labor from agriculture. And still another reason for the diminution in hired labor between 1867 and 1872 is this: in 1867, in comparison with the rest of the state, the southwest was exceptionally well supplied with hands, for the economic revolution of 1865 was slower in getting under way here than in the older part of the cotton belt or on the coast.

In Central Georgia all of the counties adjoining Bibb suffered noticeably in the loss of field hands. Houston had only 2,846 in 1872 as compared with 4,201 in 1867; in Monroe, the number decreased from 3,458 to 1,240; in

---

[1] Banks, *Economics of Land Tenure in Georgia*, pp. 67-8, 127.

Jones, from 1,750 to 1,176; in Twiggs, from 1,999 to 1,699; in Crawford, from 1,452 to 1,319. In these particular counties the attractiveness of the city of Macon in Bibb County probably accelerated other forces in drawing negroes away from the field. On the coast very few negroes were willing to hire to an employer. In Liberty County there were 1,238 hands working for white planters in 1867, and only 50 in 1872; in McIntosh, 896 in 1867, and 130 five years later. In the white counties of the north and the sparsely settled pine barrens of the south, the number of hands, always small, grew appreciably less. However, in some of the older counties of the cotton-belt there were more hands at work in 1872 than in 1867. While some counties, like Washington, Jefferson and Putnam, gained in the supply of hired laborers, the adjoining counties in the same section, Burke, Columbia, Greene, Oglethorpe, Wilkes and Warren, lost hands. The migration was local, however, for in the whole section the supply of hired labor was about the same in 1872 as in 1867.

In these years correspondents of newspapers, writing concerning agricultural conditions and prospects, made frequent note of the steady thinning-out of labor each year.[1] A correspondent from Bulloch County wrote:

Why is it that the planter with all the land and all the capital is dependent upon an independent negro, who has neither land nor money? Why is it that the farmer's wife and daughter are driven to the cook-pot, or wash-tub, when there are perhaps a half-dozen able-bodied negroes within a short distance, whom neither love nor money can induce to perform this menial service?[2]

[1] *Macon Telegraph*, January 19, 22, March 3, 17, 21, 1869; *Southern Cultivator*, November, 1868; February and March, 1869; July, 1870; February, 1871; *Savannah News*, January 21, 1868.

[2] *Southern Cultivator*, February, 1871.

NUMBER OF HANDS EMPLOYED [1]

	1867	1869	1870	1871	1872
Southwest:					
Dougherty	3140	2637	3341	1722	1669
Lee	2585	1941	2186	1634	1896
Baker	1901	1010	1389	1193	984
Mitchell	1259	1129	1161	920	1055
Terrell...................	1492	1143	1305	1431	1392
Early....................	1298	1129	1203	1190	960
Decatur	1676	983	1344	1424	1472
Thomas	1833	1474	1584	1825	1670
Brooks	1393	1344	1593	1185	1187
Lowndes................	1454	1112	1125	843	577
Calhoun	1249	791	1014	977	1098
Eastern cotton belt:					
Washington	2315	1978	2398	2886	2987
Jefferson	2108	2108	2455	2670	2610
Putnam.................	2032	2118	2230	2448	2400
Taliaferro................	1093	1070	1061	1048	1171
Hancock	2729	2232	2631	2664	2836
Morgan.................	2279	1962	1838	2146	2508
Clarke	645	1395	1594	1892	2176
Burke	4595	1109	....	2886	1462
Columbia	2789	2334	2011	914	1090
McDuffie [2]	....	....	....	1196	855
Warren.................	1795	1357	1347	1301	1267
Lincoln.................	1325	1024	1076	1216	1308
Wilkes	2345	2246	2316	2313	1915
Oglethorpe	2264	1093	1056	....	1688
Greene	1997	1215	1280	1814	1933
Elbert	1723	1669	1639	1806	964
Walton [3]	1329	1468	1620	1535	1680
Gwinnett [3]................	309	364	605	1312	1466
Jackson [3]................	312	894	931	1114	1048

The editor of the *Macon Telegraph* thought he could explain in part the unavailing clamor for more hands. In July, 1869, when one of the negro leaders was under trial in the U. S. Commissioner's court in Macon, two or three hundred negroes looked on all day. " From 2,000 to 3,000

[1] These figures are taken from the *Reports of the Comptroller General.*

[2] McDuffie county was created out of parts of Columbia and Warren counties in 1870.

[3] These counties are not properly in the cotton-belt.

bales of cotton lay in the muscles of those stout and greasy fellows, who were ' wasting their sweetness ' in the stifling atmosphere of the court room with the mercury about 90° outside ".[1] In the spring of 1868 came word from Waynesboro: " The all absorbing question is not impeachment, nor reconstruction, nor repudiation, nor the next President, but *labor*." What was to be done? Pick the best hands and the best land, sell one-half or two-thirds of the land, and as for the surplus negroes—well, let the political economist take care of them. This was the somewhat cynical advice of a dejected planter.[2]

Though figures are not available, the general proposition is incontrovertible that more and more negroes each year gave up working for wages and took up small parcels of ground to farm as tenants or as owners. By 1874 negro landholders in Georgia held taxable titles to 338,769 acres.[3] For instance, at the beginning of the season of 1869 many negroes left Macon to try farming on their own account in the country. Just outside of Augusta, in 1870, there were about one hundred negro families settled on small homesteads of an average value of $100 to $500, purchased on small installments. In early January of the same year, a city reporter of an Augusta paper noted that many freedmen were in town, trying to purchase stock to farm for themselves.[4] In Houston, a rich cotton county in Middle Georgia, several freedmen bought farms from 100 to 600 A. each, one man planting for 50 bales of cotton. A company of negroes owned together 1,500 A., and two brothers who

[1] *Macon Telegraph*, July 21, 1869.

[2] *Southern Cultivator*, April, 1868.

[3] Banks, *op. cit.*, p. 63.

[4] *Macon Telegraph*, January 13, 1869; *Augusta Constitutionalist*, January 5, 1870; Alvord, *Letters from the South*, January 13, 1870.

had saved $600 got title to 1,500 A., with credit for the balance. J. W. Alvord of the Freedmen's Bureau, a most optimistic observer of the progress of the negro in freedom, gave this glowing account of the freedmen's success in Georgia, doubtless true for some individuals, but hardly typical: " The first year they worked for bare subsistence; the second year they bought stock—mules, implements, etc.; the third year, many rented lands; and now, the fourth year, large numbers are prepared to buy. This is the record of the most industrious—others are following at a slower pace." [1]

The work of railroad construction and repair gave employment to many negroes tired of field labor. Especially was this the case in South Georgia when the Brunswick and Albany and the Atlantic and Gulf railroads absorbed much labor. From Dooly and other counties in South and Central Georgia the B. and A. R. R. in 1869 took about 5,000 hands from the production of cotton. The trades, carpentry, brick-making, etc., furnished attractions in towns to draw off a goodly number of skilled workers from the plantation. [2] Migration and emigration helped to account for the decrease in the agricultural labor supply. High wages in states further south and west continued to provide inducements to the Georgia negro. Besides, many negroes, who had been taken to the comparatively new plantations of Southwest Georgia before or during the war, strayed back to their original homes. [3] The drift of negroes to towns, the distraction of politics, the prevalence of tenancy, and the

---

[1] Alvord, *op. cit.*, January 18, 1870.

[2] *Macon Telegraph*, January 19, 22, March 17, 1869.

[3] Alvord, *op. cit.; Macon Telegraph*, March 17, 1869; *Southern Cultivator*, November, 1868; *Savannah News*, July 2, 1867, January 21, 1868; *Milledgeville Federal Union*, February 12, 1867.

exodus of women from field labor, all helped to account for the diminution of the labor supply.

Difficulties in the way of the restoration of the old plantation system in 1865-6, instead of lessening, became all the greater as time went on. In the next five years, from 1867 to the end of the reconstruction period, inroads made upon the plantation method of employment and cultivation —less supervision by the owner over the workers, and cultivation by small groups or by individuals instead of gang labor—were more strongly intrenched. The share method of payment was more used than money wage, and tenancy continued to gain hold. This does not mean that plantations in the old sense of the word disappeared. However, it was only the planter of the most skilful managing ability, with ample capital or command of credit, that was able to continue successfully the old plantation economy. A conspicuous example of a successful planter who did not have to yield to the new demands of the negroes was Colonel Lockett, in Dougherty County, who was reputed to be the largest planter in the state. He cultivated 10,000 A.—7,000 A. in cotton and the rest in corn—employed more than 300 hands and had a black population of more than a thousand on his plantation. His hands were worked under strict supervision and were paid a money wage quarterly. Field hands were classified according to the amount of work they could do and wages for each class were stipulated by the employer, to which was added one ration, consisting of four pounds of bacon and one peck of cornmeal per week to each laborer. Though the negroes did not work as they did before the war, still plantation work progressed smoothly and profits, except from the increase of blacks, were, on the whole, larger than in ante-bellum times. The remarkable success of Colonel Lockett was attributed to his unusual executive ability and notable skill in managing negroes.[1]

But the majority of planters had less success in maintaining the old routine. Frances Butler Leigh gave the following account of the method of employment on her father's plantations:

On both places the work is done on the old system, by task.[2] We tried working by the day, indeed I think we were obliged to do so by the agent of the Freedmen's Bureau, to whom all our contracts had to be submitted, but we found it did not answer at all, the negroes themselves begging to be allowed to go back to the old task system . . . In all other ways the work went on just as it did in the old times. The force, of about three hundred, was divided into gangs, each working under a head man—the old negro drivers, who are now called captains, out of compliment to the changed times. These men make a return of the work each night, and it is very amusing to hear them say, as each man's name is called, " He done him work; " " He done half him task; " or "Ain't sh'um " (have not seen him). They often did overwork when urged, and were of course credited for the same on the books.[3]

At the end of 1867, after her father's death, it became Miss Butler's duty to pay the negroes for the previous two years, dividing the proceeds of the crops according to the amount due each man. The negroes' childlike ignorance of money and of the expense of their own maintenance made it a hopeless job to satisfy each one. Miss Butler narrated her experience in paying the negroes as follows:

---

[1] *Hunt's Merchant Magazine*, October, 1869; *Ku Klux Committee*, vol. vii, p. 833 (Test.: C. W. Howard, editor of an agricultural paper, the *Plantation*.)

[2] Work by task was the rule on ante-bellum rice plantations.

[3] Leigh, *Ten Years on a Georgia Plantation*, pp. 55-6.

My father had given each negro a little pass-book, in which he entered from time to time the food, clothing and money which each had received from him on account. Of these little books there were over three hundred, which represented their debits; then there was the large plantation ledger, in which an account of the work each man had, or had not, done every day for nearly two years, had been entered, which represented their credits. To the task of balancing these two accounts I set myself, wishing to feel sure that it was fairly done, and also because I knew the negroes would be more satisfied with my settlement. Night after night, when the day's work was over, I sat up till two or three o'clock in the morning, going over and over the long line of figures, and by degrees got them pretty straight. I might have saved myself the trouble. Not one negro understood it a bit, but all were quite convinced they had been cheated, most of them thinking that each man was entitled to half the crop. I was so anxious they should understand and see they had been fairly dealt with, that I went over and over again each man's account with him, and would begin, "Well, Jack (or Quash, or Nero, as the case might be), you got on such a date ten yards of homespun from your master." "Yes, missus, massa gave me dat." "Then on such and such a day you had ten dollars." "Yes, missus, dat so." And so on to the end of their debits, all of which they acknowledged at once. (I have thought since they were not clever enough to conceive the idea of disputing that part of the business.) When all these items were named and agreed to, I read the total amount, and then turned to the work account. And here the trouble began, every man insisting upon it that he had not missed one day in the whole two years, and had done full work each day. So after endless discussions, which always ended just where they began, I paid them the money due to them, which was always received with the same remark, "Well, well, work for massa for two whole years, and only get dis much." Finding that their faith in my father's justice never wavered, I repeated and repeated and repeated, " But I am paying you from your master's own books and accounts." But the answer was always the same, "No, no, missus, massa not treat us so." Neither, oddly enough, did they seem to think I wished to cheat them, but I was powerless to help matters, one man saying to me one day, "You see, missus, a woman ai'nt much 'count." [1]

Indeed, the division of the crop among the hands according to each one's labor was by no means a simple task, even for a man. One perplexed farmer appealed to the editor of the *Southern Cultivator* to solve his problem for him, which was to divide $546.83 among four hands in this proportion: [2]

```
A, full hand, worked 12 mos.
B, ¾    "       "    11 mos. 6 das.
C, ½    "       "    10  "   9  "
D, ¼    "       "     9  "   3  "
```

Though planters exerted great effort to continue the old "associated labor" system, the plan gradually gave way to the "squad system", by which only two to eight or ten hands worked together, in many instances a single family. The squad system was much less productive on large plantations, for by it there could be no concerted action or fair division of labor. [3]

One stage in the disintegration of the ante-bellum plantation is pictured in the records of a rice plantation on the Savannah River. [4] In 1867, the owner of two plantations, unable to manage both with free labor, leased one. The lessee divided the land into five parts of 78 A. each, with an intelligent negro, experienced in rice culture, at the

[1] Leigh, *op. cit.*, pp. 75-6.

[2] *Southern Cultivator*, October, 1868.

[3] *Hunt's Merchant Magazine*, September, 1869.

[4] Copies of the records of the Manigault Plantations of East Hermitage and Gowrie, made by Prof. U. B. Phillips.

head of each division, as foreman. It was the foreman's business to superintend the cultivation in all stages until the rice was threshed and ready for market. Each foreman procured his own hands, about ten in each division. In the contracts between the employer and his foremen, the employer agreed to furnish land, trunk lumber, mules, ploughs, plantation tools, and one-half of the seed rice, bought by the employer and deducted out of the negroes' wages. The negroes were to furnish their own provisions, or if the employer furnished food the cost was to be deducted. At the end of the year, after all plantation expenses were paid, one-half of the net profits were to be divided among the negroes.

A more complete account of the process of disintegration into the squad method of cultivation, then gradually to tenancy, is given of a plantation in Oglethorpe County. For several years after the war the labor force was divided into two squads, each working as formerly under an overseer or foreman. Payment was made in a share of the crop. Gradually the squads broke up into smaller and smaller groups with less and less oversight, until finally, each man worked a separate farm, becoming a tenant. The landlord gave no direction except to see that enough cotton was planted to pay the rent (750 lbs. lint cotton to a one-horse farm, 25-30 A.).[1]

A negro much preferred to get bare subsistence out of a little patch of ground which he rented and controlled for himself than to have a neat surplus at the end of the year by working under direction. Unambitious of accumulating capital, the freedmen were all eager to have a home, a mule, cow and hogs set apart from the others. Thus, they were willing to work for a food crop for themselves and a mod-

[1] Barrow, "A Georgia Plantation," *Scribner's Monthly*, April, 1881; Brooks, *Agrarian Revolution in Georgia*, p. 45.

erate cotton crop to pay their rent.[1]   Agreements with tenants sometimes called for rent payment in a share of the
crop, and sometimes in cash.   Share tenants usually received
all the capital for their farm from the owner, and so were
subject to a certain degree of supervision since they gave no
security but their labor.   Cash tenants, who furnished stock
and all equipment except the land, reached a higher degree
of economic freedom.   Cash tenants could under certain
circumstances draw directly upon merchants for their supplies without dependence on the landlord for their credit.[2]

Before the reconstruction period came to an end schemes
of employment were so many and so varied that no regular
system prevailed.   Where planters were able to hire hands,
money wages, payment in a share of the crop, or a combination of both were used.   With the uncertainty of cotton
prices, farming was largely speculative.   Hence, share payments for labor tended to be more common than fixed money
wages.   At the beginning of 1867 the high price of cotton
stimulated competition among planters for labor and resulted in high wages for negro hands.[3]   The failure of the
cotton interests in 1867—large crop, low price, but high
cost of production—brought wages in 1868 to a considerably lower level.   In 1867 the offer of high wages by planters in the west and south, together with the expectation at
the beginning of the season of 20-25 cent cotton, was favorable to the laborer.   But in 1868, when the fall in cotton
subdued the cotton mania, labor was no longer scarce.

---

[1] *Hunt's Merchant Magazine*, September, 1869.

[2] Brooks, *op. cit.*, pp. 32-3.   In 1873 the first law was passed which
recognized this arrangement.   A Lien Law gave merchants a lien on
the crops of tenants as well as on those of farmers.

[3] *Southern Cultivator*, July and November, 1867, gives estimate of
wages, $125 and rations; Freedmen's Bureau report in *Report of the
Secretary of War*, 1867, vol. i, p. 675.

Planters who paid as much as $150-$200 for hands in 1867, did not want them at half the price in 1868. Wages paid by some planters for 1868 were $6 a month, with board for men, in Middle Georgia; $8 in Southwest Georgia, and $4 or $5 for women and boys, or their equivalent in a share of the crop. Still the share system seemed to be more commonly used, though many of the best planters had strong objections to it, because of the limitation of control over the laborer and the consequent abuse of stock it involved.[1]

A careful observer of the money-wage and crop-sharing systems in 1869 concluded that neither worked satisfactorily By shares, the worker in many instances received one-half of the corn and cotton, if he " found " himself, or else one-third or one-fourth of the crop if rations were provided. Money wages ranged from $10 to $15 per month for prime hands. The planter had more control over the wage laborer, could carry out a general system of plantation improvements, but had no way of making sure of the laborer's services during the critical crop season. The share system brought difficulties in carrying out the general work of the farm—ditching, repairing buildings, fences, clearing new lands—and tended to the abuse of stock and farm implements. Considering the merits and demerits of both systems, the planter suggested a combination of both money and share payments, the wage to secure the supervision of the laborer by the employer and the share to stimulate the interest of the worker in the crop and to hold him to the end of the harvest season.[2] This scheme was practised in many places—a kind of profit-sharing arrangement. In 1870 and 1871 conditions of employment continued much

[1] *Southern Cultivator*, January, 1868; Freedmen's Bureau Report, *Secretary of War*, 1868-9, vol. i, p. 1044.

[2] *Hunt's Merchant Magazine*, October, 1869.

the same as in the two previous years, with a strengthening of the scheme of share employment and a growing number of negro tenants.

A movement by some of the leading negro politicians to control wages took shape in a labor convention held in Macon in 1869. The leaders of the movement were the negro politicians, Jeff Long and H. M. Turner, backed by two white carpet-baggers, J. E. Bryant of Augusta and J. C. Swayze, editor of a Radical newspaper, the *American Union*. Their purpose was to organize a union among the negroes, pledged to demand as a minimum wage $30 a month for field hands and $15 for women. Results of the Macon convention were noted in various places, and naturally received unfavorable comment from newspapers, representing the employing class. In Macon there was something like a small strike among negroes, and in Dougherty County a more serious one. At a meeting in Houston County, negro laborers announced the stated wage as their minimum demand. At another meeting, the negroes presented their demands for the tenant system, by which the planter should furnish land, stock, fertilizer, food for stock, implements, and rations for hands, the negroes to work free from direction and pay as rent one-fourth of the cotton and one-third of the corn. Emissaries were sent by the Macon leaders to organize county associations among field hands, but their efforts were unsuccessful and no permanent or widespread effects were noticed from this first attempt to organize the negro field hands on a labor-union basis.[1]

It is most surprising to the reader of the daily papers and agricultural journals from 1867 to 1870, years of political ferment, to find comparatively little comment on the de-

[1] *Macon Telegraph*, October 2, 1869; *Milledgeville Federal Union*, November 16, 1869 (from *Columbus Sun*); Avery, *History of the State of Georgia*, p. 416.

moralizing effect of politics on the negro. On the coast, such demoralization was extreme and continuous, but elsewhere it was only moderate and sporadic. The first disorganization came in 1867, when registration under the Military Acts was in progress. In Houston County, where blacks predominated, registration attracted much attention from the newly enfranchised, who went in crowds, suspending labor for some days. But even then it was reported that the negroes worked better in 1867 than in 1866.[1] In 1868 laborers were slow in getting to work, refusing to make contracts for a time in the hope that something would turn up or that some relief would come from the constitutional convention in session in Atlanta. In the late summer of that year came reports from Central Georgia that much meeting in secret clubs and drilling kept the negroes in high excitement, making them slack in their plantation labor, if not entirely idle.[2] However, in the years 1867-70, the cotton crop was fairly respectable in amount. In 1870 it surpassed the largest crop raised under slavery. This would have been quite impossible had negro labor been thoroughly demoralized by the new toy of the ballot. Whether it was the fear of the Ku Klux or what it was that kept the negroes at work is beside the question here. But the fact remains that the greater bulk of the cotton crop was the product of the freedmen's labor, and the political revolution of 1867-8 brought by no means as serious a disorganization in the labor force as did emancipation in 1865-6.

At the beginning of 1867 very grave difficulties confronted the cotton planter. 1866 had ended in failure so that only about one planter in four, it was estimated, had any surplus. The failure of 1866 was assigned to many

---

[1] *Savannah News*, July 1, 1867, correspondent from Houston County.

[2] *Milledgeville Federal Union*, August 18, 1868.

circumstances: first of all, to the high price of cotton at the
beginning of the year, about 50 cents, which stimulated the
use of all sorts of land, bad and indifferent; to the late
start in planting when labor was demoralized and to the
continued uncertainty of free labor; to bad management
when negroes were rewarded with shares—too little directed
in their labor; to the fact that many old experienced planters gave up, yielding to young, inexperienced managers;
and that many soldiers, formerly overseers, got into the
business, lacking means and credit when depression came;
and in addition to all these, to many natural plagues—cut
and boll worms, rot, caterpillars, rust and rain, and everything else that cotton was heir to.[1]   Over-emphasis on cotton and the failure of provision crops brought distress and
hardship.   The general scheme of planting for 1867 was
to cultivate less land, use more fertilizer, and economize on
labor.   But with cotton at 35 cents at the beginning of 1867
the planter could not resist the temptation of another
gamble, putting in the staple heavily and again slighting
food crops.   The *Southern Cultivator* advised the planter:
" Do not let a mania for cotton planting make a fool of
you again, and prevent putting in a bountiful crop of corn.
Corn has no tax on it." [2]   But despite the warning of wise
heads, cotton was still the only term in which the planter
could think and the surest basis for credit with the merchant or factor who advanced supplies.   The motto of the
planter continued thus: " Plant more cotton, to make more
money, to buy more corn to feed upon, while we make
more cotton to get more money to buy more corn ".[3]   The
season of 1867 likewise was disastrous.   The crop itself

[1] *Southern Cultivator*, May and June, 1867; *Augusta Chronicle*, January 11, 1867.

[2] February, 1867.

[3] *Augusta Chronicle*, May 10, 1867 (from *Sandersville Georgian*).

was encouraging in bulk, almost doubling that of 1866 (1866, 255,965 bales; 1867, 495,959 bales). But the heavy crop all over the Southern states brought the price down with a tumble. In the marketing season of 1867, September to January, the New York price for middling cotton was 15¼ to 27 cents, whereas the year before it had been 32 to 40.[1]

COTTON PRICES[2]

	1865	1866	1867	1868	1869	1870	1871	1872
January		47-51	33-35	15-19	28-29	25	15	22-23
February		44-48	32-33	20-23	28-30	23-25	15	22
March		40-44	29-31	24-26	28	21-23	14-15	23
April		31-38	25-27	29-32	28	22-23	14-15	23-25
May		33-40	27-28	31-32	28	22-23	15-16	23-25
June		37-39	26-27	29-31	30-33	21-22	17-20	26
July		35-36	26-28	30-32	34	20	20-21	22-26
August		32-36	27-28	29-30	33-35	19	18-19	21-22
September	44-45	32-38	22-27	25-29	29-35	18-19	19-21	
October	49-59	39-42	18-20	25-26	26-27	15-16	18-20	
November	49-56	33-39	16-19	24-25	25-27	16-17	18-19	
December	49-51	33-34	15-17	24-26	25		15-16	19-20

The cost of producing cotton in 1867 was extremely high. A cotton expert, writing for *Hunt's Merchant Magazine,* said that every item in the cost of raising cotton had greatly advanced—as a rule prices averaged about double those of 1860 for draft animals, agricultural implements, building materials, gins, repairs, labor. Negroes lived very much more expensively than under slavery and cost more to maintain with the high price of bread stuffs and provisions. The writer estimated that a given amount of labor cost the planter twice as much as formerly. Moreover, the

[1] *Hunt's Merchant Magazine*, October, 1868.

[2] These figures are taken from the annual cotton statements in the October number of *Hunt's Merchant Magazine* and the *Commercial and Financial Chronicle* of each year.

planter was more dependent on his factor for advances to cultivate his crop. Greater dependence meant greater risk to the lender, and consequently higher interest, amounting to about two and one-half per cent per month in 1867.[1]

The immediate effect of the slump at the close of 1867 tended towards retrenchment in cotton planting in 1868 and a large planting for grains. Estimates gave it that about one-third or one-fourth less cotton was planted in 1868 than in 1867. This contraction in planting, forecasting a smaller crop, together with stimulated trade in Europe, brought almost immediate effects in the cotton market in the spring of 1868, raising the price in Liverpool from 7d. to 13d. during the planting season. Hence came a reaction on planters, who put in more cotton in late planting, favored by unusually good weather conditions.[2] In amount the Georgia crop of 1868 was considerably less than that of the previous year (357,253 bales in 1868; 495,-959 bales in 1867), but higher prices, about 25 cents, during the marketing season, more than made up for the smaller crop. Moreover, the cost of production, lower wages and less outlay for fertilizer, was considerably less in 1868 than in any year since the war. For the first time since the war, cotton interests in Georgia enjoyed some degree of prosperity—and this was the first year of the political revolution under the process of congressional reconstruction.

The success of 1868 stimulated more hope in the next year; more land was put in cotton and heavy outlay was made for fertilizer in the constantly diminishing labor supply. " King Cotton, for a dethroned monarch, still exercises a decided and positive influence in the world! "—as

[1] *Hunt's Merchant Magazine,* October, 1867.

[2] *Savannah News,* January 16, March 14, 1868; *Hunt's Merchant Magazine,* May and July, 1868.

one observer put it.[1] The result in 1869 was a crop almost
as large as in 1867—488,204 bales—which brought 25-35
cents in the marketing season.

1870 brought the record crop of reconstruction times—
726,406 bales. But the price of cotton was low—15-19⅞
—and the cost of production high. So the aggregate value
of the crop of 1870 was less than that of 1869. Tempted by
favorable prices of the crops of 1868 and 1869, planters
paid too high wages and made too heavy outlay for expensive fertilizers. Hence 1870 saw no such large surplus
accruing to the planter as the previous year brought.[2] Over-
expansion in 1870 was followed by contraction and a better
outcome in 1871. Less land was given over to cotton, more
to corn and oats, less money was spent in preparing the
ground for seed, a great decrease in the expenditure for fertilizer, favorable contracts with the negroes—all of these
circumstances greatly diminished the cost of production,
so that the crop of 1871 cost less than any crop since the
war. A fair crop in bulk, 450,539 bales, bringing 18½-
21⅛ cents, meant a favorable balance for the planter at
the end of the year.[3]

The production of sea-island cotton never regained its
own. The great plantations on the coast fell to pieces, and,
when given over to the negroes in small parcels by rent or

[1] *Hunt's Merchant Magazine*, February, 1869.

[2] *Ibid.*, November, 1870; *Commercial and Financial Chronicle*, February 11, September 9, 1871.

[3] *Ibid.*, March 11, June 3, 1871 and February 24, September 7, 1872.
Hunt's Merchant Magazine and the *Commercial and Financial Chronicle*
in October of each year give cotton statements for the year. The
cotton production in Georgia after the war was as follows: 1866—
255965 bales; 1867—495959 bales; 1868—357253 bales; 1869—488204
bales; 1870—726406 bales; 1871—450539 bales. In 1859 the crop was
700930 bales; 1860—477584 bales.

sale, produced only a fraction of the valuable long-staple cotton raised in ante-bellum times.[1]

A comparison of cotton production in the census years before and after the war shows a very decided loss in the productivity of the largest cotton-raising counties. Take, for example, the ten most important staple producing counties of the state.[2]

	1859	*1869*
Houston	28,852 bales	3,819 (?)
Stewart	25,902	13,643
Burke	23,419	14,290
Dougherty	19,580	14,034
Meriwether	18,159	8,230
Troup	17,978	9,963
Monroe	17,165	10,434
Talbot	15,366	7,020
Coweta	14,930	9,793
Harris	14,906	8,163

The same decreased production was the rule for practically every kind of agricultural product raised in Georgia. Corn, rice and other food products all declined markedly under free labor cultivation. In 1859, corn raised in Georgia amounted to 30,776,296 bushels; in 1869, 17,646,-459 bushels. In corn as in cotton the most marked falling off was in the black-belt counties. Thus:[3]

[1] The production of sea-island cotton in Georgia was as follows: 1866—7646 bales; 1868—6480 bales; 1869—9225 bales: 1870—4934 bales; 1871—1567 bales. *Hunt's Merchant Magazine,* October, 1867, 1868, 1869, 1870; *Commercial and Financial Chronicle,* September 9, 1871, September 7, 1872.

[2] *U. S. Census,* 1860, Agriculture, pp. 22-3; 1870, vol. iii, pp. 120, 126. The census gives the crop of the preceding year. The figures for the crop in Houston County for 1869 are plainly erroneous.

[3] Statistics for agricultural production in *U. S. Census,* 1860, Agriculture, pp. 22-9; 1870, vol. iii, pp. 82 *et seq.,* 120 *et seq.*

Corn Produced	1859	1869
Burke Co.	703,000 bu.	203,000 bu.
Houston	648,000	363,000
Meriwether	552,000	200,000
Monroe	547,000	241,000

In 1869 less than one-half as much rice was raised in Georgia as in 1859—22,277,380 lbs. in 1869; 52,507,652 lbs. in 1859. The utter breakdown of the coast region was responsible for the deterioration in rice culture as in sea-island cotton. The decrease in the coast counties was as follows: [1]

Rice	1859	1869
Chatham	25,934,000 lbs.	8,808,000 lbs.
Camden	10,330,000	2,877,000
McIntosh	6,421,000	4,900,000
Glynn	4,842,000	740,000
Liberty	2,548,000	1,219,000

The economic upheaval in the years after the war is shown in the decrease in other products, as well as in cotton, rice and corn.

	1859	1869
Value of live stock	$38,372,734	$30,156,317
wheat	2,544,913 bu.	2,127,017 bu.
rye	115,532 "	82,549 "
tobacco	919,318 lbs.	288,596 lbs.
peas and beans	1,765,214 bu.	410,020 bu.
sweet potatoes	6,508,541 "	2,621,562 "
molasses—cane	546,749 gal.	553,192 gal.
" —sorghum	103,490 "	374,027 "

[1] The rice production of Bryan County on the coast increased in this decade from 1,609,000 lbs. in 1859 to 2,857,000 lbs. in 1869.

CHAPTER XII

INDUSTRY, COMMERCE, BANKING

THE industrial development of Georgia belongs to the decades of the eighties and nineties. Although there was some expansion in a few lines of industry during the reconstruction period, the years from 1865 to 1872 were comparatively unfruitful in the stimulation of manufactures. During the war certain industries, notably manufacturing of war supplies and textiles, were encouraged by the abnormal demand when trade with the North was cut off. But this growth was temporary, for most of the new manufacturing establishments called into being during the war and many old ones were demolished by the Sherman and Wilson raids in the latter part of the war. Of such changes as there were, some information is to be derived from the census returns of 1860 and 1870.[1] The number of manufacturing establishments increased by nearly 2,000 in this decade, from 1,890 to 3,836. Mere numerical increase in this case is no index, however, for the greatest multiplication of establishments was in carpentering, blacksmithing and the building trades. Increase in actual numbers means not so much expansion in the industry as a change in method by which the work was done. After emancipation many skilled negroes who had been smiths or carpenters or wheelwrights on plantations set up as independent workmen. This fact will account to a large extent for the seem-

[1] Statistics concerning industries are taken from the *U. S. Census*, 1860, Manufactures, pp. 80-81; 1870, vol. iii, pp. 388 *et seq.*, 506-8.

ing increase in the number of hands employed in industry
—17,871 in 1870, and 11,575 in 1860.[1]

The great increase in the number of flour and grist mills
may also be evidence of specialization and division in industry accompanying the modification of the old plantation
régime.

Flour and Grist Mills	*1860*	*1870*
no. hands employed	620	2,356
no. establishments	378	1,097
capital invested	$1,599,515	$3,103,918
wages paid	$158,688	$337,864
value of product	$4,550,007	$11,202,029

In the textiles the manufacture of cotton gained somewhat, and woollens to a less degree. The amount of capital
employed in cotton mills and the value of the product increased about 50 per cent, and wages paid increased in
amount about 25 per cent.

	Cotton goods.[2]		Woollen goods.	
	1860	1870	1860	1870
Number establishments	33	34	11	16
Number hands	2813	2846	383	563
Wages	$415,332	$611,868	$63,348	$122,138
Value of product	2,371,207	3,648,973	464,420	471,523
Capital.....................	2,126,103	3,433,265	242,500	894,435

Muscogee County, of which Columbus was the important
center, commanding a favorable site on the fall line of the

[1] *U. S. Census*, 1860, Manufactures, p. 81; 1870, vol. iii, p. 506.

[2] *Ibid.*, p. 82; 1870, vol iii, p. 507.

Chattahoochee River, had more capital invested in manufactures in 1870 than any other county, nearly two millions. Richmond County, in which Augusta was situated, on the fall line of the Savannah River, came second, with Chatham County third. In the value of manufacturing products and in wages paid, however, Muscogee was surpassed by Chatham, Richmond and Fulton. Cotton and woollen mills and flour and grist mills were the chief industries of Muscogee.

Columbus was the largest center of textile manufacture in the state. All its important mills were destroyed by Wilson's raid in 1865, among which were those of the Columbus Manufacturing Co. and of the Eagle Manufacturing Co. At a place three miles above the city the Columbus Co. rebuilt a factory with 2,500 spindles and capacity for double that number. Its capital stock was $250,000. In the first year of re-opening it made only cotton yarn. The Eagle Co. reorganized as the Eagle-Phoenix Co. in 1866 with a capital of $450,000. In 1867 its factory building was completed with accommodations for 500 hands and 10,000 spindles to weave both cotton and woollen goods.[1] The Athens Manufacturing Co. nearly doubled its capacity in 1868, with 3,000 spindles and 75 looms, consuming 10,000 pounds of lint cotton per week and turning out 10,000 yards of cloth and 7,500 pounds of cotton yarn. In the spring of 1868 it employed 175 operatives.[2]

Next in importance to flour mills and textile manufactures was the lumber industry. Over 100 more saw-mills were in operation in 1870 than in 1860. The value of the output and wages paid both increased greatly while the capital invested remained about the same. Lumber was the most important product of the coast counties. In 1870 Camden

[1] De Bow, *Review*, June, 1867.
[2] *Atlanta Constitution*, June 26, 1868.

County produced sawed lumber to the value of $489,500; Glynn County, $435,000; McIntosh, $346,000; and Chatham, $328,000.[1]

LUMBER [2]

	1860	1870
no. establishments	410	532
wages	$438,588	$667,628
no. hands	1,871	2,976
value of product	$2,412,996	$4,044,375
capital	$1,639,217	$1,718,473

In the decade between 1860 and 1870 several industries other than those already mentioned grew markedly—among them brick and tile, rolled and cast iron, machinery, and tobacco in various forms, cigars, snuff and chewing tobacco. But the production of pig iron remained about stationary, and the tar and turpentine industry, so important later in some of the lower counties, was still insignificant with only four establishments employing 138 hands.[3] The rich marble and granite quarries of Georgia were barely touched at this time. The entire product of the state in 1870 in stone was worth $10,000 from DeKalb County; in slate, $5,550 from Polk County; in marble, $4,000 from Pickens County. The mines of Lumpkin, White and Lincoln counties produced $29,780 worth of gold quartz in that year.[4]

Of all the industries classified by the U. S. Census, seventy-one existed in Georgia in 1870, though many had only one establishment of its kind. In the number of establishments, flour and grist mills headed the list with 1,097. In 1870 there were 532 saw mills, 513 blacksmith shops, and

[1] *U. S. Census*, 1870, vol. iii, pp. 646-8.

[2] *Ibid.*, 1860, Manufactures, p. 82; 1870, vol. iii, p. 508.

[3] *Ibid.*, 1870, vol. iii, pp. 592, 604-7, 614-5, 627-9.

[4] *Ibid.*, 1870, vol. iii, pp. 761, 772.

244 shops for making boots and shoes.[1]   The returns of
the Comptroller General of Georgia, listing the taxable
property of the state, show that the wealth classified as
stocks and manufactures in 1872 surpassed the amount of
the year before the war.   In 1859, the taxable wealth of
this sort amounted to $4,428,100; in 1867 it had fallen to
$2,579,905; it then rose steadily, with a slight slump in
1871, until it reached $6,266,552 in 1872.[2]

Manufactures engaged but a small part of all the workers, for Georgia was overwhelmingly agricultural.   In 1870
nearly half a million persons in Georgia were engaged in
gainful occupation, of whom 76 per cent were in agriculture; 14 per cent in professional and personal occupations, including domestic service; 4 per cent in trade and
transportation, and 6 per cent in manufacturing, mechanical
and mining pursuits.   Of this 6 per cent, or 27,040 persons, 4,723 were carpenters or joiners, 2,846 were cotton-
mill operatives, 2,604 tailors or seamstresses, 2,262 black-
smiths, 1,375 shoemakers, 1,206 millers, and 1,215 saw-
mill operatives.   About 5 per cent of those engaged in
manufacturing and mining occupations were foreign born,
chiefly Irish and German.[3]

The labor of women and children in industry did not
become significant in Georgia until the decade or two after
the reconstruction period.   In 1870 about 8 per cent of the
total number employed in industry were women, and 7 per
cent were youths.[4]   Of the 1,498 women in industrial labor
in 1870, 1,271 were employed in textile manufactures, and
740 of the 1,295 youths were so employed.   The only other

[1] *U. S. Census*, 1870, vol. iii, pp. 507-8.

[2] Reports of the Comptroller General for the various years.

[3] *U. S. Census*, vol. iii, p. 808 *et seq.*

[4] Boys under sixteen and girls under fifteen.

industries employing women laborers to any appreciable extent were tobacco factories and shops for making articles of wear. Children were employed in brick yards, in building-material trades, in tobacco factories, saw-mills and printing shops.[1]

Let us consider now the general development of the railway system, on which the industry and commerce of Georgia so closely depended. The first year and a half after the war was devoted to the repair of damages in railway track and rolling stock. The next two years were comparatively unprogressive, but with 1869 came an active movement towards further construction under the impetus of grants of state aid, and also conspicuous steps toward consolidation among some of the older roads. The decade between 1850 and 1860 was lively in railway construction, when the mileage was more than doubled. All progress was checked during the war, but in the reconstruction period, 1865-72, the mileage of railroads increased a little over 50 per cent. Of 740 miles of new track laid in these years, the greatest additional mileage, 263 miles, was built in the year 1870-71, under the encouragement of state aid grants.[2] The railway history of the reconstruction period deals, in the first place, with the old, well-established railroads, which continued in prosperity after the temporary set-back in 1865-6; secondly, with the

[1] *U. S. Census,* 1870, vol. iii, pp. 507-8. In 1868 the state legislature incorporated 8 new manufacturing companies: 17 in 1869; 18 in 1870.

[2] Poor, *Railroad Manual,* 1868-9, pp. 20-21; 1873-4, pp. xxviii-xxix.

Railway mileage in Georgia

1850......	643 mi.	1868......	1575 mi.
1860......	1420 "	1869......	1652 "
1865......	" "	1870......	1845 "
1866......	1502 "	1871......	2108 "
1867......	1548 "	1872......	2160 "

checkered career of the state road, fearfully mismanaged
under the Bullock government, and leased in 1870 to a
private corporation; and in the third place with the sudden
rise and fall of several reconstruction railroads, nourished
on state aid and financed by Northern capitalists.

The dominating force among Georgia railroads was the
Central of Georgia under the progressive leadership of W.
M. Wadley, elected president in 1866. The main line of
the Central ran from Savannah to Macon, 190 miles, furnishing the chief outlet to the sea from the central cotton-
belt. Branch feeding lines, the Augusta and Savannah R.
R., from Millen on the main line of the Central to Augusta,
and the Milledgeville and Eatonton, were leased and operated by the Central. When the construction of the Brunswick and Albany R. R. and the Macon and Brunswick R. R.
threatened keen competition for the carrying trade from
the interior to the coast, the Central extended its control
over the main feeders of its line, by securing leases of the
Southwestern and of the Macon and Western. In 1872
the company purchased six steamers plying between New
York and Savannah, and so strengthened its control over
cotton shipment to Northern ports. The Central in financial
management continued strong and steady. Its capital stock
before the war was $3,750,000, increased to $4,666,800 in
the year after the war, and to an even $5,000,000 in 1871.
To meet the heavy expenses entailed by repairs in 1865 and
1866, bonds were issued, increasing the debt in 1866-7 to
$786,000 from $106,267, the amount of the funded debt
in 1858-9. The stock of the company was held mostly in
Georgia, and of the nine directors all except one from
Macon were Savannah business men. The bonds issued
after the war were sold in New York. In 1858-9 Central
stock paid 15 per cent dividend, in 1866-7 and 1867-8, 12
per cent, and thereafter 10 per cent. The Central with its

leased property, the Macon and Western, was the best paying railroad investment in the state.   During the years of
reconstruction its stock quotations ranged from 104 to 130,

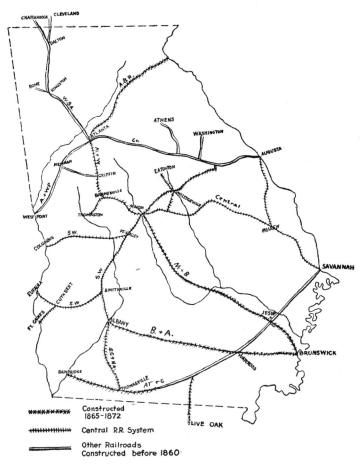

and its first mortgage 7 per cent bonds from 95 to 101.
With the increase of freight rates after the war, gross earnings increased though net earnings were smaller—$818,659
in 1868-9 as compared with $898,731 ten years earlier.

After 1870 the business of the road fell off considerably on account of competition of roads to the south, and the reduction in the cotton crop.[1]

The Southwestern Railroad tapped the rich and growing southwestern part of the cotton-belt, running from Macon to Albany, 106 miles, with branches from Ft. Valley to Butler, where the Muscogee R. R. made connections to Columbus, from Smithville to Eufaula, Ala., and from Cuthbert to Ft. Gaines—a total of 209 miles. The Ft. Gaines branch, from which iron was removed during the war, was out of commission until repaired late in 1866. On November 1, 1868, the Southwestern took over the Muscogee R. R., 50 miles, Butler to Columbus. Under the terms of consolidation, authorized by Act of March 4, 1866, the Southwestern R. R. assumed the liabilities of the Muscogee Co., exchanging its stock for Southwestern at 87½. This gave the Southwestern three points of outlet on the Chattahoochee, at Columbus, Eufaula and Ft. Gaines. In the report of the road for the first year after the war, conditions appeared favorable. Stock was held mostly within the state. Dividends were regularly paid until August, 1865, when the semi-annual payment was passed because of extra expenses from bonds and coupons past due. This road was not so badly treated by invading armies as were the Central, the Georgia, the Macon and Western and others, and so was not under so great a burden for repairs in 1865. In 1865-6 a dividend of 4 per cent was paid, 9 per cent in 1866-7, and in 1867-8 and after, 8 per cent. The Central, in leasing the Southwestern, guaranteed a dividend of 8 per cent for every 10 per cent on the Central. A comparison

---

[1] Poor, *Railroad Manual*, 1870-71, pp. 211-12; 1871-2, pp. 340-41, 445; 1872-3, pp. 116-7; 1873-4, pp. 328-9; *Hunt's Merchant Magazine*, March, 1870; *Commercial and Financial Chronicle*, July 8, December 23, 1871; January 6, 20, December 28, 1872.

of tables of earnings in 1865-6 with those of 1859-60 shows an increase in the year after the war, due, however, not to increased business but to the rise in freight and passenger tariffs. In 1865-6, the Southwestern hauled 87,250 bales of cotton; 137,696 bales in 1866-7; and with the plentiful crop of 1868, 232,343 bales. In 1866-7, when the planter plunged heavily into cotton to the exclusion of food crops, the road carried 639,538 bu. of corn. The next year, when the planters of the southwest relied more on their own products, only 149,643 bu. were carried. The annual report of the Southwestern R. R., like that of all railroads in the South, was a barometer of agricultural conditions. A full cotton crop meant heavy freight earnings, shipping cotton and bringing in goods, with free money for passenger traffic. A bad season meant little cotton to haul and consequently a slackness in goods imported and poverty not encouraging to travel.[1]

The Macon and Western R. R., connected with the Central of Georgia and with the Southwestern at Macon, going northward to Atlanta, 102 miles, and operated under lease the branch from Barnesville to Thomaston, also the Savannah, Griffin and North Alabama, from Griffin to Newnan. The Macon and Western R. R. was prosperous, paying a dividend of 8½ per cent in 1866-7, 8 per cent in 1867-8, 9½ per cent in 1868-9, and 10 per cent thereafter. In May, 1869, a dividend of 33⅓ per cent in stock was declared, raising the share capital from $1,500,000 to $2,000,000, with a second like dividend in January, 1870, making a total stock dividend equal to 66⅔ per cent on original holdings. Macon interests were largely represented on the

[1] Annual Reports of the Southwestern R. R. in *Hunt's Merchant Magazine*, January, 1867, February and December, 1868, October, 1869; Poor, *Railroad Manual*, 1868-9, p. 102; 1869-70, pp. 52-3; 1870-71, pp. 26-7; 1871-2, p. 342; 1872-3, pp. 119-20.

board of directors, with two directors from Savannah, who were also directors of the Central. Three of the eleven directors represented New York interests, and in January, 1870, Morris K. Jesup, the New York financier who played a prominent part in financing Georgia railroads in this period, was elected to the board of directors, as were also Moses Taylor and C. H. Dabney, of New York. In 1871 the Macon and Western passed over to the management of the Central under lease, by terms of which the stockholders were put on the same footing as those of the Central in matter of dividends.[1]

The Georgia R. R. was one of the oldest and most conservatively managed roads in the state. Its main line extended from Augusta to Atlanta, 171 miles, with branches from Union Point to Athens, Barnett to Washington, and Camak to Warrenton. It reached the seaboard by the South Carolina R. R. to Charleston, and connected with the northwestern systems to the Ohio and the Mississippi by way of the Western and Atlantic, Atlanta to Chattanooga, and with the gulf by way of the Montgomery and West Point and the Alabama and Florida. Like the Central, the Georgia Railway and Banking Co. closed up its banking business after the war. Heavy expenses for repairs and renewed equipment were mostly met from the reserve fund, and the bonded debt was increased only slightly. In 1866-7 and in 1868 dividends of 6½ per cent were declared. In the next year the company was able to pay 8 per cent, the normal dividend before the war. Profits were maintained at the expense of shippers through increase in freight rates. The bulk of goods carried during the years after the war

---

[1] Poor, *Railroad Manual*, 1868-9; p. 288; 1869-70, p. 109; 1870-71, pp. 252-3; 1871-2, pp. 145-6; 1872-3, pp. 120-21; 1873-4, pp. 327-9, 464; *Commercial and Financial Chronicle*, June 17, 1871, July 8, December 23, 1871, December 28, 1872.

never equaled that of the prosperous years just before the war. In 1859-60, the Georgia R. R. carried 219,774 bales of cotton. The largest amount carried during the reconstruction period was in 1870-71, 170,267 bales. However, in the year 1868-9, 1,407,326 bu. of grain were carried by the Georgia R. R., far in excess of the ante-bellum shipment. In 1871-2 net earnings fell off markedly (1870-71, $667,-539; 1871-2, $427,777), due, as the president explained, to conditions common to all Southern railroads—a want of return freight, a decrease in the cotton supply, and a decline in the prosperity of the South. The Georgia R. R. was distinctly a Georgia enterprise, with the controlling influence in the board of directors held by Augusta men.[1]

The Atlanta and West Point R. R., managed under the same presidency as the Georgia R. R., extended from Atlanta to West Point on the Chattahoochee, 86 miles, connecting with Alabama railroads to the gulf. This likewise was a Georgia enterprise, with stock held mostly in the state. Its management was conservative. It made no large bond issues after the war, met extra expenses from the reserve, paid dividends of 4 per cent in 1865-6, 3½ per cent in 1866-7, and in 1867-8, 8 per cent, equaling the dividend paid just before the war. Net earnings were largest in 1869-70—$139,058 — declining to $79,743 in 1871-2. Competition with state aid railroads, especially those of Alabama, was in part responsible for the diminished earnings of the Atlanta and West Point. The Central system, the Georgia and the Atlanta and West Point, all built before the war with private capital, were naturally vigorously opposed to the policy of opening and extending new lines under the stimulus of state

[1] Poor, *Railroad Manual*, 1868-9, p. 112; 1869-70, pp. 31-2; 1870-71, pp. 48-9; 1871-2, pp. 139-40; 1872-3, pp. 26-8; 1873-4, pp. 102-3; *Hunt's Merchant Magazine*, October, 1868, July, 1869, July, 1870; *Commercial and Financial Chronicle*, May 20, 1871, June 8, December 28, 1872.

aid. Lobbies were active at the state capitol, maintained by these companies against the bills for railway aid. In the annual report of June, 1869, J. P. King, President of the Georgia and of the Atlanta and West Point, branded the policy of state aid as unjust and oppressive, in that citizens who built their own enterprises at their own expense were taxed to build up rivals.[1] Roads were thus built at the expense of the state with little regard to public needs, leading to waste of vast capital.

The Atlantic and Gulf R. R. was the successor to the Savannah, Albany and Gulf R. R. Under the latter company the road opening the extreme southern part of the state, from Savannah to Valdosta, was built and operated before 1860. After reorganization into the Atlantic and Gulf Co., the road was extended to Thomasville and later to Bainbridge on the Flint River. A branch was built and opened for traffic in the fall of 1866 from Lawton to Live Oak, Fla., a station on the Pensacola and Georgia R. R., to tap the Florida cotton region. Later the South Georgia and Florida R. R., Thomasville to Albany, was taken over by the Atlantic and Gulf. The country traversed by the Atlantic and Gulf was poor and sparsely settled, the whole taxable property of the counties, leaving out Chatham and Dougherty, was not over fifteen millions, and the whole amount of cotton for 150 miles of the distance in 1871 was only 2,236 bales. Hence the road was not a paying investment. Its hope depended on through traffic from the southwest cotton region of Georgia to Savannah, with prospects of making connections with a through route to Mobile and

[1] Net earnings in 1859-60, $209,119. In 1868 stock was quoted at 95-100. Poor, *Railroad Manual*, 1868-9, pp. 195-6; 1869-70, pp. 29-30; 1870-71, p. 101; 1871-2, pp. 218-19; 1872-3, pp. 42-3; 1873-4, p. 28; *Hunt's Merchant Magazine*, October, 1868, October, 1869, November, 1870; *Commercial and Financial Chronicle*, November 18, 1871.

New Orleans by extension into Alabama. One million dollars of the stock of the company was held by the State of Georgia. Commissioners for the state appointed in 1872 to look after the interests of the state, reported strongly in favor of carrying out the plan of the directors to extend the road from Bainbridge to Pollard, Ala., where connections could be made with Pensacola, Mobile, and New Orleans. Thus, through connection between Savannah and Mobile could be made in 616 miles, while the distance via Montgomery and Macon was 705 miles. Common stock, to the amount of more than three and a half millions, paid no dividends, but a guaranteed dividend of 7 per cent was paid on preferred stock of about $800,000.[1]

Since the state road, the Western and Atlantic, was distinctly bound up with the political history of Georgia after 1867, its history is treated in that section.[2]

By the close of 1872 the Atlanta and Richmond Air Line was completed from Atlanta to the South Carolina boundary. The plan for a through line of transportation from Atlanta to the northeast was promoted by grants from the legislature in 1856 to the Georgia Air Line, but construction was delayed by the war. The Atlanta and Richmond Co., successors to the Georgia Air Line Co., secured aid from the state in bond endorsement to the amount of $12,000 per mile within the limits of Georgia. On completion of the first twenty miles the road received the endorsement of the state to the amount of $240,000. After the work was successfully begun, the company was able to negotiate its first-

[1] Poor, *Railroad Manual*, 1868-9, pp. 303-4; 1869-70, pp. 378-9; 1870-71, pp. 215-16; 1871-2, pp. 302-3; 1872-3, pp. xliv-xlv, 365; 1873-4, p. 230; *Hunt's Merchant Magazine*, May, 1868, July, August, 1870; *Commercial and Financial Chronicle*, March 16, August 17, December 28, 1872; *Report of the Comptroller General*, 1869, p. 16.

[2] See Chapter IX.

mortgage securities under better terms than it could secure by state endorsement. Hence the road returned to the state the bonds bearing endorsement.[1]

In order to compete with the Central for the traffic from Middle Georgia to the coast, the Macon and Augusta R. R., connecting Macon with Warrenton, a station on the Georgia R. R., was completed in 1870. The Georgia R. R. and the South Carolina R. R., wishing to divert traffic from the port of Savannah to Charleston, stood sponsors for the undertaking by endorsing the first-mortgage bonds of the Macon and Augusta to the amount of $300,000. The Georgia R. R. alone endorsed the second-mortgage loan. Rufus B. Bullock acted as president of the road until his election to the governorship in 1868. When the track was finished in 1870, rolling stock was furnished and the road was operated by the Georgia R. R., though at a loss to the stockholders. Though the Macon and Augusta secured from the legislature a promise of state endorsement of its bonds at $10,000 per mile, the company never actually received such aid. It found it could negotiate its bonds for a larger amount per mile than was authorized by the state. In December, 1871, at the close of its first year, stock of the Macon and Augusta sold for 30-35, its bonds, endorsed by the Georgia R. R., were quoted at 87-91, and unendorsed at 71-74. At the end of 1872 stock fell to 20-25, endorsed bonds remaining the same, and unendorsed rose to 82-88. Later the road became the property of the Georgia R. R.[2]

The Macon and Brunswick R. R., 185 miles, with a tenmile branch from Cochran to Hawkinsville on the Ocmulgee

[1] Report by Gov. Bullock, *Commercial and Financial Chronicle*, July 22, 1871.

[2] Poor, *Railroad Manual*, 1868-9, p. 222; 1870-71, p. 50; 1871-2, p. 470; 1872-3, pp. 509-10; *Hunt's Merchant Magazine*, July, 1870; *Commercial and Financial Chronicle*, July 22, December 9, 23, 1871; December 14, 28, 1872.

River, was completed in December, 1869, though part of the road was in operation in 1867 and about 50 miles was constructed before the war. The bonds of the company received state endorsement in 1866 to the amount of $10,-000 per mile, with an additional $3,000 later. The road was capitalized at $3,500,000, with a funded debt of $3,-750,000. Up to 1868, $400,000 endorsed bonds were issued, and by the close of 1872, $2,500,000. At the outset the enterprise was backed by Georgia men, with G. H. Hazlehurst of Macon as president (also president of the Macon and Augusta R. R.). In 1870, New York capital was introduced with Morris K. Jesup as fiscal agent as well as director. C. H. Dabney, J. Milbank and J. P. C. Foster of New York also were on the board of directors. The properties of the company in November, 1872, were advertised for sale under foreclosure of the second mortgage, and on sale the state was the purchaser, selling in 1880 to the East Tennessee, Virginia and Georgia R. R. The first mortgage bonds, 7 per cent endorsed, were quoted among active securities in the New York market in 1871 at 68-75.[1]

The Brunswick and Albany R. R. was the liveliest politically of all the reconstruction state-aid railroads. Its career was inextricably associated with that of the spectacular promoter and friend of Governor Bullock, H. I. Kimball. Under the name of the Brunswick and Florida the company was organized before the war with Northern capital, and later, by combining with the Albany and Atlantic, chartered in 1866, was planned to extend from Brunswick on the coast, across the southern part of the state through Albany to the Alabama border at Eufaula, a total distance of 242 miles. Prior to the fall of 1863, 60 miles of the road from

[1] Poor, *Railroad Manual*, 1868-9, p. 315; 1870-71, p. 415; 1871-2, p. 448; 1872-3, p. 512; 1873-4, p. 541; *Commercial and Financial Chronicle*, January 7, 28, October 28, December 9, 1871; December 28, 1872.

Brunswick to a point of junction with the Atlantic and Gulf was finished. In that year iron was removed from the road for use on other roads. Nothing was done toward restoration until 1869, when the Brunswick and Albany Co. was formed, consisting of the original bondholders. Capital stock was authorized, common, $2,548,000 and preferred, 7 per cent, $2,350,000, a total of $4,898,000, though apparently none was paid in. A funded debt amounting to $5,875,000 was authorized, of which $3,630,000 was in first mortgage 6 per cent gold bonds, endorsed by the state, and $2,350,000 in second mortgage sinking fund 7 per cent currency bonds. At the time of reorganization, Henry S. Welles of New York was President, and a little later, Chas. L. Frost, of New York. The directors in 1869, besides Welles and Frost, were Henry Clews, Treasurer and Fiscal Agent of the company, P. J. Avery, Jas. B. Taylor and J. Edwin Conant, all of New York. In December, 1870, the directorate changed decidedly, when H. I. Kimball became President. John Rice, Lewis Schofield and George Cook from Atlanta, friends or relatives of Kimball, took the place of three of the New York men. Henry Clews and H. S. Welles still remained as directors, with Chauncey Vibbard as the third New York representative. Of the official staff, E. N. Kimball, brother of H. I., was secretary, Ed. Hulburt, one of the Bullock-Kimball friends of Western and Atlantic and election experience, was general superintendent, and A. S. Whiton of New York was purchasing agent.

The company secured from the state legislature grant of bond endorsement to the amount of $15,000 per mile in 20 mile sections, with an additional $8,000 later. $3,300,000 of state endorsed bonds were actually executed in favor of the Brunswick and Albany. The political history of these bonds, with their repudiation by the state in 1872, is related elsewhere.[1] In November, 1871, the road between Brunswick and Albany was sufficiently in order for the company to commence the running of tri-weekly trains. By that time, with the change in political conditions, the flight of Governor Bullock and the financial eclipse of H. I. Kimball, the affairs of the road were in bad shape. Proceeds from bonds were exhausted, there were no signs of any real capital paid in, certificates of indebtedness were issued to the utmost limit, while the earning capacity of the road gave little hope of meeting either running expenses or interest on the enormous debt. No returns of operations or of financial condition were published. As early as October, 1871, seizures began by creditors for material furnished. The company defaulted for payment of interest on state endorsed bonds, due April 1, 1872, and went into the hands of a receiver. In November, 1872, sale was advertised under local mechanics' lien, but postponement was secured by holders of state endorsed bonds, who were trying to secure their interests after the state repudiated its guarantee. On October 15, 1873, the road was sold under foreclosure.[2]

Another one of H. I. Kimball's railroad enterprises which fell to pieces was the Cartersville and Van Wert, later the Cherokee R. R., from Cartersville on the Western and Atlantic to the Alabama border. In 1871, 23 of the total 45 miles were in operation. The road was capitalized at $12,500 per mile, with state endorsed bonds, dated June 1, 1871, to the amount of $12,500 per mile. But this, like others of Kimball's enterprises, lived only on the proceeds of bonds, and little if any of the capital was ever paid in. At the

[1] See Chapter IX.

[2] Poor, *Railroad Manual*, 1868-9, p. 337; 1870-71, pp. 115-16; 1871-2, pp. 351-2; 1872-3, pp. 555-6; 1873-4, pp. 431-2; *Commercial and Financial Chronicle*, July 22, 1871 (report of Gov. Bullock); October 28, November 4, December 2, 1871; January 20, December 7, 28, 1872.

close of 1871 the company defaulted payment of interest on its bonds, and on behalf of the state a receiver was appointed. Bonds to the amount of $275,000 were endorsed for the Cartersville and Van Wert and $300,000 more for the Cherokee under Gov. Bullock's administration. In 1878 the property was sold under foreclosure for $29,500, and again sold a year later for $22,500.[1]

The undertaking to connect Bainbridge in the extreme southwest corner of the state with Columbus by a road running parallel to and a few miles back from the Chattahoochee, 120 miles, was begun by business men of Southwest Georgia, but taken over later under the state aid epidemic by Kimball. Bond endorsement from the state was secured for $12,000 per mile. In 1871, about 20 miles from Bainbridge to Colquitt was under construction.[2]

In general, then, we may say that, during the second period of reconstruction, 1868-72, the condition of the older established railroads in Georgia was fairly prosperous. They recovered from the results of war and maintained a policy of progress. The beginnings of combination, the control of several lines of transportation by one set of interests, was conspicuous in Georgia as in the Northern states during this period. From 1868 to 1871, railroads were especially prosperous, though in general their earnings were less than in the prosperous years before 1860. In 1871-2 all the dividend-paying roads suffered a marked decrease in earnings, due to the combined influence of sharp competition from new roads, fostered by state aid in Georgia and the adjoining states, and by the depression in agricultural conditions. When railroad com-

---

[1] Poor, *Railroad Manual*, 1871-2, p. 400; 1872-3, p. 556; *Commercial and Financial Chronicle*, January 20, 1872 (report of Acting-Governor Conley).

[2] Poor, *Railroad Manual*, 1870-71, p. 252; 1871-2, p. 107; 1872-3, p. 547.

panies sought credit to improve their facilities in 1868, prominent New York capitalists took a hand, principally through managing their loans. In 1868, Morris K. Jesup took charge of the bonds of the Atlantic and Gulf, and in 1870 he became more heavily interested as fiscal agent and director of the Macon and Western and also of the Macon and Brunswick. Henry Clews was the banking agent of the Brunswick and Albany, director of the road in 1869, involved in the speculative projects of H. I. Kimball, and charged with collusion with Kimball and Governor Bullock in illegal dealings in state endorsed bonds. These years were active in new construction when almost 600 miles were added. Undue fostering of railroad enterprise by state aid with the political corruption connected with it forced the building of some lines, notably the Brunswick and Albany, ahead of any economic need, and so the companies failed as soon as political support was removed.

To the railroad builder, the merchant and the manufacturer, as well as to the farmer, one of the most crying needs was the extension of good credit facilities. State banks and private banking corporations, with few exceptions, had collapsed with the failure of the Confederacy, and it was some months before any advantage came to Georgia from the National Banking Act. The first bank in Georgia to organize under this act was the Atlanta National in September, 1865, with a capital of $100,000. A little later the Georgia National was started in Atlanta with the same amount of capital. This bank came into the political arena in 1870, when H. I. Kimball bought a controlling amount of stock. As depository for the State of Georgia the bank was involved in the crooked finance of the Bullock régime. After a suit at law brought by the state to recover funds, the bank was forced to suspend. By the end of 1867 nine national banks were in operation in Georgia, with a total paid-in capital of $1,700,000; and by the end of 1872, two more were established. National banks were organized not only in the large commercial towns but in some of the smaller ones as well. In 1871 the little town of Newnan in Coweta County organized a national bank with a paid-in capital of $62,500, and in 1872, the First National Bank of Americus was established. Individual deposits in the national banks of Georgia rose from $1,296,000 at the time of the first quarterly statement for Georgia in October, 1867, to $2,089,000 in June, 1871.[1]

Nearly all banks in Georgia during the reconstruction period were new corporations, for none survived the war in sound condition except the Central R. R. and Banking Co., the Georgia R. R. and Banking Co., and two others. In 1870 the unredeemed currency of Georgia banks, issued before 1865, was practically worthless, with the exception of the notes of these four banks.[2]

Many new banking and trust companies were incorporated under state law. There were a great many private bankers, who also did business as cotton and stock brokers and commission merchants. Bank capital in 1871 amounted to $2,384,400, far less than the amount reached before the war — $13,482,198 in 1860.[3] In 1877, there were in Georgia 39 private banks, 27 state banks, and 12 national banks.[4]

The hopeful impetus to trade in the first two years after

[1] *Hunt's Merchant Magazine,* November, 1867; De Bow, *Review,* January, 1867; *Commercial and Financial Chronicle,* July 15, August 19, 1871; July 13, December 7, 1872; Reed, *History of Atlanta,* p. 424.

[2] Quotations in *Hunt's Merchant Magazine,* November, 1870.

[3] Sub-Committee on Debts and Election Laws, *Ku Klux Committee,* vol. i, p. 235.

[4] Barnett, *State Banking,* pp. 82, 97; *Report of the Comptroller General,* 1869, p. 18.

the war received a setback in 1867 with no revival until the fall of 1868. The failure of agricultural interests in 1866 left planters still unable to meet their obligations to Northern creditors. In 1867 the general price level of agricultural products decreased about 10 per cent from the preceding year with a somewhat larger decrease in manufactured goods, whereas cotton declined about 50 per cent. Political uncertainty in the fall of 1867 and the spring of 1868 helped to retard material development. The successful cotton crop of 1868 immediately brought favorable reactions in trade conditions. In the fall of 1868 Southern buyers took more merchandise in Northern markets than at any time since 1860, with still larger purchases in the following spring. Another sign of good business conditions in 1868 was that the high-water mark in deposits in national banks was reached in September of that year, as is seen from the following figures:[1]

AMOUNT OF DEPOSITS IN NATIONAL BANKS

1867, October	......$1,296,000	1870, January	.......$1,621,000
		" April	 2,493,216
1868, February	 1,950,000	" June	 2,441,000
" May	 2,505,021	" August	 1,628,915
" August	 2,520,166	" December	 1,681,000
" September	 2,854,000		
		1871, February	 1,881,000
1869, February	 2,482,593	" June	 2,089,000
" July	 2,110,000		
" September	 2,172,000		

A mercantile review in New York noted that, contrary to expectations, a large amount of currency did not find its way back to the South to pay for the cotton crop—a sign that Southerners were buying more on credit than at any

[1] National bank statements published in *Hunt's Merchant Magazine* and the *Commercial and Financial Chronicle*.

time during the previous ten years.   This showed improved
confidence in Southern prosperity.[1]

The same review presented a keen analysis of the marked
changes in Southern trade, owing to the economic revolution of 1865.   Before the war owners of big plantations
purchased all supplies in large quantities either from Northern dealers or from a factor in the neighborhood.   After
the war the planter no longer had hundreds of dependents.
Freedmen in family groups purchased for their own wants.
Hence there sprang up a multitude of small stores, many
of which soon failed.   The better established dealers enlarged their business to cater to this new class of customers.
With the growth of village stores there developed more of
a system of commercial traveling than was known before.
" Drummers " became familiar figures in every small town.
Another change came in the quantity and kind of goods
taken by Southern merchants, now in larger quantity and
greater variety, with more demand for medium-priced
goods and less for luxuries.   The altered methods of doing
business required a larger volume of currency.   Formerly
the crops were moved by the factor, who took over the
product of a plantation on which he had made advances
during the season.   After the war the same bulk of cotton
was raised by many men, each of whom had his share of
credit with the factor or merchant.   Just as the agricultural
unit diminished in size and increased in number, so did the
credit system disintegrate.   Smaller credits in greater number by more merchants took the place of large business in
few hands.[2]

The number and amount of mercantile failures indicate
the trend of commercial conditions.   The following figures,

[1] *Hunt's Merchant Magazine*, January, June, August, October, 1868;
April, 1869.

[2] *Ibid.*, November, 1869; March, 1870.

taken from the reports of Dun, Barlow & Co., show the situation during the years of reconstruction: [1]

	Number	Amount
1868..............	73	$820,000
1869..............	30	577,000
1870..............	98	1,403,000
1871..............	42	964,000

The fact that 1869 was the best business year of this period was largely due to the highly favorable agricultural season of 1868. Political revolution, while it hindered, evidently did not make economic progress impossible.

With commercial expansion cities and towns grew rapidly. Between 1860 and 1870 the population of Atlanta more than doubled, that of Macon increased 34 per cent; Savannah, 26 per cent; and Augusta, 23 per cent. And in the smaller towns, such as Brunswick, Albany, Marietta and Valdosta, growth in this decade was even more noteworthy than in the larger cities. The migration of negroes from farm to town added largely to urban population, especially in Atlanta, Savannah, Augusta, Macon, Milledgeville, Albany and Brunswick.[2]

POPULATION

	1860	1870		1860	1870
Savannah	22,292	28,235	Brunswick	825	2,348
Atlanta	9,554	21,789	Albany	1,618	2,101
Macon	8,247	10,810	Marietta	2,680	4,376
Augusta	12,493	15,389	Valdosta	1,101	1,598

From still another standard cities and towns show an in-

[1] *Hunt's Merchant Magazine*, March, 1870; *Commercial and Financial Chronicle*, February 18, 1871; February 10, 1872. The year 1870 was a bad financial year in the country at large.

[2] *U. S. Census*, 1870, vol. i, pp. 99 *et seq.*

crease in importance during the reconstruction period. Between 1867 and 1872 taxable property in towns and cities increased from $38,000,000 to $55,000,000. In Fulton County, in which Atlanta is situated, taxable property increased 67 per cent between 1867 and 1872; Chatham County (Savannah) increased 35 per cent in the years 1867-72; Richmond County (Augusta) decreased slightly during reconstruction but increased 23 per cent between 1860 and 1872; Bibb County (Macon) increased 16 per cent in 1867-72; Muscogee County (Columbus) decreased during reconstruction, but in the whole period from 1860 to 1872 increased 21 per cent; Floyd County (Rome) in the northwest showed a remarkable increase of 113 per cent in 1867-72.[1]

In 1870 the bonded indebtedness of cities and towns in Georgia amounted to $14,383,315, the greater part of which was incurred before the war. In October, 1870, Savannah had outstanding bonds amounting to $2,318,640, most of which were issued before 1860 to develop railroads, the Southwestern, the Augusta and Savannah, and the Atlantic and Gulf. In 1866 funding bonds were issued, of which $402,800 were outstanding in 1870. Savannah 7 per cent bonds were quoted in the New York market in 1867 at 66-67; in 1871 and 1872, old 7's were quoted at 85-88 and new 7's at 83-86. Augusta bonds outstanding in 1871 amounted to $1,355,250. In 1867 Augusta 7's were quoted at 60-62; in 1872 at 83-86. Columbus 7's were at 77-79 in 1869; 70-75 in 1872. Macon 7's were quoted at 60-62 in 1867 and at 73-76 in 1872. Atlanta 7's in 1872 were sold at 72-75, and Atlanta 8's at 82-85.[2]

---

[1] *Report of the Comptroller General,* 1860, pp. 44-9; 1867, app.; 1872, pp. 35-9. City and town property, 1860 .... $35,139,145
1867 38,473,905
1872 55,219,519

[2] *Hunt's Merchant Magazine,* January, 1870; *Commercial and Finan-*

Shipping was the main business of Savannah, the chief seaport of Georgia. In the spring of 1867, Savannah had steamship connection direct with Liverpool, with New York by three different lines, two with Philadelphia, one with Baltimore, two with Charleston, two with the coast towns of Florida and Georgia, and one each with Brunswick and Darien. Activity on the wharves in 1867 was much like ante-bellum times. In 1860 the total value of exports from Savannah was nearly $18,000,000. In 1867 the exports amounted to $41,000,000, and in 1868, $50,000,000. In bulk, too, shipments from Savannah in 1867-8 compared favorably with the prosperous years before the war. While

Savannah Shipping.	1859	1868	1871
To foreign ports:			
Upland cotton	253,743 bales.	256,669 bales.	461,534 bales.
Sea-island cotton......	8,298 "	6,680 "	2,835 "
To coastwise ports:			
Upland cotton ......,...	198,523 "	234,434 "	260,549 "
Sea-island cotton......	8,489 "	5,190 "	6,839 "
To foreign ports—rice ...	6,836 casks.	—	—
To coastwise ports—rice..	31,294 "	4,291 casks.	—
To foreign ports—lumber.	29,384,315 feet.	22,844,387 feet.	—
To coastwise ports—lumber	9,543,669 "	9,152,000 "	—

shipping business progressed favorably, the wealth invested in shipping in Georgia did not recover the position it held before 1860. The taxable value of property in shipping in 1859 was $631,000 and only $200,000 in 1871. Nor did the years between 1865 and 1871 show any advance in this kind of investment. Activity in shipping brought prosperity in all lines of business in Savannah. Rents were high and property values rose steadily. The appraised value of

cial Chronicle, January 21, May 20, 1871; January 6, March 9, June 15, August 10, December 14, 1872; *Atlanta Constitution,* July 17, September 17, December 12, 1868.

[1] Advertisements in Savannah newspapers; Lee and Agnew, *His-*

real estate in 1860 was $10,000,000; about the same in 1866; but more than $15,000,000 in 1871.[1]

Before the war Macon was the railroad center of the state, with lines radiating north, east, south and west. As the center of the cotton-belt it was one of the most important interior cotton markets of the South. One of the first needs towards financial recovery after the war was the establishment of banks. Late in 1865 the First National Bank of Macon was organized. In 1869 and the years following a number of other banks were organized under state laws, and also several building and loan associations.[1]

With the growing importance of mercantile business after the war and the opening of the Richmond Air Line, Atlanta soon became the chief business center of the state. Whereas the years after the war in Savannah, Macon and Augusta were first of all a period of recovery, Atlanta entered upon a career of prosperity which she had never known before. In 1868 and 1869 the temporary rude structures which were erected after the devastation by Sherman's army gave place to substantial business buildings, and prosperity allowed citizens to build residences on a scale of luxury never before known in Atlanta. New enterprises of all sorts were started, capital flowed in, banks afforded ready financial facilities in this process of expansion, and with growing business interests many distinguished professional men moved from smaller and older towns to the promising city of the Piedmont region. The removal of the capital from Milledgeville to Atlanta in 1868 was another factor which influenced its growth. With no special advantages of water power, Atlanta had few manufactures before the

torical Record of the City of Savannah, pp. 139-40, 150; Commercial and Financial Chronicle, September 9, 1871; Sub-Committee on Debts and Election Laws, Ku Klux Committee, vol. i, p. 148.

[1] Butler, Macon and Central Georgia, passim.

war. Most of such establishments, foundries, saw-mills,
flouring-mills, were destroyed in 1864, so the field was open
to new enterprises. After 1865 there were a number of
planing and rolling mills and iron foundries, but practically no textile factories. The period of cotton manufacture
in Atlanta did not begin until the next decade. In 1866
the Chamber of Commerce, which had suspended during
the war, reorganized, and at the close of 1872 the Atlanta
Manufacturers' Association was formed. Mercantile business was decidedly more extensive in Atlanta than manufacturing. The advertising columns of newspapers were
full of announcements of grain and commission merchants,
wholesale and retail. With good railroad facilities Atlanta
was important as a distributing center, receiving grain and
meat from the West and dry-goods and manufactured articles from the East for distribution further South. One of
the chroniclers of Atlanta gives the following account of
the city in the time of reconstruction: [1]

By 1870, Atlanta, whatever may be said of Georgia, was
pretty generally " reconstructed "; Atlanta had reason to feel
rather kindly toward reconstructionists, for the city was their
headquarters during the period of military rule, and after the
civil machinery was in motion the capital of the state was lo-
cated permanently in Atlanta. The beginning of the decade
(1870-1880) witnessed unprecedented activity in Atlanta. The
town was booming, to borrow a westernism, and real estate
in desirable localities was held at fancy figures and transfers
made on that basis.

The following was a comment from one of Atlanta's
neighbors:

[1] Martin, *Atlanta and its Builders*, vol. ii, p. 69. See also Reed,
History of Atlanta.

Atlanta is certainly a fast place in every sense of the word, and our friends in Atlanta are a fast people. They live fast, and they die fast. They make money fast, and they spend it fast. They build houses fast, and they burn them down fast. . . . They have the largest public meetings, and the most of them, and they pass the most resolutions of any people, ancient or modern. To a stranger, the whole city seems to be running on wheels, and all of the inhabitants continually blowing off steam. In short, everything and everybody in and about the place seems to be moving very fast except Mayor Williams, who, the last we heard from him, was steadfast and immovable.[1]

Thus, during the years of reconstruction, while agriculture was struggling to get on its feet again and stumbling along, mercantile business and city interests shot ahead. With the growth of trade came a marked increase in urban population and a shifting of the town center from Central and Eastern Georgia to the Piedmont region, with the remarkable rocket-like rise of Atlanta, destined to be the commercial capital of the Southeast. The building of railroads and commercial expansion, as well as political influence, all helped to develop Atlanta as a center of economic importance.

[1] *Milledgeville Federal Union*, February 12, 1867.

CHAPTER XIII

SCHOOLS, CHURCHES, COURTS

EDUCATIONAL opportunities for Georgia children, except those whose parents were rich enough to pay for instruction in private schools and academies, were very limited during the period of reconstruction. Colored children were cared for in schools established by the Freedmen's Bureau and various Northern missionary societies, but white children had almost no opportunity for free instruction after the poor-school system broke down during the war, until the new public school system was put in operation in 1873.[1] Most of the funds set aside by the state for general education had vanished. Its bank stock was worthless and the Western and Atlantic R. R. under reconstruction management failed to turn into the treasury the amount of one hundred thousand dollars, which the Act of December 11, 1858, had set aside for the Poor School Fund. The only source of income for education was from state bonds issued to replace those redeemed after 1859.[2]

In 1870, opportunities for education in Georgia had not caught up with the position they had reached before the war. There were fewer schools and fewer pupils in 1870 than in 1860. At the time that the public school system was started more than half of the population of Georgia was illiterate,

---

[1] For the Poor School System, see *supra*, p. 119.

[2] *Report of the Comptroller General*, 1865, p. 23. Before the war the Educational Fund was about $150,000 annually.

and the inability to read and write was by no means confined to negroes. Among the whites 125,000 over ten years of age were illiterate and about half of this number were over twenty-one. Of blacks and whites together there were 275,000 illiterate grown men and women to whom the opportunities of the new free schools would be of no avail. Through the greater part of the black belt the proportion of illiterates to total population was over 60 per cent; on the coast and in the upper cotton-belt and in Northeast Georgia, between 40 and 60 per cent; and in the Northwest and the pine barrens, 20 to 40 per cent.[1]

The law for a common school system, passed in 1866 under Governor Jenkins's administration, never went into effect. The constitution of 1868 provided in general terms for a public school system, leaving to the legislature the task of organizing it in detail.[2] The first session of the reconstruction legislature postponed action, so the first public school law which went into effect was enacted in October, 1870, amended, January 19, 1872. The main provisions of the scheme for general education, worked out in the Act of October 13, 1870, were largely the result of recommendations made by a committee of the Georgia Teachers' Association, which met in Atlanta in August, 1869. The committee was a representative group, made up of Gustavus J. Orr of Emory College as chairman, Bernard Mallon, Superintendent of Public Schools in Savannah and later in Atlanta, John M. Bonnell, President of Wesleyan, Martin V. Calvin of Augusta, David M. Lewis, President of the North Georgia Agricultural College and former State Superintendent of Schools.[3] General J. R. Lewis was the

---

[1] *U. S. Census*, 1870, vol. i, pp. 396-7, and map, pp. 392-3.

[2] Constitution, 1868, Article VI. System of Education, " free to *all* children of the state."

[3] Stevens and Wright, *Georgia, Historical and Industrial*, pp. 386-7.

first State School Commissioner, appointed by Governor Bullock; he was followed by G. J. Orr under Democratic appointment.

By the Act of 1870, the machinery of the school system was more elaborate than in the plan formulated in 1866. The administrative head of the state schools was a State School Commissioner, appointed by the governor with the approval of the senate, and behind him was the State Board of Education, consisting of the commissioner with the governor, attorney-general, secretary of state, and comptroller-general. This board held and expended the educational fund, prescribed text-books, and acted as a court of appeal from the decisions of the commissioner. Each county constituted an educational district, with a board of education elected by the voters of the county, and a county commissioner of education, chosen by the board. Sub-districts of the county were organized, each with three school directors, or trustees, likewise elected by the voters of the district to act as a local board of education. As a school fund the legislature set aside all income from the poll tax, special taxes on shows, exhibitions, and the sale of liquors, one-half of the earnings of the state road, and all educational funds of the state not belonging to the state university. This fund was to be apportioned among the several counties in proportion to the number of children of school age, six to twenty-one years. One very important provision of the School Act was the section calling for separate schools for whites and blacks, but equal facilities for both.[1]

In August, 1872, the Democratic legislature enacted a new school law to supersede earlier ones. In general plan it followed the Act of 1870, except that it abolished the elective principle for county boards, substituting choice by

---

[1] *Acts of the General Assembly*, 1870, pp. 49-60.

the grand jury of each county from among the freeholders of the county. The school age limit was lowered from twenty-one to eighteen, with the exception of Confederate soldiers under thirty. The second law, again enforcing the principle of separate schools for whites and blacks, was less emphatic in requiring equal facilities for the two races. The same facilities, " as far as practicable ", were the words of the law of 1872.[1]

While the machinery for a state school system was in readiness in 1870, no funds were available and it was not until 1873, when the Democratic legislature brought some order out of the chaotic treasury, that public schools were actually put in general operation. In some counties schools were started in 1871, but the teachers were not paid, except where patrons advanced the pay which the state later made good. Though the comptroller general reported that nearly $500,000 was due to the education fund from poll tax, tax on liquors, shows, etc., for 1868-72, most of the amount had been diverted to other purposes by the legislature. In 1873, with a fund of $174,000 available from the state and $250,000 from county appropriations, the public school system was put in operation. In 1874, the commissioner reported that there were 1,379 schools for whites, 356 for colored children, with an attendance of 58,499 whites and 17,658 colored. In addition to the free state schools, there were schools maintained for colored children by charitable associations and also free school systems established under special laws in the counties of Bibb, Chatham, Richmond, Glynn, and in the cities, Atlanta and Columbus.[2]

[1] *Acts of the General Assembly,* 1872, pp. 64-75. Approved, August 23.

[2] *Report of the State School Commissioner,* 1872, 1873, 1874; Stevens and Wright, *op. cit.,* p. 389.

Savannah was the first city in Georgia to establish a local public school system. Started in the first year after the war with 520 pupils enrolled, the schools were enlarged each year until in 1870 there were 1,754 pupils enrolled. The estimated number of white children of school age, from six to eighteen years, in Savannah in 1870 was 3,200, of whom 2,400 were in the public schools. Of 2,400 colored children of school age, 900 were in the public schools. Besides 20 schools in Savannah, the Chatham County School Board maintained 4 schools in the county, at White Bluff, Ogeechee Canal, Isle of Hope and Cherokee Hill. In Savannah the Catholics carried on a number of schools, having about 700 pupils enrolled in 1869. In the next year these Catholic schools combined with the public school system under agreement that Catholic teachers should be preferred in Catholic schools and that the same text-books should be used except in books on history, which should be the ones commonly used in Catholic schools.[1]

The first steps toward a public school system in Atlanta were taken in 1869 and in the next year free schools were opened.[2] In Macon and Bibb County the public school system was organized in 1869 by a board of school commissioners acting with the court of ordinary.[3]

The University of Georgia at Athens felt the heavy hand of the military power upon it in 1867 because of the commencement speech of a hot-headed young student. For his junior oration, Albert Cox of La Grange chose for his subject, "The Vital Principle of Nations", making his address the vehicle for an attack on Republican reconstruction in general and on ex-Governor Brown in particular, whom he

[1] *Report of the Savannah Board of Education*, 1869-72.

[2] Reed, *History of Atlanta*, p. 334.

[3] *Macon Telegraph*, January 12, 1869.

did not name, but looked at scornfully as Brown sat on the platform with the trustees. The audience was clearly with the speaker, giving encouragement by enthusiastic applause. The board of trustees tried to repudiate responsibility for the young speaker by a resolution " that it re-affirmed its conviction of the importance of that law of the University by which party political subjects are excluded from the speeches of students at commencement ". But even then, as a result of Cox's speech, General Pope issued an order closing the university and withholding the payment of $8,000 due from the state. The Chancellor of the university secured from General Pope a revocation of the first order, but it was only after much correspondence and intercession with President Johnson and General Grant that the appropriation was restored. In 1868 the university gained in attendance 48 per cent over the preceding year, with 354 students enrolled, of whom 132 were in the high-school department. Many of those in the preparatory grades were soldiers, whose tuition was paid by the state. In 1868, it is interesting to note, the trustees established a chair of Political Science and History, to which they called Alex. H. Stephens. He declined the appointment, however, on account of ill health.[1]

Emory College, a Methodist institution at Oxford, closed its doors during the war when its endowment was swept away. Under the efforts of Bishop Pierce of the M. E. Church, South, the college was re-opened after the war, helped by payment from the state for the tuition of disabled soldiers. The college still struggled along in a hand-to-mouth existence until the Methodist bishop led a movement in 1867 to form a sustaining board of five hundred,

[1] Hull, *History of the University of Georgia*, pp. 78-80; Report of the Chancellor, *Senate Journal*, 1868, pp. 238 *et seq.*

each contributing $20 a year toward the maintenance of Emory.[1]

Mercer University, the most important Baptist college in Georgia, suffered like most educational institutions during the war. By 1862 it had practically no students, for they had all enlisted, so the college suspended. In December, 1865, the trustees held a meeting and decided to re-open the school with three teachers, all that the limited resources of the college could afford. In 1871, Mercer was moved from Penfield to Macon, on the agreement by the city of Macon to grant seven acres of land and $125,000 in bonds. Baptist schools for girls, which were forced to close during the war, again opened when peace was restored. Among these was the Monroe Female College at Forsyth and the Southern Female College at La Grange, also schools at Madison, Gainesville and Rome.[2]

Under the educational department of the Freedmen's Bureau, the work started in 1865 towards educating the negroes continued. Northern aid societies, especially the American Missionary Society and the Freedmen's Union Commission, co-operated with the Freedmen's Bureau in establishing and maintaining schools, the societies furnishing teachers and, to some extent, buildings, while the Bureau built or rented houses for school purposes. In the fall of 1865 colored schools were opened in the principal cities. During the year ending July, 1867, eighty teachers were maintained and $42,000 was spent for freedmen's schools. Sixty-five teachers were supported by the American Missionary Society, eight by the New England Branch of the Freedmen's Union Commission, and seven by the Freedmen's Aid Society of the Methodist Church. The

[1] Smith, *Life of Bishop Pierce*, pp. 496, 503.

[2] *History of the Baptist Denomination in Georgia*, pp. 241, 362.

next year one hundred and twenty-three teachers were at work in Georgia and $50,000 was spent for colored schools by various aid societies.   Up to 1868, the Freedmen's Bureau had expended for school purposes in Georgia about $100,000.   The largest number of pupils during any one month was 13,000, and in the first three years it was estimated that 30,000 colored children had learned to read, many had a fair knowledge of arithmetic and geography, some studied grammar and United States history, and a few began Latin and algebra.   The New Jersey and Pennsylvania Branches of the Union Commission, in addition to work for the freedmen, erected two houses in Atlanta and for two years supported four teachers exclusively for white children.   In Macon, too, they supported a teacher for white children, besides furnishing a large part of their clothes and books.[1]   Storrs' School in Atlanta was started in 1866 by the American Missionary Society, using one of the colored Methodist churches until a building was provided by the Freedmen's Bureau.[2]

In Savannah the Catholics had a school of sixty colored pupils taught by the Sisters of St. Joseph, a French order for African missions.   The old " Bryan Slave Mart " in Savannah was turned into a school, used by the colored education committee and by ten colored teachers under the patronage of the American Missionary Society.   The most prosperous colored people had the advantage of a private school taught by colored men, quite a respectable establishment with about 120 pupils in 1870.   In Augusta most of the colored schools were under the Baptist Home Mission

[1] Report of E. A. Ware, Superintendent of Education for Georgia, Freedmen's Bureau, in *Senate Journal*, 1868, pp. 78-9; also reports of the Commissioner of the Freedmen's Bureau in the *Report of the Secretary of War*.

[2] Reed, *History of Atlanta*, p. 324.

Society. The Richmond County school commissioners supported a school for colored children, employing for it one of the teachers of the American Missionary Society.[1]

Facilities for the education of the freedmen were not limited to primary and grammar schools. One of the foremost institutions for advanced education for the blacks, Atlanta University, was organized in October, 1867. The first building was erected in 1869, and in that year the attendance was sixty-two men and twenty-seven women. Gifts toward the work came from Northern friends of negro education.[2] About the same time was the beginning of Clark University in Atlanta under Methodist management, opened in 1869 by Rev. J. W. Lee and his wife as a primary school in Clark Chapel.[3]

The latter part of the reconstruction period marked great progress in education in Georgia, especially in the widening opportunities for negroes and in the establishment of a public school system. For the former, the friends of reconstruction were almost entirely responsible and certainly, without liberal aid from the North, the negro would not have fared so well in educational facilities. But for the public school system the reconstruction government deserves only part credit. In 1866, a common school system for the whites was outlined by the legislature to go into effect in 1868. As far as legal enactment is concerned, credit is due to the reconstruction party in the legislature of 1870, but after showing respect for common school education by putting the law on the statute books, the Republicans squandered the resources of the state until there was nothing left of their own school appropriations to carry out the work

[1] Alvord, *Letters from the South*, January, 1870.

[2] Reed, *op. cit.*, pp. 351 *et seq.*

[3] *Ibid.*, p. 371.

of education.   Putting the law into effect was left to the
Democratic administration of 1872.   Had the Democrats
been entirely hostile to the law they would have had full
opportunity to repeal or modify it.   Moreover, Georgia's
public school law was not obnoxious to the white people, as
was the law in some other states, for there was no attempt
to enforce joint instruction of whites and blacks.

The slavery issue and war brought disruption in church
organization North and South as well as political disunion.
Hence, reconstruction was a problem for churches as for
civil government in 1865.

The Episcopal Church, having an established ritual, was
subjected to military discipline in some places before its
services conformed to what was deemed the practice of
loyalty.   The military commander ordered that the prayer
" For the President of the United States and All Others in
Authority " be restored in the church service.   In Savannah, Christ Church was closed because the assistant rector,
then officiating, refused to use the prayer in the absence of
instructions from the bishop or the rector.   Later, when he
had taken the amnesty oath and promised to use the prayer
as directed, he was permitted to re-open the church for service.[1]   Bishop Elliott, of the diocese of Georgia, did not
follow the action of Bishop Wilmer, of Alabama, in with-
standing the command to restore the prayer and suffering
the churches in the state to be closed in consequence.   In
yielding to the demand, he is reported to have said that he
knew of no one more in need of divine grace than the
President and others in authority in the United States.
There was some question whether the Episcopal Church in
the Southern states should hold to its separate organization
or go back into the general organization of the United

[1] *Savannah Herald*, April 24, 1865.

States. The dioceses of Virginia and South Carolina favored the continuance of the Southern organization, but Georgia inclined to reunion under proper safeguard of her dignity. As Bishop Elliott said to a Northern bishop, " Silence, if you please, but not one word of censure ". Moreover, the Episcopal Church in the South wished the assurance that certain of its acts, especially the consecration of the bishop of Alabama and the organization of the diocese of Arkansas, acted upon after separation from the church in the North, should be accepted by the church as a whole. At a meeting held in Augusta in November, 1865, the House of Bishops and Deputies of the Episcopal Church in the Confederate States decided upon reunion with the Church in the United States.[1]

In the other great churches in which division came because of slavery or war, reunion did not take place. The Methodist, Baptist and Presbyterian churches all maintained their separate Southern organizations. The Georgia Baptist Association in 1865 passed the following resolution: " That from all we can learn of the light in which Northern and Southern Baptists look upon each other, any attempt on their part or ours, towards united effort, at this time, would be productive of trouble and confusion, and not of good." [2]

Churches everywhere except in growing towns suffered serious difficulty in maintaining their buildings and paying their pastors in the hard times just after the war. The disorganization of war times scattered many organizations, and in 1865 there were small resources for gathering forces together. The Baptists reported that in certain sections there were no church services held because the people were

[1] *Macon Journal and Messenger*, December 1, 1865; *New York Times*, November 19, 1865.

[2] *History of the Baptist Denomination in Georgia*, p. 240.

too poor to pay a preacher. In Northeast Georgia there was no preacher in the district above Athens, and in Northwest Georgia one minister supplied six churches, with conditions only a trifle less serious in the middle and southwestern parts of the state. On the coast many church buildings had been burned and not restored, congregations were scattered with no pastors to bring them together. Still, with all these hardships the Baptists were able to increase their membership and the number of their churches. Between 1868 and 1872 the number of churches increased from 1,218 to 1,973 and the number of members from 115,-198 to 146,407. In the decade between 1860 and 1870 the church property held by the Baptists in Georgia increased from about $700,000 to over a million. The Methodist Church South likewise grew rapidly in these years. More than two hundred new church organizations were established and Methodist property increased from $800,000 to a million. Presbyterians were less numerous than Baptists or Methodists and their growth was comparatively slight, as was that of the Episcopalians and other denominations.[1]

Emancipation produced a decided change in the negro membership of Methodist and Baptist churches. As slaves, negroes worshipped in churches with their white masters or had services of their own on the plantations. However, before the war separate churches for negroes were not unknown, especially in the larger towns. In 1865, as soon as the negroes were free, they began organizing churches of their own, assisted by white people, their former masters, in many instances, and helped largely by Northern missions.[2]

[1] Riley, *History of the Baptists in the Southern States East of the Mississippi*, pp. 319-26; *History of the Baptist Denomination in Georgia*, pp. 239 *et seq.*; Smith, *Life of Bishop Pierce; U. S. Census*, 1870, vol. i, pp. 506-7.

[2] *History of the Baptist Denomination in Georgia*, p. 241.

The colored Methodists went over in large numbers to the African Methodist Church, which established its first mission in Georgia after the fall of Savannah in December, 1864. In 1865, African Methodist churches were established in Macon, Atlanta, Columbus and Augusta, and in the next year work was pushed into the smaller towns and country districts. Henry M. Turner, one of the leading negro politicians during the reconstruction period, who came South as chaplain of a negro regiment of the U. S. Army, was an active organizer of the African M. E. Church before he became an organizer of Loyal Leagues and Republican meetings.[1] In fact, mission work among the negroes was not infrequently a stepping-stone to political leadership and public office.

In Atlanta, with the influx of Northerners and rapidly increasing prosperity, churches shared in the general growth. Between 1867 and 1872 all denominations were active in building. Most of the churches which had been destroyed by Sherman's army were rebuilt, and new societies were organized. During the military period the Episcopal church, of which General Meade was an active member, received a fund of $5,000 raised by General Meade among his friends in Philadelphia. As an accompaniment of reconstruction the Methodist Episcopal Church entered the field in Atlanta, starting a church for its Northern members in 1867. Negro churches, Baptist and Methodist, likewise appeared. The number of Jews in Atlanta, coming in with the re-opening of trade in 1865, was great enough to lead to the organization in 1866 of the Hebrew Benevolent Congregation, which built its first synagogue in 1875.[2]

[1] Gaines, *African Methodism in the South*, pp. 5-16; Smith, *op. cit.*, pp. 440, 456, 491.

[2] Reed, *History of Atlanta*, pp. 377-97.

Newspapers of good standing before the war took the conservative, anti-reconstruction side in 1867. The most significant of the daily papers were the *Macon Telegraph, Augusta Chronicle, Savannah News, Atlanta Intelligencer* and *Columbus Enquirer*. It was an important part of reconstruction policy to foster a favorable public opinion through the press. This was done in various ways. Under military rule newspapers were severely dealt with for publishing anti-reconstruction editorials.[1] But a more effective means of securing favorable press opinion was through patronage, not a small instrument with the publication of multitudinous official proclamations and notices. Where established papers could not be won over, the Republicans established papers of their own, kept alive by patronage from the state more than by earnings from subscribers or commercial advertisements. The first and most important paper managed in the interest of the Federal government was the *Savannah Republican,* seized under General Sherman's order in December, 1864. John E. Hayes, correspondent of the *New York Tribune* following Sherman's army, took possession of the *Republican* and continued to publish it until his death in 1868.[2] Under the editorship of Hayes it was by far the most able and influential Republican paper in the state, maintaining a fair and liberal position. In Atlanta the Republicans got control of the *New Era*. In 1866, the editor, Samuel Bard, was a strong advocate of President Johnson's policy. Early in 1867 he preached a " wait and see " doctrine. He did wait, and when he saw the chance of patronage from the military government come his way, the *New Era* became ardently reconstructionist.

---

[1] General Pope's newspaper order, *Report of the Secretary of War*, 1867-8, vol. i, pp. 325-6.

[2] Lee and Agnew, *Historical Record of the City of Savannah*, pp. 189 *et seq.*

In 1870, when disruption in the camp of the Republicans boded danger for Bullock, and Bard was among the disaffected, the paper was purchased by a group of Bullock's friends, of whom H. I. Kimball was one, to be published in his interest. The Republicans also controlled the *Augusta Republican,* the *Griffin Union* and the *Macon American Union.* The last two were edited by a notorious and troublesome carpet-bagger and agitator among the negroes, J. Clarke Swayze.

The Macon papers, the *Telegraph* and the *Journal and Messenger,* during the period after the war gave fullest accounts of agriculture and labor conditions through regular correspondents from various parts of the planting section. For political news the most useful were the Augusta and the Atlanta papers, the *Chronicle and Sentinel* and the *Constitutionalist* in Augusta, and the *Intelligencer* and the *New Era* in Atlanta. After 1868, the *Atlanta Constitution,* founded in that year, became the leading representative of Democratic political opinion, virulently hostile to the Bullock administration and particularly bitter against ex-Governor Brown.

The *Southern Cultivator,* published first in Sparta, then in Athens and later in Atlanta, was a well-edited agricultural weekly, giving special attention to reports of crops and labor conditions from all parts of the state. Several papers conducted especially for negroes appeared after 1867, most of which were short-lived. Representative of this class was the *Freedman's Standard,* a weekly paper published in Savannah by James M. Sims, a negro.[1]

In the decade 1850-60 there was very rapid growth in the number and circulation of newspapers of all sorts, daily and weekly, in Georgia, but in the next ten years there was

[1] *Milledgeville Union,* February 25, 1868.

little advance. In 1870 there were five more newspapers published in the state, but the total circulation was some thirty thousand less than in 1860.[1]

In the decade between 1860 and 1870 there was considerable shifting in the population, a movement of the blacks away from some of the white counties of the Northwest, from the pine barrens in the Southeast and from the marginal counties in the upper cotton-belt to the richer agricultural counties of Southwest and Central Georgia. In the largest cotton-producing counties, Dougherty, Lee, Houston, Sumter and Burke, there was a marked increase in the number of negroes and in most of them a decrease in the white population, as the following figures give evidence:[2]

	Whites.		Blacks.		Per cent blacks.	
	1870	1860	1870	1860	1870	1860
Dougherty..........	2093	2207	9424	6088	82	73
Lee	1924	2242	7643	4954	79	68
Houston	5071	4828	15332	10783	75	69
Burke.............	4243	5013	13436	12152	76	70
Sumter............	5920	4536	10639	4892	64	51

The general process of change resulted in the black counties becoming blacker and the white counties whiter. With few exceptions all the counties in which the negro population decreased between 1860 and 1870 were white counties. It is notable that the black counties which had

[1] *U. S. Census*, 1870, vol. i, pp. 482-3; Avery, *History of the State of Georgia*, pp. 609-23.

[2] *U. S. Census*, 1870, vol. i, pp. 20-22.

fewer blacks in 1870 were localized in two groups, the first, along the coast, including Liberty, McIntosh, and Camden, where thorough demoralization followed upon the breakdown of the rice plantations; and the other, in the upper part of the cotton belt, consisting of Elbert, Lincoln, Wilkes, Greene, and Hancock. In this older, more worn-out section of cotton land it was unprofitable to cultivate large plantations with free labor. A reduction in acreage and more intensive cultivation became the rule in that section.[1] Wages were lower than in the richer, newer southwest counties, and many negroes migrated to the more profitable fields. The Ku Klux disturbances in these counties of the upper cotton-belt may have had some part in encouraging the migration of the blacks.

With the freer opportunities that came to the blacks after emancipation, a great many found occupation in cities or else on small farms near large towns. With the importance of Atlanta as a political center under the reconstruction government the capital became a haven of joy to the black brethren. Census statistics show that there were 8,000 more negroes in Atlanta in 1870 than in 1860, but most of this increase was in the five years after the war. The following figures give evidence of the migration of negroes townward after emancipation:[2]

BLACK POPULATION

	1870	1860		1870	1860
Savannah	13,068	8,417	Chatham Co.	24,518	15,532
Atlanta	9,929	1,939	Fulton Co.	15,282	2,986
Augusta..........	6,431	4,049	Richmond Co......	12,565	8,879
Macon.	5,183	2,851	Bibb Co. ......,.....	11,424	6,831

[1] Dickson, *System of Farming.* *Supra,* chapter xi.

[2] *U. S. Census,* 1870, vol. i, pp. 20-22, 99 *et seq.*

Towns of secondary importance, like Milledgeville, Albany, Brunswick, and Valdosta, as well as the larger cities, increased rapidly in negro population.

Though Georgia took active measures in 1866 to encourage the immigration of foreigners and in 1869 appointed a Foreign Commissioner of Immigration, the foreign population of the state in 1870 was slightly less than ten years earlier. In Savannah, Augusta and Columbus there were fewer foreigners than in 1860. Atlanta was the only city to which foreigners in any numbers came after the war, though in Macon and the vicinity there was a small number of German immigrants, and of Irish in Augusta, Columbus and Macon. In 1867 the U. S. Commissioner of Immigration reported that out of a total of 228,851 immigrants, only 225 were destined for Georgia. Most of the immigration into Georgia after 1865 was from the Northern states of the Union. New York was the largest source of Georgia immigrants. In 1870 there were in Georgia 2,208 natives of New York, 829 of Pennsylvania, 615 of Massachusetts, 576 of Connecticut, 367 of New Jersey, 349 of Ohio. This is no certain index of the number of Northerners who came after the war, for many came in the prosperous decade before 1860 to try their fortunes in Georgia. The total increase in the population of Georgia between 1860 and 1870 was about 130,000, or 12 per cent, not at all commensurate with the increase before and after. The increase in 1840-50 was 31 per cent; in 1850-60, 16 per cent; and in 1870-80, 30 per cent.[1]

Population of Georgia	1870	1860
Whites	638,926	591,550
Blacks	545,142	465,698
total	1,184,068	1,057,248

[1] *U. S. Census,* 1870, vol. i, pp. 4, 5, 299, 306-307, 328-342.

This diminution in normal increase was the result of loss by war. The increase in white population was only 8 per cent, while the blacks increased 17 per cent. The loss represented more than mere numbers indicate, for the drain was primarily on the most important producing element of the community, on males between twenty and fifty years, especially on young men under thirty. The following figures present a striking record of the havoc of war: [1]

White male population.	1850	1860	1870
20–29 years	79,025	93,041	82,961
30–39 years	47,339	57,695	57,975
40–49 years	31,027	37,364	41,260
Total, 20–50 years..............	157,391	188,100	182,196

In the census year 1870, as compared with the year 1860, the birth rate was slightly less—1 :32.10 in 1870 and 1 : 31.87 in 1860. The years after the war were harder on negroes in their struggle for existence as freemen than on the whites. The death rate of blacks was considerably higher than that of whites, especially in towns and cities where negroes lived in crowded and unsanitary quarters.[2] The average size of familes tended to decrease gradually between 1850 and 1870. In 1850 the average size of family was 5.72 persons; in 1860, 5.41 ; and in 1870, 4.98.[3]

The organization of the judiciary underwent varied

[1] *U. S. Census*, vol. ii, pp. 566-77.

[2] *Ibid.*, vol. ii, pp. 532-3 ; Alvord, *Letters from the South;* mortuary reports in Savannah, Macon, Augusta, Atlanta papers.

[3] *U. S. Census*, 1870, vol. i, p. 595.

changes in 1865 and again in 1868. By the constitution of 1865 election was substituted for appointment as a means of choosing judges of the higher courts, but no material change was made in the character or jurisdiction of the various courts. Justices of the supreme court were elected by the legislature for a term of six years, and judges of the superior courts were elected by the voters of the different circuits for a four-year term. In other respects the judicial system remained much the same in 1865 as in 1860. In 1868 the constitution provided for a more elaborate judiciary. Besides the supreme and the superior courts, there were district courts, courts of ordinary and probate, and of justices of the peace. Inferior courts of the counties were abolished. Jurisdiction of the supreme and the superior courts was not materially changed. The courts of ordinary took over much of the business of the old inferior courts, and between these and the superior courts were the newly-organized district courts for each senatorial district. Another new feature of the 1868 constitution was the provision for official attorneys, an attorney general for the state, solicitors general for each circuit, and district attorneys. In 1868 appointment of judges took the place of election, and in almost all cases the term of office was extended. The governor, with the approval of the senate, had the power to appoint the supreme court justices, the judges of the superior and district courts, the attorney general, solicitors general and district attorneys, as well. Ordinaries and justices of the peace were elected. The term of office of the judges of the supreme court was extended from six to twelve years, and of superior court judges, from four to eight years.[1]

[1] Constitution, 1865, Article IV. Constitution, 1868, Article V; also W. M. Reese, " Constitutions of Georgia," *Report of the Georgia Bar Association*, 1885.

The constitution of 1868 did not confer upon negroes
the right of jury service. It left to the legislature the duty
of providing for the method of drawing " upright and intelligent persons " for juries.[1] Accordingly, in 1869 the legislature enacted a Jury Law, providing that the ordinary of
each county, with the clerk of the superior court and three
commissioners, appointed for each county by the presiding
judge of the superior court, should meet at the court house
biennially at a stated time, and select from the books of the
receivers of tax returns " upright and intelligent persons "
to serve as jurors.[2] In actual practice under the reconstruction government in but very few counties were negroes
ever drawn on juries. Since county officers were mostly
Democratic, even in 1868, they did not put the names of
negroes in the jury box, not classing them as " upright and
intelligent persons ".[3]

Considering the very broad powers of appointment in
Governor Bullock's hands and the heavy political pressure
upon him, the judges of his selection were as a general rule
able and worthy, though in many cases not up to the standard of the Georgia bench before the war. The highest office
within the patronage of Governor Bullock was that of
chief justice of the supreme court. This place was given
to Jos. E. Brown as consolation for his defeat for the U. S.
Senate. His associates were H. K. McCay and Hiram
Warner. McCay, a prominent Republican in the constitutional convention, was a lawyer of ability but had no judicial experience before his appointment to the supreme
court. Brown had been judge of the Blue Ridge circuit
before he was elected governor in 1857. Hiram Warner,.

[1] Constitution, 1868.

[2] *Acts of the General Assembly*, 1869, pp. 139-43.

[3] *Ku Klux Committee*, vol. vi, pp. 37, 266.

a native of Massachusetts, who moved to Georgia in 1821, a Union man but not a Republican, appointed for the short term, had had a long judicial career. He was justice of the supreme court when it was organized in 1845, and in 1867 was chief justice under appointment from Governor Jenkins.[1] The lack of harmony in political sentiment between Warner on the one hand and Brown and McCay on the other resulted in a divided court in almost all the important cases which reconstruction issues brought before the supreme court.

The results of war, the change in currency and the emancipation of the blacks, together with legislation for relief and homestead exemption, brought a vast bulk of litigation into court of a kind not known before the war. Earlier cases were mostly concerned with land titles or slave property, but in the reconstruction period the greatest amount of litigation arose over relief, contracts during the war in which the consideration was for Confederate currency, stay laws, and the status of freedmen.[2]

Though the extensive relief ordinance in the constitution of 1868 was stricken out by the command of Congress in the bill admitting Georgia to representation in June, 1868, various laws looking toward the adjustment of equities of contracts made during the war were enacted and came before the Supreme Court for construction. On the general principles of relief, in the ordinance of 1865, in the act of 1866 and the more comprehensive act of 1868, Jus-

[1] John W. Akin, " Memorial Address on Hiram Warner," *Report of the Georgia Bar Association*, 1897.

[2] On this subject a paper prepared by Henry R. Goetchius of Columbus, Ga., as his presidential address before the Georgia Bar Association in 1897 is most valuable. I have drawn freely on the summary he gives of the most important cases before the courts. " Litigation in Georgia during the Reconstruction Period," in *Report of the Georgia Bar Association*, 1897.

tices Brown and McCay supported the constitutionality of
the laws, on the ground that the acts touched only the remedy for enforcement and not the obligation of the contract.
In all decisions in cases involving these laws, Justice Warner was in dissent, holding that the laws impaired the obligation of contracts. Since some features of the relief acts
were ruled out by the court, in 1870 the legislature passed a
still more extensive relief measure under the guise of a
tax act.[1] It set aside from the aid of courts all debts contracted prior to June, 1865, on which legal taxes had not
been paid. In the case of Walker *v.* Whitehead, involving
this law, brought before the supreme court in 1871, Warner was again in the minority, holding that the law was not
in intent a revenue measure, but merely an attempt to nullify a certain class of debts. On appeal to the U. S. Supreme Court in the spring term of 1873, the judgment of
the Georgia court was reversed and Judge Warner's dissent sustained.[2]

In the second kind of litigation, cases concerning contracts made for payment in Confederate currency, the
supreme court sustained the position of the lower court,
leaving wide latitude to the jury in finding a specie value
for Confederate notes, not necessarily at the time of the
maturity of the note. In one such case, McLaughlin & Co.

---

[1] *Acts of the General Assembly*, 1870, pp. 401-402.

[2] The following are the most important cases involving the constitutionality of the relief acts, cited by Goetchius:

Walker *v.* Whitehead, 43 *Georgia* 539; 16 *Wallace* 314.
Slaughter *et al. v.* Culpepper *et al.*, 35 *Georgia* 25.
White *v.* Lee, 40 *Georgia* 266.
Cutts and Johnson *et al. v.* Hardee, 38 *Georgia* 350.
Graham *v.* Clark, 40 *Georgia* 660.
White *v.* Herndon, 40 *Georgia* 494.
Lott *v.* Dysart, 45 *Georgia* 355.
Mitchell *v.* Elliott, 49 *Georgia* 125.

v. O'Dowd, a set of tables compiled by a broker in Augusta, known as Barber's Tables, showing the value of Confederate currency from January 1, 1861, to May 1, 1865, estimated in gold, was admitted as evidence and accepted afterwards in cases of this kind.[1] In two cases that were argued, concerning the payment of notes calling for Confederate currency, the point was brought up that such a contract was in aid of rebellion by encouraging the circulation of Confederate notes, and so was void under the state constitution.[2] In this decision Brown was the dissenting judge, maintaining the illegality of the contract on the ground stated above. In November, 1869, a case involving the same principle was decided by the Supreme Court of the United States, Thorington *v.* Smith and Hartley, on appeal from the Alabama supreme court.[3] The binding force of the contract was upheld. The question was—"Can a contract for the payment of Confederate notes, made during the late rebellion, between the parties residing in the so-called Confederate States, be enforced at all in the courts of the United States?" Incidentally, argument arose as to the meaning of the word " dollars " in such contracts, and as to proof that notes were to be paid only in Confederate currency. Arguing that the Confederate government existed *de facto* if not *de jure,* the court decided that Confederate notes were lawful currency for those living in the Confederate States, and such contracts were therefore binding.

[1] McLaughlin *v.* O'Dowd, 34 *Georgia* 487.

[2] Miller *v.* Artemus and Georgia R. R. & Banking Co. *v.* Eddleman, 38 *Georgia* 467.

[3] Thorington *v.* Smith & Hartley, 8 *Wallace* 1. Other cases cited by Goetchius: Evans *v.* Walker, 35 *Georgia* 117, Cherry *v.* Walker, 36 *Georgia* 327, Abbott *v.* Dermott, 349 *Georgia* 226, Dean *v.* Harvey, 9 *Wallace* 15.

The validity of the various stay laws enacted by the legislature was decided adversely by the supreme court in the important case, Aycock *et al. v.* Martin *et al.*[1] This case attracted wide attention, not only because of the importance of the principle involved, but also because of the distinction of the counsel engaged in the controversy. Linton Stephens, the brother of Alex. H. Stephens, and Ben. H. Hill, two of the ablest lawyers in Georgia, argued the case before the court. Justices Warner and Harris agreed that the stay laws were unconstitutional, holding that any postponement or obstruction of the fulfilment of the contract was an impairment of the obligation. Justice Walker dissented, holding to the position taken by Brown in later cases, that the remedy in enforcement differed from the obligation.[2]

Emancipation and the results therefrom brought many cases into court, some concerning contracts for slave property, and others involving rights and privileges of freedmen. The decision of the Georgia supreme court that contracts for slave property were void, on the basis of the clause in the state constitution, was overruled by the U. S. Supreme Court.[3]

Much litigation concerning the status of freedmen came before the court. In the case of Scott *v.* State of Georgia, it decided that the intermarriage of whites and blacks was illegal.[4] In the December term, 1866, the supreme court pronounced on the competency of persons of color as witnesses. In Clark *v.* State of Georgia, a case of appeal from

[1] 37 *Georgia* 124, cited by Goetchius.

[2] Judges Iverson L. Harris and Dawson A. Walker were on the supreme bench in 1866 and 1867 before the court was reorganized in 1868.

[3] White *v.* Hart, 39 *Georgia* 306, 13 *Wallace* 646. Goetchius cites also: Shorter *v.* Cobb, 39 *Georgia* 285; Hand *v.* Armstrong, 34 *Georgia* 232.

[4] 37 *Georgia* 124. Cited by Goetchius.

a verdict for murder, which was made from testimony given by a negro witness, the court declared that the Act of March 17, 1866, gave full rights to persons of color.[1]

The most famous case of all concerning negro status was that of White *v.* Clements. The question—Can a negro hold office in Georgia?— was decided by the Supreme Court in the June term, 1869.[2] The history of the case was this: Richard W. White, a person of color, was elected clerk of the superior court of Chatham County in the election in April, 1868, defeating Wm. J. Clements. Suit for possession of the office was brought by Clements against White before the superior court, of the Eastern Circuit, Judge Wm. Schley presiding. On the question of fact the jury decided that White had one-eighth African blood, and so was a " person of color ", and on question of law the judge decided that persons of color had rights of citizens, but not the right to hold office. When the case was appealed to the supreme court, able counsel was engaged on both sides. The best Republican lawyers in the state, A. W. Stone and A. T. Akerman, took charge of White's side of the case, and Julian Hartridge and Thos. E. Lloyd, both prominent lawyers of Savannah, represented Clements. White's counsel rested their case on the following propositions:

(1) The constitution of Georgia made colored people citizens;

(2) the constitution of Georgia adopted Irwin's Code;

(3) the code provided among rights of citizens the elective franchise and the right to hold office (section 1648);

(4) all citizens of Georgia were entitled to exercise all rights as such, unless specially prohibited by law;

(5) colored citizens were not so prohibited.

[1] 35 *Georgia* 175.

[2] 39 *Georgia* 232; also a pamphlet published in Atlanta, 1869, 179 pages, giving full argument of counsel, records of the case in the lower court, and opinions of judges.

The decision of the court, Brown and McCay concurring, was that persons of color were eligible to office. Brown rested his opinion on the code, but McCay thought that the right was conferred by the constitution of 1868. Judge Warner, dissenting, took the stand that the right was nowhere conferred by the constitution—the clause conferring it had been expressly stricken out by the convention of 1868—nor was the section of the code applicable, since negroes were not citizens in the meaning of the law when the law cited (section 1648 of Irwin's Code) was adopted.

The political aspects of this case were far-reaching. The main interest was not in the clerkship of a Chatham County court, but in the relation of the decision to the eligibility of negroes to the legislature, from which they had been expelled in the preceding September. Conservative white citizens had in the decision another source for bitterness against Jos. E. Brown, for in 1868, when the constitution was before the people for adoption, he gave as his opinion that the constitution did not confer the right to office on negroes.[1]

Considering the political upheaval and uncertainty in the years following the war, the temper of the courts was remarkably conservative and steadying in its influence. With many new kinds of questions coming before the courts for adjudication, in the lack of precedent, judges had to blaze new trails. As a distinguished Georgia lawyer said, concerning litigation of the reconstruction period, there was a gradual drifting away from the enforcement of technicalities toward the administration of justice on broader principles of equity and a sense of right. The necessity of the day gave courage to break away from old forms and precedents.[2]

---

[1] *Supra*, p. 215.

[2] Goetchius, *Report of the Georgia Bar Association*, 1897, p. 103.

CHAPTER XIV

Ku Klux and Social Disorder

In the first two years after the war Georgia suffered considerably from lawlessness and social disorganization attendant upon the break-up of the old civil order, and more from difficulties arising from the new-found liberty, or license, of the freedmen. Better opportunities for work and less idleness at the beginning of 1867 encouraged the hope that conditions were growing better slowly but steadily. But the political changes of 1867 brought a change for the worse instead of the better. Much that had been accomplished toward social adjustment by these first two years of painful effort was swept aside. By emancipation the negro became a social menace to the class of poor whites. By becoming a voter he was a source of danger to the whites of all classes.

The Ku Klux Committee of Congress in 1871, the Committee to Investigate Conditions in the Late Insurrectionary States, examined into affairs in Georgia as in other states, most assiduously hunting for " outrages ". In the two volumes of testimony pertaining to Georgia it was brought out that the disturbances in the years 1868-71 were confined mostly to two sections of the state, to the extreme northwest and to a part of the upper cotton-belt. The counties especially under investigation as centers of disturbance were: (1) Dade, Walker, Murray, Chattooga, Gordon, Floyd, Bartow, Polk, Haralson, Jackson, Gwinnett, Walton; (2) Clarke, Morgan, Oglethorpe, Greene,

Taliaferro, Warren, Columbia. Conditions within these counties constitute the first twelve mentioned as one group and the others a second group.

All of the counties of the first group were predominantly white in population; in the registration under the Recon-

Population in 1860.		Registration 1867.		Vote for Governor, April, 1868.		Vote for President, November, 1868.	
		White.	Colored.	Gordon.	Bullock.	Seymour.	Grant.
Dade	White over 90 %	454	33	284	65	310	18
Walker	White over 75	1364	230	659	509	824	426
Murray	White over 75	887	118	509	350	629	338
Chattooga	White over 60	727	223	495	207	534	147
Gordon	White over 75	1340	222	787	328	894	324
Floyd	White over 60	1669	890	1223	804	1525	591
Bartow	White over 60	1976	682	1484	754	1473	668
Polk	White over 60	883	387	601	337	485	319
Haralson	White over 60	499	38	204	249	218	201
Jackson	White over 50	1138	564	576	671	1055	264
Gwinnett	White over 75	1633	341	886	505	1249	388
Walton	White over 50	1024	683	725	632	1082	382

struction Acts in 1867 these counties all had a goodly majority of white over black electors. The whites, on a straight vote, could dominate politically. Hence there was no need of a political motive to explain the attacks upon the blacks

in this section. In spite of the fact that there were many
white Republicans in North Georgia, all of these counties,
with the exception of Haralson and Jackson, were Democratic even in the first election in the spring of 1868, and
these two had Democratic majorities in the fall of that
year. "Outrages" were chiefly cases of whipping for theft,
or of attack on negroes known to associate with low white
women. Some cases were reported of negroes being
whipped and intimidated to prevent their voting. But even
this was more social than political in purpose. Political
results could not be much affected by the negro's vote, but
by it he might be inclined to think he was "as good as white
folks". Disturbances of the Ku Klux sort lasted in Northwest Georgia from the period immediately after the war
until 1871 or later. Few arrests were made of men
who were suspected of engaging in these attacks. One
such rare case occurred in Chattooga County where three
men were captured and convicted on a charge of robbery,
taking guns from negroes, for which they were sentenced
to a term of seven years in the penitentiary. The only incident of much political significance was the threat upon G.
P. Burnett, a Republican candidate for Congress in this district. In the campaign of 1870, Burnett, going from Rome
to Summerville, was visited by a band of men who fired
pistols toward the house where he was staying and warned
him not to make a speech. Burnett heeded the warning,
left town and avoided further difficulty. In Gwinnett
County bands of night riders set out after negroes who had
been stealing, simply scaring some and whipping others. In
Haralson County the most important outrage was the killing of a colored man because he had been associating with
a low white woman. In Walton County a negro woman
was whipped and warned not to " sass " white ladies. In
Floyd County a light mulatto was dealt with because he

greeted a white woman insolently—" How d'ye, Sis ".   In Murray County in March, 1869, a negro was lynched by a mob for committing rape upon a young lady, his former owner.   A year later another lynching for a similar crime took place in Dalton.[1]   In Bartow County, in 1870 a gang of night riders burned the house of a white man, a Unionist.   But this was thought to be an act of vengeance upon the victim for giving evidence against illicit distillers.   This was the kind of disturbance that occurred with some frequency in the mountainous counties of Northeast Georgia, where organizations were thought to exist for the protection of " moonshiners ".   This particular kind of informal justice, however, did not begin or end with the period of reconstruction.

The chief motive assigned for the attacks on negroes was " to control them ", " to keep them down ".   More than one case appeared where negroes were driven off when they seemed to be prospering too well in a neighborhood of poor, thriftless whites.   What was termed " impudence " to white people was a frequent cause of discipline upon the blacks, described thus: " If there is any dispute about a settlement or anything of that sort, it is not expected that a colored man will contend, in a white man's face, for anything as a white man would.   Any language that he would regard as not offensive at all from a white man would be impudence from a negro ".[2]   Or again: " It is considered impudence for a negro not to be polite to a white man— not to pull off his hat and bow and scrape to a white man, as was always done formerly." [3]   In Chattooga County a school-house for negroes, erected by a white farmer, was

[1] I have found what seem to be authentic reports of seven cases of rape by negroes upon white women in the years 1868-70.

[2] *Ku Klux Committee*, vol. vi, p. 36.

[3] *Ibid.*, p. 66.

torn down by a band of men from the neighborhood because they considered it too close to the school for white children. Lawlessness, not uncommon in North Georgia before and during the war, was aggravated by the bad habits and violence resulting from war. Personal quarrels, ending in the stabbing or killing of one or more victims, were frequent among white people.

Carpet-baggers played no political part in the northern section of Georgia. There were no political adventurers to stir up the negroes to a new sense of power, and county officers in almost all cases were Democrats. The real cause of disturbance in the northern section of the state was due fundamentally to the racial animosity of the poorer class of whites to the blacks. Emancipation removed the most important barrier between the poor whites and the negroes, and when the two classes were given political equality, the poor white, with neither economic nor political advantage, had no source of superiority except his race. The use made of this racial antagonism by leaders of both parties is explained by a witness from North Georgia before the Ku Klux Committee thus:

One great cause, I think, for the persecution of the reconstruction men and the republicans is this: There is in the country now, as there was before the war, a class of men who are bitterly opposed to the colored people, and to whom the colored people are bitterly opposed. Since the war, that feeling on the part of the non-slaveholders toward the negroes has been worse, mostly confined to that element, for most of the negroes were republicans. The shrewd, smart, cunning men of the country among the democratic masses took advantage of that feeling. While they probably would not countenance any direct, open assassination, nevertheless they took advantage of the prejudice of this class of men against the colored people and against the republicans, most of the colored men being republicans, and fanned their passions and kept them alive against the colored people, and that portion of the white people who acted with the republicans.[1]

A different situation existed in the second group of counties. Here blacks constituted 60 per cent or more of the population and in 1867 colored registered voters largely outnumbered the whites. In these counties in the neighborhood of Augusta, to the south and west, there were several notorious leaders of the blacks, some carpet-baggers and some native Republicans, who kept their influence over the negroes by inciting them against the whites. This was the cause of several of the most notorious outrages in the state. Warren County especially was the scene of much lawlessness and great activity from Ku Klux bands. In March, 1869, Dr. George W. Darden, who had killed the editor of a newspaper in Warrenton, was taken from jail and shot to death. A band of men, not trusting to the justice of the courts or fearing pardon by the governor, took the law into their own hands. It is not clear that any political motive entered into the case. More notorious than the Darden murder was that of Joseph Adkins, just two months after Darden was killed. Adkins, a Radical member of the state senate, had other qualities in addition to his politics which made him obnoxious to the white people of his community. From all accounts he was a thoroughly disreputable, low white man, consorting with negro women and inciting the passions of the negroes against white people. Though proclamations of reward were published no

---

[1] *Ku Klux Committee*, vol. vi, p. 74. References for social disorder in Northwest Georgia: *Ku Klux Committee*, vol. vi, pp. 20-4, 32, 35, 36, 38, 40, 41-5, 49-51, 56, 65, 66, 74-5, 78, 105, 131, 135-6, 351, 371, 373, 378, 391, 402, 413, 426, 493, 497, 529-30; vol. vii, p. 603; *Macon Telegraph*, March 21, 1869; *Savannah News*, March 23, 1869; *Augusta Constitutionalist*, February 13, 1870.

arrests were ever made in connection with these two murders, which figured largely in the political controversy over
the second reconstruction of Georgia.[1]

In June, 1869, General Terry, reporting that there was
no civil law in Warren County, that an insurrectionary organization terrorized the place, sent a detachment of troops
to aid the sheriff in enforcing order. The sheriff of the
county, Chap. Norris, was apparently a reason in himself
for local disturbance. He was thoroughly incompetent,
lavish in arrests and threats without evidence to substantiate his charges. His testimony before the Ku Klux Committee sounds decidedly unreliable in great part, especially
his narrative of his own experience in being shot at in Warrenton at election time in November, 1868. He tried to
make himself appear a martyr to the Republican cause in
that his life was unsafe in Warrenton on account of his
politics—this, in spite of the fact that the so-called attack
on his life was not reported until several months after it
supposedly took place, and that he remained in Warrenton
four months after he considered his life to be in jeopardy.
Major Van Voast, in command of the troops sent to Warrenton, reported to General Terry on June 6, 1869. His report showed him to be a sane, unhysterical observer of conditions, not entirely in sympathy with politicians in Atlanta
who were trying to make the conditions appear as vicious
as possible to secure renewed reconstruction and the elimination of Democrats from the legislature. Van Voast said
that Sheriff Norris seemed to think he could make arrests
without regard to law, using troops at his own discretion.
Men arrested by him were released under *habeas corpus*

[1] *Ku Klux Committee*, vol. vi, pp. 197-200, 207-8, 266-9, 283-4, 288-9,
477; *Macon Telegraph*, May 13, 1869; *Savannah News*, March 18, 1869;
reports of Gen. Terry and Maj. Van Voast, Hse. Exec. Doc., 41 C.,
2 S., no. 288, pp. 2-15.

proceedings, advised by the military and by Attorney-General Farrow. Major Van Voast reported that the existence of a Ku Klux organization in Warren and the adjoining counties was admitted by all persons. Some said its object was protection, originally started for good, but then beyond control and frequently used for personal interests. In regard to the Adkins murder, Van Voast's opinion was that it was planned, not necessarily by a large body, and he was uncertain whether or not Ku Klux were engaged in it. Adkins was undoubtedly killed for his Radical opinions, though the better element of his political opponents would not countenance murder. He had many enemies and few friends. Only three whites had voted for him in his election to the state senate. Many people rejoiced that he was out of the way though they regretted the manner of his death. Many others of the same politics as Adkins were unmolested, not regarded as obnoxious because they did not incite the negroes against the white people.[1]

In Jefferson County, a little to the south of Warren, about the time of the Adkins murder another member of the legislature was killed. Dr. Benj. Ayer, the victim in this case, was much the same sort of person as Adkins, thoroughly objectionable to the white people in the neighborhood for his intimate relations with negroes. In response to the charge made in Northern newspapers that Dr. Ayer would never have been killed if he had not been a Radical, a Macon editor replied: " True, if he had not been a Carpet-bag Radical, consorting and cohabiting with negroes at midnight and tempting them with display of his money, he would not have been murdered." [2] In Jefferson

---

[1] Report of Maj. Van Voast, *op. cit.*; also *Milledgeville Federal Union*, May 10, 1870; *Ku Klux Committee*, vol. vi, pp. 193 *et seq.*

[2] *Macon Telegraph*, April 20, 25, May 1, 1869.

County, also, Ku Klux bands dealt with obstreperous negroes by tying them up or whipping them or burning their
houses. Earlier, in November, 1867, a mob, probably not
Ku Klux, wrought speedy vengeance upon a negro who
committed rape upon a white woman. Some months later
a squad of soldiers appeared, arrested eleven white men
suspected of taking part in the lynching, and took them to
Atlanta.[1]

With many cases of violence that actually occurred there
were many more reported that never took place. Belcher,
one of the negro Republicans in Georgia, wrote to Charles
Sumner, May 14, 1869, that since his previous letter two
more colored men were made " victims of rebel treachery".
" If Congress does not interfere in our behalf, every loyal
man in Georgia that can get away, will become an exile."
The two reputed victims were later discovered to be alive
and flourishing, but in the meantime the report of more Ku
Klux murders for political purposes was spread broadcast
through the Republican journals of the North.[2]

The Ku Klux organization was formed in Augusta in
March, 1868, just before the state election. The *Augusta
Chronicle* had this note from the editor: "We learn that a
Klan has been organized in this place and that the faithful
are holding nightly meetings for the purpose of conferring
the honors of the mystic brotherhood upon such worthy ap-
plicants as may seek admission within their walls. Success
say we to the Ku Klux!"[3] And again: " Four strangers
entered a shoe store in this city on March 24th and bought
four pair of India rubber shoes. Were they for Ku Klux?

[1] Report of the Freedmen's Bureau in the *Report of the Secretary
of War*, 1868-9, vol. i, p. 1044; *Augusta Chronicle*, March 26, 1868.

[2] *Macon Telegraph*, May 25, 29, 1869.

[3] March 25, 1868.

Do they mean them 'to tread softly with', or are they for a
' bloody month' and a ' muddy day '?" [1] And a few days
later the editor mentioned a mysterious order spreading
rapidly throughout the country, carrying consternation and
dismay to craven hearts of traitors, scalawags, and bum-
mers.[2] But the Ku Klux rarely operated in cities and
no report of activities was heard from Augusta itself. A
prominent citizen of Augusta, a member of a Ku Klux band
of about forty for a part of Richmond and the southern
part of Columbia County, said that his band was never
called out as there was nothing for them to do. Negroes
knew there was such an organization and caused no trouble.
However, there was some difficulty and work for the Ku
Klux in the northern part of Columbia County.[3] In July,
1869, a body of armed men forcibly removed from jail
and put to death a freedman and his wife, accused of murder. Governor Bullock requested General Terry to send
troops to the scene of the difficulty, as the civil authorities
of the county, he declared, were in sympathy with or over-
awed by the insurrectionary organization. The governor's
offer of $5,000 reward availed nothing toward bringing the
conspirators to light.[4] In Augusta and other places at election time frays occurred between blacks and whites. In
the November election of 1868 a small riot was quelled by
troops. A negro made some insulting remarks to a white
man who responded by drawing his pistol and firing. Two
other freedmen were killed at the polls in an altercation
with some railway employees about precedence in voting.

[1] March 26, 1868.

[2] March 31, 1868.

[3] Conversation with Mr. S. M. Mays of Augusta. Stearns, *Black
Man of the South and the Rebels,* pp. 65, 249-51; *Macon Telegraph,*
January 19, 1869.

[4] *Macon Telegraph,* August 11, 1869.

Augusta, where Radicals, mostly Freedmen's Bureau and other government agents, controlled the city government in 1868 and after, was the scene of much disorder and lawlessness.[1]

In Wilkes County trouble arose because the U. S. revenue assessor of the district was a negro Republican, Belcher. People made it unpleasant for the assistant assessor, a white man named Haygood, because he was willing to work under a negro. Little boys used to run after him on the street and taunt him with such remarks as—"I smell Belcher." Troops were sent from Atlanta for the protection of the revenue officers; and the supervisor of the district, reporting the defiant attitude of the Ku Klux in Wilkes County, at the same time recommended that the resignation of Assistant Assessor Haygood be accepted.[2] The Ku Klux in Wilkes County, as in most places, were the best people, old and young alike, operating for social and political purposes as well. The young men were bolder, wishing to undertake more vigorous measures against Governor Bullock himself, but in these desires they were restrained by the older men.[3] In the neighboring county of Greene one of the Freedmen's Bureau teachers was driven away and the man with whom he boarded was taken out of his house at night and whipped.[4] And in Morgan County the band shot into the house of a negro elected to the legislature.[5]

In Clarke County the Ku Klux organization sprang up

[1] *Savannah News*, September 19, 1867; *Macon Telegraph*, January 19, 1869; *Augusta Chronicle*, November 4, 1868; Stearns, *op. cit.*, pp. 249-51.

[2] *Milledgeville Federal Union*, August 3, 10, 1869.

[3] This is from conversation with Miss E. F. Andrews of Washington, Ga., author of a *War-Time Journal of a Georgia Girl*.

[4] Alvord, *Letters from the South*, 1870, p. 22.

[5] *Ku Klux Committee*, vol. vi, p. 250.

to check growing evils in the community, to rid the county of dangerous characters and to keep the negroes in check. Mr. Hull, in his *Annals of Athens,* says that the Ku Klux in that county were not a body of fantastics out for a frolic, but a group of serious men, the most esteemed in the community. The members were organized in bands of twenty or thirty under a captain when there was work to do. Mysterious notices, understood by members but appalling to others, were nailed to barn doors. Members assembled in disguise and secret word was passed as to the business in hand. The ordinary business was to visit the house of an idle negro who was a nuisance, to terrify him by ghostly scenes, whip him into subordination, and warn him that the second visit would be more disastrous. He knew of only one such visitation in Clarke County that proved fatal. The most conspicuous case of Ku Klux action in the county was the attack on the negro, Alf. Richardson, member of the legislature, disliked by the whites on account of his insolence and his disturbing influence over the negroes. When the Ku Klux band went to Richardson's house and called him out, he refused to obey and gave fight. In the shooting that followed one of the Ku Klux band and a negro with Richardson were shot, the negro dying a few days later.[1] This same Alf. Richardson, when called as a witness before the Ku Klux investigating committee, reported many outrages on negroes, among which were cases of whipping of negro women, explained by him as follows:[2]

Many times, you know, a white lady has a colored lady for a cook or waiting in the house, or something of that sort. They have some quarrel, and sometimes probably the colored woman gives the lady a little jaw. In a night or two a crowd will come in and take her out and whip her.

[1] Hull, *Athens,* pp. 322-4; *Ku Klux Committee,* vol. vi, p. 235.
[2] *Ibid.,* p. 12.

J. H. Christy, elected to Congress from the district of which Athens formed a part, testified before the Ku Klux Committee that there was comparatively little lawlessness in Athens. Stories of violence were largely exaggerated. As to the behavior of the blacks he said:

As a general thing they behave better than I had any idea they would. As to working, they do better than I thought they would, a great many of them. There are some of them who gather about the towns and tell these cock-and-bull stories about being run off by the Ku Klux. The truth is, they come to town because they do not want to work. Generally the negroes work better than I supposed they would. A great many of them acquire property. I suppose there are from sixty to seventy-five in my town who have houses and lots. They are industrious negroes, and are encouraged and protected by the white people, who sell them lots cheap. They are inclined to become property-holders.[1]

According to the narrative of the head of the Ku Klux Klan in Oglethorpe County, Mr. John C. Reed, the organization was formed in that section in the early summer of 1868 to overcome the effects of Democratic defeat in the April election of that year. General Dudley M. DuBose, the son-in-law of Robert Toombs, was head of the Klan in that congressional district. The first appearance of the Klan in active operation was just before the November election in 1868, when they rode out to frighten the negroes. On election day the Ku Klux by their activity and their constant vigilance, aided by the absence of any powerful carpetbagger leaders of the blacks, carried things their own way. In Oglethorpe County the vote for Bullock was 1,144, for Gordon, 557; in November, 116 votes were cast for Grant, 849 for Seymour. In the state election in De-

---

[1] *Ku Klux Committee*, vol. vi, p. 243.

cember, 1870, the Ku Klux of Oglethorpe County were again busy to keep the negroes from voting. This was done in some cases by threatening prosecution of negroes who tried to vote without paying their poll tax, which requirement for suffrage had been set aside by the legislature. Outright payment for voting the right way or for refraining from voting was not uncommon. In Wilkes County the tale was told that negroes asked and received from no less a person than Robert Toombs a quarter or a half-dollar for a vote. To a U. S. detective, who must have seen the procedure, Toombs, just as he paid one lot, is reported to have said: " Sir, are you not touched by this spectacle of the unbought suffrages of a free people? " This may be only fable, but it is characteristically Toombsian, at least. Mr. Reed insists that the Klan as he knew it was political in motive and work rather than social. Yet his account of operations showed clearly that it was a force for social regulation as well, else why did the Ku Klux deal with a negro from the North because he preached intermarriage of the races, or with a white man because he lived with a negro woman? And again, he showed that the Klan was more than an instrument to turn the results from Republican to Democratic victory, in characterizing it thus: " It was a police, rather than a military force, an underground and nocturnal constabulary, detective, interclusive, interceptive, repressive, preventive—in the main—punitive only now and then, where it showed some faint resemblance to the *Vehmgericht* ".[1]

In this upper section of the cotton-belt, where the blacks could and did outvote the whites, to regain their lost supremacy meant to the white people the task of pushing the negroes out of politics by fair means or foul. Since the blacks were

---

[1] Reed, "What I Know of the Ku Klux Klan," *Uncle Remus Magazine.*

controlled by astute leaders, some negroes, some Northern
adventurers, the task of diverting the negro from political
interests was by no means easy. Hence, foul, rather than
fair means were frequently the resort of determined citizens.
With a large majority of negro voters Bullock carried every
one of these counties in the gubernatorial election in 1868.
In November of the same year, the Democratic ticket for

DECLINE IN THE REPUBLICAN VOTE

	Population in 1860.	Registration, 1867		Vote for governor.		Vote for president.	
		White.	Colored.	Gordon.	Bullock.	Seymour.	Grant.
Clarke	Black and white even	955	1156	836	1068	1197	1186
Oglethorpe ..	Black over 60 %	830	1158	557	1144	849	116
Morgan.	Black over 60	630	1229	455	1202	635	1046
Greene......	Black over 60	1002	1528	808	1632	1001	1200
Taliaferro ...	Black over 60	392	558	346	627	519	187
Warren	Black over 60	751	1219	544	1124	881	188
Columbia....	Black over 60	669	1859	457	1222	1120	1

presidential electors was successful in all but two of these
same counties. In Clarke County political reversal, brought
about by a large increase in the Democratic vote with no
corresponding decline in Republican numbers, may have
been due to the fact that citizens disfranchised in the April
election were able to vote under state laws in November.
But the result merits other explanation in Oglethorpe, Warren, Columbia and Taliaferro counties. The marked decline in the Republican vote is a certain indication that

376 RECONSTRUCTION IN GEORGIA [376

many negroes did not vote. In Columbia, for instance,
only one Republican vote was cast in November, where
there were 1,222 in April; in Oglethorpe the decline was
from 1,144 to 116; in Warren, from 1,124 to 188; in Taliaferro, from 627 to 187. Judging from results it is evident
that the Ku Klux made their work thorough in this section.

In comparison with the upper cotton-belt, other sections
of Georgia were fairly orderly, with the exception of a few
marked disturbances like the Ogeechee riot in the swamps
below Savannah, the Camilla riot in the southwest and the
notorious murder of Ashburn in Columbus. In Middle
Georgia the Ku Klux were organized but found comparatively little to do. In the spring of 1868 signs of Ku Klux
appeared in Columbus, in Macon and in Milledgeville. The
following notice was copied in a Milledgeville paper from
the *Columbus Enquirer* of March 25th: [1]

K.K.K. What are they? What about them? We noticed
these mysterious letters in chalk on many of the store doors
and windows on Broad Street on Sunday morning. We saw
no one who knew anything about how they got there. Can it
be the terrible " KU KLUX KLAN " have been riding their
pale horses about Columbus? Is it necessary to take any
heads off about here to fix the backbones of our people? We
want to know about them.

The *Milledgeville Federal Union,* in August, 1868, noted
that papers in Georgia had much to say about negroes drilling, preparing for conflict with the whites, under the incite-
ment of bad men, both white and black. But in Milledgeville and the vicinity there appeared to be no hostile demon-
stration, all was going peaceably.[2] At the beginning of

[1] *Milledgeville Federal Union*, March 31, 1868.
[2] *Ibid.*, August 25, 1868.

1869 the Grand Jury of Jasper County in Middle Georgia congratulated the people of the county on the social and material condition and the general kind feeling prevailing between the races.[1]

In Macon, according to the opinion of a negro Republican, H. M. Turner, order prevailed under a good Democratic mayor; and equally optimistic reports came from other parts of Central Georgia, with only sporadic cases of lawlessness. Some such cases occurred in Wilkinson County, where the Ku Klux interfered to show that whites and blacks should not live together. The sheriff of the county, who had a colored woman for wife, was killed, and a colored man, who had been associating with a low white woman, was severely dealt with.[2]

In Atlanta, too, the Ku Klux were organized before the election of 1868, though there is no evidence of their activity, except in arousing fear among the blacks by the publication of terrorizing notices. The following was published in the *Atlanta Intelligencer* on March 14, 1868, with an introductory note from the editor disavowing knowledge from whom or whence it came:

HEADQUARTERS MYSTIC ORDER OF THE KU KLUX KLAN,
OFFICE GRAND CYCLOPS " RED LEGION,"
ORDER OF GRAND CROSS OF MYSTERY,
MARCH 9, 1868.

CIRCULAR ORDER.

To the High and Mighty, the Grand Cyclops and Illustrious Commander of the Ku Klux Klan, the Klansmen and Brothers of the Great Circle everywhere send greeting:

I. It is meet that the Grand Cyclops of the Red Legion,

[1] *Macon Telegraph,* January 7, 1869.

[2] *Ku Klux Committee,* vol. vi, p. 359; Condition of affairs in Georgia, *Hse. Mis. Doc.,* 40 C., 3 S., no. 52.

Order of the Grand Cross of Mystery, should acknowledge the greetings and return the congratulations of the G.G.C., as announced in the General Circular, dated from Headquarters First Moon, and published to the Klansmen of the Great Circle everywhere on the first instant.

II. Klansmen! It is good to know that we are prosperous, but in the hour of prosperity remember the " poor and needy," and cease not to do justice to the afflicted and oppressed! In the pride of our strength, fail not to defend the orphan and protect the weak! In the strength of our numbers, be faithful to ourselves, true to the promptings of manhood, and square your actions upon the principles of justice and right. Be wise, cool, calm, cautious, wary, and brave. Be silent. Pass on, and heed not the growling of the wolf; but if he follows you far, ring the signal, and award the doom of the hound upon the tiger's back! To your enemies " be wise as a serpent," and, like the righteous, " bold as a lion;" to your friends, " harmless as doves," and, like the children of God, " meek and lowly." The High God of the Universe smiles approval upon your charity. Your efforts bask in the sunlight of a bright prosperity.

III. The Grand Cyclops of the Red Legion, Order of the Grand Cross of Mystery, announces to his Klan the confirmation by the Great Grand Cyclops of the sentence of the Second Grand Division, convened by order of Grand Giant Bangor, as passed upon Dloura Cidened, the Traitor.—Treachery has met with its reward, and the Red Hand of the Grand Executioner is scarce stayed from its work of swift and terrible retributive vengeance upon the cowardly slayer of the innocent.

We have welcomed in our midst the Knight Hawk Messenger of the Grand Turks, and the flesh and bone of the traitor has been offered up as a sacrifice upon the altar of the innocent and lost. Our wrath has been appeased; we have tasted and are satisfied. Homage is due and is rendered unto Him who alone can vouchsafe power to the weak and avenge the blood of murdered innocence.

By the Order of the G.C.R.L.O.G.C.M.—stella, G.S.

There was a great deal of disorder of one sort or another in Atlanta during the years of reconstruction, for it was the center towards which drifted the lowest element of both races. At a Republican torchlight procession in August, 1868, a policeman arrested a drunken, disorderly negro. When other negroes attempted to rescue the prisoner, shots were exchanged, wounding the policeman, killing one negro and wounding two others.[1] Occurrences such as this were not rare. A paper in another Georgia city, under the caption, " A Busy Day in Atlanta ", noted the following happenings of one day: a little boy " brickbatted " a colored senator; an indignant colored person shot another colored man in the National Hotel; Representative Atkins had a pitched battle with another man; and Representative Neal and Representative Rice indulged in fisticuffs on the floor of the House.[2] In Henry County, south of Atlanta, the Klan was organized and found work to do occasionally, especially in the eastern part of the county where the negroes were more obstreperous. Only one case of treatment there ended fatally, and that happened because the negro gave fight and the Klan members had to kill him or run the chances of discovery. The members of the Henry County Klan, when out on their night work, wore various kinds of disguises: some had a large coat like a linen duster, others simply turned their ordinary apparel wrong side out, tying a handkerchief across their faces, leaving the eyes uncovered.[3]

In Savannah during election time in the spring and fall of 1868 difficulties arose occasionally between whites and

[1] *Milledgeville Federal Union*, August 25, 1868.

[2] *Savannah Advertiser*, September 30, 1870.

[3] *Henry County Weekly*, April 24, 1908. Memorial number contains reminiscences of various old residents.

blacks.[1] The notorious negro leader, A. A. Bradley, who was expelled from the legislature of 1868 on the charge of having served sentence for felony in New York State, was a thorn in the flesh of the white people of Savannah. He was constantly active in organizing the blacks, in urging them to hold meetings and in stirring up their passions by incendiary speeches. To terrify the negroes, Ku Klux in Savannah posted their warnings before the April elections in 1868.[2] The Loyal League retaliated with its own threats. The following is a copy of a handbill, believed to have emanated from Bradley, circulated among negroes on the streets:[3]

Take
Notice
K. K. K.
And all BADMEN of the
City of Savannah, who now
THREATEN
the LIVES of all the LEADERS
and NOMINEES of the Republican Party, and the
President and Members of the Union League
of America. If you Strike a Blow, the
Man or Men will be followed, and the
house in which he or they takes shelter,
will be burned to the ground.
TAKE HEED! MARK WELL! !
Members of the Union.
Rally! Rally! ! Rally! ! !
For God, Life and Liberty! ! !

A large amount of crime and lawlessness in Savannah

[1] *Savannah News*, October 1, 1867; February 5, April 9, 1868; *Ku Klux Committee*, vol. vi, p. 176.

[2] *Savannah News*, April 2 and 3, 1868.

[3] *Ibid.*, April 2, 1868.

was due to the numbers of negro refugees who crowded
into the city from Florida and South Carolina and the sur-
rounding Georgia districts. They worked as stevedores or
longshoremen, or got small jobs on the wharves during the
cotton-shipping season, spending the rest of their time in
idleness and crime. In 1868, the police records of the city
noted 622 arrests of whites and 1,289 of blacks.[1] South
of Savannah, along the coast, in Glynn, Liberty and Mc-
Intosh counties, where blacks outnumbered whites, Loyal
Leagues gained full sway over the negroes by promises of
property and appeals to their superstition. Here conditions
easily encouraged vagabondage among the blacks. An
abundance of food, fish, oysters, game, plenty of lightwood,
and the existence of colonies of negro squatters along the
Sea Islands made living extremely precarious for the owners of plantations in that region. The negroes were of a
lower order of intelligence than those in the interior, dif-
fering from them in language and religion, superstitious
and easily susceptible to bad influences. From time to time
disturbances occurred on various plantations when negroes
proceeded to plunder right and left. On General Gordon's
rice plantation near Brunswick the negroes drove the overseer away and would have had everything their own way
had not the Freedmen's Bureau agent interfered with the
aid of soldiers to settle the difficulty. A friend of the
negro, a missionary from the North, was grieved to note
" the innate propensity of the negro to purloin from
others ". A Freedmen's Bureau official commented on the
prevalence of intemperance among the negroes, due to the
" whisky wagons " that traveled through the country and
the unrestrained sale of liquor in towns. Where negroes

[1] *Savannah News*, January 11, 1869; *Ku Klux Committee*, vol. vi,
p. 177; Alvord, *Letters from the South*, January 18, 1870.

received money for their wages they were free to buy liquor as they pleased.[1]

After 1867 a great change came over the negroes in their relation to their former masters. General John B. Gordon, one of the most important witnesses called before the Ku Klux Committee, spoke of the changed attitude of the negroes along the coast, attributing it to the pernicious influence of their political leaders. He said:

I believe that if you would relieve our State of these men who have come there since the war, who have no property or interest there, except what they can get out of the negroes, there would be the utmost cordiality between the two races in that State, and there would be no conflict.[2]

Frances Butler Leigh, writing of conditions on her plantations in the neighborhood of Darien and on St. Simon's Island, said:[3]

The negroes this year and the following [1868 and 1869] seemed to reach the climax of lawless independence, and I never slept without a loaded pistol by my bed. Their whole manner was changed. They took to calling their former owners by their last name without any title before it, constantly spoke of my agent as old R——, dropped the pleasant term of " Mistress," took to calling me " Miss Fanny," walked about with guns upon their shoulders, worked just as much and when they pleased, and tried speaking to me with their hats on, or not touching them to me when they passed me

[1] *Macon Telegraph*, January 6, 1869; *Ku Klux Committee*, vol. vi, pp. 305-306; Stearns, *Black Man of the South and the Rebels*, p. 54; Alvord, *op. cit.*

[2] *Ku Klux Committee*, vol. vi, p. 307. Gen. Gordon was generally believed to be, and probably was, the head of the Ku Klux organization in Georgia.

[3] *Ten Years on a Georgia Plantation after the War*, pp. 131-3.

on the banks . . . A new trouble came upon us, too, or rather an old trouble in a new shape. Negro adventurers from the North, finding that politics was such a paying trade at the South, began pouring in, and were really worse than the whites, for their Southern brethren looked upon their advent quite as a proof of a new order of things, in which the negroes were to rule and possess the land.

In the latter part of December, 1868, and in the early days of 1869, the rice plantations in the swamps along the Ogeechee River below Savannah were terrorized by the appearance of armed bands of negroes who plundered and seized loads of rice, just ready for market. The reign of terror lasted for some days. A posse of citizens was organized to aid the sheriff in quelling the disturbance, but the end did not come until General Sibley sent a detachment of troops. Fourteen of the insurgents were arrested by the military force and turned over to civil authorities, though the leaders escaped. Savannah people attributed the movement to the plot of Bradley, Sims and other leaders of the Loyal League.[1] But it was not clear that the League was responsible for this attack by the negroes on the whites any more than the Ku Klux were responsible for every act of violence committed against blacks. The editor of a Savannah paper wrote bitterly that Governor Bullock, instead of being in Georgia to put down troubles, was away looking after his own interests. The Ogeechee insurrection, heralded by the *New York Tribune* as an expression of the negroes' " rude sense of justice ", would doubtless be used by the Radicals as proof that the state was still in disorder and in need of further regulation from Washington.[2]

A conflict between white people and negroes, more ser-

[1] *Savannah News*, January 6, 8, 1869.

[2] *Ibid.*, January 5, 1869.

ious in political import than the Ogeechee trouble, occurred at Camilla in Mitchell County in the extreme southwestern part of the state in September, 1868. Notices were posted that a great Republican mass meeting was to be held in Camilla on September 19th, at which N. P. Pierce, candidate for Congress, and John Murphy, candidate for elector, would be the chief speakers. On that day a body of about 300 negroes, many of whom were armed, set out from Albany under the lead of Pierce and Murphy to march to Camilla. When the news came to Camilla that negroes were coming armed, white citizens were alarmed. The sheriff of the county met the procession a few miles out of Camilla and tried to persuade the negroes to lay aside their arms. When they refused, the sheriff returned to the town, collected a posse of citizens and met the procession as it was about to enter Camilla. As usually happens, some unknown person fired a first shot, after which shooting became general on both sides with the result that eight or nine blacks were killed and twenty or thirty wounded. The townsmen suffered slightly, several being more or less hurt. General Meade did not send troops to the scene of conflict immediately, not having confidence in the report of the Freedmen's Bureau agent. When General Meade failed to respond, Governor Bullock, in a message to the legislature (September 21st), urged the legislature to apply to the President for a military force to maintain peace in Mitchell County. According to his representation the Camilla affair was the result of a determined plan on the part of the Democrats to prevent the Republicans from holding public meetings. Instead of acquiescing in the governor's suggestion, the legislature appointed a joint committee to investigate the matter. The committee reported that evidence before it—affidavits from Mitchell County—did not sustain the governor's position. It found that the trouble was

caused by Pierce, Murphy and others trying to enter Camilla at the head of an armed company of freedmen. Civil
authorities in Mitchell County, the committee declared,
were fully able to execute law and had no need of military
assistance. Furthermore, no ill feeling between whites and
blacks resulted from the shooting affair. The report of the
committee was adopted in the Senate and in the House, and
the findings of the committee were sustained by General
Meade, who refused to interfere with troops.[1] The Freedmen's Bureau agent at Albany was quick to send reports of
the affair to the Northern press, which gave a much dis-
torted view of the difficulty. The " Camilla riot " was described thus in a journal as conservative as the *Nation*:
" The news from Georgia shows, as we expected, that the
Camilla affair was a shocking massacre. The murders continued to be committed through the afternoon and night,
the woods being scoured by hunters with dogs, and negroes shot without mercy. Their offence was Radicalism."[2]

The most notorious case in the annals of crime in Georgia
during the reconstruction period was the murder of G. W.
Ashburn in Columbus. Ashburn was much the same type
as the other Radical leaders who were murdered. Adkins
and Ayer—indeed, there seemed to be something fatal in the
initial A. Before the war Ashburn was a plantation overseer, severe and brutal. With the reversal of 1867 he went
in for politics, became a leader of the negroes in Columbus and was elected to the convention in 1867. He was the
lowest sort of white man, lived with a negro woman at a
public house, where he was killed by a band of men on the
night of March 31, 1868. A fellow Republican in Colum-

[1] *Senate Journal*, 1868, pp. 353-6, 364-9; *Annual Cyclopedia*, 1868,
pp. 315-6; Gen. Meade's report in *Report of the Secretary of War*,
1868-9, vol. i, pp. 81, 124.

[2] October 1, 1868.

bus declared that he saw a Ku Klux warning sent to Ashburn a few days before he was killed, which represented him lying in a coffin with emblems of death round about and inscribed with his name.[1] The most notable feature of the Ashburn case was the trial of nine young men of Columbus, arrested on suspicion. The trial was noteworthy, not only because of the political affiliations of the murdered victim, but also because it was the most important case in Georgia in which military justice was applied to so-called Ku Klux outrages. The case was notable, also, for the distinguished legal talent engaged on both sides. The military officers in charge of the prosecution engaged Jos. E. Brown to aid their side, while the defendants were represented by some of the ablest lawyers in Georgia—Alex. H. Stephens, Lucius J. Gartrell, Jas. M. Smith, Martin J. Crawford, H. L. Benning, R. J. Moses, J. N. Ramsey. The trial by military court, presided over by Brig.-Gen. Sibley, began in Atlanta on June 29, 1868, and proceeded until July 21st, when General Meade ordered suspension owing to the "probable immediate admission of the State of Georgia and consequent cessation of military authority ". The prisoners were turned over to the civil authorities of Columbus, released on bail, and with that their prosecution came to an end.[2]

One of the reasons most frequently assigned for the organization of the Ku Klux Klan was the need to combat the pernicious influence of the Loyal Leagues among the negroes. To a certain extent this seems to be true in

[1] *Ku Klux Committee*, vol. vi, pp. 431-2. (J. H. Caldwell.)

[2] *Ibid.*, pp. 183-5, 431-2; *Report of the Secretary of War*, 1868-9, vol. i, pp. 108, 129 (Gen. Meade) ; account of the trial in the *Atlanta Constitution* beginning June 30, 1868, and in the *New York Tribune* during July. The testimony taken during the trial was published in pamphlet form.

Georgia, that is, so far as we consider the Ku Klux in the narrower sense as a definite organization. Secret associations for the political organization of the negroes were formed in various parts of the state in 1867 in time to get ready for the first election under the Reconstruction Acts. After the presidential election in 1868 little was heard of the negro organizations except here and there in the more important towns. The April election for state officers was the season of excess of zeal among the Loyal Leagues. In Macon at a big negro mass meeting a banner was displayed bearing the warning: "Every man that don't vote the Radical ticket this is the way we want to serve him—hang him by the neck ". In Athens there were many processions and meetings where negroes swore great oaths " to vote the ticket ". At a Radical meeting in Columbus the Radical candidate for Congress threatened in unmistakable terms negroes who would fail to vote for Bullock. A negro organization in Twiggs County exacted monthly dues of 25 cents from its members—a kind of mutual aid society apparently, for it was explained to one member—" When a colored man killed a sheep or stole a hog, this money was to be applied to defending him before the law." Political meetings were considered by negroes as their first obligation. No work would be done when a " meetin " was going on. Not only the men, but negro women as well flocked to these political gatherings. The organization of the Loyal League was especially strong in the region round about Augusta, which was the center of the Freedmen's Bureau agents and of other Northern political apostles.[1] While 1867 and 1868 were the years of Loyal League strength, there was an out-

[1] Hull, *Annals of Athens*, p. 320; *Ku Klux Committee*, vol. vi, pp. 28, 48; *Savannah News*, April 1, 1868; *Milledgeville Federal Union*, April 16, 23, 1867, April 7, 14, 1868; Leigh, *Ten Years on a Georgia Plantation*, p. 97 et seq.

cropping of its activity later in connection with Bullock's attempt to reorganize the state. In May, 1869, the *American Union,* a Radical paper in Macon, edited by a notorious organizer of the blacks by the name of Swayze, published this call to " loyal men ":

Their fidelity has been repaid with contempt, and it now becomes them as men to cement their ranks more closely than ever, and—*defend themselves!* Let them not, like cowards, creep under the lash that attempted to overthrow the government of our forefathers. Let them present an unbroken front and demand a tooth for a tooth, an eye for an eye! Let them show rebels that they have the nerve to defend themselves against lawlessness. Let the whole State organize into societies—secret societies; and when rebels commit their diabolical horrors upon them, because of their opinions, retaliate at a ten-fold ratio. *For every life that is taken lay every house in ashes within five miles of that spot where such blood is spilled—shoot down every rebel who opposes you, and turn the horror back upon those who are daily repeating them upon loyal people. Do it!* and God will be your shield.[1]

To protect white citizens and to bring some order out of social chaos when the bayonet was law, when government and justice were in the hands of their opponents, the conservative whites, the old ruling class, organized the Ku Klux movement. This was primarily a movement of regulators, to administer rude justice where courts and officers of law were inadequate or distrusted, or where the standard of justice held by those in charge of the government differed from that of the regulators. This movement went on in part through the distinctive organization, known generally as the Ku Klux Klan, and in part through unofficial groups acting spontaneously as conditions demanded.[2] It

[1] *Savannah News*, May 19, 1869.

[2] " In a wider and truer sense the phrase ' Ku Klux Movement ' means

is evident that the organized body of the Ku Klux appeared and began operation in Georgia just before the election in April, 1868, for it was just at this time that Ku Klux warnings began to appear in the newspapers, which brought forth from General Meade his order No. 51, to prohibit the printing, publication or circulation of incendiary literature of any secret order to produce intimidation. At about the same time he issued another order to prevent the threatened discharge of freedmen for the purpose of controlling their votes.[1] The November election in 1868 again brought the Ku Klux into action. The Democratic majority in the presidential election in many counties which were Republican in April was due in no small part to the intimidation of negro voters. It seems that as a definite organization the Ku Klux existed in only a part of the state and that its activities were confined almost entirely to the year 1868. General John B. Gordon, reputed to be the head of the organization in Georgia, when asked by the Ku Klux Committee what he knew of any combinations known as the Ku Klux, or by any other name, that had been violating the law, replied:

I do not know anything about any Ku Klux organization, as the papers talk about it. I have never heard of anything of that sort except in the papers and by general report; but I do know that an organization did exist in Georgia at one time. I know that in 1868—I think that was the time—I was approached and asked to attach myself to a secret organization in Georgia. . . . The organization was simply this — nothing more and nothing less: it was an organization, a

Reconstruction lasting from 1865 until 1876, and, in some respects, the attitude of the Southern whites toward the various measures of almost to the present day."—Fleming, Introduction to Lester and Wilson, *Ku Klux Klan*, p. 36.

[1] *Savannah News*, April 7, 1868; McPherson, *Reconstruction*, p. 320.

brotherhood of the property-holders, the peaceable, law-abiding citizens of the State, for self-protection. The instinct of self-protection prompted that organization; the sense of insecurity and danger, particularly in those neighborhoods where the negro population largely predominated. The reasons which led to this organization were three or four. The first and main reason was the organization of the Union League, as they called it, about which we knew nothing more than this: that the negroes would desert the plantations, and go off at night in large numbers; and on being asked where they had been, would reply, sometimes, " We have been to the muster;" sometimes, " We have been to the lodge;" sometimes, " We have been to the meeting." These things were observed for a great length of time. We knew that the " carpet-baggers," as the people called these men who came from a distance and had no interest at all with us, who were unknown to us entirely; who from all we could learn about them did not have any very exalted position at their homes— these men were organizing the colored people. We knew that beyond all question. We knew of certain instances where great crime had been committed; where overseers had been driven from plantations, and the negroes had asserted their right to hold the property for their own benefit. Apprehension took possession of the entire public mind of the State. Men were in many instances afraid to go away from their homes and leave their wives and children, for fear of outrage. Rapes were already being committed in the country. There was this general organization of the black race on one hand, and an entire disorganization of the white race on the other hand. We were afraid to have a public organization; because we supposed it would be construed at once, by the authorities at Washington, as an organization antagonistic to the Government of the United States. It was therefore necessary, in order to protect our families from outrage and preserve our own lives, to have something that we could regard as a brotherhood—a combination of the best men of the country, to act purely in self-defense, to repel the attack

in case we should be attacked by these people. That was the
whole object of this organization. I never heard of any disguise connected with it; we had none, very certainly. This
organization, I think, extended nearly all over the State. It
was, as I say, an organization purely for self-defense. It
had no more politics in it than the organization of the Masons.
I never heard the idea of politics suggested in connection
with it.[1]

After 1868, most of the acts attributed to the Ku Klux
were probably the action of bodies organized locally, or
groups of citizens acting spontaneously without established
organization or connection with similar bands elsewhere—
a movement " sporadic rather than epidemic ". As we sift
the testimony brought before the Ku Klux Investigating
Committee of Congress, much of which is untrustworthy
and of doubtful historical value, it seems fair to conclude
that most of the activities attributed to the Ku Klux were
for the purpose of regulating social conditions, primarily to
frighten or otherwise deal with obstreperous or insolent negroes, to teach them their place and make them submissive
to white people. These self-constituted regulators acted on
the principle that the blacks would be all right if they were
freed from the contaminating influence of some of their
vicious leaders. Hence the murder of such men as Ashburn, Adkins and Ayer. In most parts of the state, in the
white counties and in the heaviest black counties, Ku Klux
operations were socially regulative in character. Political
regulation was attempted in that part of the state where
whites and blacks were fairly evenly balanced in numbers.
It seems hardly necessary or practicable to differentiate too
strictly between the social and the political aspects of the
Ku Klux movement; for after all, even the most direct

[1] *Ku Klux Committee*, vol. vi, p. 308.

political activities, such as maneuvers to prevent the negroes from voting and to carry a Democratic majority at the polls, were fundamentally due to the problem of race relations. Republicans were as a class objects of attack from the conservative white people because the Republican party had brought about the social revolution which the conservatives were trying to undo. The mere fact that the victims were in most cases Republicans did not mean that they were martyrs of a political persecution. Had investigators pressed their questions further they might have discovered that the victims were in most cases Baptists or Methodists, since the negroes belonged mostly to those denominations. But that would no more have proved that the Ku Klux movement was a religious persecution than that it was a political war.

It was in the upper part of the cotton-belt that race conflict in the reconstruction period assumed most acute political manifestation. And there is a reason. In North Georgia, whites were not threatened in their political control and there was no need of a struggle to maintain their supremacy. Acts of violence were attributable to racial jealousy in social and economic relations. In the parts of South Georgia where the blacks were greatly in the majority, two different sets of conditions arose. In the Southeast, along the coast, where negroes had their own way during the war, prospects for the whites were so bad that they had no hope of regaining control and so left the negroes to run things much their own way. This was the situation in Glynn, McIntosh and other counties, where negro leaders like Tunis G. Campbell ruled with a high hand. Counties in Southwest Georgia with a heavy black majority in population had quite the contrary experience. In this section negroes were not touched by new notions from invading armies, as were the blacks in the upper cotton-belt in the latter part of the war, and Radical leaders seemed not to get control of them as in other sections. In the region of the large plantations the freedmen continued with much of their old deference to the whites. That is the reason why Mr. Nelson Tift, a Democrat, was elected to Congress in 1868 from this decidedly black district. There were no Republican white leaders of any importance, the Freedmen's Bureau in this section was never strongly established, and in the absence of opposing influence, the negroes, accustomed to defer to the whites, left to the white Democrats the right of way. Moreover, the prosperous plantation owners were more friendly in their relations with the freedmen than those whites who were more nearly the economic equals of the negroes. A prominent Republican politician, who was for some time agent of the Freedmen's Bureau in Americus, controlling three large counties, gave witness to the fact that few complaints of unfair treatment of the negroes were reported to him in that region.[1] But in the part of the black belt where chances were more evenly balanced, where negroes were only slightly in majority, the ground was debatable and worth fighting for. The task of regaining political control was by no means hopeless to the whites.

The method of informal administration of justice and irregular social control, which became notorious during the reconstruction period in the South, was far from being a new invention of the time. In its simplest elements it was the adaptation of the old patrol system of slavery times to new conditions. Personal settlement of disputes without recourse to law was another symptom of the Ku Klux movement widely prevalent in the South in ante-bellum times. The *Nation* understandingly though unsympathetically noted this fact:

[1] *Ku Klux Committee*, vol. vi, p. 1083 (W. C. Morrill).

The Ku Klux Klan, let us add, is nothing new. The South before the war was one vast Ku Klux Klan. Every man was a member of the organization, and the state governments made no attempt to interfere with it, and its victims were rare because dissenters from the popular creed did not enter the South. What makes it seem so novel now is that the state governments are in the hands of the dissenters and there is a large body of them in every state.[1]

The increase in social disorder in the years after 1867 was due to racial antagonism between whites and blacks. The task of the dominant white population in the first years after the war was to keep the negro to his old labor; in 1867 to this task was superadded that of keeping the negro to a realization of his inferior social status though the law declared him equal to the white in political and civil rights and privileges. On one side was law and on the other was the social custom of generations. Ideally, it may have been a humane and civilizing act to protect the weaker race with the power of the ballot; but practically, when enfranchisement was conferred against the will of the white people and contrary to their profound sense of right and fitness, the new power left the freedmen with but little more actual freedom in 1872 than they enjoyed in 1866.

[1] September 10, 1868.

CONCLUSION

EMANCIPATION was the basic fact of reconstruction. The institution of slavery provided not only an industrial system of production, but a social organization by which two alien races managed to live together. The release of half a million slaves in Georgia meant an immediate revolution in the agricultural labor system. And the destruction of the old order brought into question social relations between whites and blacks that had been silenced for more than two centuries in the established relation of master and slave. Slavery was maintained by the capitalist owner as a profitable economic system. By the non-slaveowner it was cherished as a social order which fixed the barrier between the poverty of the white and the poverty of the black. It was this social value of slavery to the non-slaveholders that made the conflict of 1861 one of North and South rather than an industrial conflict between capitalists and non-capitalists within the South. Had slavery been only an industrial scheme, instead of being the " cornerstone " of the entire social structure, the non-slaveholders of the South would have echoed widely the protest of Hinton Rowan Helper,[1] instead of smothering it as an outcry against the eternal order of things.

The seven years of Georgia history from 1865 to 1872 mark only the beginnings of the social and economic transformation that has taken place since the war. The forces then set at work by emancipation and by the terrific eco-

[1] *The Impending Crisis.*

395]   395

nomic waste of the war have continued until the present day. The only unity that these seven years, the reconstruction period, have, apart from the entire period since 1865, comes from certain political forces, which reacted upon social and industrial life and ceased in Georgia in 1872. From 1865 to 1872, industry, social relations and politics, mutually reactive, moulded the condition of affairs in Georgia. When Democratic rule replaced Republicanism, one set of abnormal influences was put at rest. For the years to come, economic and social problems were all-engrossing, and politics, no longer a matter of self-preservation, became a diversion.

The first and immediate result of emancipation was chaos. Agriculture in 1865, when the laborers were testing their freedom, resulted only in waste. During the first seven years of experiment, the farmer, in despair of raising any crop with free labor, determined to keep the old system of cultivation and labor as nearly intact as possible. The planter himself did not organize or develop a new scheme of cultivation to utilize free labor, but yielded to changes only under sternest necessity. A very great decrease in the supply of agricultural labor with only slightly lessened demand made the laborer the master of the market. The laborer's control of the situation resulted in schemes of cultivation which freed the negro from a large measure of the supervision to which he had been subjected under slavery. The helplessness of the planter gave opportunity to the laborer to attain economic freedom.

The limitation of the labor supply, the demand of negroes to be renters rather than hired laborers, the failure in crops for several seasons, and the difficulty of obtaining credit, all tended to diminish the size of the farming unit. The greater price of labor in the cost of production made the farmer economize as much as possible in that item. Less labor, less land, more fertilizer, intensive rather than extensive cultivation was the program of the most successful planters. Very little change resulted, however, in the one-crop system of cultivation. Cotton remained king. The best land was given to cotton, and only the poorer patches devoted to food crops. There was little in the way of crop diversification. But by the end of the reconstruction period, the farmer, though he was loth to prove his prophecy false, was discovering that the staple could, after all, be raised with free labor.

From the point of view of the planter, reconstruction meant a struggle day in and day out against economic ruin, from which only the sturdiest survived. The natural advantages of rich soil and favorable climate had made profitable the wasteful economy of slave production. The planter had been protected by these natural advantages so that even the least skilful managers had been able to profit, just as the unskilful manufacturer in the North subsisted on profits from tariff protection, not earned by his foresight or managing ability. In the South, the climate was the only factor of production untouched by war and reconstruction. Even the fertility of the soil was becoming more and more exhausted each year. When the planter's capital was solely in land, not chiefly in slaves, he could not move readily from worn-out to virgin soil. Moreover, except in part of the southwestern section, the rich soil of Georgia had all been appropriated before the war.

From the point of view of the freedman, reconstruction gave an opportunity and a hope for economic betterment. The varied motives which made the negro desire forty acres and a mule were large factors, not merely in his industrial, but in his social advance, as well. The conscious desire to improve his condition, aroused by emancipation, while not universal among the freedmen, was a motive force in many which helped in the advance, not only of the negro, but of the whole community. Socially, the demand of the freedman for a farm of his own had large significance. More than any laws or moral codes the independent farm was important in developing in the negro a respect for family integrity. The change which many plantations underwent, when the negroes no longer worked together in gangs under overseers, and no longer lived in the old slave quarters, but tenanted small farms, each one with his own house on his own patch of ground, or grouped with a few others at a nearby creek or spring, was a record of social as well as economic transformation. The freer life gave added responsibility, which, as always, resulted in the weakest relapsing into a lower state, while the strong developed greater strength.

The industrial revolution of the reconstruction period was almost wholly confined to agriculture, which still remained the great economic interest of the state, despite the cataclysm following upon emancipation. The growth in other interests, manufacturing, trade, the expansion of railroads, except the great work of repair which the devastation of war occasioned, was merely a normal continuation of the process of development begun before 1860. Textile manufacturing, with the utilization of white labor from the mountain and Piedmont region, belongs to a later period of the industrial development of Georgia.

Since the economic changes of 1865-72 were mainly agricultural and had grown out of emancipation, these changes were most marked where there were the greatest number of slaves to be freed, and where the large plantation was the industrial unit. Central Georgia, the cotton-belt from the southwest diagonally across the state, with the fringe of coast counties, experienced a much greater degree of economic reconstruction than North Georgia or the pine barrens of the southeast. The grain-producing area of Northwest Georgia, after it had once recovered from the blight of Sherman's army, progressed markedly in the later years of reconstruction. Having comparatively few negroes to begin with, this section was not vitally disturbed by emancipation in its agricultural production.

While economic disturbance was less, social disorder was greater in the sections where negroes were less numerous. It was here that jealousy and rivalry were most acute, when slavery was abolished, leaving only race as a barrier between the poor white and the poor black. The race problem, one of the greatest problems which reconstruction aroused and bequeathed to a later generation, began further back than reconstruction. It began with the landing of the first negroes brought to the Colony of Virginia, but the institution of slavery, while not settling the problem, at least provided a method of adjustment whereby the negro passed from barbarism to some measure of civilization. Emancipation itself was enough to generate race antagonism between some classes of whites and blacks. But Republican reconstruction extended and intensified this racial antagonism a hundredfold. This was the most important and enduring contribution of Congressional Reconstruction.

The political results of reconstruction were, in the long run, the least important of all in the later history of Georgia. The greatest influence of Republicanism was its reaction on social relations and on economic conditions. While the Republican government for three years was both extravagant and corrupt, Georgia managed to recover rather easily from its financial abuse and mismanagement. In this respect, Georgia was decidedly less hard pressed than other Southern states in reconstruction, and it was certainly more fortunate than states where such influence as the Tweed Ring was in control. The " undoing of reconstruction " applies merely to politics, for the social and economic reconstruction of Georgia after the war continues to-day.   Politically, the greatest work of reconstruction was to constitute the negro a voter, and to make the government Republican in party politics.   In 1872, the state government was completely in control of the Democratic party. To make this political reversal possible, many negroes, by intimidation, persuasion, in some cases by their own indifference, ceased to be voters, and gradually the negro became of less and less importance in politics.   Thus the greatest political achievement of Congressional Reconstruction was undone.   But, it was not entirely undone, for the whites, in removing the political rights from the negroes, also limited their own political freedom.   The Southern white had no freedom of choice—he had to be a Democrat, whether or no.

In its largest sense, Reconstruction in Georgia meant a wider democratization of society.   Before the war, however, Georgia was far from being in the control of the " slave oligarchy ", such as is frequently pictured.   The yeoman of moderate means, who might own a few slaves, was not a negligible factor in ante-bellum life.   Alexander H. Stephens was one of this class, and Joseph E. Brown, one of the most potent leaders ever known in Georgia, was distinctly one of the " plain people ".   The change that came by reconstruction was one of degree rather than of kind.   When former leaders were set aside by the terms of Presidential and Congressional Reconstruction, the way was opened to the middle class.   The weakening of the economic supremacy of the planter class also meant that other kinds of wealth than land and slaves became the basis of social prestige.   The reconstruction period was followed by shifting, not only in class dominance, but also in sectional dominance.   The center of influence moved further to the uplands, with growing importance of the Piedmont region at the expense of the cotton-belt. The rocket-like rise of Atlanta in the Piedmont is in part illustrative of these new forces that reconstruction brought into action.

In a still more fundamental way reconstruction, with emancipation as the central fact, brought about a greater social democracy. No society, in which one-half of the members were slaves, could be democratic in any nineteenth century meaning of the term. The extension of " the people " to include the black half as well as the white half of the population, was a great step forward toward the real republic of which Georgia made a part. The greatest constructive achievement of the war, as worked out in reconstruction, was the establishment of the negro in freedom. Republican reconstruction, however, failed to establish him in permanent equality with the whites in either political rights or social privileges. While the white man was master of the slave, slavery was the master of the white man. Abolition freed the white as well as the black. But still the race problem, and the cry of Negro! Negro!—the slogan of political demagogues, who magnify and distort a very real difficulty in playing upon the passions of the less educated whites—rise to curtail freedom of thought and act. The revolution which brought about these changes was painful and costly to the last degree. As in most great changes, the benefits are enjoyed vicariously. Those who pay the price do not enjoy the product. If the revolution of Civil War and Reconstruction wrought anything of enduring value, it was in the advance toward greater social democracy. Since the transaction was a forced sale and the price extorted, not paid willingly, it was not with Georgia to reason whether or not the product of Reconstruction was worth the cost.

BIBLIOGRAPHY

Bibliographical Aids

Brooks, Robert Preston. A Preliminary Bibliography of Georgia History. Athens, Ga., 1910.
    Most complete bibliography of Georgia history published, but incomplete for the reconstruction period.

Dailey, Carrie L. List of Georgia State Publications. Atlanta, 1908.

DeRenne, W. J. Catalogue of Books relating to the History of Georgia in the Library of Wymberly Jones DeRenne, Wormsloe, Georgia. Compiled by Oscar Wegelin. Savannah, 1911. (Privately printed.)
    Mr. DeRenne's remarkable collection contains some rare pamphlets relating to the reconstruction period.

Phillips, U. B. Georgia and State Rights. Washington, 1902.
    The very full, annotated bibliography for the period before 1860 is a suggestive guide to material for the later period as well.

Phillips, U. B. Public Archives of Georgia. Annual Report of the American Historical Association, 1903, vol. i.

Phillips, U. B. Georgia Local Archives. Annual Report of the American Historical Association, 1904.
    Lists and tabulations of records in various counties and towns.

Woolley, E. C. The Reconstruction of Georgia. New York, 1901.
    The bibliography gives only the most evident authorities and public documents.

General Histories of Georgia

Arthur, T. S. and Carpenter, W. H. History of Georgia from its Earliest Settlement to the Present Time. Philadelphia, 1882.
    Of no value.

Avery, I. W. History of the State of Georgia, 1850-1881. New York, 1881.

The most important of all histories of Georgia. Though no references are given, newspapers have been drawn on for most of the material. The point of view is decidedly partisan, for Col. Avery took active part in the reconstruction of Georgia. The book is written as a vindication of Governor Brown's career. The author was editor of the *Atlanta Constitution* from 1869 to 1874, hence the journalistic character of the volume.

Evans, Lawton B. A History of Georgia. New York, 1906.
> Written for use in schools. The best complete history of Georgia in brief compass.

McPherson, J. H. T. The Civil Government of Georgia. New York, 1908.
> Brief text-book.

Mitchell, Frances L. Georgia Land and People. Atlanta, 1900.
> Chapter on the War abounds in glorification of the South and criminal charges against the North.

Smith, Chas. H., *pseud.* Bill Arp. School History of Georgia. Boston, 1893.
> Interesting chapter on " The Common People and the Aristocracy."

Smith, George Gilman. Story of Georgia and the Georgia People, 1732-1860. Macon, 1900.
> Last three chapters on Religion, Education, Cities.

(Southern Historical Association). Memoirs of Georgia. 2 vols. Atlanta, 1895.
> Civil and military history, with an account of industrial resources and biographical sketches.

Stevens, O. B. and Wright, R. F. Georgia, Historical and Industrial. Atlanta, 1901.
> Compiled by the Georgia Department of Agriculture. Follows Janes, Manual of Georgia, for the period before 1876.

Local Histories

Avery, I. W. Atlanta, History and Advantages. Louisville, Ky., 1892.
> In World's Fair Series of Great American Cities. In nature of an advertisement of the city with short historical sketch and biographical notes.

Bowen, Eliza A. Story of Wilkes County. Washington, Ga., 1870.

Butler, John C. Historical Record of Macon and Central Georgia. Macon, 1879.
> Material from local newspapers and reminiscences of old citizens.

Clarke, E. Y. Atlanta Illustrated. Atlanta, 1881.

Dutcher, Salem (and Jones, C. C. Jr.) Memorial History of Augusta, Georgia. Syracuse, N. Y., 1890.
> Contains little of interest for the period after the war.

Hull, A. L. Annals of Athens, Ga. 1801-1901. Athens, 1906.
> Disconnected reminiscences of people and events. Gives some interesting items on conditions of war and adjustment in 1865. Written as newspaper articles for the *Southern Watchman* in Athens.

Lee, F. D. and Agnew, J. L. Historical Record of the City of Savannah. Savannah, 1869.
In the war period only military events are recorded.

Martin, John H., ed. Columbus, Georgia, 1827-1865. Columbus, 1874.

Martin, Thos. H. Atlanta and its Builders. 2 vols. 1902.
Gives commercial and industrial progress of Atlanta.

Phillips, U. B. Historical Notes of Milledgeville, Ga. *Gulf States Historical Magazine*, November, 1903.

Pioneer Citizens' Society History of Atlanta. Atlanta, 1902.

Reed, Wallace P., ed. History of Atlanta, Georgia. Syracuse, N. Y., 1889.
Best history of Atlanta, but, like other local histories, undiscriminating. Material from newspapers and oral testimony.

Sholes, A. E. (compiler). Chronological History of Savannah. Savannah, 1900.

Vedder, O. F. and Weldon, Frank, (and Jones, C. C. Jr.) History of Savannah. Syracuse, N. Y., 1890.

Wilson, Adelaide. Historic and Picturesque Savannah. Boston, 1899.
Chapter on Savannah in the war by C. H. Olmstead from recollection.

SPECIAL HISTORIES, ARTICLES, PAMPHLETS.

Banks, Enoch Marvin. Economics of Land Tenure in Georgia. New York, 1905. *Columbia University Studies in History, Economics, and Public Law*, vol. xxiii, no. 1.
Deals mainly with recent conditions, but valuable for a brief historical treatment of the subject.

Barrow, David C. "A Georgia Plantation." *Scribner's Monthly*, vol. xxi, p. 830.
Account of the Barrow plantation in Oglethorpe County.

Brooks, Robert Preston. The Agrarian Revolution in Georgia, 1865-1912. Madison, Wis., 1914. *Bulletin of the University of Wisconsin, no. 639, History Series, vol. iii, no. 3.*
Important monograph contains valuable chapters on the agricultural changes after the war.

Brown, Joseph M. The Mountain Campaigns in Georgia. War Scenes on the W. and A. R. R. Buffalo, 1886.

Bullock, Rufus B. "Reconstruction in Georgia." *Independent*, March 19, 1903.
Vindication of military reconstruction by one who was the reconstruction governor of Georgia.

Bullock, Rufus B.   Have the Reconstruction Acts been fully executed in Georgia?   Speech at Albion, N. Y., Oct. 17, 1868.   pph. Washington.

Bullock, Rufus B.   Remarks of Governor Bullock before the Judiciary Committee of the Senate, Mar. 2, 1870.   Washington, 1870.   pph.

Bullock, Rufus B.   Address of Rufus B. Bullock to the People of Georgia, October, 1872.   pph.

Calvin, M. V.   Popular Education in Georgia.   Augusta, Ga., 1870.   pph.

Carter, E. R.   The Black Side.   Atlanta, 1894.
> An account by a colored preacher of the part played by negroes in the development of Atlanta.   Biographical sketches and photographs of leading negroes.

Conyngham, D. R.   Sherman's March through the South.   New York, 1865.
> By a war correspondent for the *New York Herald*.

Derry, J. T.   "Georgia in the Confederacy."   In *The South in the Building of the Nation*, vol. vii.

Dickson, David.   System of Farming, 1869.   Reprint edited by G. F. Hunnicutt, Atlanta, 1910.
> Dickson was one of the most noted farmers of Georgia.

Du Bois, W. E. B.   The Negro Landholder of Georgia.   Washington, 1901.   *Bulletin of the U. S. Department of Labor*, no. 35.
> Valuable monograph by an eminent colored scholar.

Dutcher, Salem.   How to Vote: How to Obtain Pardon.   Augusta, Ga., 1865.
> Contains extracts from official documents.

Evans, Lawton B.   "Georgia in the New Nation, 1865-1909."   In *The South in the Building of the Nation*, vol. vii.

French, S. G.   "Kennesaw Mountain."   *Southern Historical Society Papers*, vol. ix, p. 505.
> Extracts from a diary.

Gaines, W. J.   African Methodism in the South; or Twenty-five Years of Freedom.   Atlanta, 1890.

Goetchius, Henry R.   "Litigation in Georgia during the Reconstruction Period."   *Report of the Georgia Bar Association*.   Atlanta, 1897.
> Presidential address before the fourteenth annual session of the Georgia Bar Association.

Hammond, N. J.   The University of Georgia.   Atlanta, 1893.

Hedley, F. Y.   Marching through Georgia.   Chicago, 1885.

History of the Baptist Denomination. Compiled for the *Christian Index*. Atlanta, 1881.

Hood, John B. Advance and Retreat. New Orleans, 1880.
Account of the campaign in Georgia, 1864.

Howard, F. T. In and Out of the Lines; Incidents during the Occupation of Georgia by the Federal Troops in 1864-5. New York, 1905.

Hull, A. L. Historical Sketch of the University of Georgia. Atlanta, 1894.

Janes, Thomas P. Hand-book of Georgia. Atlanta, 1876.
Compilation of statistics.

Johnston, Joseph E. Narrative of Military Operations. New York, 1874.
Treats of the campaign in Northwest Georgia.

Jones, C. C. Jr. "Negro Slaves during the War." *Magazine of American History*, August, 1886.

Jones, C. C. Jr. "Sherman's March from Atlanta to the Coast." *Southern Historical Society Papers*, vol. xii.

Jones, C. C. Jr. "The Siege and Evacuation of Savannah, December, 1864." *Southern Historical Society Papers*, vol. xvii.

Jones, Charles E. Education in Georgia. Washington, 1889. *U. S. Bureau of Education, Circular of Information*, no. 4.

Jones, Charles E. Georgia in the War. 1861-1865. Atlanta, 1909.
Roster of Georgia troops, names of Georgia officers in Confederate and state armies, members of the Confederate Congress, etc.

Kennaway, John H. On Sherman's Track, or The South after the War. London, 1867.
By an Englishman who traveled in Georgia in November, 1865.

Lewis, D. W. Report on Public Education. Milledgeville, 1860.
Appendix gives school statistics for 1860.

Manigault, Louis. Records of a Rice Plantation in the Georgia Lowlands. MSS.
Original records are in private possession. A copy, made under the direction of U. B. Phillips, is in the Georgia Historical Society Library in Savannah.

Nichols, George Ward. Story of the Great March. New York, 1865.

Phillips, U. B. Georgia and State Rights. Washington, 1902.
Monograph of unusual excellence. Deals with the period before 1861. Valuable for political and economic maps and for its comprehensive bibliography.

Phillips, U. B. History of Transportation in the Eastern Cotton Belt to 1860. New York, 1908.
Contains good map of transportation routes in Georgia in 1860.

Pierson, H. W. Letter to Charles Sumner with statement of Outrages upon Freedmen in Georgia. Washington, 1870.
> Testimony taken from negroes by a Northern clergyman.

Power, S. F. "The Last Battle of the Late War" (West Point, Ga.) *Southern Historical Society Papers*, vol. xxii.

Radical Rule. Military Outrage in Georgia. Arrest of Columbus Prisoners with Facts connected with their imprisonment and release. Louisville, Ky., 1868.

Reed, John C. "What I Know of the Ku Klux Klan." *Uncle Remus Magazine*, January through November, 1908.

Riley, B. F. History of the Baptists in the Southern States East of the Mississippi. Philadelphia, 1898.

Savannah Board of Education. Annual Reports of Public Schools for the City of Savannah and the County of Chatham. 1869-1872. Savannah.

Sherman, William T. "Gleanings from Despatches." *Southern Historical Society Papers*, vol. xiii.

Sherwood, Adiel. Gazetteer of Georgia. Atlanta, 1860.
> Contains tables of railroads, factories, newspapers, etc. in Georgia before the war, with a map of the state in 1860.

Smith, Charles H. Bill Arp's Peace Papers. New York, 1873.

Smith, G. G. History of Methodism in Georgia and Florida from 1785 to 1865. Macon, 1881.

Stearns, Charles. The Black Man of the South and the Rebels, or the Characteristics of the former and the recent outrages of the latter. New York, 1872.
> Written by a "Northern teacher, missionary, and planter, and an eye-witness of many of the scenes described." Lived on a plantation in Columbia County after the war. Native of Massachusetts.

Stephens, Alexander H. Reviewers Reviewed, a Supplement to the War between the States. New York, 1872.
> Appendix contains material on the reconstruction period.

Turner, Henry G. "Georgia." In *Why the Solid South?* (Edited by Hilary A. Herbert.)

Woolley, Edwin C. The Reconstruction of Georgia. New York, 1901. *Columbia University Studies in History, Economics, and Public Law*, vol. xiii, no. 3.
> Deals with the political and constitutional aspects of reconstruction.

GEORGIA BIOGRAPHY, MEMOIRS, CORRESPONDENCE, SPEECHES.

Andrews, Eliza Frances. War-Time Journal of a Georgia Girl, 1864-1865. New York, 1908.
> Sprightly narrative of life in the last year of the war.

Andrews, Garnett. Reminiscences of an Old Georgia Lawyer. Atlanta, 1870.
> Andrews was a prominent Unionist in a strong secession district. Nothing of importance on reconstruction.

Avary, Myrta Lockett, *ed.* Recollections of Alex. H. Stephens. New York, 1910.
> Contains Stephens' Prison Journal, which he kept while a prisoner at Fort Warren, Boston, from May 11 to October 26, 1865.

Avery, I. W., *ed.* In Memory—Alexander H. Stephens. Atlanta, 1883.

Bell, Hiram P. Men and Things. Atlanta, 1907.
> Disjointed reminiscences.

Boykin, Samuel, *ed.* Howell Cobb. Memorial Volume. Philadelphia, 1870.
> Brief biographical chapter with eulogies by various persons.

Caldwell, John H. Reminiscences of the Reconstruction of Church and State in Georgia. Wilmington, Del., 1895.

Candler, A. D. and Evans, C. A., *ed.* Cyclopaedia of Georgia. 3 Vols. Atlanta, 1906-
> Sketches of places and people. Published by subscription—hence eulogistic.

Clark, Richard H. Memoirs. *ed.* Lollie Belle Wylie, Atlanta, 1898.

Cleveland, Henry. Alexander H. Stephens. Philadelphia, 1866.
> Contains letters and speeches of Stephens.

Campbell, Tunis G. Sufferings of the Rev. T. G. Campbell and his family in Georgia. Washington, 1877. pph.

Cobb, Howell. Correspondence. MSS. in private possession in Athens, Ga.
> Many of Cobb's letters have been published in the Annual Report of the American Historical Association, 1911, vol. ii.

Cobb, T. R. R. Correspondence. 1860-1862. (Ed. A. L. Hull) *Southern Historical Society Papers*, vol. xxviii, and *Publications of the Southern History Association*, vol. xi.

Felton, Mrs. W. H. My Memoirs of Georgia Politics. Atlanta, 1911.

Fielder, Herbert. Life and Times and Speeches of Joseph E. Brown. Springfield, Mass., 1883.
> Highly eulogistic.

Gay, Mary A. H. Life in Dixie during the War, 1861-1865. Atlanta, 1897.
    Deals with Georgia—written from recollection.

Gordon, John B. Reminiscences of the Civil War. New York, 1903.

Hill, B. H. Address before the Georgia Branch of the Southern His-
    torical Society, Atlanta, Feb. 18, 1874. *Southern Historical Society
    Papers*, vol. xiv.

Hill, B. H., Jr. Senator Benj. H. Hill of Georgia. Life, Speeches, and
    Writings. Atlanta, 1893.
        Contains important speeches of the reconstruction period and
        Hill's "Notes on the Situation," 1867, written for the *Augusta
        Chronicle*.

Johnston, Richard Malcolm and Browne, William Hand. Life of
    Alexander H. Stephens. Philadelphia, 1878.
        Contains important letters and speeches.

Knight, Lucian Lamar. Reminiscences of Famous Georgians. 2 vols.
    Atlanta, 1907.

LeConte, Joseph. Autobiography. *ed.* W. D. Armes. New York, 1903.

Leigh, Frances Butler. Ten Years on a Georgia Plantation Since the
    War. London, 1883.
        Very valuable description of conditions on sea-island planta-
        tions, written by the daughter of Fannie Kemble, whose *Journal
        of a Residence on a Georgia Plantation in 1838-1839* contains the
        well-known account of slavery as she saw it.

Northern, W. J. (*ed.*) Men of Mark in Georgia. 6 vols. Atlanta, 1907-8.

Norton, F. H. Life of Alexander H. Stephens. Alden, N. Y., 1883.

Pendleton, Louis. Alexander H. Stephens. Philadelphia, 1907.
    In series of American Crisis Biographies.

Phillips, U. B. (*ed.*) Correspondence of Robert Toombs, Alexander
    H. Stephens and Howell Cobb. *Annual Report of the American
    Historical Association*, 1911, vol. ii. Washington, 1913.

Phillips, U. B. The Life of Robert Toombs. New York, 1913.
        Best account yet published of Toombs and his time. Com-
        paratively little material for the period after the war.

Scott, W. J. Biographic Etchings of Ministers and Laymen of the
    Georgia Conference. Atlanta, 1895.

Scott, W. J. Seventy-one Years in Georgia—An Autobiography.
    Atlanta, 1897.

Smith, G. G. Life and Times of George Foster Pierce. Sparta, Ga.,
    1888.
        Pierce was for many years Bishop of the Methodist Church,
        South, in Georgia.

Sparks, W. H.   The Memories of Fifty Years.   Philadelphia, 1870.

Speer, Emory.   Lincoln, Lee, Grant and other Biographical Addresses.
New York, 1909.
> Contains address on Joseph E. Brown, delivered at Emory
> College, June 7, 1905.

Stovall, Pleasant G.   Robert Toombs.   New York, 1892.

Toombs, Robert.   Letters to Alex. H. Stephens.   MSS.   Copies made
by U. B. Phillips.
> Views of Toombs on some of the political issues of Recon-
> struction.   Most of these letters have been published in *Annual
> Report of the American Historical Association,* 1911, vol. ii.

Trent, Wm. P.   Southern Statesman of the Old Regime.   New York,
1897.
> Essays on Toombs, Stephens and others.

Waddell, Jas. D.   (*ed.*)   Biographical Sketch of Linton Stephens.
Atlanta, 1877.
> Linton Stephens was the brother of Alex. H. Stephens.   The
> volume contains a few letters and documents of interest.

Wadley, Rebecca.   A Brief Record of the Life of William M. Wadley
written by his Eldest Daughter.   New York, 1906.   (Privately
printed.)
> Wadley was President of the Central of Georgia R. R., 1866-
> 1882, an important agent in the railroad history of Georgia after
> the war.

Georgia Public Documents

Acts of the General Assembly, 1860-1873.

Georgia Senate.   Journal, 1860-1873.

Georgia House of Representatives.   Journal, 1860-1873.

Journal of the Public and Secret Proceedings of the Convention of the
People of Georgia held in Milledgeville and Savannah, 1861.
Milledgeville, 1861.

Journal of the Proceedings of the Convention of the People of Georgia,
in Milledgeville, October and November, 1865.   Milledgeville, 1865.

Journal of the Proceedings of the Constitutional Convention of the
People of Georgia, Atlanta, 1867-1868.   Augusta, 1868.

Harrison, Z. D., *ed.*   Constitution, Ordinances, and Resolutions of the
Georgia Convention, 1867-1868.   Atlanta, 1868.

Clark, R. H., Cobb, T. R. R. and Irwin, D., *ed.*   The Code of the State
of Georgia, 1861.

Irwin, D. Code of 1865. Revised and corrected. Pub. 1867.

Irwin, D., Lester, G. N., and Hill, W. B. Code of 1868. Pub. 1873.

Confederate Records of the State of Georgia. Compiled and published under the authority of the Legislature by A. D. Candler. Vols. I-IV, VI. Atlanta, 1909-11.

Annual Reports of the Comptroller General. 1860-1873.

Annual Reports of the Officers of the Western and Atlantic R. R., 1866. Published later in the Journal of the Senate.

Georgia Reports. Decisions of the Supreme Court of Georgia.

Report of the Commissioners on Freedmen's Code, submitted to Governor Jenkins. December 19, 1866. pph.

Reports of Committees
    Report of the Finance Committee on the report of N. L. Angier, Treasurer, on the condition of the treasury. Macon, 1869.
    Report of the Joint Committee to investigate the condition of the Western and Atlantic R. R. Atlanta, 1869.
    Proceedings of Committee appointed to investigate charges made by Angier against Bullock. Report of the committee.
    Testimony taken by the committee to investigate the official conduct of Rufus B. Bullock. Report, 1872.
    Report of the Committee of the Legislature to investigate the Bonds of the State of Georgia, 1872.
    Reply of Henry Clews and Company to the Annual Report of N. L. Angier, 1872.
    Evidence taken by the joint committee of the legislature, appointed to investigate the management of the State Road under the administration of R. B. Bullock and Foster Blodgett. Atlanta, 1872.
    Majority and Minority reports of the Committee to investigate the fairness of the State Road Lease. Testimony, 1872.

GEORGIA NEWSPAPERS

Guides to newspaper collections
    Bulletin of the Library of Congress.
        List of newspapers in the Congressional Library.

    Harden, Wm. List of newspaper files in the Library of the Georgia Historical Society, Savannah. In *Gulf States Historical Magazine*, March, 1903.

    Owen, Thos. M. List of newspaper files in the Carnegie Library, Atlanta. *Gulf States Historical Magazine*, May, 1903.

Phillips, U. B.   Georgia and State Rights.   Bibliography, pp. 219-20.

> Gives a list of Georgia newspapers and their location for the ante-bellum period. Some of those cited belong to the reconstruction period as well.

ATHENS

Southern Watchman (weekly)

> In the office of the Clerk of the Superior Court of Clarke County are files from 1865, occasional numbers missing.

ATLANTA

Atlanta Constitution (daily)

> Complete file in the office of the *Constitution,* beginning June 17, 1868.
> In Carnegie Library, Atlanta, complete file from January, 1869.
> In The Library of Congress, file beginning July 16, 1871.

Atlanta Daily New Era

> In Carnegie Library, Atlanta, October, 1866 to June, 1867; January, 1868 to December, 1871.
> In Library of Congress, January 1, 1868 to Dec. 4, 1869; Aug. 3, 1870 to Dec. 31, 1871.

Daily Atlanta Intelligencer

> In Carnegie Library, Atlanta, January, 1869 to April, 1871.
> In Library of Congress, June 6, 1865 to Nov. 21, 1866; Jan. 1, 1867 to Dec. 25, 1867.
> Complete office file in private possession in Atlanta.

Daily True Georgian

> In Carnegie Library, Atlanta, June 28 to Dec. 24, 1870.

Atlanta Daily Sun

> In Carnegie Library, Atlanta, May 18, 1870 to Dec. 31, 1872.
> In Library of Congress, August 23, 1871 to Dec. 31, 1872.

Southern Confederacy (daily)

> In Carnegie Library Atlanta, March, 1861 to May, 1863.

AUGUSTA

Augusta Daily Chronicle and Sentinel
> Complete file in the office of the *Chronicle.*
> In the Ordinary's office, Augusta, file beginning July, 1868.
> In the Library of Congress, May 24, 1865 to Dec. 30, 1865; June 2 to Nov. 1, 1866.

Augusta Daily Constitutionalist
> Complete file in the office of the *Chronicle.*
> In the Ordinary's office, Augusta, file beginning July, 1868.

Augusta Daily National Republican
> In the Ordinary's office, Augusta, July to December, 1868.
> In the Library of Congress, Jan. 1 to Dec. 31, 1868.

Augusta Daily Press
> In the office of the Ordinary, Augusta, January to April 18, 1869.

COLUMBUS

Daily Sun
In Library of Congress, Oct. 1 to November 25, 1865.
Columbus Enquirer
Complete file in the office of the *Enquirer*.

MACON

Macon Daily Journal and Messenger
Macon Daily Telegraph
The valuable files of these two papers were burned or damaged by water in the *Macon Telegraph* building on Nov. 3, 1910. Only a few volumes were saved.

MILLEDGEVILLE

Milledgeville Federal Union (weekly)
Complete file in the office of the *Union-Recorder*, Milledgeville.
Southern Recorder
File, 1865-1868, privately owned in Atlanta.

SAVANNAH

Daily Advertiser
Incomplete file in the library of the Georgia Historical Society, Savannah.
Daily Herald
In the office of the *Savannah News*, file from Jan. 11, 1865 to April 1866, when it was merged with the *News*.

Savannah Daily News and Herald
In the office of the *Savannah News* is the file of the *Morning News*, beginning January, 1866, merged with the *Herald* in April, 1866. In 1869 the name was changed to *Savannah Morning News*. In the Library of Congress, Jan. 1 to Dec. 31, 1870.

Savannah Daily Republican
In the office of the *Savannah News*, July 1 to Dec. 30, 1865. The Library of Congress has the office file, July 1, 1861 to Dec. 30, 1865; July 2, 1866 to Dec. 31, 1872.

Southern Cultivator. A Practical Newspaper for the Farm, the Garden, and the Family Circle. Monthly. Published at Athens, Ga.
Complete file in the office of the *Cultivator* in Atlanta.

SCRAPBOOKS

Brown Scrapbooks
This is a very valuable collection of clippings from newspapers from all sections of the state, pertaining to the political career of Joseph E. Brown from 1855 to his death. The collection was made by Mrs. Joseph E. Brown and is now owned by a member of the Brown family. The clippings are carefully marked with the names and dates of the papers from which they are taken.

Howard Scrapbooks
In Carnegie Library, Atlanta. Compiled by F. T. Howard. The usefulness of the clippings is impaired by the omission on many of them of the names and dates of the papers from which they are taken.

New York Times, established 1851.

New York Herald, established 1835.

New York Tribune, established 1841.

The Nation, New York, established 1865.

Harpers Weekly, New York, established 1857.

Townsend Library of Newspaper Clippings.
> In Columbia University Library. A vast collection of clippings dealing with the Civil War and Reconstruction from the most important New York papers.

American Annual Cyclopaedia and Register of Important Events, New York; after 1874, continued as *Appleton's Annual Cyclopaedia.*

De Bow's Review, New Orleans, Charleston, Washington, 1846-64; New York, 1866-70.

Hunt's Merchant Magazine and Commercial Review, New York, 1839-70.

Commercial and Financial Chronicle. New York, established 1865.
> In January, 1871, *Hunt's Merchant Magazine* and the *Commercial and Financial Chronicle* were merged together. The former was a monthly, the latter a weekly.

Poor, H. V. *Manual of the Railroads of the United States*, New York, 1868.

Alvord, J. W. Letters from the South relating to the Condition of the Freedmen. Washington, 1870.
> Alvord, General Superintendent of Education of the Freedmen's Bureau, spent a little more than a week in January, 1870, in Georgia on a tour of inspection. Letters are addressed to Maj. Gen. O. O. Howard.

Andrews, Sidney. The South since the War. Boston, 1868.
> Andrews was the Washington correspondent for the *Boston Advertiser* ("Dixon") and for the *Chicago Tribune* ("Israel"). He was in Georgia from Oct. 24, to Dec. 3, 1865.

Schurz, Carl. Report on conditions in the South, submitted to President Johnson in the fall of 1865. *Sen. Exec. Doc.*, 39 C., 1 S., no. 2. Also letters of Schurz in the Johnson Papers in the Library of Congress, MSS.
> Schurz's point of view as ardent advocate of negro rights prevented a dispassionate observation of conditions in the South on his part.

Grant, U. S. Brief report of a rapid tour of inspection in the South in 1865 [appended to the above report of Carl Schurz.]

Nordhoff, Charles. The Cotton States in the Spring and Summer of 1875. New York, 1876.

Reid, Whitelaw. After the War; a Southern Tour. May 1, 1865 to May 1, 1866. Cincinnati, 1866.

Somers, Robert. Southern States Since the War, 1870-1871. London, 1871.

Trowbridge, J. T. Picture of the Desolated States, 1865-1868. Hartford, 1868.

Truman, B. C. Report of affairs in the Southern states. *Sen. Exec. Doc.*, 39 C., 1 S., no. 43.
Truman, sent by the President to investigate conditions in the Southern states in 1865-6, was one of the most fair-minded of Northern travelers in the South. His report and his letters to the *New York Times* are of special importance.

Watterson, Henry. Letters to President Johnson in Johnson MSS.
Report of Watterson's views on conditions in the South in 1865.

Books and Articles Dealing with the South and Reconstruction

Atlantic Monthly, 1901. Articles on Reconstruction.

Banks, Enoch Marvin. Labor Supply and Labor Problems. *Annals of the American Academy*, January, 1910.

Beard, J. M. Ku Klux Sketches. Philadelphia, 1877.

Blaine, James G. Twenty Years of Congress from Lincoln to Garfield. 2 vols. Norwich, Conn., 1893.

Brown, William Garrott. The Lower South in American History. New York, 1902.

Bruce, Philip Alexander. "The Rise of the New South." Philadelphia, 1905. *History of North America*, vol. xvii.

Clews, Henry. Twenty-eight Years in Wall Street. London, 1888.

DuBois, W. E. B. "Reconstruction and its Benefits." *American Historical Review*, July, 1910.

Dunning, William Archibald. Essays in the Civil War and Reconstruction. New York, 1904.

Dunning, William Archibald. Reconstruction, Political and Economic, New York, 1907.

Fleming, Walter L. Documentary History of Reconstruction. 2 vols. Cleveland, Ohio, 1906-7.

Fleming, Walter L. "Prescript of the Ku Klux Klan." *Southern History Association Publications*, vol. vii, 1903.

Grady, Henry W. "Cotton and its Kingdom." *Harper's Magazine*, October, 1881.

von Halle, Ernst. Baumwollproduktion und Pflanzungswirthschaft in den Nordamerikanischen Südstaaten. Zweiter Teil. Sezessionskrieg und Rekonstrucktion, 1861-1886. Leipzig, 1906.

Hammond, M. B. The Cotton Industry. New York, 1897.

Kelsey, Carl. The Negro Farmer. Chicago, 1903.

King, Edward. The Great South. Hartford, Conn., 1875.

Ingle, Edward. Southern Sidelights. New York, 1896.

Lester, J. C. and Wilson, D. L., *ed.* W. L. Fleming. Ku Klux Klan, its Origin, Growth, and Disbandment. 1905.

McPherson, Edward. Political History of the United States of America during the Period of Reconstruction. Washington, 1875.

Meade, George Gordon, *ed.* The Life and Letters of George Gordon Meade. 2 vols. New York, 1913.

Moore, Frank, *ed.* Rebellion Record. 12 vols. New York, 1861-8.

Peirce, Paul Skeels. The Freedmen's Bureau. *University of Iowa Studies*, vol. iii, no. 1. Iowa City, 1904.

Pennypacker, I. R. General Meade. New York, 1901. Great Commander Series.

Phillips, U. B. "The Decadence of the Plantation System." *Annals of the American Academy*, Philadelphia, January, 1910.

—— "Conservatism and Progress in the Cotton Belt." *South Atlantic Quarterly*, January, 1904.

—— "The Economic Cost of Slaveholding in the Cotton Belt." *Political Science Quarterly*, June, 1905.

—— "The Economics of the Plantation." *South Atlantic Quarterly*, July, 1903.

—— "The Origin and Growth of the Southern Black Belts." *American Historical Review*, July, 1906.

—— "The Plantation as a Civilizing Factor." *Sewanee Review*, July, 1904.

—— "Racial Problems, Adjustments and Disturbances." In the *South in the Building of the Nation*, vol. iv.

—— *ed.* "Plantation and Frontier." *Documentary History of American Industrial Society*, vols. i and ii.

Pollard, E. A. The Lost Cause Regained. New York, 1868.

Reed, John C. The Brothers' War. Boston, 1905.

Rhodes, James Ford. History of the United States, 1850-1877. 7 vols. New York, 1906-10.

Schurz, Carl. Reminiscences. 3 vols. Vol. iii edited by Frederic Bancroft and W. A. Dunning. New York, 1907-1908.

—— Speeches, Correspondence and Political Papers. *ed.* Frederic Bancroft. 6 vols. New York, 1913.

Schwab, J. C. Financial and Industrial History of the South during the War. New York, 1901.

—— "The South during the War." In *Cambridge Modern History,* vol. vii.

Sherman, William T. Memoirs. 2 vols. New York, 1892.

Sinclair, William A. The Aftermath of Slavery. Boston, 1905.

Stone, Alfred Holt. "The Negro and Agricultural Development." *Annals of the American Academy.* January, 1910.

Taylor, Richard. Destruction and Reconstruction. New York, 1883.

Watkins, James L. King Cotton—Historical and Statistical Review, 1790-1908. New York, 1908.

Williams, G. W. History of the Negro Race in America. 2 vols. New York, 1883.

Wood, Robert C. Confederate Hand-Book. New Orleans, 1900.

U. S. Documents

Congressional Globe for the 39th, 40th, 41st and 42d Congresses.

Reports of the Department of Agriculture.

Reports of the Secretary of the Treasury.

Reports of the Secretary of War.

War of the Rebellion, Official Records of the Union and Confederate Armies. Series 1, vols. 9, 12, 24; pt. 3, 47, pt. 3, 49, pts. 1 and 2, 53; series iv, vol. iii.

39 Congress, 1 Session
  Senate Executive Documents, nos. 2, 26, 37.
  House Executive Documents, nos. 11, 34, 70, 99.
  Reports of the Committees of the House of Representatives, vol. ii, Report of the Joint Committee on Reconstruction.

2d Session.
  Senate Executive Document, no. 2.

40 Congress, 2 Session.
  House Executive Documents, no. 291.

3 Session.
  House Miscellaneous Documents, p. 52.

41 Congress, 1 Session.
  Senate Executive Documents, no. 3, 41.
  Senate Report of Committees, no. 58.
  House Miscellaneous Documents, no. 34.

2 Session.
  Senate Executive Document, no. 13.
  House Executive Documents, no. 82, 288.

3 Session.
  Senate Reports of Committees, no. 308.

42 Congress, 2 Session.
  Senate Reports of Committees, vol. ii, pts. vi and vii. Report of the Joint Select Committee to inquire into the Affairs of the late insurrectionary states. Ku Klux Report, Georgia testimony. Referred to in foot-notes as *Ku Klux Committee.*

43 Congress, 2 Session.
  Senate Executive Document, no. 23.

Biographical Congressional Directory, 1774-1911. Washington, 1913.

Census, 1860, 1870, 1880.